ARTHURIAN STUDIES XIX

LAȜAMON'S *BRUT*

The Poem and its Sources

ARTHURIAN STUDIES

ISSN 0261–9814

LAƷAMON'S *BRUT*
THE POEM AND ITS SOURCES

Françoise H.M. Le Saux

D.S. BREWER

First published 1989 by D.S. Brewer, Cambridge

D.S. Brewer is an imprint of Boydell & Brewer Ltd
PO Box 9, Woodbridge, Suffolk IP12 3DF
and of Boydell & Brewer Inc.
Wolfeboro, New Hampshire 03894–2069, USA

ISBN 0 85991 282 5

British Library Cataloguing in Publication Data
Le Saux, Françoise H.M. (Françoise Hazel Marie), *1957–*
    Laȝamon's Brut: the poem and its sources. – (Arthurian
    studies; ISSN 0261–9814; v 19
    I. Title   II. Series
    821'.1'09
    ISBN 0-85991-282-5

Library of Congress Cataloging-in-Publication Data applied for

♾ The paper used in this publication meets the minimum
requirements of American National Standard for Information
Sciences – Permanence of Paper for Printed Library Materials,
ANSI Z39.48–1984.

Printed and bound in Great Britain by
Woolnough Bookbinding Ltd, Irthlingborough, Northants

Contents

Contents

Preface

> The question of sources other than the *Roman de Brut* must probably be left at 'non-proven'.

This statement by Håkan Ringbom, in his *Studies in the Narrative Technique of* Beowulf *and Lawman's* Brut, is a good summary of the state of research on Laȝamon's sources when I first took an interest in the subject, in 1980. The possible sources of the poem had mostly been discussed in a fragmented form; the bits of the puzzle brought by different critics did not fit in together, and the overall image was one of confusion. Herbert Pilch's noteworthy attempt to put the issue within a consistent perspective failed to clarify the situation, and the student or the critic who wished to go further in his or her appreciation of the *Brut* was faced with the paradox of a poem hailed by some for its originality, but whose relationship with the other literary works of its time was strikingly neglected. A comprehensive and (if possible) objective study of Laȝamon's sources was long overdue.

The first step was obviously to investigate the English poet's handling of his main source, Wace's *Roman de Brut*, and determine what principles guided the composition of the English *Brut*. It thus became possible to distinguish between different sorts of variation from the *Roman*, thereby providing us with norms against which to gauge the probability of further, secondary sources. These additional sources then had to be identified, in the various fields suggested by the poem: historical, literary, religious writings (or tales) in Welsh, English, Latin, French, and perhaps even Scandinavian. The passage from one language into another made this task somewhat difficult, as borrowings of this nature cannot be detected to any great extent by verbal overlap; moreover, the very act of associating one text with another is necessarily tinged with some degree of subjectivity. I have however endeavoured to follow as strictly as possible the rules of chronological and contextual consistency, and attempted to assess the implications of the influence of a given work on an overall reading of the *Brut*.

This study could never have been completed without the help and advice of a host of people: the librarians of the Bibliothèque Cantonale et Universitaire de Lausanne; the assistants of the computing department,

vii

and especially Marc-Olivier Christinat; and of course my friends and colleagues of the departments of Medieval French and English, who took a keen interest in the progress of my research. But above all, my thanks go to Professor Ian J. Kirby, who directed this thesis, to Professors Derek S. Brewer, Roy F. Leslie and Brynley F. Roberts, for their guidance; to Neil Wright, who kindly allowed me to consult the proofs of his forthcoming edition of the Variant Version of the *Historia Regum Britanniae*; and to my parents, for their unfailing support.

1

Laȝamon's *Brut*: Dates and Manuscripts

Laȝamon's poem is to be found in two manuscripts, MS Cotton Caligula A ix, and MS Cotton Otho C xiii, both kept at the British Library, and former property of the collector Sir Robert Cotton. The better of the two texts, MS Caligula A ix, is a small quarto written on vellum, containing 259 leaves, and consisting of two portions which Sir Frederic Madden, the first editor of Laȝamon's *Brut*, considers were originally distinct.[1] The first contains the *Brut*, covering 192 leaves: the writing is in double columns, generally of 34 lines each, and in two interchanging (and therefore coeval) hands. A number of Latin glosses in the margins appear to have been part of the original design of the manuscript: from fol.49 (verso), they are adorned with the same red ink as in the body of the text. These glosses, in black ink, have in many parts been cut away by the bookbinders, but what remains is consistently historical information concerning a character or episode in the *Brut*, either adding to or correcting what is said in the poem. The margins also bear the proper names, in red ink, which appear in the text; these inscriptions are made by the same hand(s) as the body of the work.

The second part of the volume, Madden suggests, was written at a later period than the first. It is also in two different hands, and contains three poems by the thirteenth-century poet Chardri;[2] a short prose Chronicle in French, from the arrival of the Saxons to the reign of Henry III; a number of short English poems of a religious or moral nature; and that masterpiece of early Middle English literature, *The Owl and the Nightingale*.[3]

---

[1] Sir Frederic Madden, *Laȝamons Brut, or Chronicle of Britain* (hereafter Madden). See vol. 1, Preface, p.xxxiv.

[2] i.e., a life of St Josaphaz, *La Vie des Sept Dormanz*, and *Le Petit Plet*. Of the poet himself, nothing is known, except that he apparently lived in England in the later years of the twelfth century or at the beginning of the thirteenth. His name may be an anagram of Richard. See John Koch ed., *Chardry's Josaphaz, Set Dormanz und Petit Plet*, especially pp. v–xxv, and Brian S. Merrilees ed., *La Vie des Set Dormanz by Chardri*, Introduction.

[3] In the order of the manuscript, *The Owl and the Nightingale* precedes the religious verse.

MS Otho C xiii is a quarto, written in the same hand throughout, in double columns of 38 lines. It originally comprised some 155 leaves, but suffered greatly in the 1731 fire at Ashburnham House, and now consists of only 145 leaves of varying condition. Most damaged are the first fifty leaves, and the end of the manuscript (from fol. 110 onwards). It contains only the *Brut*. The Otho version is an abbreviated recension of the poem, which Madden considers may have been written partially from recitation.[4]

The 'Brut' portion of the Caligula manuscript was dated by Madden to the early part of the thirteenth century, and the latter portion to 'a later period, probably at the close of Henry the Thirds reign';[5] the Otho manuscript he does not specifically date, but by implication places it towards the end of the thirteenth century.

The dating of the two manuscripts takes on great importance in considering the *Brut*, for internal evidence as to the date of composition of the poem is limited. Madden points out four passages which he suggests may allude to 'contemporary events':

a mention of the ruined state of the city of Leicester (*Brut*, 1458–9), which may refer to its destruction by the forces of Henry II under the Justiciary Richard de Lucy, in 1173;[6]

Brut, 1335–7: 'Eoverwic' has become 'ȝeork' due to the foreign pronunciation of northern men 'nawiht ȝeare', 'not long before' the composition of the poem;

Brut, 15949–64: account of the establishment of the 'Rome-feoh' (i.e., Peter's Pence), ending on what Madden understands as a doubt as to the continuance of the payment

> Drihten wat hu longe   þeo laȝen scullen ilæste[7]

and therefore suggests it is an allusion to King John's resisting the Pope's mandate for the collection of the tribute in the year 1205;

Brut, 22–3: the Prologue says that Wace presented his book to 'þare æðelen Ælienor, þe wes Henries quene þes heȝes kinges'.[8]
From the use of the past tense, Madden deduces that Henry must have

---

[4] Madden, p.xxxviii.
[5] Sic. In quotations I have kept Madden's idiosyncracies of language.
[6] Madden, p.xviii.
[7] *Brut* 15964. 'Lord knows how long the law will last'. The *Brut* is quoted from the Brook and Leslie edition.
[8] 'The noble Eleanor, who was the queen of Henry the high king'.

been dead at the time these lines were written (which brings us to 1189), and possibly Eleanor as well. As Eleanor died in 1204, 'the date will correspond very accurately with the time when the *Rome-feoh* was forbidden'.[9] Moreover, Madden considers that if Eleanor had been living in England at the time Laȝamon wrote those lines (she only retired to Aquitaine after the accession of King John), she would not have been mentioned so briefly.

To these four passages, Madden adds a number of external arguments in favour of the poem having been written or completed at the beginning of the thirteenth century, notably the fact that up to 1203, England was still united to Normandy, and that English composition was not likely to have been encouraged before the separation.

These arguments, however, are not entirely convincing. Rudolf Imelmann pointed out that the 'Rome-feoh' passage is better understood as meaning that the tribute was still being paid, without any prospect of a near abolition;[10] whilst the Prologue passage gives no real indication as to whether Eleanor was alive or not. That the poem was completed by 1205, however, Imelmann has no doubt; he quotes a message of King John, dated from 29 April 1205, to John of Cornhill:

> Mittas etiam nobis statim visis litteris Romantium de Historia Angliae.[11]

These words were understood by Le Roux de Lincy as referring to Wace's *Roman de Brut* (of which he was the editor); Imelmann however suggests that this Historia may have been Laȝamon's *Brut*. Such was also G.J. Visser's opinion:

> Considering the hurry of the king to get the book and the fact that Wace's *Brut* was fifty years old at the time, it is much more likely that King John asked for the newly finished work of Laȝamon.[12]

In the midst of this general tendency to place the *terminus ad quem* at the beginning of the thirteenth century were a few dissenting voices which placed the *Brut* well back in the twelfth century. This, one may note, had been the current opinion before Madden's investigations; early nineteenth century scholars had tended to date the *Brut* by adding what they

---

9 Madden, p. xx.
10 Rudolf Imelmann, *Laȝamon. Versuch über seine Quellen*, especially p. 9.
11 'Send us immediately the writings we saw of the Romance of the History of England'.
12 G.J. Visser, *Laȝamon's Brut. An Attempt at Vindication* (hereafter *Vindication*), p. 10, note 1. To Imelmann's and Visser's views on this subject, one may object, first, that one may doubt whether King John knew English; and secondly, that the material contained in Laȝamon's poem was usually referred to as the history of Britain, not of England.

considered a reasonable number of years to the date of completion of Wace's *Roman de Brut*. For example, George Ellis, in his *Specimens of the Early English Poets* (1801) conjectures the date of completion of the *Brut* to be 1185, on the assumption that it must have taken Laƺamon about thirty years to write his poem. An early *terminus ad quem* was also advocated in 1932 by H.B.Hinckley (on more scientific grounds than his predecessors, however).[13] Hinckley rejects Madden's arguments point by point: the passage on the renaming of York he considers too vague; the Leicester calamity is already present in Wace; the exclamation at Peter's Pence he agrees with Imelmann in seeing as a cry of exasperation; and last, since Eleanor is said to be a noble queen, the poem must have been written before her rebellion against her husband in 1173. Hinckley therefore suggests that the *Brut* must have been written while Henry II was still alive, and completed before 1173; allowing two years for Laƺamon to obtain a Wace text would provide a *terminus a quo* of 1157, whilst, considering that nothing points to the period 1166–1172, and that a date of composition posterior to 1172 'is not worth considering', the *terminus ad quem* must be 1165, within the period where Eleanor was still bearing children to Henry II.

Hinckley's opinion did not find much support. It was opposed from the outset by G.J.Visser, who pointed out that Hinckley's argumentation was valid only for the period immediately following the queen's disgrace in 1173. If Laƺamon wrote during the reign of King John, as suggested by Madden, the detail would lose all its significance. Moreover, notes Visser, the term 'noble' is probably little more than an *epitheton ornans*.[14]

The weakness of the elements used to date the poem with any precision was further underlined by J.S.P.Tatlock, in his *Legendary History of Britain*.[15] Tatlock accepts only one of Madden's arguments – that the past tense used in the Eleanor passage must indeed mean that the poem was written after Henry II's death in 1189. He agrees with Hinckley that nothing can be deduced from it as to whether the queen was alive or not, and that the reference to Peter's Pence 'merely may imply marveling at the several centuries' duration of the payment, or impatient dislike of this foreign tax'. Tatlock therefore suggests new grounds on which to date the poem, with two additional arguments which make him place the *Brut* between 1189 and 1199.

The first argument is the reference on line 14297 of the *Brut* to 'an Arður' who will come to help the 'Anglen':[16]

[13] H.B.Hinckley, 'The Date of Laƺamon's *Brut*', *Anglia* 56 (1932): 43–57.
[14] G.J.Visser, *Vindication*, pp. 9–10.
[15] J.S.P.Tatlock, *The Legendary History of Britain* (hereafter *Legendary History*), esp. pp. 503–7.
[16] This 'Anglen' Tatlock understands as 'Angles'; I.J.Kirby has demonstrated, however,

It is impossible not to see an allusion to Arthur of Brittany (1187 – 3 April 1203), posthumous child of Geoffrey, Henry II's second son, by Constance daughter of Conan IV, count of Brittany, and murdered as historians believe by King John.[17]

The name of the young prince was probably chosen, Tatlock notes, in order to 'convey hopes of independence'; he finds a parallel between Laȝamon's words and a remark made by the chronicler William of Newbury, to the effect that the name was imposed by the Bretons themselves, who nourished great hopes in the child. Moreover the young prince Arthur had good grounds to claim the English crown: Richard had declared him his heir in 1190, in default of a child of his own (thus passing over his own brother John). And though when Richard died nine years later there seemed no chance of Arthur becoming king of England, 'at any time earlier an Englishman may have anticipated this'.[18] The fact that the Arthur of the English *Brut* is more closely connected with Brittany than in Wace or Geoffrey (he is brought up in Brittany, and has to be fetched from there), Tatlock sees as a confirmation of his hypothesis that Laȝamon must have written during the reign of Richard I.

Tatlock's second argument is based on the account of the 'tailed' people of Dorchester, who earned their affliction through their bad treatment of St Augustine. The term used by Laȝamon, 'cued' (14772), translates Wace's 'cué' (13735–41). The taunt that Englishmen bore tails was flung at Richard I's crusaders in 1190, in Sicily, notes Tatlock, and one particular incident at Messina became especially notorious.

For these two reasons, Tatlock places the composition of the *Brut* between the *termini* of 1190 and 1199.

The consensus was thus established in favour of a date of composition of 'around 1200'; and the matter met with no further discussion until Herbert Pilch's reassessment of the material in 1960.[19]

Pilch suggests (pp. 15–17) that the accepted date of composition for the *Brut* ought to be revised, to be placed earlier in the twelfth century, on the strength of the following arguments:

Brut, 12112–5: Caerleon seems to have been bewitched. This may refer to the successive destructions of the town in 1171, 1173 and 1175.

---

that it could equally mean 'England', in the context of the *Brut* (see his 'Angles and Saxons in Laȝamon's *Brut*').

[17] J.S.P.Tatlock, *Legendary History*, p.504.

[18] J.S.P.Tatlock, *Legendary History*, p.505.

[19] See for example Dorothy Everett, 'Laȝamon and the Earliest Middle English Alliterative Verse', p.25; Fernand Mossé, *A Handbook of Middle English*, p.152; H.Ringbom, *Studies in the Narrative Technique of Beowulf and Lawman's Brut* (hereafter *Narrative Technique*), p.58; N.Bogholm, *The Laȝamon Texts, a Linguistical Investigation*; Herbert Pilch's *Laȝamon's Brut. Eine Literarische Studie* (hereafter *Literarische Studie*).

Brut, 14276–80. Laȝamon follows the older tradition, whereby Arthur goes to the fairy island of Avalon to be healed of his wounds, rather than to Glastonbury to be buried. This, considers Pilch, points to a date of composition prior to 1191, the date indicated by Giraldus Cambrensis' account of the 'discovery' of the grave of Arthur and Gwenhwyfar at the Abbey of Glastonbury.

Brut, 23. The use of the preterite in the Eleanor passage need not indicate that the king was dead at the time the poem was written – just that such was the case after the poem was completed. Pilch assumes here that the Prologue was written last.

Brut, 11179–81. Laȝamon's description of the relics of the Irish saints Columkille, Brendan and Bride suggests that the poem was written after 1185, when the supposed grave of these saints was 'discovered'.

Finally, the archaic language of the poem confirms that the poem must have been written at an earlier date than that postulated by Tatlock or others.

The argumentation of Pilch and his predecessors is subjected to close scrutiny by E. G. Stanley in 'The Date of Laȝamon's *Brut*'.[20] Tatlock's interpretation of 'an Arthur', Stanley feels, could at most be supporting evidence to a more weighty argument; there is no indication that the English shared the hopes of the Bretons regarding Arthur of Brittany, while the construction where a proper noun is used with the indefinite article (with the generalizing meaning 'comparable to the individual in question') has other parallels in Middle English literature. The story of the fish tails and the English cannot be accepted as significant, because it is taken over entirely from Wace, who wrote some fifty years before the incident at Messina. As for Pilch's arguments, Stanley rejects them on the grounds that Laȝamon could have kept to the older version of Arthur's end out of choice, and that the Glastonbury discovery did not wipe out popular belief.

The *Brut*, suggests Stanley, was written well into the thirteenth century. In a previous article, he had already noted a resumption of the payment of Peter's Pence in 1226;[21] but he had refrained from postulating a later *terminus ad quem* because it would not have been compatible with the then accepted date of the Caligula manuscript. But this dating had since been challenged by C. E. Wright, who in his work on English vernacular hands from the twelfth to the fifteenth centuries considered that the

[20] *Notes and Queries* 213 (1968): 85–88.
[21] *Notes and Queries* 209 (1964): 192.

MS Caligula A ix was written 'about A.D. 1250'.[22] N.R. Ker concurred with such an opinion in his facsimile edition of *The Owl and the Nightingale*: 'Wright's dating 'probably a little after A.D. 1250' seems to me on the early side.'[23] Ker then proceeds to demonstrate that this date given by Wright to the second part of Caligula, containing *The Owl and the Nightingale*, is also valid for the first part of the manuscript (containing the *Brut*), which had always been accepted as an earlier script than the second. The difference between the hands of the two sections, considers Ker, is one of kind, not of date:

> Cotton's habit of binding unrelated manuscripts together is well known, but in the present instance the similarities of script, layout and number of lines suggest strongly that ff. 195–261 belonged from the first with the 'Hystoria brutonum' (Laȝamon).[24]

The presence of an Anglo-Norman prose chronicle from the Saxon conquest to the reign of Henry III would indeed seem to confirm that the second part of the manuscript bore some relationship to the first: the prose chronicle takes over where Laȝamon stops, more or less. This, however, cannot be said to shed any light on the English poem, except that the second section of the manuscript may have been designed to complete it. If so, the similarity in layout and in the number of lines noted by Ker would not be astonishing; the second part would presumably have been produced by the same scriptorium as the first. The exact relationship between the different scripts of the Caligula manuscript in terms of date is difficult to assess: as stressed by Wright, paleography is not an exact science, and where no internal evidence is available, the dating of vernacular manuscripts 'is to be regarded for the most part as tentative only'.[25] But that the hands of the *Brut* section must be mid-thirteenth century is apparent from their clearly differentiated c's and t's; Ker's hypothesis that the difference in the Caligula scripts must be a matter of skill is therefore highly probable.

But whatever the relation between both parts of Caligula, this shifting forward of the date of the manuscript by almost half a century necessitated a renewed outlook upon the internal evidence offered by the *Brut*. E.G. Stanley thus notes that the thirteenth century series of dates provided by the interruptions in the payment of Peter's Pence could no

---

22 C.E. Wright, *English Vernacular Hands From the Twelfth to the Fifteenth Centuries*. MS Caligula A ix, and more specifically the part containing Laȝamon's *Brut*, is the sixth item of the book.
23 N.R. Ker, *The Owl and the Nightingale. Reproduced in Facsimile from the surviving manuscripts Jesus College Oxford 29 and British Museum Cotton Caligula A ix*, p.ix.
24 Ker, p.ix.
25 Wright, p.xvi.

longer be ruled out as irrelevant; Laȝamon's mention of the vicissitudes of Caerleon upon Usk also offers a wider range of dates – 1171, 1173, 1175, 1217 and 1231 – than had previously been envisaged. None of this evidence, however, provides a sure *terminus ad quem*, considers Stanley, who concludes (p. 88): 'the only probable *terminus ad quem* is the palaeographical dating of the manuscripts'. The *terminus a quo* Stanley places after Henry II's death in 1189, on the strength of the past tense in the Prologue passage, which he accepts must indicate that the king was deceased; he finds confirmation of this in Pilch's observation concerning the relics of the Irish saints, which firmly place the *Brut* after 1185.

One may make a number of reservations about both *termini* postulated by Stanley. The *terminus a quo* is based on the Prologue, which, as suggested by Pilch, was probably written in its actual form after the completion of the work only; and within that Prologue, on a passage which could well have been 'updated' by a later scribe, the crucial verb being embedded in the verse, and therefore easy to modify. The date of the death of Henry II thus cannot be accepted as a conclusive *terminus*. The only truly safe element for determining the *terminus a quo* is the date of the Invention of the relics of the Irish saints mentioned in the *Brut*, which took place a few years before Henry's death. In practice, however, this four-year difference is so minimal that it may be disregarded. As regards the *terminus ad quem*, satisfying oneself with the date of the manuscript is debatable: a surviving manuscript is generally the copy of an older manuscript of which nothing will be known, and which may itself have been a copy. In the case of the Caligula manuscript, though, one may agree with Stanley in considering that it cannot have been very far removed from the authorial text of the *Brut*:

> The archaic language of the Caligula text seems less in keeping with the language of the second half of the thirteenth century than that of Otho, and must, to a great extent, go back to the poet: if there had been many intermediate copies the author's language is unlikely to have escaped modernization to the extent to which it has escaped in Caligula.[26]

This brings the discussion to the language of the Caligula version of the *Brut*, which is distinctly archaic for a thirteenth-century text. The contrast with the modernized language of the Otho text is striking, and pleads strongly in favour of an authorial text which antedated the Caligula manuscript by several decades, as both Otho and Caligula are roughly contemporary manuscripts. Such an opinion, however, cannot be confirmed to any great extent, for our corpus of early Middle English

---

[26] E. G. Stanley, 'The Date of Laȝamon's *Brut*', p. 85.

texts is too limited to be able to draw any precise conclusions from the linguistic or metrical evidence offered by the *Brut*.[27]

But to leave matters at that, and state that the poem was written between 1190 and 1275, is somewhat unsatisfactory, for in so doing one is disregarding the potential information contained within the Prologue. As long as it was believed that the Caligula manuscript was copied at the beginning of the thirteenth century, the debate as to the exact implications of the phrase 'Ælienor, þe wes Henries quene' was of necessity restricted to considerations as to whether Henry II was still alive at the time the line was written. The revised date of Caligula, however, extends the possible period of composition over the reigns of five kings, two of whom were called Henry.[28] If one admits no earlier *terminus ad quem* than the date of 1275, one is faced with the question why the Henry of the Prologue is not distinguished from Edward's immediate predecessor: especially as both had queens named Eleanor, and could thus have been all the more easily confused. It could be argued that the mention of Wace among the sources of the poem is sufficient to identify the king in question as Henry II; however, Wace's disappearance from the Otho version of the Preface suggests that the Anglo-Norman poet was not well known among thirteenth-century English scribes. It is therefore most improbable that the *Brut* should have been written after 1272. Likewise, if Laʒamon had written under Henry III, one would expect the poet to have differentiated the Henry of the Prologue from the reigning monarch; and I am in complete agreement with E. G. Stanley's argument (made in connection with *The Owl and the Nightingale*):

> From lines 1091 f. .... it emerges that the poem was written after the death of Henry II in 1189. Since King Henry is not referred to as 'old King Henry', or by some similar distinguishing mark, it is clear that the poem must have been written before the accession of Henry III in 1216.[29]

This argument is all the stronger in the case of the *Brut* as the reference to King Henry is embedded in what was obviously thought of as a serious piece of historical writing, while the 'king Henri' of *The Owl and the Nightingale* appears in a tale told by the birds, as fiction within a fiction. If

---

[27] See the introduction to G. L. Brook's *Selections from Laʒamon's Brut*, pp. xv–xvi.

[28] i.e. Henry II, Richard I, John, Henry III and Edward I.

[29] E. G. Stanley ed., *The Owl and the Nightingale*, Introduction, p. 19. The lines referred to are in the Nightingale's refutation of the Owl's accusation that her song entices women to adultery, exemplified by a reference to the tale of the 'Laüstig', where the wronged husband takes vengeance on a nightingale. The lines read:

> þat underyat þe king Henri
> Iesus his soule do merci!

'King Henry came to hear of it, Jesus be merciful to his soul!'

the king in *The Owl and the Nightingale* could conceivably refer to Henry III (supposing that the date of composition of the poem was roughly the same as that of the Caligula manuscript), the 'Henry' of the Prologue of the *Brut* can only refer to Henry II, husband of Eleanor of Aquitaine.

To this strong internal argument in favour of a *terminus ad quem* of 1216, we may add the cumulative argument of the contents of the Caligula manuscript itself. Such evidence must be used with caution, for none of the items within Caligula offer a really secure basis for dating (with the exception, I suggest, of the *Brut* itself); however, learned opinions converge in dating most of the items of Caligula to the beginning of the thirteenth century. We have seen that E. G. Stanley considers that *The Owl and the Nightingale* must have been written before 1216; of the Anglo-Norman poet Chardri we know nothing, but both his language and internal evidence point towards the early thirteenth century;[30] while the French chronicle, as noted above, stops short of the reign of Henry III, which presumably indicates that it was compiled and completed around 1216. If indeed the second part of Caligula was designed as a sequel to the first, it would follow that the *Brut* must also have been completed before 1216: for certainly, a chronicle of contemporary events, following an account of the early history of Britain, would not have stopped several decades before its compilation; and if it was a copy of an earlier work, surely it would have been brought up to date?

I shall therefore assume in the following considerations that the *Brut* was written between 1185 and 1216.

There remains to investigate the relationship between the two versions of the *Brut*, in order to justify the choice of one text as the basis of study rather than the other.

That the Caligula manuscript must be closer to the authorial text than the Otho manuscript in linguistic terms has been confirmed beyond doubt by E. G. Stanley;[31] and to that extent, it is logical that one should base any analysis on the Caligula rather than the Otho manuscript. However, as Otho displays a number of differences from the Caligula text other than those proceeding from the modernizing of the lexis of the poem, it is necessary to have a closer look at the text.

The major characteristic of Otho is that it is not only a modernized version of the poem, but also an abridged one. An early attempt to find the principles underlying the pruning of the Otho scribe was made by Theodore A. Stroud in 1952.[32] The Otho-scribe, considers Stroud (p. 42), was

---

[30] See Koch, *Chardry's Josaphaz* and Merrilees, *La Vie des Set Dormanz*, referred to above, note 2.

[31] See Stanley, 'Laʒamon's Antiquarian Sentiments'.

[32] Theodore A. Stroud, 'Scribal Editing in Lawman's *Brut*', *Journal of English and Germanic Philology* 51 (1952): 42–8.

methodical, both in familiarizing himself with his copy before revising, and in re-arranging passages to put first things first. He
succeeds in preserving practically every narrative unit in the poem,
while omitting numerous irrelevant, clumsy or unintelligible
lines.

The aim of Stroud's article was to establish whether the omissions of
the Otho-scribe are indicative of a 'defective appreciation of poetry', or to
external circumstances such as the necessity to economize parchment, or
the possibility (first advanced by J. S. P. Tatlock) that the Otho-scribe may
have copied the *Brut* partly from memory. Stroud dismisses Tatlock's
hypothesis, on the grounds of the great similarity between the Otho and
Caligula texts, and further notes that the lines in Otho generally take up
more space in the 'mutilated' parts of the poem. Whilst admitting that the
Otho-scribe 'ends up deleting the products of genius', Stroud rejects
(p. 48) the idea that he was 'prosaic by nature':

> he operated, more or less ineptly, according to poetic principles at
> times antithetical to those of Lawman ... But that his behaviour can
> be validly characterized as anti-poetic seems very dubious; he
> seems on the contrary to be a poet, seeking with simple means to
> enhance the most ennobling and poetic myth of his culture.

Stroud's vindication was elaborated upon by W. J. Keith in 1960.[33] Having first established that the writer of Otho must have worked from a text
very close to Caligula, if not practically identical with it, Keith proceeds
to classify the omissions from the 'standard' text (that is, in practice, the
passages in Caligula that are not present in Otho), which make Otho
some 16% shorter than the Caligula text. He thus notes that Otho deletes
primarily repetitive or 'uninteresting' material, such as messages, 'back
references', rhetorical repetition, didactic or learned details, and poetic
descriptions. Keith also points out a tendency of the Otho scribe to 'distinguish far more stringently between heroes and villains', which results
in a number of alterations of assessment of different characters.[34] In certain cases Keith considers that Otho's pruning is an improvement on
Caligula, because of the greater conciseness thus obtained: though it
often results in destroying the effect of a given episode. Laȝamon, concludes Keith, was 'mediaeval', loving detail and digression, and his work
is 'poetic story'. The reviser, on the other hand, was 'far more modern' in

---

[33] See W. J. Keith, 'Laȝamon's *Brut*: the Literary Differences Between the Two Texts',
Medium Aevum 29 (1960): 161–172.
[34] See Keith p. 169. Keith notes more specifically that favourable comments on enemies
(such for example as Julius Caesar) tend to be omitted, and the account of their adventures
are often cut down.

his sense of form and relevance, with 'a more serious and professional view' of his task:

> The digressions are excised, the unhistorical comments omitted ...
> Neat and professional as he is, he gives us a historical chronicle.[35]

The result, notes Keith, is less personal in a way, through the deletion of Laȝamon's comments, yet more personal in another, in that the scribe's alterations suggest a partial approach to history.

These results were questioned by A. C. Gibbs in the sixth chapter of his Cambridge Ph.D.[36] Stroud, he claims, has over-stressed the pattern of abridgement of the Otho text, while Keith's analysis has not been made on a large enough scale to prove that all the differences between both texts are indeed the result of a conscious choice. Moreover, the Otho-scribe could *not* have worked on the Caligula manuscript itself, because of the differences in the prologues, where Laȝamon's father is variously called Leuca and Leovenað, and where the poet himself is said to have been attached to the church of Areley, in one case, and to a 'cniþte' in the other.[37] The Otho scribe must have been writing partly from memory: Gibbs agrees on this point with Madden and Tatlock. The additional material in Otho is minute (only 80 half lines over the whole of the poem), and quite unimportant – a few descriptive formulas, minor additions which supply gaps in the Caligula text, or regularize the metre of a line following the deletion of archaic phrases:

> From these passages, we receive the impression of the 'Otho' scribe as a modernizer ... It is clear enough that the language has changed in the sixty or seventy years between the composition of the *Brut* and its copying by the Otho scribe. His alterations are brought about by sheer incomprehension as well as a desire to bring the work up-to-date ... He preserves the old style by default, in that he had not the confidence or the inclination to carry through his modernizing process on a large enough scale.[38]

As regards the omissions of the Otho text, Gibbs contends that

---

[35] Keith, p. 172.

[36] A. C. Gibbs, 'The Literary Relationships of Laȝamon's *Brut*', pp. 243–69.

[37] One could postulate a reading error in both these cases: 'Leucais' and 'cniþte' could well result from a misreading of 'Leouenaðes' and 'chirechen', from an earlier manuscript (possibly Laȝamon's holograph) where these words could have been abbreviated. The modification of the beginning of the words is easily explained by a faulty decoding of ambiguous letter-shapes. This hypothesis would confirm Gibbs' theory of a third copy, and solves the problem of why Laȝamon's father should have been called by a nickname in the Otho-text, as suggested by Tatlock (*Legendary History*, p. 511, note 113).

[38] Gibbs, pp. 245 and 250.

Stroud's units are too large to be significant, while Keith's hypothesis of a rationalizing process in the characterization of the Otho text meets with too many counter-examples to be convincing. What a close examination of the whole of both texts *does* reveal is rather 'a frequently random and irrational process', which appears to have operated to the detriment mainly of Laȝamon's additions to Wace, but without any recognizable method:

> I cannot see that the scribe understood what Laȝamon was trying to do, or the style in which he wrote. Nor does he leave a sufficiently clear impression on his copy for us to conclude that he had any real ideas about these things himself.[39]

Gibbs makes it clear that the Otho text is inferior to the Caligula text both in terms of material conservation and literary value, and that the few additions or modifications brought to the 'standard' text are negligible. The omissions in Otho follow no regular pattern, and what is retained remains extremely close to Caligula (and therefore, one assumes, to the authorial text) in content if not in lexis. Gibbs does however note one area in which the Otho scribe was fairly consistent in his omissions: in lines of moral comment. Considering that both Otho and Caligula were written down within the same 25-year period (1250–1275), Gibbs calls attention to the possibility that these comments may have been *added* by the Caligula scribe: 'We cannot, I suggest, be certain that their *inclusion* is not a characteristic of the "Caligula" scribe.'[40] But, as underlined by generations of literary critics, including Gibbs himself, Laȝamon was obviously a strong moralist, and these comments are but one manifestation of a more generalized tendency, also found in his proverbs or the speeches of his characters, for example.

It thus appears that, though the Otho and Caligula versions both descend from extremely close originals, and may have been copied from the same manuscript (possibly even from Laȝamon's holograph), because of the very principles which guided the scribal teams in their work, the Caligula text must be considered as most faithful to the authorial copy. The use of the Otho text will therefore be restricted in this work to cases of conflicting readings. Quotations from the *Brut* will consistently be taken from the most recent edition, that of Brook and Leslie.

---

[39] Gibbs, p. 269.
[40] Gibbs, p. 220.

2

The Prologue; or: The Acknowledged Sources

It is a paradox not unusual in medieval studies that some of the most puzzling source-problems arise in connection with those works whose sources have been acknowledged by the author. Convention demanded that an authority be referred to, regardless of actual facts; with the result that the critics are frequently confronted with the question of how seriously to take a writer's claim to having used a given work. A perfect example of this is Geoffrey of Monmouth's *liber vetustissimus*, which one may be fairly confident never existed (at least, not as he describes it); or, on a different level, Chaucer's claiming of 'Lollius' as source for his *Troilus*, though he made no use of it when writing his poem. The problems which arise in connection with the books mentioned by Laȝamon in his Prologue are of a similar nature: what exactly were they, and to what extent were they really used?[1]

Laȝamon describes the genesis of his work in the following words: after deciding that he would like to tell the noble past of England,

---

[1] I follow here my predecessors in assuming that the Prologue of the *Brut* was written by the author of the poem. One may object that there is room for doubt: the Prologue is written in the third person (but so is Wace's), and it follows to some extent the pattern of the conventional Prologues to 'auctores'. The 'unworthiness' topos is missing; on the contrary, the work is presented as competent and authoritative, and worthy to be repaid in prayers. However, one fails to see how anyone but the author could have given such information as to the sources of the work. The Otho text indicates quite clearly that the link between Wace's *Roman de Brut* and the English *Brut* was not felt at all, and it is improbable that a work deleted by one scribe should have been added by another. Similarly, while a copyist could conceivably write a Prologue requesting prayers for the author, the personal touch in asking the reader to pray for the souls of Laȝamon's father and mother as well is more likely to come from the poet himself. Moreover, on a stylistic level, the Prologue makes use of the same devices as the rest of the poem (notably, a blend of anaphora and alliteration preparing important scenes or statements), and neither the language nor the general feeling of the passage suggest that it was written by someone else than the author of the poem itself.

Laȝamon gon liðen   wide ȝond þas leode
& bi-won þa æðela boc   þa he to bisne nom
He nom þa Englisca boc   þa makede Seint Beda
An-oþer he nom on Latin   þe makede Seinte Albin
& þe feire Austin   þe fulluht broute hider in
Boc he nom þe þridde   leide þer amidden
þa makede a Frenchis clerc
Wace wes ihoten   þe wel couþe writen
& he hoe ȝef þare æðelen Ælienor
þe wes Henries quene   þes heȝes kinges
Laȝamon leide þeos boc   & þa leaf wende
he heom leofliche bi-heold   liþe him beo Drihten
Feðeren he nom mid fingren   & fiede on boc-felle
& þa soðere word   sette to-gadere
& þa þre boc   þrumde to are.[2]

These lines state that the poet had three written sources, which he found after extensive travel; three books in three different languages – English, French and Latin – which provided the basis for a work of 'soðere word', that is, a work of some scientific pretensions. In this case, history.

The first reaction of the medievalist to such claims is generally one of dubious caution. On the one hand, such prologues and references tend to be conventional, more or less fictitious appeals to authority. On the other hand, assuming that the Prologue does indeed provide serious information, how are we to interpret such subjective notions as 'wide', 'leode', 'sette to-gadere'? Does this mean that Laȝamon searched the whole of England for his material, or only part of it? Could his 'leode' have included neighbouring Wales? Or could it refer merely to Worcestershire? And to what extent can one consider the different works mentioned as actively significant, as opposed to having been used for occasional reference only?

Part of this last question is readily answered. The book by the French clerk named Wace is the *Roman de Brut*, a mid-twelfth century Anglo-Norman verse adaptation of Geoffrey of Monmouth's *Historia Regum Britanniae*, which may be recognised immediately as Laȝamon's main

---

[2] *Brut*, Prologue, lines 14–28. 'Laȝamon travelled widely throughout this land, and obtained the noble books which he took as example. He took the English book that Saint Bede made; he took another in Latin, that Saint Albin made, and the fair Austin, who brought baptism here. He took and placed between them the third book, made by a French clerk named Wace, who knew how to write well; and he had given it to the noble Eleanor, who was the queen of Henry the high king. Laȝamon took these books, and turned over the leaves; he considered them with respect, may the Lord be gracious towards him! He took a pen with his fingers and wrote on parchment, and put the true words together, and compressed the three books into one'.

source. The English *Brut* follows the *Roman de Brut* very closely; so closely, in fact, that it is generally accepted that there was no other major influence on the structure and contents of the poem. The two other references can therefore only allude to sources of secondary importance.

These two minor sources have been the object of heated debate, due, in part, to the fact that they have not marked the *Brut* to any great extent, but mainly because of the Prologue's confused description of them. Madden, who first tackled the problem, identified 'þa Englisca boc þa makede Seint Beda' as a translation of Bede's *Ecclesiastical History*. This identification was confirmed by Richard Wülcker,[3] and until quite recently was widely accepted. Any doubts were easily removed:

> Laȝamon's attribution of the Anglo-Saxon translation to Bede is not so surprising as it may appear at first, for the translator mentions himself nowhere, and the text begins with: 'Ic Beda Cristes þeow and mæssepreost sende gretan ðone leofastan cyning...'.[4]

That Bede should have been quoted by a work dealing with the history of England is far from surprising – the *Ecclesiastical History* was after all the most prestigious authority on the history of the English people, and Laȝamon being both English and learned (though the actual scope of this learning is a matter of debate), he must certainly have been familiar with the work. But the poem betrays no definite sign of such knowledge. On the contrary, notes Madden:

> so far from making it form an integral portion of his own poem, or even make it occupy a prominent place in it, he seems to have taken nothing from it except the story of Pope Gregory and the Anglo-Saxon captives at Rome. Indeed, in several instances he is quite at variance with Bede, even when not translating from Wace.[5]

The subsequent works of Richard Wülcker were moreover to prove that even that single episode of Pope Gregory could not have been taken from Bede, but must have been derived from some oral source.[6] Laȝamon's non-utilization of Bede was however considered as quite normal; for, as remarked by J.S.P.Tatlock:

> Lawman is specially unlikely to have used Bede much to supplement Wace because Bede, being concerned mostly with religion, is confused and hard to follow as to secular history.[7]

---

[3] Richard Wülcker, 'Über die Quellen Layamons', *Beiträge zur Geschichte der Deutschen Sprache und Literatur* 3 (1876): 524–55.
[4] G.J.Visser, *Vindication*, p.11.
[5] Madden, Introduction (vol.I), p.iv.
[6] Wülcker, pp.526–36.
[7] J.S.P.Tatlock, *The Legendary History of Britain*, p.488.

He may, suggests Tatlock, have used the *Ecclesiastical History* to obtain the correct forms of Anglo-Saxon names corrupted by Wace; but proper names are notoriously inconclusive evidence, and cannot therefore be considered as positive proof that Bede was used, or at least consulted by the English poet.

The Latin book by 'St Albin' and 'þe feire Austin' is, to quote Madden, 'more difficult to identify':

> it [is not] easy to understand how St Austin, who died in the year 604, and Albinus, Abbot of St Austin's at Canterbury, who died in 732, should be conjoined in the same work.[8]

This apparently puzzled the copyist who wrote the Otho version of the *Brut*, for – as noted by Madden – he 'here departed designedly from his original and ascribed the second book to Albin, and the third to Austin', omitting Wace altogether in the process. As Albinus is mentioned in Bede's prologue as having helped him in his research for material, Madden suggests that the Latin text by 'Seinte Albin' is no other than the Latin version of Bede's *Historia Ecclesiastica*:

> [Laȝamon] has not distinguished between the contributors and the writer, and having first erroneously given the Anglo-Saxon version of the work to Bede, he proceeds next to assign to Albinus and Austin (whose *Interrogatories* inserted in the first book seem to favor the notion) the Latin text of the *Ecclesiastical History*.[9]

This hypothesis led certain critics to assume severe limitations – if not total incompetence – on the part of the English priest. The implicit conclusion drawn by J. S. P. Tatlock, in his *Legendary History of Britain*, is thus that Laȝamon's grasp of Latin was so weak that he could not recognize 'St Albin's' book as the same work as his English Bede:

> While, being a churchman, of course he knows some Latin, he shows no intimacy with it, and this may be why ... he used Bede so little, even why he procured the English version.[10]

The identification of the book by 'Seinte Albin' and 'þe feire Austin' as

---

8 Madden, Introduction, p. xii.
9 Madden, Introduction, p. xii.
10 Tatlock, pp. 494–5. There is no reason, however, to think that the English poet's Latin was actually inadequate. Tatlock points out (note no. 35, p. 490) that 'Lawman oftener inflects Latin names than Wace does, and quotes liturgical bits', which demonstrates at least some familiarity with Latin texts. Tatlock further suggests (p. 491) that Laȝamon may have used the English translation of Bede's *Ecclesiastical History* to obtain correct forms of Anglo-Saxon names corrupted by Wace; but the evidence in favour of this hypothesis (a few proper names) is scarce.

Bede's *Ecclesiastical History* therefore confronts us with problems which far exceed a mere bibliographical note: if we accept it, we also have to accept a certain image of Laȝamon himself, that of a cleric who did not know Latin well enough to read even a very well-known work, and who quotes as authorities manuscripts he neither used nor understood. Or, alternatively, that of a man who possessed the necessary skills, but quoted more or less at random works of which he knew little more than the title-page. A current practice, in the Middle Ages, but which jars strangely with the earnest quality of the Prologue. In the first case, one is led to doubt the probability of the poet's acquaintance with even very widespread material, such as Geoffrey of Monmouth's *Historia Regum Britanniae*, for example, let alone more specialized sources of knowledge. Rudolf Imelmann's thesis – that the whole of the English *Brut* is a close translation of an expanded version of Wace's *Roman de Brut*, to the exclusion of any other sources[11] – may be considered a logical, if extreme, consequence of such an outlook, as indeed J.S.P.Tatlock's condescending portrait of

> a man ... enthusiastic and loyal, but a man who had seen little of the great world ... not ill educated, still less crude, but a man little acquainted with the advance of civilisation. ... Sometimes he makes a general observation about life ... sometimes perhaps with a smile, much oftener causing us to smile as one might suppress a smile over the reflections of a growing boy.[12]

The obvious result of such an attitude is a devaluation of the poem, whose deviations from Wace will tend to be assigned to an intermediary source, or to misunderstanding, rather than to artistic choice or deliberate adaptation for a specific audience. Significantly, F.L.Gillespy's analysis of the *Brut*, the first to be concerned with its literary aspect rather than with rhetorical technicalities, deliberately ignores the question of sources;[13] while G.J.Visser, a staunch admirer of the English poem, refuses to get involved in this particular issue by stating:

> We need not discuss the plausibility of this [i.e. the identification of the Latin book of St Albin and St Augustine as Bede's *Ecclesiastical History*], as Wülcker concludes ... that Laȝamon made no use of the Latin book at all.[14]

---

11 See Rudolf Imelmann, *Layamon. Versuch über seine Quellen*.
12 Tatlock, *Legendary History*, pp.509 and 514–5. Strangely enough, Tatlock does not seem to have been aware of the contradiction between these views and his theory (based mainly on the breadth and accuracy of Laȝamon's knowledge) that the poet may have travelled as far as Ireland.
13 F.L.Gillespy, 'Layamon's *Brut*: a Comparative Study in Narrative Art', *University of California Publications in Modern Philology* 3 (1916): 361–510.
14 Visser, *Vindication*, p.11.

The outlook on the *Brut* was such that a discussion of its possible sources would have been a barrier rather than an instrument towards critical appreciation.

The closely related issue of what one may call the 'personality of the author' comes to the fore in the openly ethical considerations of R.H. Fletcher, confronted with what he suspects may be interpreted as a moral taint on Laȝamon's character:

> This does not indicate any attempt on his part to deceive his readers. He wants them to know that he took all possible pains to secure authorities; but evidently when he got to work he found that details from Bede's story would not combine well with Wace's, and so fell back upon the latter.[15]

Even this experienced medievalist felt uneasy in front of what, in appearance, is a perfectly respectable medieval commonplace, and put it down to an anachronistic sense of scholarly standards, rather than questioning the hypothesis that made Laȝamon unwittingly acknowledge the same work twice under different names, and then not use it.

A possible key to the problem was provided in 1969 by E.G. Stanley, in his article 'Laȝamon's Antiquarian Sentiments'. He first notes a general confusion between the names Albin and Alcuin, to the extent that they were considered as variants of the same name: Laȝamon's mysterious book could thus be understood as containing the work of *Alcuin* and Austin, rather than *Albin* and Austin. Stanley then considers Laȝamon's possible connections with the centre of learning which produced the 'tremulous hand' scribe, who worked in Worcestershire during the first half of the thirteenth century. After a survey of the manuscripts available, Stanley ventures to suggest that

> perhaps Laȝamon had really seen some book containing works by both Albin/Alcuin and St Augustine (of Hippo, presumably), for such books existed, even in the vernacular.[16]

However, considers Stanley, he did not make much use of it, and continues, with overtones somewhat reminiscent of Fletcher:

> Whatever the explanation, it looks as if there is something sham rather than honestly erroneous about Laȝamon's antiquarian learning; we may not wish to go so far as to accuse him of improving his

---

15 R.H. Fletcher, *The Arthurian Material in the Chronicles*, p. 148.
16 E.G. Stanley, 'Laȝamon's Antiquarian Sentiments', *Medium Aevum* 38 (1969); p. 32.

list of sources to excite admiration for learning, but he does seem to be the kind of antiquary who pretends to himself that he is more fully conversant with his authors than is really the case.[17]

This suggestion solves the gruelling problem of a double attribution to Bede, while allowing – however cautiously – some amount of familiarity of Laʒamon with his hypothetical second source. This new area of investigation was taken up by P. J. Frankis in his article 'Laʒamon's English Sources'.[18] While following former criticism in accepting also a supplementary, oral source for the passage,[19] Frankis sees in Laʒamon's account of Pope Gregory and the English slaves traces of Ælfric's homily on Pope Gregory, notably in lines 14699–14701 of the *Brut*:

> þa com he in are strete   þat strahte to Rome
> þa isah he leden   of Englisce leoden
> þreo swiðe fæire men   faste ibunden[20]

when compared with Ælfric's

> brohton heora ware to romana byrig and Gregorius eode be ðære stræt to ðam engliscum mannum.[21]

This phrase, stresses Frankis, is one of the few independent additions by Ælfric to the English Bede, which he follows very closely, 'retaining numerous phrases verbatim' (note 16). The weakness of this specific argument, however, is obvious: the mentioning of a street in a scene taking place in Rome, the most important town in Christendom, is far from unexpected. Frankis further detects in those passages of the *Brut* dealing with idolatry, witchcraft and divination a number of parallels, both verbal and syntactical, with two other homilies of Ælfric, *De Falsis Diis* and *De Auguriis*.[22] None of these correspondences, in isolation,

---

[17] Stanley, 'Antiquarian Sentiments', p. 32.

[18] In *J. R. R. Tolkien, Scholar and Storyteller, Essays in Memoriam*, pp. 64–75.

[19] i.e., some oral form of the legend recorded in the *South English Legendary*, which agrees with Laʒamon's account in mentioning that there were three slaves involved in the scene.

[20] 'When he came into a street that led to Rome, he saw three exceedingly fair men of the English nation being led, tightly bound'.

[21] 'They brought their wares to the city of Rome, and Gregory went along the street to the Englishmen'; Frankis, p. 69. This parallel is also noted by Herbert Pilch, in *Layamon's Brut. Eine Literarische Studie*, p. 67, note 218a; but it is not discussed in any way. The texts referred to by Frankis are *The Homilies of Ælfric*, ed. J. C. Pope, vol. II, and *The Sermones Catholici or Homilies of Ælfric*, ed. B. Thorpe. The homily 'Sti Gregorii Pape Urbis Romane Incliti' is quoted from Thorpe, vol. II, p. 120.

[22] *De Falsis Diis*, 104–209, which shows some parallels with the account of Brutus' visit to the temple of Diana (*Brut* 569–637) and 556–9, which may have inspired the description of the destruction of pagan idols by King Luces (*Brut* 5079–81). Frankis further suggests that the names of the idols Apolin and Dagon (*Brut* 4030 and 2695) may also have been derived

would be convincing, admits Frankis, for whom it is the cumulation of such evidence that is significant.

> The similarities are of a kind that suggest the poet's recollection of an earlier reading of the homily rather than his writing with a copy of the Old English text beside him

considers Frankis (p. 65), thereby confirming the opinion of E. G. Stanley that while Laʒamon knew enough of the work to be conscious of its influence on him, he was not familiar enough with it to quote it at length, or did not think it desirable to do so.

In view of the somewhat tenuous nature of these isolated agreements between Ælfric's homilies and the *Brut*, Frankis also investigates the material possibility for Laʒamon to have found a composite book containing English material in thirteenth-century Worcester, the closest centre of learning to the poet's parish.[23] He concludes that

> in Worcester, Laʒamon could have had access to Ælfric's *Catholic Homilies* and *Lives of Saints*, including *De Auguriis* and *De Falsis Diis*, and also Felix's *Life of St Guthlac*.[24]

He notes moreover that N. R. Ker's *Catalogue of Manuscripts Containing Anglo-Saxon* mentions at Worcester two manuscripts such as described by E. G. Stanley:

> Both contain not only Ælfric's translation of Alcuin's *Interrogationes Sigewulfi*, beginning 'Sum geþungen lareow... albinus gehaten' ... but also the two homilies especially used by Laʒamon, *De Falsis Diis* ... and *De Auguriis*, the latter of which claims to quote Augustine ... To substitute for Laʒamon's Latin book by St Albin and St Augustine of Canterbury an English book with pieces deriving from Alcuin and St Augustine of Hippo ... may seem cavalier, but it may not be an unjustifiable assumption for a world in which Ælfric and Alcuin were interpreted as variant names for the same person.[25]

---

from *De Falsis Diis*. The expansion on the theme of witchcraft and divination (*Brut* 7734–40 and 7880) he puts in parallel with *De Auguriis*. These parallels, however, converge on points too commonplace to be significant. See below, chapter 7.

23 Worcester is only some eleven miles from Areley Kings.

24 Frankis, p.71. Frankis suggests that the names Æðelbald and Ælfwald, given by Laʒamon to the two brothers who killed Gratian (*Brut* 6114–49), may have been borrowed from Felix's *Life of St Guthlac*.

25 Frankis, p.74.

One would certainly agree that such a state of affairs could account for the confusion in names; the switching from a Latin text to an English one, however, is more dubious, despite E. G. Stanley's remark that such composite manuscripts existed 'even in the vernacular'. Moreover, none of the somewhat vague parallels mentioned by Frankis preclude indebtedness to a Latin religious source rather than an English one. Probability would therefore seem in favour of a Latin manuscript.

After going to some lengths to prove the likelihood of Laȝamon's claims of a source by Albin and Austin, Frankis proceeds to suggest that the reference may be a mere topos. His arguments, however, are based on invalid parallels. Laȝamon's claim to authority cannot be equated with Geoffrey of Monmouth's, Chrétien de Troyes', Wolfram von Eschenbach's or Marie de France's references to fictitious written sources: for on the one hand, we have people 'justifying' their fiction through unverifiable sources, and on the other, a man who is writing 'soðere word' – or who believes he is. Nearly all of Laȝamon's additions belong to the *amplificatio* of medieval rhetorics; his subject-matter remains scrupulously that of his source, Wace's *Roman de Brut*, and he therefore has no need of a 'cover-up'. On the contrary, it is to his advantage to name well-known, verifiable authorities, rather than spurious or obscure works. To ignore this fact in discussing the Prologue to the *Brut* is to presume a remarkable lack of shrewdness on Laȝamon's part. Whether or not the book was used, whether or not we may detect echoes of it in the poem, it is therefore reasonable to assume that the Latin book by Albin and Austin must have existed, either as a now lost composite manuscript, or – more plausibly – as the explicit sub-text to a well-known authority (Bede). As such, it should probably be understood as a 'pedigree' to the work, rather than as a source in the modern sense of the word.

Whilst there are good reasons to believe in the reality of the sources mentioned by Laȝamon, the Prologue falls short of truth in one respect at least: these three books were not made into one. Wace's *Roman de Brut* stands out, virtually unchanged, and the bulk of Laȝamon's expansions to Wace's material is not taken from the authorities named as guarantors to the seriousness of the *Brut*. We are therefore confronted with a twofold problem: what were those unacknowledged sources of Laȝamon's, and how were they integrated within Wace's subject-matter and framework? Moreover, how far afield are we entitled to search for these sources, which, we are told, the poet collected 'wide ȝond þas leode'? In the following discussion I shall assume as a working hypothesis that Laȝamon, being a cleric, must have been acquainted with at least the Latin school set-texts, and probably with the more widespread Latin material available at his time; his translation of Wace shows that he had the ability to read other French texts; the very language of the *Brut* suggests the possibility of some influence of older English texts; while the proximity of Areley Kings to Wales would provide a route of transmission for Welsh material. All the relevant texts from these four cultural fields will therefore receive close attention in connexion with the *Brut*.

3

From Wace to Laȝamon

Every text is unique and, at the same time, it is the translation of
another text. No text is entirely original because language itself, in
its essence, is already a translation: firstly, of the non-verbal world
and secondly, since every sign and every phrase is the translation of
another sign and another phrase. However, this argument can be
turned around without losing any of its validity: all texts are
original, because every translation is distinctive. Every translation,
up to a certain point, is an invention and as such it constitutes a
unique text.   Octavio Paz[1]

It is recognized by all that Laȝamon's *Brut* is a translation of Wace's
Roman de Brut, and a fairly faithful translation at that. J.S.P. Tatlock notes
that the English poet 'almost never inserts wholly new episodes or incidents, except amplifications of what he has found in Wace'.[2] These
amplifications, state Madden, Tatlock, and, more recently, H. Ringbom,
result in a massive inflation in length: Wace's 14,866 lines are more than
doubled, with very little additional material to account for the fact. Yet
the translating technique of Laȝamon, which is clearly the key to his
attitude towards Wace's text, has generally been glossed over. The reason
for this silence is undoubtedly that earlier critics felt that translation was
too menial a task for a poet such as Laȝamon. Madden significantly states
that the English poet must not be considered as a '*mere* translator';[3] and
Tatlock's description of how he imagined Laȝamon's translation technique stresses the poet's virtual disregard for his source text:

> Since in a poet's retelling of a narrative by another the taking of the
> matter by the teller must be followed by digestion and assimilation,
> we infer that he took in good-sized masses of Wace's poem and let

[1] *Traduccion: literatura y literalidad*, Barcelona: Tusquets Editor, 1971, p.9. Translated
quotation by S. Bassnett-McGuire, *Translation Studies*, p.38.
[2] Tatlock, *Legendary History*, p.489.
[3] Madden, I, p.xiv; my italics.

24

them settle down in his imagination and stimulate its own creation; hence his great expansion, especially after the early part (often too great to suit our taste); hence also his frequent small changes in order, his occasional contradictions of Wace, and forgetful dropping of very good passages, his constant insertion of precise numbers, fresh proper names, and other concrete detail.[4]

One may notice that not once in this passage does Tatlock use the verb 'to translate'. Moreover, if indeed Laȝamon rewrote the *Roman de Brut* after taking in 'good-sized masses' of it, he must have had a remarkable memory, for the *Brut* can be read line by line beside the *Roman* almost throughout the early part of the poem, and in a great number of passages of the latter part (though admittedly not so often in the Arthurian section, with its frequent adjuncts of new material).

Implicit in such an attitude is the belief that the act of translation is a purely mechanical process, a matter of merely giving different names to the same things, which is of an entirely different nature to poetic creativity. Modern translation theory, however, has demonstrated the fallacy of such a view. On the one hand, the simple 'renaming' of things in a different language has been shown to be virtually impossible, for there is no such thing as identical equivalents: from one language to another, even the simplest word will undergo some change in connotation or associative power. Translation is therefore an attempt to find the *closest* possible equivalent, but the final result will never be *exactly* the same.

In the quest for the closest possible equivalent, there are two basic orientations, towards a formal equivalence on the one hand, and a dynamic equivalence on the other. Eugene A. Nida defines these terms in the following way:

> Formal equivalence focuses attention on the message itself, in both form and content. In such a translation one is concerned with such correspondences as poetry to poetry, sentence to sentence, and concept to concept. Viewed from this formal orientation, one is concerned that the message in the receptor language should match as closely as possible the different elements in the source language ... A translation of dynamic equivalence aims at complete naturalness of expression, and tries to relate the receptor to modes of behaviour relevant within the context of his own culture; it does not insist that he understand the cultural patterns of the source-language context in order to comprehend the message.[5]

An example of a formal-equivalence translation is the 'crib' intended for

---

4 Tatlock, *Legendary History*, p. 489.
5 Eugene A. Nida, *Towards a Science of Translating*, p. 159.

students; as pointed out by Nida, such a translation would require numerous footnotes to make the text fully comprehensible to the lay reader; and such is the sort of translation which Madden obviously had in mind with his 'mere' translator. In this respect, he was a child of his time. Susan Bassnett-McGuire, in her outline of the history of translation, notes:

> The main currents of translation typology in the great age of industrial capitalism and colonial expansion up to the First World War can loosely be classified as follows: 1) translation as a scholar's activity, where the preeminence of the SL (= source language) text is assumed *de facto* over any TL (= target language) version; 2) translation as a means of encouraging the intelligent reader to return to the SL original; 3) translation as a means of helping the TL reader to become the equal of ... the better reader of the original, through a deliberately contrived foreignness in the TL text; 4) translation as a means whereby the individual translator who sees himself like Aladdin in the enchanted vaults ... offers his own pragmatic choice to the TL reader; 5) translation as a means through which the translator seeks to upgrade the status of the SL text because it is perceived as being on a lower cultural level.[6]

It is readily perceptible that Laȝamon's poem fits into none of these categories; yet it is interesting to note that Madden's judgement is based on a negative recognition – the *Brut* belongs to neither the first nor the second of these types, that is, it is not of the literal or 'learned' sort, whilst Tatlock has clearly tried to force the *Brut* into the fourth category, based on a principle of very free translation. Both critics therefore intuitively see the *Brut* as what would now be called a dynamic-equivalence translation, characterized mainly by its naturalness:

> A dynamic-equivalence (or D–E) translation may be described as one concerning which a bilingual and bicultural person can justifiably say, 'That is just the way we would say it'.[7]

The frequent underlining of Laȝamon's 'Englishness' by critics is an indication of the poet's success in this respect. Moreover, another characteristic of the dynamic-equivalent translation is the necessity to 'draw out' the SL message, in order to make the TL message equivalently meaningful. Almost all good translations tend to be longer than their originals, notes Nida, who further explains:

---

[6] Susan Bassnett-McGuire, *Translation Studies*, p. 71.
[7] E. Nida, *Towards a Science of Translating*, p. 166.

Some redundancy must be built into the message. Thus the form of the original message is almost always expanded, both as the result of differing patterns of obligatory features and because of cultural diversity. Even so there is an almost inevitable loss of meaning, for a translator can rarely do complete justice to the total cultural context of the communication, to the emotive features of meaning, and to the behavioural elements, for a shift of setting provides a widely varying range of consequences to any communication.[8]

This loss of meaning from the French *Roman* to the English *Brut* was noted by Tatlock, who like many other Laȝamon critics puts the fact down to a fundamental inferiority of thirteenth-century English society:

> Lawman has translated not only his language and style, but also his cultural background, from those expected among mid-twelfth century Normans to those of more primitive people.[9]

Naturalness (in this case, 'Englishness'); a certain loss of meaning (in this case, the loss of Wace's cultured 'Frenchness'); expansion of the source-message: these three distinctive features of Laȝamon's *Brut* may thus be accounted for to some extent by the translation process. The expansion aspect, however, requires a closer examination.

The first edition of the *Brut* by Sir Frederic Madden numbers 32,241 lines; or, to be more precise, 32,241 *half*-lines, as Laȝamon's verse-form is derived from the Anglo-Saxon long line. The more recent edition of Brook and Leslie correctly prints the poem in long lines, with the result that the poem 'shrinks' to 16,095 lines.[10] The question therefore arises: does Wace's octosyllabic line correspond to Laȝamon's half line, or to his long line? Depending on the answer, the whole outlook on the *Brut* is bound to be modified. Laȝamon expanded Wace's text, that much is certain – the *Roman de Brut* numbers 14,866 lines – but in one case, he more than doubled it; in the other, he added just over 1000 lines. And in view of his sizeable additions to Wace's material, in the Arthurian section especially, this second option would imply that far from expanding throughout his poem, as suggested by Madden, Laȝamon must have considerably *compressed* certain episodes of Wace. Among the critics who have been able to use Brook and Leslie's edition of the *Brut*, Håkan

8 E. Nida, *Towards a Science of Translating*, p. 174–5.
9 Tatlock, *Legendary History*, pp. 488–9.
10 This figure does not correspond to what a division by two of Madden's lines would lead one to expect, because Madden used a composite line-numbering, which gave a number to each half-line, whether it occurred in both manuscripts or only in one. Brook and Leslie number the lines of the Caligula manuscript only.

Ringbom follows his predecessors in this matter,[11] considering that Laȝamon's long line is roughly equivalent to Wace's octosyllabic couplet. He therefore sees the ratio between both texts as being 2:1, like Madden or Tatlock. However, the content potential of a French octosyllabic couplet appears to be far greater than that of Laȝamon's long line. Let us consider, for example, the passage where Brutus is admiring Britain. Wace reads:

> Vit les mores, vit les boscages,
> Vit les eues, vit les rivages,
> Vit les champs, vit les praeries,
> Vit les porz, vit les pescheries.[12]

This corresponds in the English *Brut* to:

> bi-heold he þa wateres   & þa wilde deor
> bi-heold he þa fisches   bi-heold he þa fuȝeles
> bi-heold he þa leswa   & þene leofliche wode
> bi-heold he þa leswa   & þene leofliche wode
> bi-heold he þene wode hu he bleou   bi-heold he þat corn hu hit
>   greu.[13]

In this case, the French octosyllabic line corresponds almost exactly to the English long line. Both contain two 'ideas'; had Laȝamon's long line been equivalent to Wace's couplet, the English text ought to have comprised four elements per line – twice of what we actually have. In non-descriptive passages, such clear-cut parallels are more difficult to find; the passage from one language to another has often necessitated extensive rephrasing, and general alterations in syntax and word order. Where comparison remains possible, however, the 1:1 ratio remains frequent. To the two lines of Wace:

> A sun aiol l'unt fait livrer
> Pur nurrir e pur doctriner[14]

correspond two lines in Laȝamon:

---

[11] See Håkan Ringbom, *Studies in the Narrative Technique of Beowulf and Lawman's Brut* (henceforth, *Narrative Technique*).

[12] Wace, 1211–4. 'He saw the moors, he saw the woodlands, he saw the waters, he saw the shores, he saw the fields, he saw the pastures, he saw the ports, he saw the fisheries'. All quotations of Wace's *Roman de Brut* are taken from the edition of Ivor Arnold.

[13] *Brut*, 1005–8. 'He beheld the waters and the wild beasts; he beheld the fish, he beheld the birds; he beheld the meadows and the fair woodland; he beheld the wood, how it was blossoming; he beheld the corn, how it was growing'.

[14] Wace, 1407–8. 'They have had him taken to his grandfather, to be brought up and educated'. These lines occur in the Locrin episode, and refer to Madan.

> & to Corinee hine sende   in-to his londe
> þat he hine sculde wel i-teon   & tuhlen him teachen.[15]

A more complex instance may be found in the following passage, taken from the account of Ebrauc's reign:

> Il assembla un grant navie
> Si prist de ses homes partie[16]

which becomes:

> He lætte bi sæ-flode   ȝearkien scipen gode
> vmben ane stunde   þa scipen ȝaru weoren
> & he dude þer-inne   his drihtliche cnites.[17]

If Wace's octosyllabic couplet were really equivalent to one long line, we would expect Laȝamon's long lines to represent an expansion of double the original information. Yet, as in Wace, one line is taken to state that Ebrauc assembled a fleet; and it takes another to mention the manning of them. The ratio here is clearly 1:1, not 2:1. It is apparent, moreover, that the two ideas expressed by Wace in two of his octosyllabic lines could not have been condensed satisfactorily in one long line. D.P. Donahue, in his thesis on thematic and formulaic composition in the *Brut*, suggests that this is due to a number of constraints unknown to Wace. His analysis of the scene where Leir questions his daughters thus shows that sixty out of ninety-two lines of the English poem parallel the corresponding lines in Wace, essential idea by essential idea: and the reason for this Donahue identifies in Laȝamon's use of end-stopped lines:

> Because of the structure of Lawman's lines, Lawman's ideas are generally not run on. He used a subject-verb structure in the first half of most of his lines. In doing so, he limited the function of the second half of these lines to modifying either the subject or the verb that appeared in the first half. Ordinarily, the fact that his lines were dominated by this pattern made it necessary for Lawman to use a full long-line to state each idea ... Even when a thought continues for several lines each line is end-stopped. The continuity of thought is picked up and maintained in each succeeding line through the

---

15 *Brut*, 1209–10. '[Locrin] sent him to Corineus, into his land, so that he should well educate him, and teach him manners'.
16 Wace, 1503–4. 'He assembled a great fleet and took part of his men'.
17 *Brut*, 1316–8. 'He had good ships prepared by the sea. After some time the ships were ready, and he placed his noble knights therein'. Line 1317 provides additional information not found in Wace, and therefore is not taken into consideration.

introduction of a new subject and/or verb or repetition of the old.[18]

This style, notes Donahue, is used throughout the poem, including the long-tailed simile sections. Laʒamon's unit of thought is the long line, just as Wace's is the octosyllabic line – a fact partially noted by Ringbom, when he states that Wace is more concise than Laʒamon, due to the limited space afforded by the octosyllable, and that there is 'a very strong trend in Wace to make each line a self-contained unit'.[19]

That Laʒamon's long line could not contain as much information as Wace's octosyllabic couplet must therefore be regarded as a fact. Technical constraints specific to the English poet make his long line roughly equivalent to one of Wace's octosyllabic lines in terms of content potential, even though the English long line undeniably has a greater syllable and word potential. The inadequacy of assimilating the long line to the octosyllabic couplet was also felt by Ringbom:

> The fact that all sections show an increase makes one doubt whether the information capacity of Lawman's half-line really was quite the same as that of Wace's line.[20]

However, he fails to grasp the full implications of this remark, and his study of Laʒamon's 'expansion rate' is marred by his using units in both poems which do not correspond.

Ringbom's attempt to express the passage from one poem to another in terms of the relative length of the different episodes therefore needs to be revised. In terms of a 1:1 equivalence, 69 of Ringbom's 114 sections thus show an increase, ranging from 0.9% (one line, in a passage on minor kings; Wace 13925–14026, *Brut* 14923–15025) to 353.6% (the account of Arthur's northern conquests and his return to Britain; Wace 9703–30, *Brut* 11210–336). Two sections have exactly the same length (the first years in Britain, Wace 1169–316 and *Brut* 967–1114; Luces and his preparations, Wace 11059–124 and *Brut* 12614–79). In 44 sections, Wace's text is the longer, in proportions varying from 1% (Brutus's voyage to Logice; Wace 611–701, *Brut* 548–637) to 83.2% (Arthur's feast at Caerleon, Wace 10337–620 and *Brut* 12187–12341). A table of the comparative length of each major episode of the *Brut* yields the following results:[21]

---

[18] Dennis P. Donahue, *Thematic and Formulaic Composition in Lawman's Brut*, pp. 13–14.

[19] Ringbom, *Narrative Technique*, p. 111.

[20] Ringbom, *Narrative Technique*, p. 107–8.

[21] For practical reasons, I have compressed Ringbom's 114 sections (see *Narrative Technique*, pp. 105–110) into 26. There is no real information loss in so doing: the 114 sections are too numerous to allow an overall view of the matter, yet too general to give a precise idea of the true nature of the expanded (or compressed) passage. Moreover, Ringbom's division of the text is often arbitrary (some sections end in the middle of a speech, for example).

Subject matter	Wace	Laȝamon	Length difference
Aeneas, Ascanius, Brutus before arrival in Britain	9–1050	36–891	197 (−)
Brutus in Britain, Locrin, Camber, Albanactus	1051–440	892–1254	27 (−)
Guendoleine to Bladud	1441–654	1255–449	19 (−)
Leir and Cordoille	1655–2066	1450–886	25 (+)
Margan, to Rival and successors	2067–139	1887–957	2 (−)
Ferreus, Porreus, Judon	2140–202	1958–2023	3 (+)
Stater, to Dunwale	2203–312	2024–139	7 (+)
Belin and Brennes	2313–436	2140–237	26 (−)
Gurguint to Lud	2437–790	2238–561	30 (−)
Cassibelaune (Caesar's invasions)	2791–4840	2562–4484	127 (−)
Tenauntius, Kimbelin	4841–82	4485–581	55 (+)
Wider, Arviragus, Marius, Coil	4883–5208	4582–5031	123 (+)
Luces to Coel	5209–652	5032–504	29 (+)
Constantin, Octaves, Maximian, Constantine	5653–6468	5505–6472	153 (+)
Vortigern and Vortimer	6469–7652	6473–8100	444 (+)
Aurelius	7653–8284	8101–905	172 (+)
Uther	8285–9008	8906–9892	263 (+)
Arthur (a) to the conquest of France (incl.)	9009–10174	9893–12079	1021 (+)
(b) to his death	10175–13294	12080–14297	902 (−)
Constantin to Malgo	13295–374	14298–399	21 (+)
Carric and Gurmund	13375–682	14400–694	11 (−)
Augustine's mission (to the Bangor massacre)	13683–926	14695–922	15 (−)
Minor kings	13927–14005	14923–15006	15 (−)
Cadwallan	14006–656	15007–864	207 (+)
Cadwalader	14657–842	15865–16078	28 (+)
Yvor and Yuni, conclusion	14843–866	16079–95	6 (−)

This procedure makes no allowances for any shifting of material and obliterates any parenthetical remarks or general changes in narrative technique; however, it shows a clear trend towards compression at the beginning of the English *Brut*. This is visible in the first, preliminary section, but also in more celebrated passages such as the Belin and Brennes episode, or the account of Caesar's invasion. From the period of the birth of Christ onwards (Kinbelin) starts a strong movement towards expansion, culminating in the first part of the Arthuriad (1021 lines longer than in Wace, an increase of 87.5%). The latter part of Arthur's career (the campaign against Rome), however, shows a sharp decrease in length, to the extent that the total length of the Arthurian episode, surprisingly, is only 2.7% longer than its counterpart in Wace. The next section to display a major expansion in length is the reign of Cadwallan; with an addition of 207 lines (= 31.8%) as compared with the Wace-text, it would appear to be the core of the latter part of the poem.

From the length of its various sections, the English *Brut* would thus seem to have as centre and culmination the *beginning* of Arthur's reign, for whom the preceding reigns, all considerably expanded, serve as pedigrees. Arthur's Roman campaign, however, does not appear to have had the favour of Laȝamon, who minimized it to an extreme (in terms of length, at least). By comparison, Wace's account of this section is well over twice the length of that of Arthur's early exploits: the relative importance of the two phases in Arthur's life is simply reversed in the English poem. And the post-Arthurian section, which may be said to carry the 'moral' of the poem, polarizes around the reigns of Cadwallan, the king responsible for the slaying of St Oswald, and Cadwalader, the very last Briton king, who is told in a divine vision to leave Britain to the Angles. Despite his clerical status, Laȝamon does not appear to have taken too much interest in the mission of Augustine, which is somewhat cut down.

This general survey suggests that even though the *Brut* scrupulously follows the order of events of Wace's *Roman de Brut*, the poem has a different inner structure through the shifting of weight from one episode to another. This, of course, does not mean that sections were uniformly expanded or compressed; as noted above, the very procedure of comparing the relative length of two poems implies a number of limitations, especially when (as in our case) the size of the works makes a detailed analysis of every part of the poem somewhat difficult.[22] In order to complete the picture, it is therefore necessary to resort to a different methodology, namely, an investigation of the general principles governing Laȝamon's omissions or expansions; this will also provide us with some sort of norm to distinguish 'organic' from 'non-organic' variation with the *Roman de Brut* in the following chapters.

Omissions

The opinion that the *Brut* systematically expanded the Wace text has meant that most critics have discussed Laȝamon's additions to his

---

[22] In print, that is. It would take a reader of preternatural patience to read such a study to the end.

source, but have barely touched upon the question of his omissions; I shall therefore dwell upon the matter at some length.

Laȝamon's omissions or contractions fall into three main categories:

(a) omission of technical description

(b) omission of redundant material, or material not of direct relevance to the plot

(c) omission of details inconsistent with the portrayal of a given character or episode.

The first category of omissions concerns more especially battle descriptions, where Wace's wealth of technical terms and war machinery is consistently replaced by the 'clash-of-arms' motif. There are a number of examples of such a substitution (which often results in a general compression of the passage) throughout the *Brut*; the first case occurs in the description of the siege of Sparatin (Wace 319–36; *Brut* 310–20), where the description of the war machinery is deleted, as well as the technicalities of the battle, to be replaced by the various sub-themes of the 'battle' narrative formula.[23] Of a similar nature is the omission, in the account of the counsel between the besieged Trojans in Tours (Wace 984–94; *Brut* 843–5), of Wace's tactical considerations; or, in the Arthurian part of the poem, the absence of reference to general strategy in Laȝamon's account of Evander's troop movements.[24]

This apparent lack of interest in the technical aspects of warfare is accompanied by a tendency towards compressing battle scenes in general, and toning down of slaughter scenes in particular. The battle of Sparatin, mentioned above, is thus condensed into five lines in the *Brut*; Laȝamon deletes the mention that the Greeks who manage to escape from Brutus' trap end up falling off cliffs or getting drowned (Wace 468–83, *Brut* 402–11); the battle-scene between the Romans and the army of Belin and Brennes is reduced to the simple statement that all the Romans were killed.[25] The onslaught between the Romans and the

---

23 See below on Laȝamon's narrative technique. Other instances of Laȝamon's cutting down of technical detail may be found in Wace 3033–48, *Brut* 2837–844 (siege of Rome); Wace 11159–62, *Brut* 12703–4 (enumeration of the different kinds of foot-soldiers in Arthur's army deleted); Wace 11947–70, *Brut* 13317–30 (the battle description stressing the technical superiority of Petreius and his Romans is deleted); Wace 12339–57, explaining the battle formation, is entirely deleted in the *Brut*, as is Wace 13541–58, describing the fortifying of Cirencester by the besieged inhabitants of the town, and the war machines used by Gurmund.

24 Wace 12176: Evander groups his troops because he realises that he cannot get to the prisoners.

25 Wace 2997–3027, *Brut* 2822–8. The English poem replaces the battle description by three lines on the prowess of the Britons. Other instances of this tendency may be found at Wace

Britons at Caesar's first invasion is likewise reduced to a few sub-themes (the clash of arms, rolling heads) to concentrate immediately on the figure of Caesar himself (Wace 4005–36; *Brut* 3727–30).

These omissions bring about a corresponding stress on the *issue* of the battles, the *result* of a given tactical choice, the prowess of a given warrior rather than the fate of a whole army. The same is true of the second category of omissions, that of redundant or 'irrelevant' material. There is a general reluctance in the *Brut* to give minor characters too much importance, or admit details which slacken the pace unnecessarily. Most of the omissions or compressions in the earlier part of the *Brut*, before Brutus' arrival in Britain, belong to this category. Thus, Wace 86–88

> Mais al tomulte e al desrei
>
> ...
>
> En la grant presse la perdi[26]

becomes in the *Brut* (line 109):

> Inne þane fehte   his feon heo him binomen.[27]

These lines, which occur in a parenthesis explaining Ascanius' parentage, have clearly been remodelled to avoid too much stress on past events more or less unconnected with the 'story'; and one may notice that the English *Brut* (113) replaces Wace's line 86 by a mention of Ascanius' loyalty to his half-brother, thereby firmly placing the narrative in a future-oriented perspective. A certain reluctance to give too much importance to minor characters or events may also explain Laʒamon's omission of Wace 581–2, where the Greek king Pandrasus says it is a consolation that his daughter Ignogen should be given to a man of such prowess as Brutus, and of Wace's mention (605–10) of his generosity to the departing Trojans. Similarly, the whole of the speech of Goffar in

12227–32, *Brut* 13507–8 (the Roman débâcle is condensed to two lines); Wace 12817–28 (rhetorical battle description) is deleted to proceed immediately to the single combat between Walwain and Luces; Wace 12967–76, describing the slaughter of the fleeing Romans, is deleted, to go on directly to Arthur's honourable treatment of Luces' corpse; Wace 13087–90, describing arrows piercing heads, eyes, etc., is omitted; Wace 14419–24, *Brut* 15599–601: the wholesale massacre of the civilian population, including women and babies, is deleted, and the focus narrowed to the 'ferde'; Wace 14695–8, the reasons for the flight from plague-stricken Britain, are deleted; Wace 9679–94, describing the helpless flight of the Irish in front of Arthur, is condensed in *Brut* 11146–52. And the most striking slaughter scene of the *Roman de Brut*, that of the monks of Bangor, covers just three lines in Laʒamon (14920–2) where Wace (13913–24) provides an ornate piece of rhetorical narrative. The descriptions of Briton difficulties are omitted or toned down with noteworthy regularity. See Wace 3099–3111, *Brut* 2887–90; Wace 11947–70, *Brut* 13332; Wace 12869–73, entirely deleted; Wace 13571–87, *Brut* 14570–5.
[26] 'But in the tumult and the disturbance, (when Eneas got out of Troy), he lost her in the great turmoil'.
[27] 'In the fight, his enemies took her from him'.

front of Tours is deleted (Wace 953–62; *Brut* 831–2); Goffar's reaction, which in the *Historia Regum Britanniae* (ch. 20) is described in detail, had already been considerably abridged by Wace, presumably for the same reasons. Laȝamon's omission of all mention of mothers mourning their dead children (Wace 7879–4) in Aldad's considerations about what to do with the defeated Hengest, may also be due to the desire to avoid Hengest's humanity (and that of his mother) mitigating the reader's condemnation of him.[28] A similar tendency towards minimizing the characterization of certain major enemies is found in the Roman campaign episode, where Laȝamon deletes Wace's (positive) parenthetical portrait of Luces (12451–8) and his internal debate on whether to flee or not, when he knows of Arthur's position (12463–72).[29] A most striking instance of this tendency is the case of Modred, whom the English poet characterizes exclusively through statements of moral condemnation. Wace's attempts to explain Modred's actions because of his awareness of his guilt towards his uncle are systematically deleted (Wace 13054, 13073–6); the image of a tragic Modred, cornered into battle by his own conscience, unable to believe that Arthur could possibly pardon a crime as heinous as his (Wace 13155–62) is obliterated from Laȝamon's poem, where Modred is totally lacking in human dimension. All sympathies must be with Arthur, and no chances are taken in that respect. The similes with which Wace (11519–21 and 11551–2) enhances his description of the giant of Mt St Michel, comparing him first to a boar hurling itself at the hunter, then to an oak-tree uprooted by the wind, are likewise omitted by Laȝamon: partly because of the emblematic value of the boar, too closely connected with Arthur, the 'aper Cornubiae', to be used of one of his enemies; but also, one suspects, because the rhetorical effects connected with the giant were felt to deflect somewhat the attention from Arthur himself. One may further notice that the story of the giant Rithon and his mantle of beards,[30] which in the French poem is meant to give a fuller appreciation of the strength of the Mt St Michel giant, disappears completely from the English *Brut*.

The wish of the English poet to keep the focus on the main character of the episode sometimes expresses itself, in battle-scenes, by the omission of the names of minor figures. The central role of Caesar, in the account of the first Roman invasion of Britain, is thus enhanced by Laȝamon's omis-

---

[28] The reference to bereaved mothers is explicitly taken from the Scriptures (Samuel's beheading of Agag). It is therefore all the more interesting that Laȝamon should have omitted it.

[29] The short description of Guitard of Poitiers (Wace 10117–8) is also deleted by Laȝamon, who just mentions that he refused to submit to Hoel.

[30] Wace 11565–92. One of the manuscripts collated by Arnold also omits the story of Rithon (MS J., Bibliothèque Nationale, fonds français 1416; late C13, Northern dialect); the omission is however more extensive than that of Laȝamon (Rithon is not even mentioned), and need not indicate an alternative manuscript tradition.

sion of Wace's description of the killing of Labienus by Nennius, with Caesar's sword; Nennius' victims remain anonymous Romans. Similarly, where Wace (11857–74) describes Gawain hacking off the arm of one of Marcel's cousins, Laȝamon merely states (13272–3) that whenever the Britons turned back, the Romans were the worse for it. The fights between Guitard of Poitiers and the king of Africa, and between Holdin of Flanders and King Alfatin of Spain (Wace 12727–42) disappear entirely to give place directly to the encounter between Leir of Boulogne and an admiral of Babylon, the eventual slaying of Leir being the motivation for Gawain's entering into the narrative. Laȝamon further ensures that the focus remains on Gawain – who may be considered as the true hero of the Arthurian campaign against Rome, far more than Arthur himself – by deleting the mention of the death of the three Britons Balluc, Cursal and Urgent.[31]

These compressions or omissions in connection with minor characters not only restrict the focus to the main characters, but also result in an acceleration of the rhythm. Håkan Ringbom, in his considerations on point of view, tempo and time in the *Brut*, points out quite correctly that the question of whether the tempo of the *Brut* is fast or slow depends on what poem we compare it with; but it is difficult to agree with his apparent identification of conciseness with speed, which makes him conclude that Wace's tempo is more rapid, because 'in comparison with its source the English *Brut* is quite elaborate'.[32] In fact, as noted by Ringbom, not only are retarding devices extremely rare in the English poem (with the notable exception of the messenger-theme), but those details or remarks which, though appearing in Wace, are not essential to the flow of events, or break the rhythm of an episode, are regularly omitted by Laȝamon. Wace's characteristic 'ne sai' is thus systematically deleted, as are the remnants of the annal-like time rubrics scattered by Geoffrey through his *Historia*.[33] Excessively didactic passages also tend to be cut down: Wace's elaborate description of the mermaids, their sweet song, and the dire fate of those who listen to it, followed by an explanation of their allegorical meaning, is drastically compressed into six lines in the English poem (Wace 733–64; *Brut* 663–8). Similarly, Wace's learned lesson in word formation (13799–803), explaining how the final o of *cerno* disappeared according to the rules of philology, is omitted, as is Wace's

---

[31] The disappearance of Wace's rhetorical battle scene (12817–28) to give way directly to the single combat between Walwain and Luces, clearly proceeds from the same wish to make Gawain the pivot of the episode. This emphasis on Gawain is even rendered at Arthur's expense: Wace's scene of Arthur's prowess giving courage to his men at the encounter with Luces (Wace 12887–920) is entirely deleted, and replaced by the standard sub-themes introducing a battle-scene (horns and trumpets blowing).

[32] H. Ringbom, *Narrative Technique*, pp. 135–7.

[33] See Wace 1247–50; 3827–9; 14837–8 (time rubrics). Instances of Wace's discarded 'ne sai' may be found on lines 4093, 4838, 7264 and 13614 of the *Roman de Brut*.

information as to the specificities of the Gaulish or English political system. Laȝamon does not bother to repeat Wace's note (9905–8) that Gaul had neither 'rei ne seinnur' in Frolle's day, nor does he retain the comment that many English kings in Cadwalan's day only really held counties (Wace, 14401–2), or that Æthelstan did not hold sway over Wales or Cornwall (Wace 14760), a fact implicit in the context. The 'unnecessary' details of local geography provided by Wace (12285–6) before the battle of Saussy are likewise deleted, as are many of Wace's more rhetorical passages. Wace's lyrical description of the beauty of the night and the moonshine making the weapons of Belin's army gleam (Wace 2997–3007) is omitted, partly because it delays the glorious outcome of the battle (i.e., the conquest of Rome; the battle-scene proper is reduced to the simple statement that all the enemies were killed), and partly because the ambush is shifted in time, in the English poem, and takes place during the day. The French poet's consideration of the changing names of the cities of Britain also shrinks to almost half its original length, through the omission of the four-times repeated mention that new invaders did not know the language of the country, and thus perverted the names they heard (Wace 3762–84; Brut 3543–55). Wace's elaborate effects on 'pais' (Wace 7211–12) are deleted, while the scene of Brian's hunt for venison is considerably shortened through Laȝamon's deleting of Wace's synonymic doublets (Wace 14207–13; Brut 15255–8). The description of Arthur and his companions riding to the lair of the giant of Mt St Michel (Wace 11333–5) is similarly reduced to one line, through the omission of the rhetorical effects of the French text. Wace's rhetorical attack on gambling (lines 10557–88) disappears entirely from the English poem, where gambling is not even mentioned among the pastimes of Arthur's court, as does also the accumulation of musicians, jongleurs, instruments and stories which Wace describes as having entertained the Britons at Arthur's coronation feast (Wace 10543–56).[34]

The English poet would thus appear to have had a marked aversion from delaying devices of any nature, especially in connection with battle-scenes. All details interfering with a swift outcome of the encounter are deleted or shifted; important battles are moreover prepared by a build-up of tension which admits no side glances, and requires a sustained narrative tempo. Some of Laȝamon's omissions are thus accompanied by slight changes in structure; a good example of this is the account of Brutus' preparation of his ambush against Pandrasus. In Wace (385–428), Brutus first tells Anacletus what to say to the Greek knights; Wace then describes Brutus preparing his trap and reports Anacletus' words to the Greeks in direct speech. In the English poem (356–77), Brutus *dictates* to

---

[34] This may however be due to a lacuna in Laȝamon's Wace-manuscript; Arnold notes that lines 10543–88 do not appear in eight of the manuscripts he collated.

Anacletus the very words he is to say, in direct speech; Wace's scene of Anacletus approaching the Greek warriors therefore becomes redundant, and is deleted: we are immediately told that Brutus' ruse worked. Only then is Brutus' trap described, leading on to the onslaught.[35] Similarly, Corineus' boasting of his strength during the battle between the Trojans and the men of Goffar (Wace 853–900; *Brut* 766–93) disappears from the English poem, as it retards the outcome of the battle – the centrepiece of the encounter, the single combat with Suard, is yet to come. All of the speeches placed by Wace in the middle of a battle are thus either deleted or shifted by Laȝamon. This unwillingness to break the rhythm of battle scenes is especially noticeable in the Arthurian section, where boast-speeches of any length are placed before the onslaught, or after the victory, but never during the fight.

One may also assign to a wish to keep up a sustained tempo the omission of Wace's list of the areas Arthur asks Hoel to conquer for him (Wace 10107–112; Laȝamon just mentions them once they are conquered); the condensing of Wace 12477–518, where Luces makes a long speech to his men describing the situation and exhorting them to battle (*Brut* 13662–87 deletes the tactical considerations of Wace 12499–516 entirely); the deletion of such passages as the eulogy of the fighting qualities of Kei and Beduer (Wace 12589–96) in the middle of a battle, or the celebrating of the 'bunté, curteisie, pris de chevalerie' (Wace 12764–6) of Gawain and Hoel, which Laȝamon replaces by epithets such as 'swiðe stið-imoded mon' (13829, 'very stern-minded man'), easier to integrate within a swift-moving narrative. Likewise, the omission of Wace 12001–4, where Bos sets out to see which of the Romans is Petreius before launching an attack on him, is probably due to the fact that the English poet presumably felt that the enemy leader ought to have been conspicuous enough anyway, and that to report such a precaution would have delayed the outcome of the campaign unnecessarily. Wace's account of Arthur's giving Ewein the crown of Scotland following the death of his uncle Anguissel (Wace 13189–200) breaks the narrative flow which leads from the surrendering of Winchester and Arthur's vengeance on the town to his pursuing of Modred and the final battle, and therefore also disappears from the English poem.

The third category of omissions are made for the sake of inner con-

---

[35] This shift of material, describing military movements in action rather than beforehand, as part of tactical considerations, is indicative of a more general reluctance to dissociate cause and effect. Similar shiftings occur in lines 1019–36 of the *Brut* (Wace 1223–46), where the change in names of the towns of Britain is mentioned only *after* Corineus has secured the island for Brutus and his people by defeating Geomagog; and at the end of Arthur's Roman campaign, where Laȝamon inverts the order of events given by Wace (the *Roman* has Arthur send his people to different abbeys to be buried *before* sending Luces' corpse to Rome with a taunting message). These inversions are best explained by the English poet's distaste for departures from supposed chronological order.

sistency rather than for formal considerations. They may be dictated either by inner contradiction, when a given detail in Wace goes against what 'common sense' would expect in a given situation or of a given character; or because it may jar with the overall ideological pattern imprinted on the *Brut* by Laȝamon. These principles function most noticeably in Laȝamon's reworking of the speech of Tonuenne, in the Belin and Brennes episode. The two brothers are about to engage in battle when their mother interposes herself, and tries to bring the younger brother (who is in the wrong) back to reason. In Wace, she does so by reproaching Brennius for his misdeeds and chiding him for having come back to Britain with weapons rather than gifts for his brother. This unconvincing part of what is supposed to be a reconciliation speech (Wace 2753–66) is deleted in the English *Brut*. Wace's mention that Gorlois was expecting help against Uther from Ireland (Wace 8649–50) is presumably omitted to avoid imputing treachery to the duke, who is consistently described in positive terms. Similar 'editing' is also conspicuous in the Uther episode, where Wace's 'courtly' detail of the rough soldier Uther falling in love with Ygerne before having even seen her (Wace 8577–82) is omitted, as is Gawain's defence of 'druerie' (Wace 10765–72) at a war counsel, just before the solemn decision to wage war upon Rome, or the tears and kisses at the recognition scene between Brian and his sister (Wace 14283–4), when they are supposed to be pretending they do not know each other.

The wish to present a given character in a more favourable light may also explain the omission of Cadwan's boasts that he will destroy Northumberland and kill or destroy Elfrid (Wace 13969–76): the English *Brut* replaces this passage by a mention (14970–2) that Ælfric has it reported to him that Cadwan was making threatening speeches against him; the whole issue thus becomes more vague. Similarly, a number of details of the Oswi episode (his submitting to Cadwalan, Penda's accusation that he has sent to Germany for Saxon troops, his attempts to make peace with Penda before deciding to fight it out)[36] are left aside, clearly with the intention of securing the reader's sympathy for Oswi.

The most systematic editing of Laȝamon does not concern isolated characters, however, as much as one specific abstract entity: the legitimate inhabitants of Britain. It has already been pointed out many a time that Laȝamon depicts the Britons in a more favourable light than Wace, until the arrival of the Angles, who then 'inherit' the land; but what is striking is that the upgrading of the Britons is effected by pruning down potentially unfavourable traits, rather than adding elements in their favour.[37] Battles are often depicted in a vaguer way in the English *Brut* in

---

36 Wace 14499–514, 14555–60 and 14613–24.
37 Favourable comments are also added by Laȝamon on occasion, of course; the ambush of

order to avoid having to show the Britons in a difficult position. Wace's
description, in the Belin and Brennes episode, of the Britons being cut
down by the Romans (Wace 3099–111) is replaced by a terse

> þer wes ballu riue   Bruttes þer fullen
> Belin and Brennes   burstes þare hæfden.[38]

The ensuing tactical retreat is not motivated, in the English poem, by
the heavy losses of the Britons, but as a reaction to the taunting of the
Romans, a passage added by Laȝamon (2891–7). In the battle scene between Arthur and Luces, Laȝamon avoids mentioning the difficulties of
the Britons (Wace 12869–73), and the main onslaught, with its single
combats and temporary reversals of fortune, is entirely deleted, so that
only the Roman flight remains. Similarly, in the account of Caesar's
second defeat, Wace's stress on the valour of the outnumbered Romans
and the losses they inflicted on the Britons is totally reversed: Laȝamon
(3957–60) underlines the *Roman* losses, insisting (3969–79) that Caesar
only managed to escape thanks to a stratagem; and where Wace states
(4311) that 'Cassibelan fu mult joius' ('Cassibelan rejoiced greatly') at
Caesar's departure, Laȝamon (3995–4015) has him lament the fact that his
prey is gone. After Caesar's final victory, the link with Rome is underplayed; Wace's mention of Coil's Roman education and his loyalty to
Rome is reduced to the bare statement that he knew Roman law well.[39]
The Britons are shown to be free agents even under the reign of Severus:
where Wace has him subdue the Britons through his cruelty (Wace
5281–4), Laȝamon (5126–36) has them rally to him because they are so
impressed by the perfect discipline of his troops. Wace's negative statement (8871–4) that the Britons lacked discipline because of their arro-
gance becomes in the English *Brut* the result of their contempt for the
ailing Uther, who was unable to show all the regal authority that was
needed (*Brut* 9684–8). This pro-Briton bias also expresses itself through a
reticence to retain details which detract from the glory of the Britons:
Wace's mention that the fleeing Saxons had thrown off their armour to
get away more easily, so that they only had their swords to defend themselves against Hoel (Wace 9383–6), is omitted in the *Brut*, as is Wace's
explaining of Arthur's first victories over Modred by the lack of experience of Modred's men (Wace 13112–8).

This movement towards increased dignity for the Britons culminates
(as is to be expected) in the Arthurian section. Their superiority is ab-

---

Belin's, referred to above, is a case in point, where the battle-scene is replaced by a three-
line expansion on the valour of the Briton knights (*Brut* 2822–8); no other explanation is
given for the outcome of the encounter (all the Romans are killed).
[38] *Brut* 2888–9. 'There, death was rife; there, Britons fell; there, Belin and Brennes had
losses'. See also above, note 25.
[39] Wace, 5202–6; *Brut* 5029.

solute, to the extent of making totally redundant Wace's expansions of
Arthur's virtues to explain his success. The rhetorically marked passage
where Wace tells of the massive defections of the French to Arthur, and
their reasons for doing so (Wace 9947–54), is replaced by the bare statement that all submitted to Arthur whom he looked upon (*Brut* 11688):
they have no choice. Similarly, the 'courtly' reasons for the general flock-
ing to Arthur's coronation (Wace 10331–6) become futile in a context
where all are summoned 'bi heore life' ('by their life', *Brut* 12135). As a
result, Wace's scene of Arthur distributing gifts to his foreign guests
disappears; all those who have answered Arthur's summons are of
necessity his men, and the gift-giving is therefore restricted in the English poem to Arthur's own knights.[40] The whole tone in the *Brut* is more
solemn: Wace's description of the clothes at the queen's procession
(10407–16) is replaced by ceremonial, more in keeping with so serious an
event as the crowning of the king, and, as noted above, the description of
the distractions during the festivities is reduced to a minimum. This
increased dignity of the English *Brut* is perceptible throughout the
Roman campaign. Arthur's dream is given an aura of mystery and impending doom through its not being given any definite interpretation
(Wace 11267–74 says it predicts Arthur's victory over a giant). Wace's
comments as to the expectations of the Britons concerning the outcome of
the campaign are also carefully avoided by Laȝamon.[41] The reasons given
by Wace for Arthur's going to Mt St Michel alone – to avoid frightening
his men, and because he does not need help anyway – disappear from the
English poem, with their implicit slur on the valour of Arthur's men, as
does Arthur's confession, after his fight with the giant, to having been
afraid.[42] The grotesque story of the giant Rithon (Wace 11565–92) is likewise upgraded into an unspecified encounter with a *king* Riun (*Brut*
13036–7).

The Briton heroes also have a more dignified attitude in battle; the
gory details given by Wace in his account of the single combats during
the fight against Luces, for example, are regularly deleted by the English
poet. Evander thus kills Borel by throwing his spear through his throat,
in Wace (12195–7); Laȝamon (13479–80) just mentions he was slain, and
deletes Wace's scene (12245–8) of the agonizing Borel being found on the
battlefield. The slaughter of Kei's men (Wace 12648) remains unmentioned in the English poem, where they are left to pierce their way

---

40 Wace, 10591–620; *Brut* 12337–40. Eleven of the manuscripts collated by Arnold omit lines
10601–20.
41 Wace 12260–2 states that the Britons expected to be victorious, after winning a battle
where they were fighting one to seven. Incidentally, these figures are also deleted by
Laȝamon, who merely mentions the heavy losses and great courage of the Britons (*Brut*
13482–5).
42 Wace 11327–32 and 11561.

through the fight to carry their lord's body off the field; and the savage conduct of Wace's Hirelgas, who hacks to pieces the corpse of his uncle's slayer (Wace 12695–708), gives way to Laȝamon's Ridwathlan, whose vengeance takes on the more dignified form of straightforward slaying in battle.

It is readily perceptible that the bulk of Laȝamon's omissions concern material connected with battle-scenes. It seems that Laȝamon felt justified in modifying such passages to fit the general drift of the narrative: in other words, tactical details were apparently not considered by him as 'serious' historical data, and could therefore be reshaped to some extent. The main consequence of this, for our concern, is that any divergence between Laȝamon and Wace about the progression of a given fight need not indicate indebtedness to a conflicting authority.

The other area touched by Laȝamon's omissions is what one may call 'cultural' elements: details of *étiquette* (Brennus' gifts), descriptions of finery or entertainments (as for example at Arthur's coronation), or such niceties as 'druerie'. Whether or not this indicates a conscious rejection of Wace's courtly seasoning of the poem will be discussed in the following chapter.

To sum up: the overall pattern of Laȝamon's omissions first reveals a tendency towards a swifter tempo than his source; a fondness for structuring his episodes around one main hero, to the glory of whom minor characters will frequently be sacrificed; and last, a general survey of the omissions in the poem suggests a binary structure to the *Brut*, the core of which would appear to be the first part of the reign of Arthur and the reign of Cadwallan.

Additions and Expansions

Laȝamon's additions, expansions or modifications cover virtually the whole of the *Brut*. They may be divided roughly into three categories:

(a) modifications due to the change of language. In order to render Wace's ideas (which, as noted by Ringbom, are expressed very concisely, due to the limitations of the octosyllabic line), the English poet has sometimes to resort to paraphrase, or has to provide additional contextual elements. Wace's

> Unches ne fist altre prüesce

is thus glossed as

and al he leas his wurðscipe   for þon win-scenche
ne dude nauer oðer god   ne greiðe on his þeode.[43]

Laȝamon takes two half-lines to express the personal and social connotations of the concept of 'prüesce', and a third one to render the ironical comment – getting drunk was the beginning and end of this king's qualities. The passage to the English language seems to have brought with it greater explicitness: Wace's 'locus amoenus'-type descriptions are also filled out, and the reasons for which the land is considered to be desirable are clearly stated; positive adjectives tend to be added to nouns. 'Les boscages' thus become 'þene leofliche wode', 'the fair wood'; the 'praeries' are 'swiðe mære', 'really splendid';[44] the appeal of 'les champs' is rendered by the image of growing corn.[45] These additions are of no concern for the present argument, though a thorough study of them would be a valuable contribution to our knowledge of the comparative grammar, syntax and lexis of early Middle English and Medieval French, and give us a better understanding of the poetic atmosphere and attitudes in both literatures.

(b) modifications or additions resulting in a change of emphasis, or introducing ideas and incidents not present in, nor suggested by Wace's *Roman de Brut*. If one excepts the Arthurian passages, these additions tend to be limited in scope; but they are numerous enough for it to be impractical to provide a list of them, as well as ultimately confusing.[46] Any relevant passage will therefore be discussed below, in whatever chapter it best appears to belong.

(c) expansions, additions or modifications dictated by Laȝamon's narrative technique and aesthetic preferences.

It is often difficult to draw the line between the second and third categories of additions; so much so, in fact, that some critics have been tempted to minimize one at the expense of the other. Rudolf Imelmann represents one extreme: for him almost everything is to be explained by the influence of an additional source, a hypothetical expanded Wace. J. S. P. Tatlock represents the other extreme: 'very nearly everything came from Wace and Lawman's own imagination'.[47]

43 Wace 3656, 'He never accomplished any other feat'. *Brut* 3455–6; 'He lost all his honour through wine-drinking; he was never any good for anything else, nor did he profit his country'.
44 Madden translates 'mære' as 'spacious'; this, however, is considered as questionable by Kurath and Kuhn in their *Dictionary of Middle English*. The more common meaning of the word is 'splendid', 'fine'.
45 Wace 1211 and 1213; *Brut* 1004, 1007 and 1008.
46 Herbert Pilch's attempt to discuss Laȝamon's variations from Wace in a list following their appearance in the poem has shown the limits of such a method.
47 Tatlock, *The Legendary History*, p. 487.

Among modern critics, Herbert Pilch rejects both attitudes, on the grounds that they are methodologically trivial: for neither are based on objective arguments.[48] Yet Pilch does not come up with a truly satisfying methodology either.

It would seem, then, that as the *contents* of Laƶamon's additions do not necessarily betray their origins (with the exception of those few Arthurian passages), it is necessary to fall back on their *form*, that is, on their following or not a recognizable pattern which may be considered typical of the English *Brut*. And such a procedure requires a thorough investigation of Laƶamon's narrative technique.

That Laƶamon used formulas of one sort or another to compose his poem was accepted virtually from Madden onwards. The formulaic nature of certain phrases, such as 'feollen þæ fæie', was easily recognized, and eventually led to J. S. P. Tatlock's article on epic formulas in Laƶamon:[49] an important work, but of little use for assessing units exceeding the long line. Herbert Pilch then pointed out that certain scenes always seemed to follow a stereotyped model: 'Immer wieder kehren die gleichen Formeln, Syntagmata, Rhythmen und Lautfiguren'.[50] This is especially so in the descriptions of battles, notes Pilch. However, we have to wait till 1968 for the implications of such observations to be fully grasped, with H. Ringbom's *Studies in the Narrative Technique of Beowulf and Lawman's Brut*. Ringbom sees definite traces of a formulaic composition method in the English *Brut*, and notes

> an exasperatingly large proportion of half-lines recurring elsewhere in different syntactic form, although semantically they remain closely related.[51]

These half-lines, notes Ringbom, are clearly related, but too loosely to be classified as formulas or formulaic systems according to Old English usage. He thus widens his outlook to units larger than the half-line, and introduces into Laƶamon criticism the notion of *theme*, originally defined in 1938 by Albert B. Lord as

> a subject unit, a group of ideas, regularly employed by a singer, not merely in any given poem but in the poetry as a whole.[52]

Ringbom adapts this concept (which had previously been profitably

---

[48] Herbert Pilch, *Literarische Studie*, pp. 78–81.
[49] J. S. P. Tatlock, 'Epic Formulas. Especially in Layamon', *PMLA* 38 (1923): 494–529.
[50] Herbert Pilch, *Literarische Studie*, p. 213. 'The same formulas, syntagmatic forms, rhythms and assonance patterns are always recurring'.
[51] H. Ringbom, *Narrative Technique*, p. 70.
[52] See Albert B. Lord, 'Homer and Huso II: Narrative Inconsistencies in Homeric and Oral Poetry'.

applied to Old English poetry) to the *Brut*, defining the theme as recurring topics or scenes, which can in turn be split up into several motifs, or sub-themes. This new tool enables Ringbom to analyse the themes of Feasts and Voyages in Laȝamon's *Brut* with considerable insight.

The 'Feast' theme in the *Brut* is thus shown to comprise up to nine sub-themes: (1) the blowing of trumpets or horns; (2) the laying of the table; (3) the sitting down to table; (4) the bringing of water; (5) the serving of food and drink; (6) drinking and eating; (7) music and singing; (8) distribution of gifts; (9) phrases denoting happiness.

Laȝamon's feasts are of a very conventional character, notes Ringbom. They do not vary much in length, and are described in the same terms whatever the historical period. This Ringbom contrasts strongly with the corresponding passages in Wace, where each banquet has 'some flavour of its own' (p. 90). Similarly, Laȝamon's descriptions of voyages (and more specifically sea-voyages) betray an extensive reshaping of his source; all technical terms, notably, are excluded.[53]

The third theme singled out by Ringbom, that of 'Arrivals with greetings', is in fact little more than a sub-theme; the analysis of the encounters 'introduced by a direct speech beginning with a salutation' amounts to examining various speech-acts in a specific context.[54]

Ringbom's observations are carried one step further by Dennis Patrick Donahue, in his *Thematic and Formulaic Composition in Lawman's Brut*. Donahue first rejects Ringbom's definition of Laȝamon's themes as 'frequently recurring stereotyped descriptions of similar scenes', to view them as elements of composition. The theme is thus shown to be

a conceptually stable unit of composition that Lawman could use flexibly. That is, though the poet drew from the same pool of sub-themes to compose all the instances of a particular theme, he could elect to use all or just some of these subthemes, he could choose from among at least several formulas to verbalize the concept underlying each subtheme, and could use the theme straightforwardly or metaphorically.[55]

The formula Donahue also defines as flexible,

---

53 The sub-themes noted by Ringbom for the 'Voyage' theme are: going to the shore; embarkation; the setting of sails; other nautical details; going with the waves; going forth; singing of *scops*; happiness; reaching the shore or harbour.
54 See Ringbom, pp. 98–103.
55 Dennis Patrick Donahue, *Thematic and Formulaic Composition in Lawman's Brut*, p. 10. This more positive approach to Laȝamon's narrative technique is due to Donahue's rejection of a rigid approach to the oral-formulaic theories of composition, following Parry's own development from emphasizing the idea of composition by analogy (1928–30) to a growing awareness, following extensive work on South Slavic song, of the flexibility of formulaic composition, both in quality ('fullness') and in quantity ('length'). See Donahue, pp. 3–11.

a word group composed in part of words that remain constant (key words) and in part of words that change as the context changes (context words).[56]

Formulas are thus distinct from compositional devices (i.e., repeated structural patterns, tag lines, certain word pairs) in that they can be (and are) used to state specific concepts.

Donahue focuses his analysis on three themes: the Feast theme, the Single Combat theme, and the Transferral of Kingship theme; and he comes to the conclusion that what is reused by Laȝamon in presenting a given theme is not so much particular formulas as a group of concepts:

Only sometimes did he verbalize a concept by re-using a particular phrase in exactly the same words and form.[57]

Moreover, notes Donahue, themes are used in the *Brut* to develop mood and plot. The feast theme is thus lavishly full in the victory celebrations of Cassibelaune, but is reduced to four lines of background information in the scene of Uther's flirtation with Igerne.

Donahue's examination of the Single Combat theme is of especial interest. Not only are its eight sub-themes used with great flexibility, in the *Brut*,[58] but the presence of similes in 'Combat' passages suggests that this stylistic feature is an inherent part of Laȝamon's technique. Just as given sub-themes may be expanded, repeated or omitted, so are the similes of the *Brut* more or less elaborate. They are usually connected with the first sub-theme, notes Donahue: the fierceness of a warrior's attack is described by comparing the man to an animal. The reversed comparison is used metaphorically to describe the fate of vanquished enemies, such as Childric or Baldulf. Moreover, an examination of Bedever's fight against the king of Media shows clearly that Laȝamon recomposed the scene he found in Wace.[59] It thus appears that in a number of passages, and notably those comprising a strong descriptive element such as the 'Combat' theme, the 'Feast' theme or the 'Voyage' theme, we are not dealing so much with translation as with re-creation; those parts of the narrative which carry no special authority are transposed into a different set of conventions. To postulate additional sources to account for discrepancies between the *Roman de Brut* and the

---

[56] Donahue, p. 10. Tatlock's 'epic formulas' cannot therefore be considered as narrative formulas, according to Donahue's definition, but are rather compositional devices.
[57] Donahue, p. 131.
[58] The eight sub-themes identified by Donahue are (p. 143): (1) rush to battle; (2) naming of the weapon being used; (3) the raising of the weapon; (4) striking of the blow; (5) mention of the armour worn; (6) breaking of weapon; (7) serious wound or death blow given or enemy routed; (8) the victory yell is given.
[59] See Donahue, pp. 229–252.

English *Brut* within the limits of these conventions is therefore unnecessary.

Donahue's demonstration of the flexibility of the themes of the *Brut* and of the fact that the composition of these themes does not depend upon exact repetition raises the question whether Laȝamon had at his disposal non-descriptive themes occurring in sufficiently differentiated contexts for the verbal overlap to be minimal. Such indeed seems to be the case for what is certainly Laȝamon's most important single expansion device: the 'Messenger' theme. H. Ringbom, in the introductory considerations to his section on 'Arrivals with Greetings' (p. 98), notes that in both Wace and Laȝamon, 'kings and their messengers are continually travelling'. The role of the messengers takes on much more importance in the English *Brut*, however. Where Wace merely states that some piece of information came to the ears of a given character, Laȝamon consistently mentions the channel through which the tidings come. Brutus thus hears of Diana's shrine 'þurh his sæ-monnen', through his sailors (*Brut* 584); 'þurh his sæ-monnen' (669) also is he made aware of the danger of the sirens; and when his boats approach Spain, he is told so by a 'steoresman' (a steersman, 677). The Britons are warned of Caesar's second attack by 'sæ-liðende men' (seafaring men, 3900);[60] Wanis and Melga also hear of Gratian's death through 'sæ-liðende men' (6157); and Vortigern pretends he has heard of imminent attack through 'chæpmen', merchants (6645), while Edwine learns where Brian's sister is through spies. Most often, though, information comes through a 'sonde' or 'ærendrake' – a messenger. The envoy, in the English poem, is sometimes given a name (for example, Maurin, *Brut* 10100, or Patric, *Brut* 10155). The number of messengers on a given mission and their social status may also be mentioned; in the majority of cases, they are knights or knights' sons, who tend to go in twos or twelves. They may furthermore be qualified as wise.[61] At their fullest, these 'messenger' scenes may depict the envoys, often bearing a written message, addressing whoever they were sent to, exposing their errand, and giving a full account of their message (these sub-themes are often in direct speech).[62] The reaction of the recipient of the message is then described in more or less detail. He may seize the writ, like Pandrasus (*Brut* 244), swoon (Godlac), turn colour, become angry, remain speechless, etc. The ensuing action is then related – the

---

[60] Wace 4244 reads at the corresponding passage: 'ne sai cum il ourent oï' – 'I do not know how they heard of it'.
[61] See *Brut* lines 2383; 4113; 4516; 4540; 4718; 5285; 5297; 6714; 9262; 12802; 13070; 14097. Wace either mentions nothing in the corresponding passages, or refers in non-specific terms to a messenger, or the fact that information was transmitted.
[62] For the link between greetings and direct speech, see Ringbom, *Narrative Technique*, pp. 98 sqq.

gathering of a hustings or the raising of troops, for example. In a few cases, the outcome of the errand may be delayed by having the same messengers sent back and forth, with answers or confirmations (i.e., the first sub-themes are repeated): thus, in the Belin and Brennes episode, during the build-up towards a fratricidal battle (*Brut* 2354–9), and in the embassy of Gabius and Prosenna to the two kings;[63] or during Arviragus' parleying with Claudius (*Brut* 4718–50); or the dealings between Bassian and the Picts.[64] The exchange of messages during the difficult period when Rome decides to withdraw its help also displays a repetition of various sub-themes.[65] The introduction of the 'messenger' theme may reshape an episode almost out of recognition, such as in the passage where Vortigern manipulates the Picts to get them to kill Constance, and finally has them all slaughtered once they have done their dirty work. The scene starts with Vortigern sending two knights to invite the Picts to a feast (*Brut* 6714–5); the English poem thus provides a formal setting where Wace provides no prior explanation. During the ensuing drinking session, in both texts, Vortigern makes the Picts believe he has to leave court because of Constance's meanness towards him. Laȝamon then depicts Vortigern ostentatiously departing from the town (thereby securing himself a good alibi), while in Wace he remains suspiciously close to the scene of events. The Picts present Constance's head to Vortigern as soon as he is killed, in Wace; in Laȝamon, the Picts first send a messenger to inform him of the good news; Vortigern sends them answer not to budge, has messengers go about to summon a hustings, then goes to London where he has the hapless Picts slaughtered as they present Constance's head to him. In Wace, the hustings is called *after* Vortigern has been presented with the king's head. The 'messenger' theme thus becomes a device to underline Vortigern's responsibility in the affair, and his utter deviousness.

The reason for the proliferation of the 'messenger' theme in the English *Brut* is, on the one hand, a general tendency of Laȝamon's to present events in a logical sequence, with clearly perceptible motivations for a given act, the consequences of which must in turn be explicitly defined. Only rarely, for example, is a king shown going to battle without a prior

---

[63] Laȝamon (2630–728) shows the Roman earls equipping themselves, journeying four days, asking for the king's tent, and delivering their message on bended knee; we are then shown Belin's reaction, his acceptance of Rome's submission, and his sending back the earls as messengers to fetch hostages and tribute. The scene (which has no equivalent in Wace) ends with the earls going to Rome, then riding back to Belin and Brennes again, having fulfilled their mission, and having gained time for their compatriots.

[64] *Brut* 5296–305: Carrais' messengers are sent to the Picts; they return with their answer; they are then sent to Bassian, whose reaction is described.

[65] *Brut* 6292–305: an appeal is sent to Rome for help; the answer is given to the messengers; the tidings are brought back to Britain; general reaction of sorrow.

mention of his raising the necessary troops,[66] nor do big assemblies gather without being called.[67]

On a more basic level, however, the importance of intermediaries seems to be due to a specificity of Laȝamon's syntax, which often makes him render Wace's verbal forms by more elaborate constructions. Wace's 'ad... deffiez' ('he has defied', 7081) is thus translated by 'sende... word' ('he sent word that', *Brut* 7312); Wace's 'venir fist' (7313) becomes 'he lette his men riden widen and siden & lette him to bonnen ...' (*Brut* 7687–8);[68] Wace's 'requist cunseil' ('requested counsel', 7341) becomes 'sende after witien... & bad' ('sent for wise men... and asked', *Brut* 7731). The most frequent formula verbalizing the 'messenger' concept,

> x sende his sonde   ȝeond þe londe – (x sent his messengers
> throughout the land)

is thus the regular translation for Wace's more abstract 'mander',[69] as well as for verbs with equivalent meanings such as 'apeler', 'enveier', 'assembler', or 'enquerre'.[70] The intrusion of the grammatical object – the letter, messenger, spy, guide, sailor – provides the starting-point for more conscious expansion. The messenger figure is now explicitly present: he exists within the narrative. His actions must be accounted for, he may be shown interacting with other characters, and depending on the importance of his errand, may take on a more or less marked personality. Where the grammatical object is a writ rather than a person, the letter also takes on the dimension of a palpable, physical link. In the Leir episode, Wace's 'mander' becomes a letter sent through messengers to the king of France (*Brut* 1574): we are thus shown the message arriving at the court of

---

66 Tatlock notes over 20 cases of the 'raising of troops' formula verbalized by 'ferde ... ærde'. See 'Epic Formulas', p.500.

67 See *Brut* 4492–9, 7242, 10194–6, 11128–32, etc. In this last instance, the 'summons' formula is verbalized by the rhyming pair 'beoden... ȝeond þeoden', 'to bid... throughout the land'.

68 'He had his men ride far and wide, and had summoned to him ...'.

69 This rhyming pair was analysed by Tatlock, 'Epic Formulas', pp.506–7. Instances of the French 'mander' being rendered by the 'sonde ... londe' verbalization may be found in the *Brut* on lines 741–2; 1561; 1574; 1808; 3045; 3086; 6675; 7230; 8434; 12130; 12647; 14104; 14218–20; 14228; 14882–3; 14973; 15416; 15557; 15923; 15932. In none of these cases does Wace make any mention of messengers.

70 i.e., to call, to send, to assemble, to enquire, to fetch. See for example *Brut* 2475, 4957, 5269, 6876, 7242, 7525, 9114, 14310 (raising of troops); 213–4, 4492, 6308, 7500, 9292, 11551 (calling of an assembly); 4937, 6101 (calling of a new king); 5655; 6086; 6176; 6221; 6360–1; 7754; 8488 (appeal for information or help). The 'mander' concept is not always explicit in the Wace-text corresponding to some of these lines, and I have included among these examples cases where the basic formula undergoes some variation (in its second element especially). Other instances of 'mander' translated by a Verb + Object + Subordinate Clause may be found at *Brut* 2244, where Delgan sends Godlac 'stille boc-runen'; Wace 2577 becomes 'Gudlac him sende word bi ane wise monne' (*Brut* 2383), and Wace 6109, 'heore sonde heo [n]omen sone', 'they quickly took their messengers' (*Brut* 6057).

Aganippus (*Brut* 1595) and his listening to it; his answer is then sent to Leir 'mid writ & mid worde' ('with writ and with word', 1607), an expression translating, once again, Wace's 'mander'.[71]

In most of these cases, the addition made to Wace in terms of contents is negligible; it merely provides the English poet with the opportunity to give extra depth to the psychology of a given character, and to introduce direct speech.[72] Moreover, the use of formulas allow a number of rhetorical effects. The accumulation of the 'sende... sonde' verbal pairs in the account of Arthur's campaigns against Orchenie, Godland, Weneland and Norway, or at his calling of the Caerleon assembly, contribute towards the feeling of Arthur's invincibility and power; and the recurrent mention of the messengers sent by the Britons, when Rome decides to help them no longer, underlines the pathos of the situation. There are however a number of instances where the 'messenger' theme becomes a central element within the narrative. The passages thus distinguished often elaborate on Wace extensively. This is especially true of those scenes involving prophets (Teleusin and Merlin), a few of the 'messenger' passages of the Arthurian section, and the beginning of the Penda episode.

The scene where Penda's envoy negotiates peace with Cadwalan (*Brut* 15485–531) is perhaps one of the most revealing of Laȝamon's composition technique, despite the fact that we find none of the standard verbal formulas associated with the 'messenger' theme. The term 'sonde' is replaced by the (conceptually equivalent) description of Penda's messenger:

> þa nom Pendan enne cniht
> þe wes swiðe wis mon   and wel cuðe speken.[73]

That the focus is on the individual (further characterized as 'treowe', 'loyal', 15496), rather than the function, becomes obvious during the negotiation with Cadwalan: the man is not named, but he is the pivot of the scene, offering terms that Penda had not specified (or at least, not explicitly), and a worthy interlocutor for Cadwalan. One may still see the imprint of the *Roman de Brut* on the passage, in its following the sequence submission/homage/marriage:

---

[71] *Brut* 1607, Wace 1819. The alliterating word pair 'writ ... word' may also be found translating Wace's 'mander' on line 5181. It occurs elsewhere in the *Brut*, always in a 'messenger' context, on lines 5237, 5646 and 6181.

[72] The delivering of messages in direct speech thus makes it possible for Laȝamon to build up tension before potential strife, through the vivid report of boasting speeches. See for example the answer of Gorlois to Uther, *Brut* 9272–9.

[73] *Brut*, 15485–6. 'Then Penda took a knight who was a very wise man and knew how to speak well'.

Ne pot mie estre delivrez
Dissi qu'il fist al rei humage
E prist de lui sun eritage.
De sun fieu li ad fait ligance,
E pur faire ferme aliance
E pur faire entr'els ferme amur
Prist Chadwalein une sorur
Que Peanda aveit, mult bele,
Gente e curteise damisele.[74]

However, one may note that in the English poem, the 'marriage' element is almost presented as a favour of the knight's to the king, after having obtained Cadwalan's acceptance of Penda's offer to become his vassal. The offer does indeed come from Penda, formally (*Brut* 15515, 'ȝet *he* wulle mare': 'yet *he* wishes to do more'); but it is the knight's man-to-man advice, and his skilful stressing of the desirability of Penda's sister through the mention of her royal French suitor, that makes Cadwalan eager to marry her. The importance of the intermediary is further underlined by the fact that the king offers the knight 'al Deuene-scire' to secure Helen;[75] and it is the knight who fetches the maiden and hands her over to Cadwalan – not Penda.

In no other part of the *Brut* is a messenger figure given such independence, functioning as a character in his own right. In most cases, Laȝamon's 'intermediaries' are described only within the restricted limits of their errand.[76] Thus, the heathen man who, in the *Brut*, helps Gurmund at the siege of Cirencester, is characterized only by the graspingness that motivates his action.[77] Messengers, envoys, spies or informants are generally subordinated to their message, and act as foils for the main character of the episode. The 'messenger' theme thus provides a quasi-ritualistic introduction to scenes featuring prophets. Both Teleusin and Merlin have to be sought out by the kings who wish to consult them – and this they do with the utmost respect; Wace's

Li preia li reis e requist
Qu'alcune chose li deïst,[78]

---

74 Wace, 14382–90. 'He could not be freed until he made homage to the king and took his inheritance from him. He recognized him as overlord for his lands, and to make a firm alliance and to establish strong bonds of affection between them, Chadwalein took a sister of Penda's as wife, a very beautiful, noble and courteous damsel'.

75 *Brut*, 15529.

76 This remark is only valid for those intermediaries not mentioned by Wace, of course.

77 This very limited characterization is all the more striking as this heathen man is central to the episode: he comes to offer his services to Gurmund (functioning as his own messenger), in direct speech; and on Gurmund's acceptance of his terms (in direct speech, once again) he is shown catching the sparrows and preparing the shells that will destroy Cirencester. The credit for the falling of the town is entirely his.

78 Wace, 4861–2. 'The king prayed and requested of him that he tell him something (about

which looks very much like an order, becomes in the English *Brut* a
request to come to court carried by a delegation of 'wise twalf cnihtes'
(4540). Laȝamon also provides a scene where Kinbelin greets Teilesin
with a solemn oath:

> A-nan swa þe king hine imette   fæire he hine igrette
> Swa me helpen min hefde & mi chin   wulcume ært þu Teilesin
> & leouere me is þine isunden   þenne a þusend punden.[79]

In response to this, Teilesin formally agrees to interpret the portents
which trouble the king.

This procedure generates an aura of mystery around the seer, who
appears as an elusive and powerful being. This is especially true of
Merlin. Where Wace states that Aurelius 'fist ... enveier pur lui' ('had
him sent for', 8016) at Labanes, a distant 'fontaine' in Wales, in the
English poem the king not only sends his messengers, but 'bad
æuerælcne mon axien after Mærlin' ('bade every man to ask after Merlin')
with the promise of ample riches;[80] and the messengers find him only
after extensive travelling north, south, east and west. The two knights
who eventually find him give him a formal greeting, deliver their message, and receive Merlin's answer; he agrees to help, but refuses treasure,
with the mysterious statement that

> ich wuste þat ȝe comen
> & ȝif ich swa walde   ne mihte ȝe me finden.[81]

The prophet is then escorted to Aurelius' court; the marks of honour
bestowed upon him by the king are expanded upon – Laȝamon has
Aurelius ride out to greet Merlin, for example.

The 'messenger' theme is further used to demonstrate Merlin's ability
not to be found. After Uther's coronation, Merlin thus disappears from
the Wace-text until he is needed again to win Ygerne; Laȝamon explains
the prophet's absence from the following stretch of narrative as the result
of his own free choice:

> Merlin him æt-wende   nuste he nauere whidere
> no nauere a worlde-riche   to whan he bicome
> ...

the future)'.
[79] *Brut*, 4543–5. 'As soon as the king met him, he greeted him fairly: "So help me my head
and my chin, you are welcome, Teilesin, and your safety is worth more to me than a
thousand pounds".'
[80] *Brut*, 8488–92.
[81] *Brut*, 8516–7. 'I knew that you were coming, and if I had so wished, you would not have
been able to find me'.

þe king lette riden   widen & siden
he bad gold & gersume   ælche farinde gume
wha-swa mihte finde   Merlin an londe
þer-to he læide muchel lof   ah ne herde he him nawhit of.[82]

Whereas Wace has Merlin reappear at Uther's beck and call (*Roman* 8682: 'fist mander e venir Merlin'), Laꝫamon repeats the ritual 'quest', and having previously stated the inability of messengers to find the prophet, he introduces an informant-figure, a hermit living in the same forest as Merlin, and who fulfils the 'sonde' function of the 'messenger' theme. His being a hermit rather than a knight, a spy, or a merchant can in no way be accounted for merely in terms of composition technique;[83] but his function of Merlin's 'sonde' to Uther may be gathered by his greeting words:

Sæie þu mi leofe freond   wi naldest þu me suggen
þurh nanes cunnes þinge   þat þu wældest to þane king
Ah ful ꝫare ich hit wuste   anan swa ich þe miste
þat þu icumen weore   to Vðere kinge
and what þe king þe wið spæc   and of his londe þe bæd
þat þu me sculdest bringe   to Vðere kinge.[84]

Merlin thereupon gives further proof of his powers, by stating the nature of Uther's problem, and prophesying Arthur's birth. Laꝫamon's use of the 'messenger' theme in this passage is therefore an indirect way of describing the central character, rather than a straightforward means of information transmission.

The same is true of a number of passages featuring Arthur: thus, Laꝫamon's interpolation, in his account of Arthur's war with Luces, of a wounded knight who tells the Briton king of the movements of the Roman troops, and advises him to submit:

Ah lauerd Arður quað þe cniht   ich þe wulle cuðen her-riht
þat betere þe is freondscipe to habben   þene for to fihten
for aꝫan þine tweie   heo habbeoð twælue.[85]

82 *Brut*, 9070–7. 'Merlin disappeared; he never knew whither, or to whichever kingdom of the world he had gone ... The king had men ride wide and far; he offered gold and treasure to any traveller who could find Merlin in the land; to this he added great praise, but he heard not a thing of him'.
83 The detail is not suggested by Wace. See below, chapter 4, for further discussion of this passage.
84 *Brut*, 9388–93. 'Tell me, my dear friend, why you would not tell me, for any kind of thing, that you intended to go to the king? But I knew very quickly, as soon as I missed you, that you had come to King Uther; and what the king said to you, and how much of his land he offered you, in order for you to bring me to King Uther'.
85 *Brut*, 13077–9. 'But, lord Arthur, said the knight, I will tell you straightaway that you had better have a settlement than fight, for against two of yours they have twelve'.

In Wace, words to the same effect are put in the mouth of peasants and spies.[86] Arthur's courage seems all the greater (comparatively) in the English text, for his disregarding the advice of a seasoned warrior, who has lost best part of his 'folc' in battle. But it is at the turning-points of Arthur's career that the potentialities of the 'messenger' theme are exploited to the full, allowing the king to express himself (in direct speech) more fully than in Wace. The first passage occurs at the end of the battle of Lincoln, Arthur's first major victory against the Saxons. In Wace, the decision of the Saxons to submit, and Arthur's agreement to let them go, covers ten lines (*Roman* 9211–20). The decision and the terms suggested by the Saxons are introduced by 'Cunseil pristrent que ...' – 'They took counsel that'; no delegation is mentioned, just the result: 'Artur ad cel plai graanté' – 'Arthur has granted this request'. In Laȝamon this is expanded into a formal counsel situation, where Colgrim suggests to Childric that they should submit to Arthur in order to depart with life; Childric accepts on condition that Baldulf and the other Saxons are in agreement; then all acclaim the decision, and twelve knights are sent in delegation to Arthur (beginning of the 'messenger' theme). The envoys then deliver their message. Up to here, we have no real addition in substance to Wace's text, with the exception perhaps of the positive image of Arthur given during the Saxon deliberations, and the request by the envoys that they be allowed to announce their defeat to their people.[87] The counsel scene may be explained by Laȝamon's tendency to provide specific information where Wace prefers general statements, while the envoys repeat in substance what was decided at the counsel, in other words. The function of the 'messenger' theme is here to motivate Arthur's first major speech in the *Brut*, with his triumphant laugh, and an elaborate long-tailed simile, that of the hunted fox. Arthur is thus defined as a hunter from the outset, and the predatory nature of the king marks the treatment of his character throughout the poem, while suggesting an underlying irony that the hunter should have let his prey get away, in this case.

The most dramatic use of the 'messenger' theme is however found with the announcing to Arthur of Modred's treason. Wace's lapidary

> Arthur oï e de veir sot
> Que Modred fei ne li portot [88]

is turned into a full-scale scene, with a wealth of delaying devices which result in a build-up of tension. Between the arrival of the knight bearing

---

[86] Wace, 11625–36. The report is made in reported speech, and the odds are one to four, not two to twelve.

[87] This last element is discussed below, in chapter 6.

[88] Wace, 13031–2. 'Arthur heard and knew in truth that Modred was not loyal to him'.

the bad news and his actually delivering his message, we have Arthur's second dream, announcing in obscure terms that which the knight fails initially to tell him.[89] Dramatic irony is further enhanced by the dismissal of the portent by Arthur's knight:

> Lauerd þu hauest un-riht
> ne sculde me nauere sweuen   mid sorȝen are\<c\>chen
> ...
> ȝif hit weore ilu[m]pe   swa nulle hit ure Drihte
> þat Modred þire suster sune   hafde þine quene inume
> ...
> þe ȝet þu mihtest þe awreken   wurð-liche mid wepnen.[90]

Arthur answers that for nothing in the world could he imagine Modred betraying him; and only then does the messenger reveal the treason. The following sub-theme, the recipient's reaction, is extended to include not only Arthur but his men; it shows the ensuing hush among Arthur's followers, and the general outrage. The decision/answer sub-theme is likewise duplicated to include a speech by Arthur, announcing his intention of punishing the traitors, and by Gawain; both speeches are then acclaimed by the Britons. Messengers occur once again as central agents in the account of the campaign against Modred. Laȝamon's addition of the delaying device of the lack of wind keeping Arthur's fleet at Whit-sand is reinforced by his creation of a 'for-cuð kempe', a 'wicked warrior' (*Brut* 14095) who sends his swain to Wenhauer to warn her of Arthur's coming. The collusion between Modred and the queen is made manifest as she hastens to tell him the news, while a plausible channel of information is thus provided to account for Wace's 'Modred sot ...' (13053;

---

[89] This second dream of Arthur's may be considered an elaboration of the 'messenger' theme, though the medium of transmission is neither a human being nor a letter. The contents of the dream are emblematic of what is to happen; it announces in clear terms Modred's and Wenhaver's treason, Walwain's death (symbolized by his falling and breaking both his arms), and Arthur's bitter-sweet revenge. The mystery of his fate after killing Modred is expressed by the obscure symbolism of the lioness and the fish. The lioness could conceivably represent Argante, the queen who takes Arthur over the waters to tend him (the medieval bestiaries give no particular significance to the female lion), and his being saved by a fish could perhaps indicate salvation, considering the Christian overtones of such a symbol. Herbert Pilch's suggestion (*Literarische Studie*, 56–60) that the dream may be derived from Welsh tradition is based on an early sixteenth-century text, 'Breuddwyt Arthur', which has nothing significant in common with this passage of the *Brut*. (See F. Le Saux, unpubl. M.A., pp. 67–70). Likewise, the dream found in the prose *Lancelot* is only superficially analogous to that of the *Brut*.

[90] *Brut*, 14022–3, 14026–7 and 14031. 'Lord, you are wrong: one should never give a dream a sorrowful interpretation ... Even if it had so happened – God forbid – that Modred, your sister's son, had taken your queen ... you could yet avenge yourself honourably by force of arms'.

'Modred knew that'). Modred reacts by sending messengers to Childric, telling him to

<blockquote>wide senden sonde   a feouwer half Sex-londe [91]</blockquote>

to raise men for him; and throughout the hostilities, we are told that messengers came to Modred every day from Arthur's army (as many details unmentioned by Wace). The reader is thus being prepared for Arthur's sad end, through the stressing of the treachery surrounding him.

The messenger theme, which on its simplest level is reduced to a transitive construction followed by a conjuncted clause, translating a French verb followed by a subordinate clause, is thus Laʒamon's major device for providing explicit causal relationships between the actions and decisions of given characters. It is frequently (in fact, nearly always) used to introduce speeches, the more striking of which tend to be the pre-battle, 'Hohnrede' type speeches. Integrated within the narrative, it may also serve as a delaying device to create tension. The 'messenger' theme, with its various sub-themes, may therefore be considered as one of the most important 'building-blocks' of Laʒamon's construction technique, both in terms of function – the theme is very versatile – and in terms of mere length. It is the major single expanding device of the whole of the English *Brut*. Thus, the mention of a messenger, or the description of the reaction of the recipient of a message, or the fact that he or she makes a speech, cannot be considered as a relevant indication as to Laʒamon's indebtedness to a source other than Wace's *Roman de Brut*. The nature of the messenger, or the contents of a given speech, may however be significant.

It appears from these considerations that Laʒamon's work was composed according to different aesthetic principles from its source, though in terms of content it remains a recognizable translation of Wace's *Roman de Brut*. The 'poetic' element in the *Roman* has been replaced by an approach more congenial to the English poet and his language, to the extent that the English *Brut* is in effect a re-creation on the same theme as the *Roman*. Indeed, it is recognized that there is no other way to translate poetry effectively. The divergences between Wace and Laʒamon are most flagrant where the French poet elaborates his own source, Geoffrey's *Historia Regum Britanniae*.[92] Descriptions are rendered with different techniques, while a different sense of rhythm has made the English poet subtly reshape Wace's poem, placing narrative pauses at different places,

---

[91] *Brut*, 14108. 'To send messengers widely to the four corners of Saxony'.
[92] This is probably due to the nature of those passages: where the poets felt that they were dealing with 'amplificatio' rather than solid facts, they took more liberties with their source.

and introducing different linking devices (most notably, the 'messenger' theme). Moreover, the English poem sets a different tone, through Laȝamon's higher sense of the dignity of his subject matter – the excision of Wace's disparaging comments on the peasantry, for example, may be seen as a symptom of this – and his obvious feeling that there was a *meaning* to it all. To this, one may add Laȝamon's more concrete approach to his material, possibly due in part to the greater syntactic explicitness of Middle English than of Medieval French, which makes him state where-bys and wherefores which in Wace remain implicit, and are the starting-point of the great majority of the expansions of the *Brut*.

As noted above, Laȝamon's translation aimed primarily at a dynamic equivalence of his source-text; and such was to be expected, for Wace's authority lies in what he says, not in the way he says it. The prologue of the *Brut* explicitly states that the substance of the poem is 'soðere word', thereby implying that its sources will have been followed in the measure *only* that they themselves conform to this ideal of veracity. Hence, the acknowledgement of several sources, and the warning that the *Brut* is to some extent a synthesis. Yet, as is unanimously recognized by critics, the final result is clearly derived from Wace. This apparent contradiction is resolved to a great extent by Ronald H. Bathgate's operational model of the translation process: source-language text – tuning – analysis – under-standing – terminology – restructuring – checking – discussion – target language text.[93]

The core of this framework, for our concern, is in the first steps of the process, from tuning to restructuring. *Tuning* Bathgate defines as 'getting the feel of the text to be translated':

> If the text is difficult or of a type which is less familiar to [the translator], he may want to read some background literature ... or talk to the author (if available) or some other adviser.[94]

The 'difficulty' attached to Wace's *Roman de Brut* was obviously that errors may have crept into Laȝamon's copy of the work; and such errors would have gone against the purpose of the poet, which was to produce a historical treatise. Moreover, as a poem, Wace's *Roman de Brut* gives great importance to characters whose fame had made them transcend their purely historical status. Arthur and Merlin are two cases in point. A competent translator, who knows he cannot have entire confidence in the text he has before him, due to the always present spectre of scribal error, yet cannot consult the author, must necessarily do some amount of

---

93 Ronald H. Bathgate, 'A Survey of Translation Theory', *The Incorporated Linguist* 20 (1981): 113–4.
94 Bathgate, p. 113.

double-checking with what 'background literature' is available, and, if feasible, glean additional information that will further clarify the source-language text in his own mind: Laȝamon's reference to different works in his Prologue is best understood as reflecting this stage of his work.

The second stage, analysis, consists in splitting each sentence into translatable units – of this no trace should remain; and in a third phase, 'the translator will generally put it together again in a form which he can understand or respond to emotionally'.[95]

In the 'terminology' phase, keywords and phrases in the sentence are reconsidered, to ensure that the translation is 'in line with standardized usage and is neither misleading, ridiculous nor offensive for the target-language reader'.[96] Finally, the 'restructuring' phase focuses on the target language: it is the moment where *form*, as opposed to content, comes into its own. These different phases in the process of translating take on varying importance depending on the translator, and the sort of translation he or she wishes to achieve; moreover, this process need not be a conscious one. However, they underlie the very act of translation, and Laȝamon must have gone through them, as must anyone wishing to express the sense of a text in another language. Moreover, the recomposing implicit in Bathgate's operational model becomes essential in dealing with poetry. The translator, whom Nida describes as ideally having 'a truly empathic spirit' with his origo-text, must be a poet himself to do so competently: translation becomes conscious re-creation.

The material of potential use for an enquiry into the different influences on the English poet thus appears as limited, and the chances of recognizing echoes of a given work with any amount of certainty are tenuous. Laȝamon has reworked even his main source to such an extent that one may expect his incidental or complementary reading to have been at least equally 'digested'. Where some degree of similarity between the English *Brut* and a work other than Wace's *Roman de Brut* becomes apparent in the following discussion, the internal evidence will as much as possible be reinforced by external evidence. The implications of such indebtedness on an overall reading of the *Brut*, and its congruence with the general trends of the poem, will also have to be taken into consideration.

---

95 Bathgate, p. 114.
96 Bathgate, p. 114.

4

The French Connection

Laȝamon's attitude towards his main source has been described in terms both of extreme faithfulness, and of conscious rejection. The faithfulness to the general layout and contents of Wace's *Roman de Brut* is acknowledged by all critics. The rejection of the *manner* of Wace's work, and more especially of that hallmark of French culture, the courtly ideal, was stressed primarily by those critics advocating a 'nationalistic' Laȝamon, until it became a commonplace in all studies of the *Brut*. Even R.H. Fletcher, who supported Rudolf Imelmann's theory of an expanded Wace-manuscript as the only source for the *Brut*, remarks in his *Arthurian Material*: 'For the courtly French tone of Wace's poem he substitutes the less elegant but more sturdy Saxon tone'.[1] The measured terms of 'tone' and 'substitution' become under the pen of Gwyn Jones a sweeping statement: 'he rejected French influence'.[2]

At the root of this unanimity, we have Laȝamon's apparent distaste for French loan-words. Madden was first to note that

> if we number the words derived from the French (even including
> some that may have come directly from the Latin) we do not find in
> the earlier text of Laȝamon's poem so many as fifty, several of which
> were in usage, as appears by the Saxon Chronicle, previous to the
> middle of the twelfth century.[3]

While Madden clearly considers these figures as astonishingly low, K.F. Sundén seems to take the opposite view, stating that there are 'not a few' romance loan-words in the *Brut*; and A.C. Gibbs goes as far as to say that the 'influence of French romance is generally underestimated', be it in matter, language or style.[4] The attitude of earlier critics therefore

---

1 R.H. Fletcher, *Arthurian Material in the Chronicles*, chapter 5, p.166.
2 Gwyn Jones, introduction to *Wace and Layamon. Arthurian Chronicles*, Eugene Mason transl., p.xi.
3 Madden, vol.1, introduction p.xxii.
4 K.F. Sundén. 'Notes on the Vocabulary of Laȝamon's *Brut*', p.286, and A.C. Gibbs, 'The Literary Relationships of Laȝamon's *Brut*' (hereafter 'Literary Relations'), p.98. There is no

appears to have been marked to a great extent by subjectivity and *a priori*.

Such a discussion is necessarily influenced by the idea these scholars had of the translating process, and of the standards they expected of Laȝamon as a translator. As noted above, the generation of Madden considered translation as a somewhat inferior, quasi-mechanical process: however, to express the sense of a word in such a way that it fits into another set of socio-linguistic norms is by no means a simple process; to express the sense of an abstract concept in other cultural terms is often virtually impossible. In such cases, the translator is confronted with a treble choice: either he selects the closest equivalent in the target culture, and transposes *every element* in order to create in the target reader of the translated version an emotional impact which approximates to that of the initial reader on reading the initial text (i.e., the 'full translation' option); or else, he may choose to transliterate certain attributes of this abstract concept, with the result that his text will be 'closer' to the original, but will have an exotic flavour to the target reader; or last, he may opt for zero-translation, and decide to quote, making only minimal changes, thereby producing an alien concept, couched in alien terms, for his target-reader to digest.[5] Laȝamon's option in the *Brut* appears to be that of 'full translation'. To render the concept of Fortune and her wheel, for example, he resorts to the Anglo-Saxon concept of *weal*, *good* fortune, and avoids expressing the related concept of transitoriness in the cyclical terms (Fortune's wheel) which are not connected with it in his target culture – English.[6] One may agree in this respect with the observation made by Tatlock in his *Legendary History*:

> the poetic form and feeling of the French original are almost wholly transformed into what the less experienced islanders were used to.[7]

Whilst correctly identifying this process as transformation – in other words, translation – Tatlock's assumption that the conventions and outlook of the origo-text are lost is oversimplifying the matter. For significantly, it is the only major abstract concept added by Wace to his source (namely, 'courtoisie') which lends arguments in favour of a conscious rejection of French culture by Laȝamon; the limited number of French

---

unanimity as to the exact number of romance loan-words in the *Brut*. D. S. Munroe, in his 'French words in Laȝamon' numbers a total of about 150 romance loans for both manuscripts; no list exceeds 160. One may note that some of these loans have no equivalent in the corresponding passages of the *Roman* (cf. l.11858, 'cheisil').

[5] See Eugene A. Nida, *Towards a Science of Translating*.
[6] Compare Wace 1913–36 and *Brut* 1704–9.
[7] Tatlock, *Legendary History*, p.485.

loan-words in the English text are further seen as confirmation of this tendency.

To talk of rejection, however, implies that Laȝamon had the choice between 'quoting' such passages and 'translating' them; that is, between partial or zero-translation and full translation. For such a choice to be possible, or at least viable, his target readers must be assumed to have been sufficiently familiar with this 'alien' concept to understand and respond to passages only minimally adapted to their native culture. Was this really the case? K. F. Sundén's remark that there are 'not a few' Romance loan-words in the *Brut* suggests that, on the contrary, he felt that the French influence on the vocabulary of the *Brut* was greater than one would have expected. Håkan Ringbom concurs:

> Though too few texts from the time before 1200 have survived for us to say anything definite about the French influence on the vocabulary of early Middle English, it seems that the French impact had not yet made itself fully felt on the West Midlands dialect in which Lawman wrote ... His dialect did not possess the courtly vocabulary or way of thought. Instead, he had to make use of words existing in the English poetic tradition.[8]

Walter Schirmer's examination of Wace's 'courtly' terminology confirms moreover that

> die englische Sprache des 12. Jhs. hatte keine angemessenen Ausdrücke zur Übersetzung des höfischen Wortschatzes, den Wace stolz zur Schau trägt ... Auch für bekanntere und allgemeinere Dinge tauchen die Lehnwörter erst viel später im Englischen auf.[9]

The very word 'curteisie', notes Schirmer, is not attested until well into the thirteenth century.[10] The relative lack of French words in the *Brut* must thus be ascribed to the fact that the audience Laȝamon was writing for was not sufficiently 'frenchified' to admit them. This argument becomes less effective the later one places the date of composition of the *Brut*, and the testimony of the Otho-text shows that in mid to late thirteenth-century England the vocabulary of the Caligula-text did in-

---

8 H. Ringbom, *Narrative Technique*, p. 59.
9 'The English language of the twelfth century had no adequate expressions to translate the courtly vocabulary which Wace proudly displays ... Even for better-known and more ordinary things, loan-words appear much later only in English'. Walter F. Schirmer, *Die frühen Darstellungen des Arthurstoffes*, p. 61.
10 Schirmer dates the first attested form of the word in English to 1280. Kurath and Kuhn note that 'courteisie' is first attested in the *Ancrene Wisse* (c. 1230); however, we must wait till *circa* 1300 for the word to reappear in another English text.

deed seem contrivedly Germanic. Yet, considering the length of the poem, the Otho-scribe did not substitute such a great number of French words for the original English ones, especially if one bears in mind that he probably set to work some fifty years after the completion of the *Brut*, during which time French influence was leaving its mark on even the more conservative dialects. There are therefore good reasons for believing that Laȝamon's limited use of French words was not a symptom of cultural xenophobia, but simply the consequence of their not being comprehensible to the speakers of his brand of English.[11]

This unavoidable limitation was felt by certain critics to be a sign of cultural inferiority. Tatlock's 'less experienced islanders' become with Walter Schirmer barbarians: Wace's courtly world is thus regularly opposed to Laȝamon's 'heroisch-barbarische' outlook. At the root of this subjective reaction, there seems to be an anachronistic response to the English language.[12] Such at least was the conclusion of A. C. Gibbs after a close analysis of the Ygerne passage in the English *Brut*:

> On balance, Laȝamon's telling of this story seems no less influenced by convention than Wace's. However, the courtly romance is a Romance, if not a French invention. The terms which eventually passed into our language, and which we use today to talk about the convention, are French terms. Is this not the ultimate reason for our calling Laȝamon's treatment primitive and naïve?[13]

This perceptive remark draws one's attention to the fact that throughout the Middle English period the English Arthurian romances retain specific traits. W. R. J. Barron thus notes that the overall effect of classifying the English examples

> is largely negative, presenting the English Arthurian romances as shattered fragments of a foreign tradition, ineffectual in imitation, wrong-headed in innovation.[14]

Yet, stresses Barron, 'that is not how they read'; and when R. S. Loomis

---

[11] Whether this conservativeness is inherent in the English language of the time, or merely indicates that the *Brut* was written for a non-frenchified audience, is hard to resolve. On the one hand, the West Midland area is noted for its linguistic conservativeness; on the other hand, French words are very frequent in the *Ancrene Wisse*, which was written in roughly the same area and within the same time-slot as the *Brut* (See E. J. Dobson, *The Origins of Ancrene Wisse*, pp. 114 sqq.). All things considered, however, I would tend to favour the idea that the vocabulary of the *Ancrene Wisse* was influenced by the fact that the work was written for a specifically aristocratic audience.

[12] As well, of course, of being indicative of the greater prestige that French once enjoyed.

[13] Gibbs, 'Literary Relations', p. 216.

[14] W. R. J. Barron, 'Arthurian Romance: Traces of an English Tradition', p. 5.

states that Laȝamon belonged to a milieu 'where the softening influences of woman-worship and courtesy were unknown',[15] one is led to ask 'Is that how the *Brut* reads?' And the answer is: 'No more than the *Roman* itself'.

On the subject of the treatment of love and of chivalric behaviour, Gibbs notes that the only points of rejection of the French conventions are, on the one hand, that the English poet 'thinks automatically of marriage' as the outcome of the love situation, and on the other, that he refuses to condone the courtly divorce of feats of arms from political aims. Laȝamon's handling of love-situations is in fact more consistently 'court-ly' than that of Wace.[16]

One may debate whether Laȝamon's systematic addition of reasons for military campaigns (where Wace mentions none) is indeed due to moral considerations, as suggested by Gibbs, or to a more general tendency to underline, and, if necessary, to provide motivations for all important actions in the *Brut* (be they political or no). However, the treatment given by our 'uncourtly' poet to women in his *Brut* is indeed worth mention-ing. F. L. Gillespy was first to note the attention given to the characteriza-tion of the mother of Merlin, of Ygerne or of Rouwenne, further stat-ing:

> The most cursory examination will suffice to show that Laȝamon displayed no inclination to exclude romantic elements from his work. Several of the elaborated episodes have love motives (either principal or subsidiary).[17]

This is true; though it must be noted that some of Laȝamon's most forceful scenes involving women tend to be in a non-courtly context. He thus gives a vivid picture of women as victims of the violence of men. King Goffar's threat to drown all the Trojan women; the rape of Ursele and the slaying of her companions; the carving off of the noses of the kinswomen of those responsible for the brawl at Arthur's court; the debasement of the Briton noblewomen and the cutting off of the breasts of the maidens by Gurmund and his men; the plight of widows and orphans are as many elements added to the French narrative by the English poet.[18] Women are far from being put on a pedestal – they remain flesh-and-blood creatures throughout the poem. Laȝamon's expansion

---

[15] R.S. Loomis, 'Layamon's *Brut*', in *The Arthurian Legend in the Middle Ages* (= ALMA), p. 107. Loomis's statement betrays a confusion between the conventions of a purely literary game and social reality; there is no reason to believe that 'woman-worship' was ever practised in actual fact, even in France (see J. F. Benton, 'Clio and Venus: An Historical View of Courtly Love').

[16] Gibbs, 'Literary Relations', pp. 217–8.

[17] Gillespy, pp. 422–4.

[18] *Brut*, 752–5; 6037–45; 11398–400; 11785–9; 14538; 14654.

of the speech of Merlin's mother not only comprises a glimpse of the virgin bower and of the supernatural seducer (in true courtly style), but also a realistic description of the young woman's pregnancy, her changing body and her going off her food.[19] Arthur's magnanimity in his Scottish campaign is moreover expressed through his pity for the Scottish women who come as suppliants – another addition to Wace.[20] This last instance is representative of Laȝamon's depiction of women in the *Brut*, in that the Scottish suppliants, though powerless, are *active*. The savage behaviour of the Briton women dressed as men, in the Wanis and Melga episode, is an extreme example of this. A number of Laȝamon's major expansions involving female characters show the women speaking or interceding. In the Leir episode, the discussion between Gornoille and her husband is initiated and led by the woman, as is that between Regau and her husband. And their advice is acted upon. The intercession of Belin and Brennes' mother takes on a heightened dramatic and emotional dimension in the English *Brut*, through the focusing on Tonuenne herself. The *Roman*'s repetition of 'remenbre tei', 'remember', with its intellectual, backward focus, is replaced by 'leo', 'see', appealing to Brennes' immediate perception. Laȝamon's Tonuenne also omits to mention what Brennes ought to have done (for example, bring presents), but merely touches on his past actions, reminding him of his oath of allegiance to his brother (a detail unmentioned by Wace), whilst linking the whole issue to herself:

> Biðenc o ðire mon-schipe   bi-ð[e]nc o ðire moder
> bi-ðenc a mire lare   þu eært mi bærn deore.[21]

Where Wace presents Tonuenne's baring of her breasts as a way of stressing her own importance, and reminding both brothers that they came from the same body, Laȝamon has her present her body in order to stress her responsibility in whatever might happen. Should Brennes lose his 'monscipe' through perjury, his shame would necessarily reflect on the mother that bore him:

> Leo wær here þa wombe   þe þu læie inne swa longe
> Leo war here þa ilke likame.   Ne do þu me neuere þane scome
> þat ich for þine þinge   mid sæxe me of-stinge.[22]

Through Tonuenne's linking of her own life and honour with that of her

[19] *Brut*, 7845–9. Laȝamon's greater realism in the treatment of his material is considered by Barron, p. 9, note 12, to be part of his 'Englishness'.
[20] *Brut*, 10912–43.
[21] *Brut*, 2504–5. 'Consider your honour, consider your mother, consider my teaching. You are my dear child'.
[22] *Brut*, 2508–10. 'See here the womb in which you lay so long; see here the very same body. Never do me such shame that I should stab myself with a knife because of your deeds'.

sons, the impact of her words on Brennes gains in credibility, whilst her own attitude – outspoken, yet pleading, with tears running down her cheeks – is more in keeping with the situation than her reasoning in Wace, which culminates with

> Bels filz Brennes, que penses tu ?[23]

A similar scene of a woman interposing herself between two enemies is the object of some elaboration in the account of the opposition between Arviragus and Rome. Arviragus' queen, the Roman-born Genuis, first attempts to convince her husband to make peace with Vespasien, for her sake and that of her son, and in the name of the compact sworn to her father Claudius.[24] As the half-convinced king and his knights get ready for combat the following morning, the queen rides between both armies and reconciles the two parties. Genuis, like Tonuenne, thus appears as a 'freoðuwebbe', the peace-weaver of Old English tradition; like Tonuenne she underlines, both in her words and her actions, her involvement in what is happening, and the importance of the virtues of faith and truth. By comparison, Wace's Genuis remains shadowy, and the whole of her initiative is dismissed in two lines:

> La reïne les acorda,
> Genuïs, ki mult s'en pena.[25]

To these two 'peace-weavers' correspond two 'black' figures, women who choose to reject the virtues of faith and truth advocated by Tonuenne and Genuis, and who kindle antagonisms instead of appeasing them: Rouwenne and Wenhauer. Both are described as exceptionally beautiful women, who turn traitor at a crucial moment of Briton history. The first epithets qualifying Rouwenne are 'fæirest wimmonnen' and 'wimmon swiðe hende'.[26] Her duplicity is then shown in two episodes not to be found in Wace: first, in her poisoning of Vortimer at a feast called under false pretences (from which point she is called 'swicfulle', 'luðere', 'ufele'), and then in her deceiving her own husband Vortigern into believing that Vortimer is going to besiege him in Thwoncaster.[27]

Laȝamon's Wenhauer is also depicted in a more negative way than Wace's Ganhumare; and it is striking that while Wenhauer gains in stature and immediacy, all of Wace's comments describing the feelings of her paramour, Modred, are deleted. As in the case of Rouwenne, the first

23 Wace, 2811. 'Handsome son Brennes, what do you think of it?'
24 In a speech some twenty lines long; see Brut 4891–914.
25 Wace, 5135–6. 'The queen reconciled them, Genuis, who was most upset'.
26 Brut, 7148 and 7177.
27 Brut, 7434–974.

mention of Wenhauer is positive, and corresponds in all points to the
courtly convention. She is of noble stock, and endowed with beauty as
well as good manners.[28] This part of the picture is directly derived from
Wace, though Laȝamon expands a little on Arthur's love for her (the
motivation given for the king's staying in Cornwall all winter). Wenhauer remains a shadowy figure, restricted to her beautiful imago as
queen, until the beginning of the campaign against Rome. Then, the
woman appears behind the function, and she is firmly linked with
Modred the arch-traitor, of whom it is said

> treouðe nefde he nane   to nauer nane monne.[29]

When Laȝamon states

> Ardur bi-tahte   al þat he ahte
> Moddrade and þere quene   þat heom was ique[m]e [30]

the implication is that they are already in league; neither of them ought to
ever have been born, both were a bane to the country, both, suggests
Laȝamon, lost their souls as a result, and are hated by all. Wace, in the
corresponding passage of the *Roman de Brut*, only mentions that Modred
secretly loved the queen: Ganhumare's feelings are not touched upon at
this point, nor are they ever in the French narrative, until the very end
where we are told that she enters into a convent, overcome by shame.
Otherwise, the queen remains a passive, shadowy character. On the
other hand, Modred's feelings are analysed with some perception,
especially in the inner conflict between his desire for reconciliation with
Arthur, and his awareness of the enormity of his crime. Laȝamon re-
verses this state of affairs. Wace's considerations on Modred's motivations or feelings are systematically omitted; his characterisation, in the
English *Brut*, is limited to his evil nature. The only potentially positive
remark about him – that he was loved – leads to emptiness: this was so
only because he was Gawain's brother. On the other hand, Wenhauer is
described as a woman in love, who has totally espoused the cause of her
unworthy lover. On receiving the news of the return of Arthur by a
'for-cuð kempe' (a scene not in Wace), she hastens to warn Modred, 'þat
wæs hire leofuest monnes'.[31] And when she takes the veil, it is not out of
shame, but out of despair at Modred's obvious defeat. Laȝamon's Wen-

---

[28] The description of Wenhauer is to be found in lines 11091–8 of the *Brut*. The expression
'of tuhtle swiðe gode' ('of manners very good', 11087) appears to be an attempt to
paraphrase 'courtoise'.
[29] *Brut*, 12712. 'Loyalty he never had any, towards any man'.
[30] *Brut*, 12726–7. 'Arthur gave all that he possessed to Modred and the queen; that was
agreeable to them'. The Otho manuscript reads 'him' for 'heom'.
[31] *Brut*, 14095–102. 'Who was to her the most beloved of men'.

hauer shows as few signs of remorse or moral standards as Rouwenne herself; and while her incestuous marriage to Modred can hardly be equated with courtly love, it comes close to the forbidden love of a Tristan (who was also in love with his uncle's wife), or, to stay within the *Brut*, the irresistible blind passion of a Locrin, a Godlac or an Uther.

Laȝamon may thus be considered as more sensitive than Wace in his treatment of women; he certainly gives them more prominence in his narrative, even if this prominence is not of a courtly nature: but then, neither do the corresponding episodes in Wace owe anything to courtly convention. Where courtly elements occur in Wace, their being retained or not depends on how consistent they are with the context. The incongruity of Wace's courtly refinements to express Uther's unthinking craving for Ygerne, for example, is obvious, and the deleting of lines such as

> Ainz que nul semblant en feïst,
> Veire assez ainz qu'il la veïst,
> L'out il cuveitee e amee,
> Kar merveilles esteit loee [32]

obeys the most basic rules of internal logic. For Uther has nothing of a disembodied lover; as for the courtly ideal of discretion in love, it is so little followed by him that all at the banquet notice what he is up to. Laȝamon's dispensing with the wholly rhetorical passage where Uther expresses his love in Ovidian tones may also be due to it being out of character, as well as distracting the reader from the urgency of the situation.[33] The whole passage is condensed into three lines, where Uther plainly states his case to Ulfin asking for help:

---

[32] Wace, 8579–82. 'Before he had made any show of it, indeed before he had ever seen her, he had desired and loved her, for she was greatly praised'.
[33] The passage reads (Wace, 8657–67):
> Ulfin, dist il, conseille mei,
> Mis conseilz est trestut en tei.
> L'amur Ygerne m'ad suspris,
> Tut m'ad vencu, tut m'ad conquis,
> Ne puis aler, ne puis venir,
> Ne puis veillier, ne puis dormir,
> Ne puis lever, ne puis culchier,
> Ne puis beivre, ne puis mangier,
> Que d'Ygerne ne me suvienge;
> Mais jo ne sai cum jo la tienge.
> Morz sui se tu ne me conseilles.

'Ulfin, he said, advise me, all my hope is in you. Love for Ygerne has taken me by surprise, it has totally overcome me, totally conquered me; I can neither come nor go, wake nor sleep, rise up nor lie down, neither drink nor eat without thinking of Ygerne. But I do not know how to get her. I am dead if you do not counsel me'.

> Ulfin ræd me sumne ræd   oðer ich beo ful raðe dæde
> swa swiðe me longeð   þat ne mai i noht libben
> after þere faire Ygærne.[34]

Any refinements in characterization in the English poem are concentrated on the person of Ygerne, who, by contrast, appears as the ideal courtly lady. She greets Uther's attentions agreeably ('She him lovingly beheld'), but without giving a hint as to her true feelings ('but I know not whether she loved him')[35] – an attitude also implicit in Wace's

> Ygerne issi se conteneit
> Qu'el n'otriout ne desdiseit.[36]

But whereas Ygerne all but disappears from the *Roman de Brut* as an independent factor from this point, Laȝamon completes the portrait of the future mother of Arthur. He first specifies (9287–8) that Ygerne, 'wifene æðelest', is Gorlois' 'leofmon', the closest English equivalent for the courtly 'amie'. The relationship between the two spouses is therefore described in terms of mutual attachment. Moreover, Ygerne is shown to be compassionate:

> Ygerne wes særi   & sorh-ful an heorte
> þat swa moni mon for hire   sculden habben þer lure.[37]

That her love is not to be bought by presents is attested by Ulfin – an indispensible quality according to the courtly code – as is her fidelity:

> for Ygærne is wel idon   a swiðe treowe wimmon
> swa wes hire moder   & ma of þan kunne.[38]

It has been suggested that Ygerne's chastity was out of keeping with her image as courtly heroine. Such claims, however, result from an overselective reading of the French romances that have come down to us. Chrétien's Enide remains faithful to her Erec: yet *Erec et Enide* is undoubtedly a courtly romance, as is *Cligès*, where Fénice goes to extraordinary lengths to avoid being possessed by any other being than her beloved. Ygerne's truth to Gorlois, whom she greets (or at least, thinks she is greeting) as 'monne me leofest', is not necessarily at odds with

---

[34] *Brut*, 9341–3. 'Ulfin, give me some advice, or I shall very soon be dead; I long so exceedingly for the fair Ygerne that I cannot live'.

[35] *Brut*, 9254. 'and [heo] hine leofliche biheold ah inæt whær heo hine luuede'.

[36] Wace 8595–6. 'Ygerne behaved in such a way that she neither encouraged nor rejected him'.

[37] *Brut*, 9290–1. 'Ygerne was pained and sorrowful in her heart, that so many men because of her should there be lost'.

[38] *Brut*, 9359–60. 'For Ygerne is well-bred, a very loyal woman; so was her mother and others of that kindred'.

the courtly ideal, while being morally more acceptable to the priest Laȝamon.[39]

The opposition between courtly Ygerne and Uther is further elaborated upon in Laȝamon's rewriting of the scene at Tintagel. Uther answers Ygerne's 'winsome words' (9491) by a blunt statement, followed by a command:

> ... ich æm bi nihte   bi-stole from þan fihte
> for æfter þe ic wes of-longed   wifmonne þu ært me leofuest
> Buð in to bure   & let mi bed makien.[40]

And when the news of Gorlois' death arrives at Tintagel, whereas in Wace Uther/Gorlois reassures Ygerne by saying he will make peace with the king, in Laȝamon he leaps out of bed proffering menaces against Uther, and departs from the castle without even taking leave of his 'wife', merely asking his attendants to tell her not to mourn. The Uther of the English *Brut* is consistently characterized as a rough-hewn soldier, and the rejection of Ovidian conventions in connection with him must therefore be ascribed to the English poet's aversion from conflicting elements in a key character, rather than to a more general hostility to things courtly.

In such conditions, it is worth considering whether the same principle governs the modifications of the second passage generally quoted as evidence for Laȝamon's conscious rejection of French culture: the quarrel between Cador and Gawain. We are at a crucial moment: Rome has just sent an ultimatum to Arthur, war is imminent. But not just any war: Rome is the greatest power in the world of the *Brut*; the matter is serious. Moreover, this campaign is going to be the indirect cause of Arthur's downfall: without it, Modred would never have been made regent of Britain. The decision that is to be taken in the tower, following the arrival of the Roman envoys, is a weighty one; and it is understandable that Laȝamon should have felt the lighthearted joking between Cador and Gawain to be out of place. The issue at hand is either peace or war: what has love to do with the matter? The English *Brut* therefore changes the tone, the contents and the setting of the exchange. The *setting* is no longer the staircase leading to the counsel room, but the hall itself. All the lords are already seated, and all are silent for fear of Arthur, when Cador formally denounces the mollifying effects of idleness. The emphasis on

---

[39] And also, it would seem, to his audience. It is well known that later Mediaeval English literature also tends to favour tales of conjugal love, such as Chaucer's *Franklin's Tale*. One may add that Laȝamon's attitude may be closer to that of the French 'advocates' of courtly love than was once assumed (see D. W. Robertson Jr., 'The Concept of Courtly Love as an Impediment to the Understanding of Medieval Texts').

[40] *Brut*, 9497-8. 'I have by night stolen away from the fight, for I was longing for you: you are to me the dearest of women. Go into the chamber and have my bed made'.

idleness is also present in Wace, where the word 'uisdive' is the object of anaphora over four lines, as well as being repeated a number of times throughout the passage. Walwain's rejoinder on the virtues of love in peace is due to Cador's linking of 'uisdive' with 'lecheries' and 'drueries' (10745–6). As neither of these elements appear in the English version of Cador's speech, they do not recur in Walwain's corresponding answer either.

This change in setting explains to a great extent the change in tone. Cador could no longer denounce idleness 'en suzriant' in the midst of such a tense assembly; moreover, within the context of the English *Brut*, Cador's speech becomes a formal counsel, advocating war for the sake of war, thereby justifying Walwain's strong reaction. Where in Wace the debate is restricted to the private level, in Laȝamon we are dealing with politics, and Walwain correspondingly replies in wider terms of ethical principle and national economy:

> for god is grið & god is frið   þe freoliche þer haldeð wið
> and Godd sulf hit makede   þurh his Godd-cunde
> for grið makeð godne mon   gode workes wurchen
> for alle monnen við þa bet   þat lond við þa murgre.[41]

The third passage where Wace displays his knowledge of courtly manners occurs in a more congenial context: at the festivities following Arthur's crowning, immediately preceding the arrival of the Roman ambassadors which caused the counsel mentioned above. Wace begins by stating the excellence of the Britons over all people in courtesy and courage; mentions that all people of quality wore only one colour; and that no knight, however high his birth, could have a noble lady as 'amie' unless his knighthood had been proven three times: thus, concludes Wace, were the knights more valiant and the ladies more chaste.

In some respects, Laȝamon's rendering of this passage reads as more courtly than that of Wace. The women are 'wunliche on heowen' (Wace does not mention their personal beauty), 'hah-lukest iscrudde' (elegant), 'alre bezst itoȝene' (well-bred).[42] These three aspects underlined by Laȝamon sum up quite neatly the attributes of a 'courtoise dame'; indeed, 'alre bezst itoȝene' looks very much like an attempt to paraphrase the French 'courtois', similar to the 'of tuhtle swiðe gode' used to translate the word 'courtois' in the description of Wenhauer. The vow to wear clothes of one hue Laȝamon further explains as a distaste for variegated cloth (which, throughout the Middle Ages, was worn predominantly by

---

[41] *Brut*, 12455–58. 'For good is peace and good is concord for whoever supports it of his own free will; and God Himself made it, through His divinity. For peace makes a good man work good works; for all men are the better for it, the land is the more prosperous for it'.
[42] *Brut*, 12298–9.

'jongleurs' and jesters), and extends this distaste to everything unre-
fined: '& elche untuhtle heo talden unwurðe'.[43]

Yet, Laȝamon falls short of the standards of theoretical courtly love
(such as defined in Andreas Capellanus' *De Amore*) by translating Wace's
'amie' by 'brude' ('bride').[44] The reward for prowess is not merely love,
but wedded love. A. C. Gibbs suggests that Laȝamon may not have recognized the courtly element in this case;[45] a closer reading of the Wace-text,
however, suggests that the passage could not have been kept as it was.
For Wace's

> E les dames meillur esteient
> E plus chastement en viveient [46]

implies that the 'druerie' granted to the thrice-proven knights was of the
sort that endangered chastity. In the outlook of the priest Laȝamon, it
could therefore not be properly applied to *married* women; wholesale
adultery would have turned Arthur's court into a den of iniquity. And
honourable love directed towards unmarried women of a noble rank
implied marriage.

The idea of prowess leading to marriage is far from being alien to
medieval French 'courtly' literature. The gallant knight errant frequently
ends up marrying the damsel in distress. Thus, Chrétien's Perceval
finally marries his Blancheflor, and so does Yvain marry Laudine. Even
in Old Provençal literature, the homeland of *fin'amor*, the knight Jaufre
ends up marrying his Brunissen. To conclude from such passages that
Laȝamon belonged to a milieu where the conventions of courtesy were
unknown is therefore a gross error.[47] The Romance tradition of love
offered a number of facets, from which a perceptive poet could take his
pick.

Other omissions of 'courtly' elements by the English poet are mostly
restricted to technical chivalric terms which presented obvious translation problems, such as 'bohorder' or 'escremir', which Laȝamon attempts to render by more general terms such as 'ærnen', to ride, or the

---

43 *Brut*, 12304. 'And all bad manners they considered despicable'.
44 *Brut* 12313. The word 'brude'/'burde' also has the more general meaning of 'lady', and
could therefore be considered as the exact translation of Wace's 'amie'. However, the
preceding sentence, which states that the ladies would never accept an unproven knight as
lord, indicates quite clearly that we are dealing with a marriage situation, and that 'brude' in
this case must mean 'bride'.
45 Gibbs, 'Literary Relations', p. 217.
46 Wace, 10519–20. 'And the ladies were more worthy and lived the more chastely for it'.
47 Indeed, from a modern point of view, Laȝamon depicts his female characters with far
more respect than his source. He thus omits Wace's mention that the breasts of the elderly
mother of Belin and Brennes were 'flaistres de vieillesce e pelues' (2724), and even has the
adventurer Hengest refer to his wife as 'a Sexisc wimmon of wisdome wel idon' (*Brut*,
7058).

phrase 'to play under shield'. Other modifications tend to go in the direction of increasing dignity: the lords at Arthur's coronation feast no longer play with stones, but with more civilised balls.[48] The omission of Wace's parenthesis on the evils of gambling may also be due to the desire to 'keep up the standard', so to speak; though the passage may have been missing in his source already.[49] The absence of Wace's enumeration of the different sorts of instruments which were to be heard at the festivities may also be due to an omission in the source; but it may also have been felt to be too technical, as well as disrupting the rhythm of an episode which, in its English version, goes gradually from a very slow pace, with the description of the ceremonial at Arthur's coronation, to general turmoil, at the arrival of the Roman ambassadors.

Whatever the reason, however, the evidence at hand seems to indicate with some clarity that Laʒamon was well acquainted with the courtly conventions and that, even though he did not choose to follow Wace's placing of the courtly elements in the poem, he was sufficiently familiar with them to use them in other, more relevant contexts. A most striking instance of this is the reappearance of the theme of love-by-hearsay (deleted from the Uther passage) in an entirely independent expansion of Laʒamon's, at the beginning of the Penda episode. Cadwallan has taken Penda prisoner: Penda has to submit. Where Wace merely states:

> E pur faire ferme aliance
> E pur faire entr'els ferme amur
> Prist Chadwalein une sorur
> Que Peanda aveit, mult bele,
> Gente e curteise damisele,[50]

Laʒamon provides a long scene, based on his favourite narrative formula, the 'messenger' theme. The captive Penda sends a knight to Cadwallan, offering his submission; the knight greets Cadwallan, presents his errand, and receives a favourable answer. The knight thereupon offers himself as surety, and extols the beauty and virtues of Penda's sister:

> ane suster he haueð hende   in þan æst ende
> nis nan feirure wifmon   þa whit sunne scineð on
> þe king of France Leouwis   ʒirneð hire ful iwis.[51]

---

[48] Wace, 10528: 'pierre geter'; *Brut*, 12328: 'driuen balles'.
[49] Lines 10543–88 of the *Roman*, which cover the whole section on gambling and on the variety of musical instruments at Arthur's festivities, are missing from nine of the manuscripts collated by Arnold.
[50] Wace, 14386–90. 'And to make a firm alliance and establish solid bonds of affection between them, Chadwalein took (as wife) a sister that Penda had, a most beautiful, noble and courteous damsel'.
[51] *Brut*, 15516–8. 'He has in the East end a beautiful sister: no woman is fairer, that the bright sun shines on. Louis, the king of France, desires her very greatly'.

By marrying her, continues the knight, Cadwallan could obtain the support of her kindred and rule over the whole of England. Cadwallan responds enthusiastically, and promises the knight all Devonshire if he is successful as a go-between – 'all for the love of Helen' ('al for Heleine lufe', 15530). The young lady is then brought to him, the wedding is celebrated, and Penda is released.

The inclusion of a love element in what Wace presents as a purely political decision shows that the impact of the conventions of Romance literature on the author of the *Brut* is not as negligible as was once thought; it is apparent, moreover, that these conventions could be expressed in English. The evidence at hand denies that Laȝamon was opposed to French culture, or unable to render 'sophisticated' concepts through the medium of his mother-tongue. Traces of French works other than the *Roman de Brut* could therefore conceivably be found in the English *Brut*.

That such traces are few, and of very inconclusive a nature, may be gathered from the lack of critical interest in that direction. F. L. Gillespy was the first to state that

> Old French traits ... appear to be negligible, so that from the point
> of view of narrative technique the French *Brut* must be considered
> as solely representative of the Old French line of influence.[52]

G. J. Visser was less categorical. Wace must have been Laȝamon's *principal* Norman source; but

> Laȝamon must of course also have perused other Norman works,
> which, for instance, are responsible for the names of such heathen
> gods as Tervagant, Dagon and Apollin.[53]

These 'other works' Visser apparently felt were too marginal and elusive to be sought after fruitfully. To these technical considerations, one may add that a poet who was felt to have rejected French culture, and who openly states that the Normans came to Britain with 'nið-craften', was not likely to have introduced more elements than necessary from that alien culture. And it is a fact that France and the French do not always appear in a very good light in the English *Brut*. The first encounter with French rulers, in the Brutus episode, is hostile: and King Goffar of Poitou and his French lord have the worst of it. France appears mainly as an obstacle and a stepping-stone towards Rome (for Belin and Brennes, Maximian or Arthur); but it is also a haven where Briton exiles such as Cordoille, Porreus or Brennes find support and strength. Moreover, most

52 Gillespy, p. 497.
53 Visser, p. 92.

of the mentions of France in the English poem are also in Wace, as is the outcome of the different confrontations between French and Britons. Expansions or modifications relative to France proper to Laȝamon are few.

The first case – which strictly speaking is not truly an expansion – occurs in the Brutus episode, where France has a 'kaisere' who has twelve companions: 'þa Freinsce heo cleopeden dusze pers'.[54] These 'dusze pers' mentioned in connection with a French emperor immediately call to mind what is generally referred to as the 'Matière de France', centred around the emperor Charlemagne. The 'dusze pers' also appear in Wace; but their impact on the reader is very different:

> Gofier, ki en out grant pesance,
> Pur querre aïe ala en France
> As doze pers ki la esteient,
> Ki la terre en doze parteient.
> Chescuns des duze en chief teneit
> E rei apeler se feseit.[55]

Wace's 'doze pers' mean no more than 'twelve noblemen of equal rank'. The word 'pers' is unmarked, and in no way refers to the title of these petty kings; Laȝamon correctly translates it by 'iferen', 'companions' (ll. 810, 812). The statement that 'the French called them *dusze pers*' may therefore be said to be an addition to Wace: the French words, quoted, take on connotations that they did not have in the *Roman*. This may be a mistranslation: the English poet knew of the *chanson de geste* genre, and jumped to the conclusion that the 'doze pers' were the same as Charlemagne's worthy retainers. Some knowledge of the *chanson de geste* genre would not be astonishing on the part of an Englishman: William of Malmesbury attests that the 'Cantilena Rollandi' was one of the first French works to have been brought to Britain by the Norman invaders, as it was sung by the soldiers before the battle of Hastings, 'ut martium viri exemplum pugnaturos accenderet'.[56]

In such conditions, the genre must have had a quasi-emblematic significance for the Normans, and the English population must have met with the *chanson de geste* fairly early, from the Conquest onwards. There is also, however, a possibility that Laȝamon's 'mistranslation' was fully conscious; in which case, his 'dusze pers' can only be ironical. For all

---

[54] *Brut*, 813.
[55] Wace, 921–6. 'Gofier, who was greatly upset by this, went to seek help in France from the twelve peers who lived there, and who shared the land in twelve. Each one of the twelve was independent, and was called king'.
[56] 'So that those who were about to fight should be spurred on by the warlike example of the hero'. William of Malmesbury, *Gesta Regum Anglorum*, W. Stubbs ed., vol. 2, book 3, paragraph 242.

their valour, neither the 'kaisere' nor his 'dusze pers' are able to withstand Brutus and Corineus. The heroes of the Normans are inferior to
those sung by Laȝamon, is the obvious implication.

This inferiority of the French is indeed apparent throughout the poem.
Not only do the Briton heroes (or, it would seem, their Roman rivals)
have no apparent difficulties in conquering the land, but the French
themselves lack resolution. At the news of Caesar's defeat, after his first
attempt to invade Britain, Laȝamon provides us with a glimpse of the
reactions of his French underlings:

Ælc Frensc-mon þe wes aht hæfð hine seolfne bi-þoht
and seide to his iuere Ne wurðe he nauere isæle
þe nu and auere-mare buȝe [to] Cesare
þe Bruttes habbeð ouer-cumen & of heore londe idriuen
Nulle we him nauere hæren ne hælde for ure hærre
a[c] wih him we scullen ure freo-scipe mid fehte bi-tellen
for ne sunde we na bliðere þenne beoð þa Bruttes
þe hine habbeoð ut idriuen & his cnihtes <i>slæȝen.[57]

The substance of this speech is derived from Wace, but the explicit
comparison with the Britons is Laȝamon's, while the outcome of the
episode shows clearly that the French do *not* compare with the Britons.
Caesar does not even need to resort to arms to bring them into subjection
again: gifts and bland words will be sufficient. However, Wace's account
of the episode is no less uncomplimentary. In fact, the words he uses to
qualify the French – 'felun', 'orguillus', 'coveitus',[58] are far more pejorative than anything we find in the English poem. And whereas in Wace
the French derive their rebellious strength from the rumour that the
Britons are going to help them against the already weakened Caesar, in
Laȝamon it is an upsurge of national pride that makes them raise their
heads and proffer 'beots' which they will not accomplish. The French
thus appear as upgraded: they are decidedly inferior to the Britons, but
they are not the non-entities described by Wace.

In the Arthurian section, the conquest of France is presented by
Laȝamon as a gracious concession on Arthur's part to the whim of his
men – a decision taken in an off-hand manner, as a matter of no great
import:

[57] *Brut*, 3821–28. 'Each Frenchman who was brave thought things over and said to his
companion: 'May he never be prosperous, he who now and ever again shall bow to Caesar,
whom the Britons have overcome and driven from their land. We will never obey him, nor
accept him as our lord, but we shall obtain our freedom from him in battle; for we are no
weaker than are the Britons who have driven him out and slain his knights''.
[58] Wace, 4165–7.

Lauerd Arður faren we   to Francene riche
and iwinnen al þat lond   to þire aȝere hond
...
þa andswarede Arður   aðelest kingen
Eouwer wille ich wulle don   ah ær ich wulle to Norweien.[59]

Throughout the episode, France appears as the extension of something else – an extension of Rome, through Frolle, then of Britain, once all the chief cities and provinces have been allotted to one or other of Arthur's companions. The only element of resistance (in Wace as in Laȝamon) is Duke Guitard of Poitiers, and even he ends up submitting to Arthur. Otherwise, the French people seem opportunistic cowards, whose shortcomings are expressed through the description of their leader, Frolle. That Frolle, a Roman, should be considered representative of the people he governs, is indicated in the English *Brut* by the title given to him – 'king'. Whereas Wace states 'n'i aveit rei ne seinnur' (9906), thereby implying a headless nation, Laȝamon reestablishes a 'normal' hierarchy, with at the top of the social ladder the king, the emanation of his people.

The first reaction of Frolle to the news of Arthur's invasion is one of fear, in the English poem. 'Laðliche of-fered', 'horribly afraid' (11689), he immediately asks for help from Rome, and obtains 25,000 knights. Significantly, neither Wace nor the *Historia* include this help from Rome, but mention a massive Gaulish defection from Frolle to Arthur. This passage, in Wace, is the object of considerable stylistic adornment, and is expanded to include the reasons for this defection (Arthur's courtesy, generosity, etc.): it is entirely deleted by Laȝamon, who only mentions the huge size of Arthur's army. The ensuing battle, which ends in a massacre and Frolle's retreating to Paris, marks in Laȝamon the beginning of a campaign. He provides an account of the fighting which motivates Arthur's first battle-speech on French soil, and his description of the sorrow in besieged Paris focuses on Frolle, who becomes the mouthpiece of the feelings of the Parisians.[60] On the other hand, the inhabitants of Paris are reduced in the English poem to a background rumour, with no personal existence: Wace's flourished description of the 'refugees' crowded in the town (9965–9) is deleted, and when the Parisians cry out to Frolle to make peace, Wace's direct speech becomes reported speech. The 'voiceless' mob is contrasted all the more to Frolle through the constant stressing in the English poem of his personal fears and motivations,

[59] *Brut*, 11523–4 and 11528–9. 'Lord Arthur, let us go to the kingdom of France, and win all the land into your own hand ... Then answered Arthur, noblest of kings: "I will do as you wish, but beforehand I will go to Norway".'
[60] Stating for example (*Brut*, 11740): 'Leouere me weore þat ich iboren nære', 'I would rather never have been born'.

and his speaking in direct speech. As a result, the English version of the story reads not as the conquest of Paris, but as a personal encounter between Arthur, 'ærhðe bi-deled', and Frolle, 'laðliche of-fered'.[61]

The attitude of the two kings, unspecified by Wace, is strongly contrasted by Laȝamon. Whereas Arthur greets Frolle's covenant with enthusiasm, Frolle hears of Arthur's decision with consternation:

> for ȝif hit wuste Frolle   þe king wes ane France
> þat Arður him ȝetten wolde   þat he iȝirnd hafde
> don he hit nolde   for a scip ful of golde.[62]

Frolle's suggestion was sheer bluff: 'to soðe he hit wende þat Arður hit wolde for-saken'.[63]

Arthur's response forces him to keep his word (Laȝamon uses the word 'beot' twice in this connection), but he would have preferred not to. Frolle is therefore depicted as lacking in heroic stamina as compared to Arthur; but he is not *unheroic* for all that. Laȝamon's description of him is positive:

> Neoðeles wes Frolle   to fihte swi[ð]e kene
> muche cniht & strong mon   and modi on heorten.[64]

Moreover, having proffered his beots, Frolle does his best to fulfil them, an attitude which meets with Arthur's approbation: 'for hit bicumeð kinge þat his word stonde'.[65]

Before the duel, Laȝamon adds a long scene describing the preparation of Arthur and his men. The king first bids his men to spend the night in prayer for him to obtain victory. As moral justification for this victory, Arthur states his good intentions:

> auere-ælche ærmen mon   þe æð scal iwurðen
> and wurchen ich wulle   muchel Godes wille.[66]

The following morning, we are given a description of Arthur donning his armour, with a special mention for his sword Caliburn, and his spear,

---

[61] *Brut*, 11750. The tryst between the two kings for sovereignty over a country recalls the situation in the first branch of the *Pedeir Keinc y Mabinogi*, where Arawn and Hafgan also fight for preeminence: though it must be stressed that Laȝamon adds nothing significant to his source at this point.

[62] *Brut*, 11822–4. 'For if Frolle, who was king of France, had known that Arthur would grant him what he had requested, he would not have done it for a shipful of gold'.

[63] *Brut*, 11820–1. 'In truth, he thought that Arthur would renounce (to fight)'.

[64] *Brut*, 11825–6. 'Nevertheless Frolle was very brave in battle; a sturdy knight and a strong man, and stout-hearted'.

[65] *Brut*, 11841. 'For it is fitting for a king, that his word should be kept'.

[66] *Brut*, 11848–9. 'Every poor man shall be the happier, and I shall accomplish the will of the great God'.

which once belonged to Uther and was made in Carmarthen by a smith
called Griffin. Arthur then rides towards the meeting-place, followed by
an impressive procession of Briton warriors, led by Walwain. No less
than thirteen of Arthur's allies are mentioned by name in this passage,
while

> Folc þer wes afoten   swa feole þusend monnen
> þat nas nauere na swa wit-ful mon   a þissere weorlde-richen
> a nauere nane spelle   þat mihte þa þusend telle
> bute he hauede mid rihte   wisdom of Drihtene
> oðer he hafde mid him   þat him hafde Mærlin.[67]

Laȝamon's expansions stress Arthur's stature as a warrior (he is elated
at the thought of battle), as a Christian (he makes everyone pray for him),
as a king (his link with Uther and the royal family of Britain is recalled
through his spear) and as a semi-supernatural being, not only through
his prestigious and mysterious weapons, but also through the explicit
reference to Merlin. The scene is given added solemnity through the
procession of kings, knights and soldiers following Arthur, and it is
significant that Wace's detail of the exchange of hostages before the duel
is deleted in the English poem, probably because it would have spoiled
the impressiveness of the picture.

Laȝamon's account of the duel also betrays considerable reworking,
not so much in the description of the fighting proper as in the framework
surrounding it. Laȝamon expands Wace's statement that the fight took
place 'dedenz l'isle', to include a description of Arthur, and then Frolle,
being led by boat to the island, where they are left. This slow, dignified
movement is then contrasted to the agitation of the people of Paris,
climbing up on walls, halls, bowers and towers in order to see the fight: a
detail already present in the French text, but underlined in the *Brut* by the
four-fold repetition of 'heo clumben uppen'. As in Wace, the keyword to
the passage is fear: but where in the French version the Parisians appear
in a decidedly opportunistic light, not caring who wins, providing

> Que cil venque que pais lur tienge
> Si que mais guerre ne lur vienge,[68]

in the English poem they join the Britons in prayer;[69] but for their own

---

[67] *Brut*, 11894–8. 'There was of foot-soldiers so many thousand men, that there was never in
this world a man so learned that he could tell, in any language, the number of thousands,
unless he was endowed with righteous wisdom by the Lord, or unless he had the powers
which Merlin had'.
[68] Wace, 10023–4. 'That he should win who would ensure them peace, so that never war
come to them'.
[69] The way this is expressed in the *Brut* interestingly diverges from Wace by its stress on
the humility with which the Britons pray to 'Godd þene gode' (*Brut*, 11923, 'the good God',

king. They are not beneath having feelings of loyalty.

The actual fight between the two kings is roughly the same in Geoffrey, Wace and Laȝamon. The English version, however, deepens the tension by delaying the onslaught with a description of the preparation of the two opponents on the island, and by exaggerating and expanding on Wace's statement that it was not easy to tell which would win, for they were both good warriors:

> Næs he næuere ifunde   a næuere nane londe
> nan swa wiht-ful mon   þat hit wuste ær þan
> whæðer of þan kingen   ouer-cumen sculde liggen
> for beien heo weoren cnihtes kene   ohte men and wihte
> muchele men on mihte   and a maine swiðe stronge.[70]

Frolle is a worthy adversary for Arthur, and Laȝamon therefore describes his death with more dignity than Wace. Where the *Roman de Brut* shows the brains and the blood of Frolle splattered all around him after the mortal blow, Laȝamon merely states

> uppen þan gras-bedde   his gost he bi-læfde.[71]

The importance of this victory is emphasized in the English poem by the addition of a speech made by Arthur, first establishing his status as law-giver,[72] then ordering the people to come and pay homage to him, and receive their new laws:

> For nu scullen Romanisce laȝen   to þan gru[n]de reosen.[73]

This passage clearly shows that the conquest of France is but a prelude to the conquest of Rome in the English poem. The victory over Frolle leads to a 'beot' which in content merely echoes other passages of the poem, but is placed at a very significant moment:

rather than 'le Rei de glorie', 'the King of glory') and to 'hali his moder', the ultimate recourse of the sinner. This enhances the solemnity of the scene; it also implies that Arthur cannot be certain of divine favour. The incident is thus placed out of the realm of political morality, which justified Arthur's previous campaigns against the Saxons. This is not a crusade.

[70] *Brut*, 11932–6. 'One could never have found, in any land, a man so wise that he could have known beforehand which of the two kings would lie defeated; for they both were brave knights, worthy men and active, men of great might, and of exceedingly great strength'.

[71] *Brut*, 11969. 'On the grass-bed he left his life'.

[72] The importance of peace is particularly stressed: the word 'grið' is repeated twice in the passage. First in Arthur's order that the Romans depart 'mid griðen', and then in his commanding the population to 'halde grið uppen leome & uppen lif' ('to hold peace upon life and limb', *Brut* 11975 and 11977). Law-giving is a recurrent theme in the *Brut*; Gibbs (pp. 207–8) notes that the mention of a king's upholding the traditional laws is almost as universal a formula in the English poem as bravery in battle.

[73] *Brut*, 11984. 'For now shall the laws of Rome fall to the ground'.

> Her-after ful sone   scal his cun of Rome
> heren tidinge   of Arðure þan kinge
> for ich heom wulle wið speken   and Rome walles to-breken
> and munegie heom hu king Belin   Bruttes ladde þider in
> and iwon him þa londes alle   þat stondeð into Rome.[74]

Whereas in Wace the conquest of France is just a postscript to Arthur's Scandinavian exploits, which at the most provides motivation for the Roman ultimatum, in Laȝamon it becomes a foretaste of the conquest of Rome: it legitimates Arthur's status as successor of Belin and Brennes. The delivering of Paris to Arthur is thus described with a ceremonial befitting the symbolic importance of the gesture: Arthur is led in by 'wit fulle men', who

> bitahten him halles   bitahten him castles
> betahten him ful iwis   al þa burh of Paris.[75]

One cannot say, therefore, that Laȝamon's vision of France in this episode is entirely negative. Frolle is undoubtedly less perfect a hero than Arthur, but his end is a worthy one; as for the people he governs, they have more dignity than Wace's inconsequential Parisians who pray for peace, whoever wins the duel, then rush to open the town gates to Arthur whilst lamenting Frolle's death.

To draw any conclusions as to Laȝamon's attitude towards France from the testimony of such passages would be unconvincing, for it is clear that France as such does not really exist. Even in the Julius Caesar episode, Gaul is already under Roman domination. Laȝamon's kinder treatment of the French people would appear to be another instance of the English poet's broader social outlook, which also expresses itself through Arthur's concern for the 'poor folk' and a general lack of disparaging comments on the peasantry, for example.[76] Any clues as to Laȝamon's attitude towards France must therefore be sought in his rare authorial comments, only one of which is relevant to our present purpose: the often-quoted reference to the Normans and their 'nið-craften':

> Seoððen her com vncu[ð] folc   faren in þessere þeode
> & nemneden þa burh Lundin   [an] heore leode-wisen
> Seoððen comen Sæxisce men   & Lundene heo cleopeden

[74] *Brut*, 11987–91. 'His Roman kindred will hear tidings of Arthur the king very soon after this: for I am going to speak with them and break down the walls of Rome, and remind them how King Belin led the Britons in there, and won for himself all the lands that extend to Rome'.
[75] *Brut*, 11995–6. 'They delivered to him the halls, they delivered to him the castles, indeed, they delivered to him all the town of Paris'.
[76] Compare *Brut* lines 11035–8; 13055; 13109; 13595–6 to the corresponding passages in Wace.

þe nome ileste longe   inne þisse londe
Seoððen comen Normans   mid heore nið-craften
and nemneden heo Lundres   þeos leodes heo amærden
Swa is al þis lond iuaren   for uncuðe leoden
þeo þis londe hæbbeð bi-wunnen   and ef[t] beoð idriuen
                                            hennene.[77]

The corresponding passage in Wace reads:

Puis sunt estrange home venud,
Ki le language ne saveient,
Mais Londoïn pur Lud diseient;
Puis vindrent Engleis e Saisson
Ki recorumpurent le nun,
Londoïn Lundene nomerent
Et Londene longes userent.
Norman vindrent puis e Franceis,
Ki ne sourent parler Engleis.
...
Des languages as gens estranges,
Ki la terre unt sovent conquise,
Sovent perdue, sovent prise,
Sunt li nun des viles changied.[78]

One may notice that to describe this phenomenon of the renaming of
towns, Wace uses the pejorative word 'to corrupt', while Laȝamon
applies the pejorative 'nið-craften' to one specific instance: that of the
passage from English to French. The English *Brut* extends the negative
judgement on the Normans' renaming of London to their works as a
whole: they not only imposed a foreign culture on the land, but destroyed the people who lived there. The true import of Laȝamon's remark
becomes clearer on comparing it with an earlier passage in the *Brut*,

[77] *Brut*, 3543–52. 'Afterwards there came foreign people to this land, and they named the
town Lundin, in their own manner. Then came Saxon men, and they called it Lundene; the
name lasted long in this land. Then came the Normans with their evil ways, and they named
it Lundres. They massacred this people. So has all this country fared because of foreign
people who have conquered the land, and then are driven away again'. 'Beoð idriuen', at
line 3552, can have present or future reference: this central passage could therefore also be
understood as 'they *will* be driven hence'. The 'nið-' element in 'nið-craften' means 'evil',
'dreadful' (see Kurath and Kuhn); as an adjective, it is attested in the passage of the *Brut*
under consideration, and in the *Ormulum*, where it qualifies the torments of Hell.
[78] Wace, 3762–70 and 3776–9. 'Then foreign men came who did not know the language, but
said Londoïn instead of Lud; then the English and the Saxons came, who corrupted the
name again; they called Londoïn Lundene, and long used (the name) Lundene. Then came
the Normans and the French, who did not know how to speak English ... Through the
languages of the foreign peoples who have often conquered the land, often lost it, often
taken it, the names of the towns have been changed'.

dealing with the same subject of the changing names of the towns of Britain:

> Soððen þa leodene   longe þer-after
> leiden adun þene noma   & Trinouant heo nemneden
> ...
> Seo[ð]ðen com oþer tir   & neowe tidinde
> þat men heo clepeden Lundin   ouer al þas leode
> Seoððen comen Englisce men   & cleopeden heo Lundene
> Se[ð]ðen comen þa Frensca   þa mid fehte heo bi-wonnen
> mid heora leodðeawe   & Lundres heo hehten.[79]

This passage follows Wace in all points except two. The first is the poets' position towards the French language: Wace is speaking from within the language, whereas Laȝamon sees it from outside. It would not have been possible for the English poet to make a literal translation of Wace's

> Londenë en engleis dist l'um
> E nus or Lundres l'apelum.[80]

The second difference is that Wace consistently equates change with corruption: 'Puis ala li nuns corumpant'; 'bien pert par corruptiun', 'Puis unt cest nun Lud corumpu'.[81] This aspect is totally deleted by Laȝamon. That violent conquest should have been mentioned in connection with French only, is significant: Wace's comment on the destruction of the good towns wrought by different invaders (1239–46) is thus narrowed to the more recent happenings. One may infer some bitterness on the poet's part against the Normans, who seem to be equated to some extent with the French. Whether this animosity against an oppressing political authority is a valid argument in favour of a wholesale rejection of French culture is a different matter. On the one hand, both of the passages just quoted stress the transitoriness of political supremacy, and Laȝamon was certainly well aware that what the Normans did to the English was no different from what the Saxons had done to the Britons; it is significant that the expression 'ufele craften' reappears in the *Brut* to describe the Saxon ways (though the term appears in the mouth of a Briton, and a bad

---

[79] *Brut*, 1019–20 and 1027–31. 'Subsequently, the people – long afterwards – changed its name, and they named it Trinovant ... Afterwards came another rule and new customs, so that men called it Lundin, over all the country. Subsequently came English men, and they called it Lundene. Afterwards came the French, who conquered it with fight in their customary manner, and they named it Lundres'.

[80] Wace, 1237–8. 'They say 'Lundenë' in English, and we now call it Lundres'.

[81] Wace, lines 1225, 1229, 1234. 'Then the name went corrupting'; 'it appears clearly, by corruption'; 'then they corrupted the name Lud'.

counsellor at that).[82] Saxons and Normans are put in parallel as evil peoples who usurped the rights of the legitimate inhabitants of Britain – the Britons, then the Angles.

The destructive nature of the Norman conquest is then twice under-lined in the *Brut*; but it must also be stressed that the Conquest was indeed a traumatic and bloody experience, and that as a historian (and an English one at that), Laȝamon could hardly have referred to it otherwise. One may note, moreover, that even a pro-Norman historian such as William of Malmesbury hinted that the union between Britain and Nor-mandy was unnatural, like the woman with two bodies he refers to in the second book of his *Gesta Regum*.[83]

Laȝamon's remarks may thus be read as bare statements of fact, and the animosity which underlies them lies on a strictly political level. The very fact that the *Brut* is a reworking of an Anglo-Norman poem is a clear indication that the English poet took an interest in both the language and the literary developments of the new rulers. The accuracy with which Laȝamon did his work shows that he had all the competence necessary to understand and appreciate French works other than his main source. As suggested above, he was probably familiar with the *chanson de geste* genre, and while the possible influence of further genres or works is harder to ascertain, there is no doubt that Visser was correct in stating that Wace was only the *principal* Norman source, and that 'Laȝamon must of course also have perused other Norman works'.[84]

Visser bases his opinion on the fact that the names of the heathen gods Tervagant, Dagon or Apolin must be derived from French sources, though he does not suggest any specific work. If Apolin is clearly derived from Apollo, and Dagon is an idol mentioned in the Scriptures,[85] Ter-vagant is certainly quite common in medieval French literature. Jean Bodel's *Jeu de Saint Nicolas* also includes the three gods Tervagun, Mahom and Apolin, who appear to have been well-established in French popular culture as 'typical' heathen idols. Such names were part of general knowledge, and probably crossed the Channel with the Nor-mans, though chronologically it would not have been impossible for Laȝamon to have known Bodel's play (the *Jeu de Saint Nicolas* was first produced in December 1200). However, the most definite signs of French influence appear in Laȝamon's expansions dealing with the theme of forbidden love (such as in the Delgan and Godlac episode) and in his treatment of secret encounters (such as that between Brian and Galarne).

---

82 i.e., Margadud, *Brut*, 15803.
83 See William of Malmesbury, *Gesta Regum Angliae*, W. Stubbs ed., pp. 259–260.
84 Visser, *Vindication*, p. 92.
85 Mamilon is more of a mystery. The name may perhaps have been derived from Mammon.

Herbert Pilch was the first critic to note analogies between the French *Tristan* and certain episodes of the *Brut*, though the possible significance of such parallels was obscured by his providing a number of other analogues (from Celtic sources, mainly). The first instance is found in the Delgan and Godlac episode, where Laȝamon considerably expands the French text, and introduces material not found in Wace. The starting-point is Laȝamon's tendency towards a better characterization of women, joined to his custom of providing the motivations for a given action (through the compositional device of the 'messenger' theme). Wace describes the feelings of Gudlac's unnamed 'amie' in the following way:

> La dame ert assez bele e gente,
> Mais li plaiz li desatalente.
> Ele out, lunc tens aveit passé,
> Le rei de Danemarche amé,
> Gudlac, qui mult rout li amee
> Si li deveit estre dunee,
> Mais Brennes l'en ad desturbé;
> E ele ad a Gudlac mandé
> E tut le conseil descovert
> Que Brennes l'ad e il la pert,
> E, si forment ne se purchace,
> Jamais ne girrat en sa brace.[86]

Gudlac therefore attacks the fleet of Brennes; 'par aventure' he captures the queen's ship and carries her off. They are then caught in a storm (elaborately described by Wace) and are thrown on the shores of 'Engleterre'.

Laȝamon's version of the story comprises all the usual elements of courtly convention. The love between Delgan and Godlac is repeatedly stressed:

> heo hauede enne leoue-mon   þa heo swuþe ileoued hæfde
> þene king of Denmark   þe leof hire weis on mode.[87]

Wace's 'ad … mandé' is expanded; the English poet specifies both the means of communication (letters) and the contents of the message, first

---

[86] Wace, lines 2439–50. 'The lady was very beautiful and becoming, but the settlement displeased her. She had for a long time been in love with the king of Denmark, Godlac, who also loved her greatly, and she was to have been given to him; but Brennes changed these plans. She sent a message to Godlac and revealed the situation to him, that Brennes had her and he had lost her, and that unless he reacted vigorously, she would never lie in his arms'.
[87] *Brut*, 2239–40. 'She had a lover, whom she had loved greatly – the king of Denmark, who was dear to her in mind'.

given in reported speech, but ending on an emotional farewell in direct speech:

> þa sende Dalgan   þa quene in-to Denemarke
> & guðde Godlacke   þa wes hire gome deore
> stille boc-runen   heo senden him to ræden
> ...
> Sone hit mæi ilimpen   þanne ihc hunnen liðe
> þah þu habben blisse and grið   ne speke ich þe nauere-
>   more wið
> and ihc sende þe gretinge   of mine gold ringe [88]

If the explicit mention that Brennes exerted conjugal rape on Delgan goes one step further in realism than Wace's account, one may notice that the opposition between the inflicted husband and the chosen lover, the secrecy surrounding the exchanges between the lovers, and the use of a ring as a token of recognition, are recurrent themes in Romance literature. Godlac's reaction to Delgan's message, in a scene unparalleled in Wace, is also typical of a courtly lover. In true Ovidian manner,

> þ<a> Godlac isæh þis   wa him wes ful iwis
> Stille he wes iswoȝen   on his kine-stole
> Me warp on his nebbe   cold welle-watere.[89]

The swooning lover then turns into a valiant warrior, calling his men to battle. They recognize the queen's ship by its silken sail – 'sulkene wes þat seil-clæð' (2270), capture the queen (and with her, the treasure – a realistic detail not in Wace), and steer back towards Denmark. Then, as in Wace, they get caught in a storm. Laȝamon follows Wace faithfully in the depiction of the storm itself: the darkening sky, the raging wind, the rough sea, the fearful waves. But the account of the effects of the tempest on the ships is greatly modified. Wace's technical terms are deleted; only the breaking ropes are mentioned. We are immediately told that 53 ships sank, their sails turning into the sea. And Godlac, in order to save himself, grasps a battle-axe and hews the mast in two, so that both mast and sail fall into the waters. In Wace also masts get broken, but through the strength of the wind. Herbert Pilch thus states:

> Die von Layamon neu eingeführten Motive erinnern lebhaft an Tristan D 1165–1770. Dort kehren sowohl die Übersendung des

---

[88] Brut, 2242–44 and 2250–52. 'Then Delgan the queen sent to Denmark, and warned Godlac, who was her dear man; secret letters she sent him to read ... The moment will soon come for me to depart; may you have joy and peace: I will never speak with you again, and I send you my greeting by my golden ring'.
[89] Brut, 2253–5. 'When Godlac saw this, he was exceedingly sorrowful. He fainted senseless on his throne; cold well-water was thrown over his face'.

Ringes als Hilferuf wieder wie der zerhauene Mast und das besondere Segel, das die Anwesenheit des Geliebten auf dem Schiff
anzeigt.[90]

However, these parallels are of a very general nature. The exchange of
rings as love-tokens or as signs of recognition is a very common theme in
medieval literature. The silken sails of Delgan's ship have no exact correspondence in *Tristan*. Pilch's suggestion that the detail may have arisen
from a misunderstanding of the Thomas text is attractive,[91] but the silken
sails of the ship of the royal bride could equally be due to Laȝamon's taste
for luxurious accessories for his heroes. As for the mast, one may note
that in *Tristan* (1592–3), it breaks with the wind, as in Wace, not as the
result of the hero's effort to save himself and his lady.[92] Yet, one can only
agree that the passage is reminiscent of *Tristan*. This is due mainly to the
similarity of the situations: a couple of young lovers separated by an
unwanted marriage; the royal rank of the protagonists; the secrecy surrounding the affair; the importance of the sea, and finally, the ring. These
elements are not proper to *Tristan*, but to the modern reader they evoke
the story immediately. Was this however the case with Laȝamon who,
one may notice, never mentions the name of Tristan once in his poem?

Another motif possibly reminiscent of *Tristan* is pointed out by Pilch
in the Belin and Brennes episode: that of the harp. Brennes, like Tristan,
attains social recognition in a foreign land through his musical skill at the
harp. The motif reappears in a less courtly manner in the Arthurian
episode, where Baldulf disguises himself as a fool to get into York:

> he lette sceren half his hæfd   and nom him ane harpe an
> hond
>
> He cuðen harpien wel   an his child-haden
> & mid his harpe he ferde   to þas kinges hirede
> & gon þær to gleowien   & muche gome to makien.[93]

The rough treatment the 'crosse' (fool) Baldulf receives at the hands of his

---

[90] Herbert Pilch, p. 35. 'The new motives introduced by Laȝamon are strongly reminiscent
of Tristan D 1165–1770. There also appear the sending of the ring as an appeal for help, the
hewn down mast, and the special sail which indicates the presence of the beloved on the
ship'.
[91] *Tristan* 1743–6: 'Nequedant jo l'ai si veüe / Que pur la sue l'ai coneüe' ('As soon as I saw
it, I knew it was hers'). Pilch plausibly suggests that 'pur la sue' may have been misread 'pur
la seie' ('because of the silk').
[92] The storm scene in Thomas' *Tristan* is in fact derived from this passage of Wace's *Roman
de Brut*.
[93] *Brut*, 10133–6. 'He had half his head shaved and took a harp in his hand – he had learned
how to play the harp well in his childhood – and with his harp he went to the kings host,
and started to play there, and fool around'.

audience contrasts strongly with the enraptured delight of those listening to Tristan or Brennes; though the initial situation – passing one's self off as a professional harper to gain access to a given place – is similar. This instance, however, is directly derived from Wace. Herbert Pilch suggests that this importance of musical skills, and especially of harp-playing, is ultimately taken from Celtic tradition; and indeed the harp enjoys a prominent position in Welsh literary, historical and legal documents. The harp was one of the three possessions a man could not be deprived of; the magician Gwydion, in the *Pedeir Keinc y Mabinogi*, disguises himself as a bard on several occasions; and we know that learning to play the harp was part of the education of young Welsh noblemen. However, neither the harp as an instrument, nor the importance given to music, are exclusively Welsh features. Bede's account of how the herdsman Cædmon received the gift of poetry shows quite clearly that in Anglo-Saxon society as well, proficiency at the harp was a valued social accomplishment. Moreover, the existence during the Middle Ages of a number of wandering musicians whose skill gained them access to different European courts could well have suggested such expansions, without needing to postulate a literary source; and one may note that legend has it that King Alfred the Great himself once posed as an itinerant minstrel.[94]

There remains, though, that the motif tends in the English *Brut* to appear in a 'courtly' context – the only 'realistic' appearance of the harp-motif is taken directly from Wace – and the same may be said of the ring-motif, which appears in the episode of Brian and Galarne. In this case, the protagonists are not lovers, but brother and sister: however, the similarities with the Tristan legend are in some ways more striking even than in the Godlac passage. On the one hand, the ring is linked with a distinctive relish for disguises. Brian first sets out as a merchant, with his companions; a disguise often used in the Tristan-legend, be it by the hero himself, during his second voyage to Ireland, or by the faithful Caherdin on his mission to Isolde.[95] Brian then assumes the character of a pilgrim (following the Wace-text), and comes as a beggar to Edwine's hostile court, where he hopes to be helped by his sister Galarne. Though Galarne is not Edwine's queen, Laȝamon explicitly states that she was forced to be his mistress:

94 Closer to Laȝamon's time, a similar story was told of Hereward, one of the figureheads of the resistance against William I.
95 These instances are to be found in Gottfried of Strassburg's version of the story; Thomas' account of these episodes is no longer extant. However, there is good reason to believe that it was very similar to that of Gottfried, as 'Thômas von Britanje', 'der âventiure meister was' ('Thomas of Britain, who was the master of *aventure* tales') is specifically referred to as source in Gottfried's Prologue (150–1).

> to bure me ladde   to þas kinges bedde
> þe king dude vnwisdom   þat he þat ilke maide nom
> for þe wifmon a   was þes ilke kinges iua.[96]

She is therefore in a situation reminiscent of Isolde's, even though the ultimate issue here is political (she is going to help her brother kill Pellus), not amorous. In both cases, the man who comes in disguise is dearer to the two women than their 'lords', and in both cases they use the same subterfuge to show their recognition. The scene in Wace covers some 14 lines:

> Sa suer est d'une chambre issue
> E Brien l'ad bien cuneüe;
> En ses meins un bacin teneit,
> A la reïne ewe quereit.
> Brien s'enbati en sa veie
> Qu'ele le cunuisse e veie;
> La suer ad le frere entercié,
> Mes il li ad dit et cluignié
> Qu'ele ne face nul semblant
> Qu'il li partienge tant ne quant.
> Il la baisa e ele lui,
> Asez plurerent ambedui.[97]

Laȝamon puts the incident in a more formal setting, that of the king's dole:

> þe king him gon to þeinen   mid alle his here-cnihten
> þæ quene bar to drinken   & alle hire bur-lutlen
> þa i-lomp hit seoððe   þe[r]-after ful sone
> þat Galarne þat maiden   com hire ȝeongen
> bolle heo hafde an honden   þer-mide heo bar to dringen.[98]

Galarne thus appears in an official function, assisting the queen in her 'largesse'; the gift of the ring consequently passes unnoticed:

[96] *Brut*, 15215. 'She was led to the chamber, to the king's bed; the king did a foolish thing in taking that maiden, for the woman was that king's enemy ever after'. Wace merely states that she was taken to his chamber.
[97] Wace, 14273–84. 'His sister came out of a room, and Brian recognized her well; she was holding a basin in her hands, she was fetching water for the queen. Brian put himself in her way, so that she would recognize and see him; the sister caught sight of her brother, but he told and gestured for her not to show in any way that they were anything to each other. He kissed her and she kissed him, and they both cried enough'.
[98] *Brut*, 15367–71. 'The king started the serving, with all his attendants; the queen carried the drink, and all her maidens. It then happened very soon afterwards that the maiden Galarne came near; she had a bowl in her hand with which she carried the drink'.

þa isæh heo Brien þer   deore hire broð[er]
on wræcches monnes liche   þeh he weoren riche
Anan swa þat maiden hine i-sæh   sone heo him to bæh
and droh of hire uingre   an of hire ringe
and salde him an honde   ænne ring of rede golde
and þus sæide Galerne   þat goð-fulle maide
Haue þis gold wræcche   Godd þe wurðe milde.[99]

One finds a very similar scene in Thomas' *Tristan*:

Que Tristran ert ben s'aparçut
Par sun gent cors, par sa faiture,
Par la furme de s'estature;
En sun cuer en est esfreée
E el vis teinte e colurée,
Kar ele a grant poür del rei;
Un anel d'or trait de sun dei,
Ne set cum li puisse duner,
En sun hanap le volt geter.[100]

The outcome is different, due (in the French poem) to the intervention
of Brengvein, who has the 'leper' thrown out; but we find the same
elements in a similar context: the wretched clothes, the jostling and
pushing of the crowd of beggars,[101] and the gift of the ring as a sign of
recognition which leads (or fails to lead, in the *Tristan*) to reunion. One
may object that the disguise motif is already in Wace, and that the pushing about of Brian is just the sort of realistic touch that Laȝamon relishes.
The combination of these different elements, however, is significant, as
is the stress on secrecy in the ensuing conversation between Brian and
Galerne. In Wace, brother and sister openly kiss each other with tears
before thinking of hiding away to talk; in Laȝamon their public exchange

99 *Brut*, 15372–8. 'Then she saw Brian there, her dear brother, looking like a poor man, even
though he was rich. As soon as the maiden saw him, she quickly drew near him and took off
her finger one of her rings, and put into his hand a ring of red gold; and thus said Galerne,
the good maiden: 'Have this gold, poor man; may God be gracious to you'.
100 Thomas, *Les Fragments du Roman de Tristan*, B.H.Wind ed., p.108 (Fragment Douce;
lines 552–60). 'She well realised that it was Tristan, by his noble person, by his appearance,
by his bearing; she felt fear in her heart, and her face has changed colour and blushed, for
she fears the king greatly; she takes a gold ring from her finger, but doesn't know how she
could give it to him; she wants to throw it into his cup'. This parallel is also noted by Pilch in
his *Literarische Studie*.
101 Tristan's treatment by the 'serjant' of Marc's court is no gentler than that of the disguised Baldulf, or Brian in the crowd of beggars:
Li uns l'empeinst, l'altre le bute,
E sil metent hors de la rute,
L'un manace, l'altre le fert.
(Fragment Douce, lines 537–9). 'One pulls him, the other pushes him, and they get
him out of the way, one threatens him, the other hits him'.

is limited to the gift of the ring, and the thanks of the 'lome monne'. The feeling of impending menace is greater in the English poem, and in that respect also does the scene resemble that of *Tristan*:

> þa heo to-gadere hafden ispeken   sone heo gunen to-delen
> for nauer neoðer nalde   for his æfne wiht of golde
> þat þe king hit wusten   þat heo to-gaderen weoren
> for sone heo weoren for-don ba   oðer of-slaȝen oðer
>
> an-hon.[102]

This fate Tristan and Isolde were many a time close to sharing also. By contrast, in Wace, Brian's sister does not seem to have any great fears for herself, only for her brother: 'de lui ert en grant freür'.[103]

Whilst the separate elements of this scene could be explained away, either as 'organic' expansion, or as exaggeration, or as a reworking of motifs found elsewhere in the French *Roman de Brut*, the overall effect is too similar to Thomas' *Tristan* to be overlooked.

If Laȝamon was influenced by the *Tristan* legend, it could well account for the lack of recognition of the courtly element in the *Brut* by successive generations of critics. For *Tristan* may to some extent be considered as a counter-current within the love ideal that was emerging in Wace's day. The ill-fated passion of Tristan and Isolde has little in common with the highly codified social game described by Andreas Capellanus. Isolde is no distant lady to her Tristan. Gillespy, in her considerations about the treatment of love by Laȝamon, notes that the English poet's love-scenes 'have an oddly modern tone':[104] this may readily be explained by the fact that modern ideals of love are closer to what we find in the *Tristan* than to the well-bred ritual of the *De Amore*.[105] Likewise, love in the English *Brut* is predominantly a passion, something potentially destructive (Locrin and Astrild, Uther), and a source of suffering (Delgan, Godlac, Uther, even Guinevere) unless it can express itself within the institution of marriage. In such an outlook on love, women become active participants. Whereas the characterization of the courtly lady on her pedestal is hindered by convention, the passionate lover has to be described in more detail: her feelings and motivations are at least as important as those of her paramour. Laȝamon's greater interest in the characterization of women would thus appear to follow the same principles as those under-lying the *Tristan*; and the cumulative effect of the parallels between the

---

[102] *Brut*, 15390–3. 'When they had spoken together, they quickly parted, for neither would ever have wanted for his own weight in gold that the king should come to know that they had been together, for they both would have been swiftly executed, slain or hanged'.
[103] Wace, line 14294. 'She was greatly afraid on his account'.
[104] Gillespy, p. 483.
[105] See Denis de Rougemont, *L'amour et l'occident*.

English *Brut* and different episodes of the *Tristan* certainly suggests that Laȝamon was acquainted with the legend.

In what form could Laȝamon have known the legend? The closest version to the two passages of the *Brut* under consideration is that of Thomas. In other versions of *Tristan*, Iseut rejects her lover disguised as a leper, and has him beaten up. According to Bédier, such must have been also the reading of the archetype (reconstructed by him on the basis of the agreements between the different versions).[106] In Thomas, Iseut recognizes Tristan, and attempts to give him her ring: but Brengvein stops her, and the 'leper' is thrown out. If the Brian/Galarne scene is reminiscent of *Tristan* at all, it must therefore be derived from the Thomas text.

We know nothing precise about Thomas, except that he was an Anglo-Norman writer, and possibly a cleric. In terms of chronology, his poem was accessible to Laȝamon: it was composed between 1155 (after Wace's *Roman de Brut*) and 1170 (before Chrétien de Troyes' *Cligès*), and we know it circulated on British soil. In fact, the English poet could conceivably have found a copy of Thomas' *Tristan* in the same library as the *Roman de Brut*: the influence of Wace on Thomas' *Tristan* is established, and it would be pleasant to think that Laȝamon worked on the same Wace-text as Thomas – though this, of course, is mere day-dreaming.

To sum up: the analogies pointed out by Pilch between the *Brut* and Thomas' *Tristan*, though inconclusive in the Belin and Brennes episode, and of a somewhat general nature in the Delgan and Godlac episode, become more significant in the recognition scene between Brian and Galarne. Laȝamon's expansions in these passages are not derived from Wace, yet they have a distinctly 'courtly' tone. They do not betray any influence of the *fin'amor* conventions, as exemplified by Chrétien's *Lancelot* or Andreas Capellanus' *De Amore*, but throughout the *Brut* we find a depiction of the love-relationship that is closely akin to that of the *Tristan*, with its stress on reciprocity in passion. Moreover, as noted by Bédier, though *Tristan* is on a superficial level a tale of adultery, its dramatic impact and the suffering of the two lovers can only be explained by a very high idea of marriage on the poet's part:

> La légende est fondée tout entière sur la loi sociale, reconnue comme bonne, nécessaire et juste. Elle est fondée sur le mariage indissoluble.[107]

This attitude we find in Laȝamon's disapproving attitude towards Locrin's abandonment of Gwendoleine, his rightful wife, and his approv-

106 J. Bédier, *Le Roman de Tristan par Thomas*, pp. 270–6.
107 J. Bédier, *Le Roman de Tristan par Thomas*, p. 166.

ing comments on the harshness of different kings in maintaining the laws of their land. The moral outlook is the same.

In terms of the general economy of the *Brut*, there are also good reasons for Laȝamon to have taken an interest in the Tristan legend. On the one hand, the legend was thought to be of Welsh origin. Thomas explicitly refers to a certain Breri as authority for his version of the tale: this Breri is probably the same as 'famosus ille fabulator Bledhericus', 'that famous story-teller Bledhericus', mentioned by Giraldus Cambrensis in his *Descriptio Kambriae*,[108] or the Bleheris of the Perceval continuation. And the evidence of the *Brut* shows that Laȝamon took Welsh tradition quite seriously. Moreover, in a number of versions of the Tristan legend, the hero is connected with King Arthur, a fact which could have induced Laȝamon to take a 'historical' interest in the story. In Welsh tradition, Tristan thus figures among the Three Powerful Swineherds of the Island of Britain, a triad where we are told that Tristan kept the swine of King March while the swineherd was carrying a message to Essyllt; and that Arthur tried in vain to get one of those pigs from him, by ruse or by force.[109] The episode of the blades related by Eilhart of Ogberg, one of the early redactors of the Tristan legend, also features Arthur and his knights.

This is not the case in Thomas' poem, where Tristan is shifted in time, in order to magnify King Mark, who thus becomes king of Cornwall *and* England. Another reason, suggests Bédier, is that

Combinant la fable de Tristan avec la pseudo-histoire de Wace, Thomas a prétendu conférer à son roman une sorte de dignité historique.[110]

The Tristan legend, which was ascribed to Wales, the theoretical fountain-head of Laȝamon's historical material, and was traditionally connected with Arthur, the main hero of the *Brut*, had therefore the added attraction, in the Thomas version, of being in accord with (or at least, not in contradiction with) Wace, whilst betraying the stylistic influence of the *Roman de Brut*. It thus combined respectability of a sort with the attraction of supplementary information about an era dealt with by the *Brut*: more than enough to arouse Laȝamon's curiosity.

Laȝamon thus appears to have been well informed of the literary achievements of his Anglo-Norman masters. That he appreciated what he found is attested by the 'French tone' of a number of his expansions.

---

[108] Giraldus Cambrensis, *Opera*, VI, J. F. Dimock ed., ch. xvii.
[109] Rachel Bromwich, *Trioedd Ynys Prydein*, triad no. 26 (pp. 45–54): 'Tri Gwrdueichyat Enys Prydein'.
[110] 'Through combining the fable of Tristan with Wace's pseudo-history, Thomas attempted to confer upon his romance some sort of historical dignity'. Bédier, p. 101. Bédier equates Wace's Gurmund with Tristan's king Gormon of Ireland.

The fact that the modern reader, used to connecting this tone with French lexis, finds it difficult to muster the same emotional response when 'courtly' concepts are expressed in English words, is irrelevant. The French influence on the *Brut* cannot be said to be restricted to Wace, and it is more pervasive than was once thought.

5

Geoffrey of Monmouth

Geoffrey of Monmouth's *Historia Regum Britanniae* was certainly one of the best-known works in Laȝamon's day; and, being the source of Wace's *Roman de Brut*, it is also ultimately the source of the English *Brut*. For Laȝamon not to have been aware of this would be somewhat astonishing – everything indicates that he was a man of considerable curiosity, even if certain critics have questioned the extent of his learning. One would therefore expect Laȝamon to have been personally familiar with the text of the *Historia*, which was widely read, and tremendously popular. To quote G. J. Visser:

> A priori there seems no reason why Laȝamon should not have been acquainted with this epoch-making work that has left its traces on so many medieval poems and chronicles.[1]

But there is little evidence within the poem to substantiate such an assumption. Richard Wülcker, who first investigated the *Brut* in order to find traces of a cross-checking of Wace's text against Geoffrey's *Historia*, thus came to the conclusion that Geoffrey's work had no influence at all on Laȝamon's poem, except perhaps the seventh book of the *Historia*, containing the Prophecies of Merlin.[2] Such was also the opinion of R. H. Fletcher, who, whilst pointing out that 'there is a little evidence looking in the contrary direction', states:

> It seems nearly certain that if Layamon had drawn directly from Geoffrey's *History*, he would have named it among his sources in his introductory lines, unless – what does not appear very probable – he thought, or believed his readers would think, that it was too untrustworthy.[3]

Wülcker had suggested that the Prophecies of Merlin quoted by

---

[1] G. J. Visser, *Vindication*, pp. 11–12.
[2] Richard Wülcker, 'Über die Quellen Layamons', p. 543.
[3] R. H. Fletcher, 'Some Arthurian Fragments from Fourteenth Century Chronicles', p. 91.

Laȝamon may be due to independent Welsh popular tradition; Fletcher considers this 'dangerous' (p. 93), and, noting that all the passages quoted in the Brut either correspond to Geoffrey's seventh book, or agree with Wace, postulates that some of Merlin's prophecies had passed from Geoffrey's work into popular lore.

Rudolf Imelmann's position was somewhat different. As Imelmann considered that Laȝamon was a hack who slavishly transposed into English a French work of outstanding merit compiled from a number of sources (the most important being Wace's Roman de Brut and a lost work of Geffrei Gaimar on the same subject), there is no question of Laȝamon having used the Historia. Any agreement between the English Brut and the Historia against Wace's Roman de Brut can only be explained by Laȝamon's hypothetical source. From our point of view, Imelmann may therefore be disregarded; though one may note that he does not rule out the possibility of his hypothetical Norman compiler having used the Historia.

Perhaps as a reaction to this consensus against Laȝamon having used the Historia – 'Why should that which seems quite natural in a French poet be deemed impossible in the English priest?' – G. J. Visser, in his Vindication, takes the opposite viewpoint. Laȝamon, he contends, did make use of the Historia, to some extent. In favour of this opinion, Visser investigates eleven Laȝamon/Geoffrey parallels which may indicate a connection between both works:[4]

(1) Brut, 316, we have a mention of 'Grickisce fure', which corresponds to Historia ch. 11 (I, vii), 'Greco igne', where Wace reads (327) 'granz fuz'. Visser does not exclude the possibility of a corruption in the printed Wace-text he used; the edition of Le Roux de Lincy was notoriously unreliable. The only variant noted in the critical edition by Ivor Arnold is 'gros fuz'; but Herbert Pilch points out that the corresponding passage of the Münchener Brut reads 'feu gregois'.

(2) Brut 965, 'Geomagoges lupe' corresponds to Historia ch. 21 (I, xvi), 'Saltus Goemagog', where Wace (1167–8) reads

> Li leus out puis le nun e a
> Del gaiant qu'illuec trebucha.[5]

Visser suggests that 'lupe' may be a translation of Geoffrey's 'saltus'. As the name of the giant is also mentioned by Wace, however, Laȝamon may have derived his 'Geomagoges lupe' from the story itself.

---

[4] The Historia Regum Britanniae is quoted from the edition of Neil Wright. The references indicate, first, the chapter in Wright's edition; then, in brackets, the book and paragraph following Acton Griscom's division of the text.

[5] 'The place afterwards had and still has the name of the giant who fell there'.

(3) *Brut* 7763 and *Historia* ch. 106 (VI, xvii) agree against Wace (7363–66) in representing Vortigern's messengers as arriving tired at Carmarthen.

Visser's conclusion that Laȝamon drew on Geoffrey here fails to convince; the tiredness of the messengers is an obvious expansion, as Wace mentions in the preceding lines (7359–60) that they had journeyed through many regions.

(4) *Brut* 7835–44 and *Historia* ch. 107 (VI, xviii) represent Merlin's mother speaking of maidens in her chamber and the beauty of the youth who came to her. Wace includes no such details.

Laȝamon's text does indeed look like an elaboration of the *Historia*, though none of its elements, taken in isolation, could be said to be truly significant. The maidens in a lady's bower are a fairly commonplace 'background' detail; as for the 'þing ... swulc hit weore a muchel cniht al of golde idiht', the creature who looked like a knight all dressed in gold could be an elaboration of Wace's 'fantosmerie'. Beauty and gold would then be understood as indicating the supernatural nature of the nightly visitor. However, the cumulative effect confirms Visser's feeling that 'it is much more likely ... that Layamon is here indebted to Geoffrey' (p. 13).

(5) *Brut*, 8475–83 and *Historia* ch. 128 (VIII, x) imply that Aurelius did not know of Merlin until Tremorien mentioned him, while Wace's language does not convey that impression.

In fact, Wace's way of putting things (8003–5) is neutral: 'Tremorius ... li rova que Merlin mandast', 'Tremorius advised him to send for Merlin', followed by a eulogy of Merlin to the king. The 'impression' noted by Visser is due to the fact that Laȝamon makes Tremorius speak in direct speech, whereas in Wace we have reported speech.

(6) *Brut* 8488–97 and *Historia* ch. 128 (VIII, x) say that Aurelius sent messengers for Merlin all over the kingdom, whereas according to Wace (8013–16) he sent at once to the right place; both Laȝamon and Geoffrey mention that Merlin often visited or bathed in his favourite fountain. Visser suggests that Laȝamon must either have had another source besides the *Historia*, or given free rein to his imagination, in this passage. That Laȝamon elaborated freely in this scene is a fact; it features for example the messenger motif (see above, chapter 3). Visser also admits the possibility of an expansion from Wace, 'besides consulting Geoffrey' (p. 15).

(7) Both *Brut* 9546–53 and *Historia* ch. 138 (VIII, xx) state that Gorlois was sallying out of the castle when he was killed, while Wace (8743–7) implies that he remained inside. In fact, Wace states that Gorlois was killed whilst defending the castle against the assault of Uther's men ('al defen-

dre fu ocis'). Whether the defence took place inside or outside the castle gates is not specified. The image presented by Wace (8743) of attackers setting off 'senz faire eschele e senz conrei', and unexpectedly surrounding the fortress would certainly suggest that Gorlois was killed on the battlements; however, the very disorganisation of the besieging troops could lead the reader to suppose that Gorlois attempted to take advantage of the situation by fighting in the open. In that case, the battle-motif would be an expected addition in Laȝamon's poem. The borrowing from the *Historia* is therefore not as 'clear' as suggested by Visser.

(8) Geoffrey ch. 147 (IX, iv) says that in ascending the hill at the battle of Badon, Arthur lost many men. Laȝamon (10661–2) states he lost 500, while Wace mentions no loss at all.

As noted by Visser, both Geoffrey and Laȝamon mention a fact that is absent in Wace. However, the losses on the Briton side are implicit in Wace 9306: 'Mais cil nes pourent sustenir' ('but they could not sustain it'). Laȝamon could merely have added a figure, a fact underlined by Imelmann in his discussion of this passage (pp. 89–90). This seems all the more probable as, in the *Historia*, the Briton casualties are mentioned to stress their strategic disadvantage; all such considerations are absent from Laȝamon, where the loss of his men serves as motivation for Arthur's outburst of berserk fury.

(9) *Brut* 11082–3, and *Historia* ch. 152 (IX, ix) mention Lot's two sons, Gawain and Modred. Wace knows only the first. 'The most logical conclusion is that we here come across a Geoffrey-reminiscence' (Visser, p. 13): however, that Modred was Gawain's brother is commonplace in Arthurian literature.

(10) R. H. Fletcher ('Arthurian Fragments', p. 94) is of the opinion that *Brut* 13530–2 and 13964–5 are based on *Historia* ch. 112 (VII, iii): 'Tremebit Romulea domus seuiciam ipsius', 'The house of Romulus will tremble before his ferocity'. Imelmann (p. 90) pointed out that this correspondence is not word-perfect, as the recurrent theme in Laȝamon is that the walls of Rome shall fall; the connection, however, is clear.

(11) *Brut* 14200–2 and *Historia* ch. 116 (VII, iv) both include Merlin's prophecy of the destruction of Winchester.

Of these eleven cases, only six may be considered as potentially significant, and three are dubious (nos 1, 7 and 9). All the cases that plead strongly in favour of Laȝamon's indebtedness to the *Historia* are related in one way or another to Merlin and his prophecies. Visser cannot therefore be said to have proven Laȝamon's indebtedness to the *Historia* as a whole. No one bothered to refute him, apparently, but no one took his argumentation into account either – possibly because in disproving Imelmann's 'compilation' theory, he had stepped on too many important toes for comfort.

The question was next taken up by J.S.P. Tatlock, in his *Legendary History of Britain* (1950), where he dismisses the idea on four counts:

(a) Laȝamon does not mention Geoffrey's *Historia*, nor his 'liber vetustissimus', while he cites Bede, though using him little.

(b) 'Having Wace, even if an adequate Latinist, why use the less congenial Geoffrey?'

(c) The scholarly world has a near consensus that Laȝamon did not use the *Historia*.

(d) The dozen or so agreements of Laȝamon's 'immensely long' poem with Geoffrey and not Wace are without exception 'the veriest trifles', and it is not plausible that they should have been borrowed by 'so sensitive a poet, so released and free-handed a paraphraser', while disregarding 'things more important'. Those agreements must therefore be ascribed to 'accident, common knowledge, obvious addition or omission of detail'; some details may have come to Laȝamon's knowledge through acquaintances who had read Geoffrey's *Historia*.

However, continues Tatlock, there are 'several undeniable echoes' of Geoffrey's Prophecies of Merlin, which had been omitted by Wace on the grounds that he could not interpret them (*Roman de Brut* 7535–42). 'These echoes Lawman quotes as prophecies of Merlin'.[6] The term 'echoes' indicates that Tatlock does not rule out the possibility of Laȝamon's knowledge of these prophecies by hearsay, though he further suggests that

> it is likely enough that Lawman, while ignoring the part of the *Historia* paraphrased by Wace, would be interested to read the part ignored by him.[7]

Tatlock points out five passages in the *Brut* derived from the Prophecies of Merlin; three of these – Merlin's twice-repeated prophecy that Arthur would make the walls of Rome fall, and the prophecy of the destruction of Winchester – had already been noted by Visser. The two remaining passages (9411–12 and 11494–500) are close parallels to *Historia* ch. 112 and 115 (VII, iii):

[6] J.S.P. Tatlock, *Legendary History*, pp. 489–491.
[7] Tatlock, *Legendary History*, p. 490.

In ore populorum celebrabitur & actus eius cibus erit narrantibus
... Pectus eius cibus erit egentibus, et lingua eius sedabit
sicientes[8]

> of his breosten scullen æten   aðele scopes
> scullen of his blode   beornes beon drunke
> ...
> þat gleomen sculden wurchen burd   of þas ki[n]ges
>   breosten
> and þer-to sitten   scopes swiðe sele
> and eten heore wullen   ær heo þenne fusden
> and winscenches ut teon   of þeos kinges tungen
> and drinken & dreomen   daies & nihtes.[9]

This last instance certainly seems conclusive; moreover, the Prophecies were available not only as a separate book of the *Historia*, but were
frequently added to Wace-manuscripts, as attested by Ivor Arnold (introduction, pp. vii–xiv). The copy of the *Roman de Brut* kept at Durham
Cathedral, C IV 27.1, a thirteenth-century Anglo-Norman manuscript,
includes an interpolation of 670 lines containing a French translation of
the Prophecies of Merlin; MS Lincoln Cathedral no 104 (Anglo-Norman,
C13) also adds some ten folios of prophecies (in French), at the Vortigern
passage.

The publication in 1951 by Jacob Hammer of the edition of a variant
version of Geoffrey of Monmouth's *Historia Regum Britanniae* introduced
a new element of complication into the discussion. That different manuscripts of the *Historia* sometimes had different readings was already
known; but these differences tended to be minimized. Acton Griscom, in
the introduction to his edition of the standard, or 'Vulgate' version of the
Historia, writes (p. 21):

> Geoffrey undoubtedly altered his book in minor details as it
> became popular and demands for additional copies arose. The
> changed relations of his patrons compelled him to rewrite his
> dedicatory epistle, and criticism apparently led him to warn rival
> historians not to talk or write of things about which they were
> ignorant.

Hammer's edition shows clearly that the Variant Version is far from

[8] 'He will be celebrated in the mouth of peoples and his deeds will be food to the story-
tellers. His breast will be food for those in need, and his tongue will satisfy those who are
thirsty'.
[9] 'Of his breast noble poets shall eat; of his blood shall men be drunk', and, (Merlin said)
'that entertainers would make a table of the king's breast, and excellent poets would sit
down at it and eat as much as they wished before leaving it, and they would draw wine from
the tongue of this king, and drink and have pleasure day and night'.

varying 'in minor details' only; it is, to quote Hammer, 'a different re-cension'.[10] This 'recension' provides some additional material, of which Hammer mentions four instances:

(a)   The statement that Ascanius carried the household gods of his father from Lavinium to Alba Longa, whence they returned to Lavinium.

(b)   The mention of the muddy and watery state of Britain, which neces-sitates the building of roads and bridges by King Belin.

(c)   The consuls Gabius and Prosenna set out to gather troops from Italy and Apulia to assist the besieged Romans.

(d)   A brief description of Ireland (developed by Wace, 3315–20 of the *Roman de Brut*), when King Gurgiunt sends the Basclenses to Ireland.

Hammer points out a fondness for biblical phraseology in the Variant, and a tendency to tone down or omit certain unpleasant details, such for example as the rape of Helen's old nurse by the giant of Mont St Michel, or Cad-wallo's eating a slice of Brian's thigh in place of venison. Moreover, the two versions of the *Historia* differ in their handling of speeches, which tend to be either slightly abbreviated or paraphrased in the Variant Version, and even, in some places, omitted altogether (see Hammer p. 10). Hammer also de-tects in the Variant a 'tendency to go back to older sources', more speci-fically Bede's *Ecclesiastical History*, notably in the account of the conquest of Britain by Caesar (*Historia* 54), the description of Britain (ch. 5), and the murder of Maximianus by Valentinianus.

The overall plan of the Variant Version, however, remains that of the Vulgate; and Jean Frappier, in his review of Hammer's edition, notes the lack of fundamental divergences from one text to the other:[11]

> J'ai comparé des passages assez étendus et assez variés de la *vulgate* (édition Faral) et de la *Variant Version*; de cette enquête je garde l'impression nette que celle-ci est originale seulement par une refonte presque continue de la phrase et par le resserrement du récit. Les coupures me semblent plus fréquentes et plus importantes que les additions. Nulle part je n'ai découvert de trace d'une invention vraiment personnelle.

From the outset, it was accepted that the Variant Version was not Geoffrey's work; its exact position in relation to the Vulgate *Historia* was more contro-

---

[10] Jacob Hammer, *Geoffrey of Monmouth. Historia Regum Britanniae. A Variant Version Edited from Manuscripts.* The following points are made by Hammer in his introduction, pp. 8–16.
[11] *Romania* 74 (1953): 125–8.

versial. The extant manuscripts date back to the thirteenth century: does that mean that the Variant Version was a rewriting of the Vulgate, or could it have been a first redaction of the *Historia*, or even, perhaps, the 'liber vetustissimus' referred to by Geoffrey?[12]

In this debate, Wace's *Roman de Brut* takes on a special prominence. Margaret Houck, whose *Sources of the Roman de Brut* had hitherto been the unquestioned authority on the subject, had already noticed a number of discrepancies between Wace's text and the *Historia* (in its Vulgate version).[13] These she explained partly by indebtedness to Landolfus Sagax, for additions in the first 105 lines of the *Roman de Brut*, and partly by Wace's own genius. In the light of the Variant Version, however, Houck's observations pointed in a different direction. Robert A. Caldwell, after a systematic comparison between Wace's text and that of the Variant *Historia*, was able to show that part at least of the *Roman de Brut* agrees consistently with the Variant Version.[14] Most of the additions attributed by M. Houck to indebtedness to Landolfus Sagax are conclusively shown to be explicitly stated, or suggested, in the Variant Version. Moreover, in one case (the length of the reign of Ascanius), Wace agrees with the Variant Version against Landolfus Sagax.[15]

Caldwell also notes a similar consistency in the omission of matter, from the beginning to the end of the works. Thus, neither Wace nor the Variant Version mention the altars of Jove and Mercury, when Brutus consults the oracle of Diana; both works display a general toning down of sexual aberrations (Membricius's homosexuality is unmentioned) and other distasteful details (such as souls being sent 'ad tartara').[16] This consistency can hardly

---

12 For a detailed discussion of the manuscripts, date, peculiarities and impact of the Variant Version, see the introduction to Neil Wright's recent edition.
13 Houck notes for example a number of additions in the first 105 lines of the *Roman*: 52: Turnus is 'sire e dux' of Tuscany; 70–2: Lavinium, built by Aeneas, is named after Lavinia; 82: Postumus is reared by his half brother Ascanius; 84–5: Ascanius' mother is Creusa, daughter of Priam of Troy; 91–6: Ascanius builds Alba Longa, and leaves Lavinium to Lavinia; 97–104: the household gods return to Lavinium from Alba; 105: Ascanius rules for 34 years, as in the Variant Version of the *Historia*; Landolfus Sagax, the source then postulated for Wace's information in this part of the poem, reads 38 years.
14 See Robert A. Caldwell, 'Wace's *Roman de Brut* and the *Variant Version* of Geoffrey of Monmouth's *Historia Regum Britanniae*', *Speculum* 31 (1956): 675–82.
15 Further 'additions' of Wace which agree with the Variant Version are: 772: Brutus meets Corineus *in Spain*; 3001–7: the light of the moon reveals the shields and weapons of Belinus' men to the Romans (in the Vulgate Version, the battle takes place by day); 3827: the invasion of Britain takes place 60 years before the Incarnation; 3966 and 4226: Caesar's first expedition to Britain counts 80 ships, and his second 600; 8148–9: Merlin moves his lips as if saying prayers, when he moves the Giants' Circle; 10711–20: uproar of Arthur's guests at the Roman ambassadors (mentioned in the Variant, but in a less elaborate form); 13179–85: Modred flees from Winchester to Southampton, then goes to Cornwall by ship. Only one addition is not suggested in the Variant Version, and that is Wace's elaborate summary of Caesar's continental conquests, and his reasons for invading Britain (*Roman de Brut*, 3827–94).
16 Another instance of this tendency may be found in the absence of any mention of

have been accidental, considers Caldwell, who suggests (p. 678) that Wace had the Variant Version 'constantly before him as he wrote'. In support of this view, Caldwell points out other agreements 'not likely to be the result of coincidence', the most significant of which are:

Wace 6487–94. After the death of Constantine, Wace has Vortigern deliver a speech to the nobles, urging that they make Constant king. The Variant says that he made such a speech, while the Vulgate has him go directly to Constant at Winchester without a word to the nobles.

When Hengist and Horsus arrive, both Wace and the Variant specify that they are men of an unknown tongue; both agree in Hengest's statements that men reproduce more abundantly than any animal in his country, and that he and his companions worship the gods of their ancestors.

The Vulgate's catalogue of Roman leaders in Arthur's Roman wars is omitted both by Wace and the Variant.

Both Wace and the Variant give the historically correct information that St Augustine was received in Kent by Æthelbert, who accepted the faith and was baptized, where the Vulgate proceeds immediately from Augustine's landing to his rebuff by the Celtic clergy.

There are striking similarities, both in matter and in wording, between Wace's and the Variant's description of the Great Pestilence of Britain (Wace 14674–98).

To these passages, Caldwell also adds a number of verbal echoes. Wace's use of the Variant Version, stresses Caldwell, does not exclude his having used other sources – a number of references, such as those to the Round Table, for example, cannot be accounted for by the Variant – and more specifically, it does not exclude indebtedness to the Vulgate:

> He clearly used the Vulgate as well as the *Variant*, though probably not until he got to Book VIII of the Latin text. Passages suggesting the Vulgate rather than the *Variant* are scattered and insignificant before the reign of Vortigern; but from Merlin's prophecy of Vortigern's death to the end of the work, the Vulgate is used unmistakably and somewhat frequently.[17]

Caldwell substantiates his statement with a sizeable list of examples, the most striking of which is the presence in Wace's *Roman de Brut* of the story

---

Ethelfrid's dismissal of his first wife, thus leaving Cadwallo and Edwin's upbringing as brothers unexplained in both texts.

[17] See Caldwell, p. 680.

of Brian and the 'venison' which he obtained by cutting his own thigh – an episode which does not figure in the Variant. Caldwell's conclusion is clear (p. 682):

> Wace employed two main sources in the composition of his *Roman de Brut*, the *Variant*, which he used principally, and the Vulgate, with which he supplemented the *Variant*, especially in the latter part of his work. That there were two such sources is precisely what Gaimar tells us in the epilogue to his *Estoire des Engles*.

This conclusion brought about a strong reaction from Pierre Gallais, who maintained on the contrary that the Variant could only be a late recension, based on the Vulgate with modifications from Wace.[18] At the root of this position, we have clearly a case of hurt feelings. 'Wace n'est-il donc qu'un compilateur?' cries out Gallais, betraying our modern confusion between poetic ability and 'imagination' or 'originality'. To wipe out this imagined blot on Wace's honour, Gallais proceeds to a count of all the divergences, omissions and additions from one text to the other, over some 4300 lines of Wace's poem (9005–13298). However, his strictly mathematical approach fails to take into account the relative importance of these different features; moreover, the passage in question, which covers Arthur's reign, can hardly be considered a representative choice, especially as Caldwell had amply demonstrated that the influence of the Variant was virtually obliterated in the latter part of the *Roman de Brut*. Gallais also brings forth arguments of a more general nature:

> Il n'est pas vraisemblable que, quinze ans après la parution de l'*Historia*, une seconde version en courût, dont l'auteur s'était ingénié à récrire presque complètement l'oeuvre de Geoffrey, à en remanier constamment le vocabulaire et la syntaxe.[19]

Moreover, how could one imagine Geoffrey allowing his masterpiece to be tampered with, 'et cela avec une application (ou un sans-gêne) qui frise le mépris'? And how could one accept the idea that Wace worked with two different sources, without checking to see which was the 'authentic' one? Admittedly, if the Variant was prior to the Vulgate, part of the problem would be solved, but the hypothesis is 'insoutenable', claims Gallais, 'car elle réduit Geoffrey à un plat et sot remanieur'.[20]

As can be seen, Gallais' argumentation is based on a sentimental preconception of the excellence, in modern terms of originality as well as of talent, of the authors whose names have come down to us as Robert Wace and

---

18 Pierre Gallais, 'La *Variant Version* de l'*HRB* et le *Brut* de Wace', *Romania* 87 (1966): 1–37.
19 P. Gallais, 'La Variant Version ...', p. 7.
20 P. Gallais, 'La Variant Version ...', p. 9.

Geoffrey of Monmouth; and on the mistaken assumption that a medieval author was as protective of his work, and as critical towards his sources, as his contemporary counterparts.

The different arguments of Gallais and Caldwell were reassessed in 1977 by H. E. Keller, in an article entitled 'Wace et Geoffrey de Monmouth: problème de la chronologie des sources'.[21] Keller points out a number of difficulties in such a discussion, the main one being the virtual impossibility of determining the original version of Wace's *Roman de Brut*. Scribes frequently interpolated material, added notes and glosses, and, in this case, a scribe may have compared the text to either the Vulgate or the Variant, and made modifications accordingly. However, states Keller (p. 13):

> On peut retenir, sans trop d'erreurs, que Wace a dû suivre principalement la *Variant Version*, bien qu'on ne puisse plus déterminer, dans l'état actuel de nos connaissances, s'il a utilisé un texte composite à partir de la prophétie de Merlin concernant la mort de Vortigern, tel que nous le trouvons, par exemple, dans le MS Harley 6358 du British Museum, ou si ce tournant coïncide avec sa première connaissance de l'*Historia* de Geoffrey, qui correspondrait donc à un stade relativement avancé de son travail.

Whichever alternative one chooses – a composite text, or, more convincingly,[22] a merging together of both versions by Wace himself from Merlin's prophecy onwards – the complexity surrounding Wace's main source further complicates any attempt to define Laȝamon's relationship to the *Historia*. If we assume that Laȝamon *did* use the *Historia*, we are faced with three possibilities:

(a) Laȝamon used the Variant Version.

In this case, the influence of this text would be undetectable throughout the first part of the work; neither would it be readily noticeable in the latter part of the English *Brut*, for the Variant Version differs from the Vulgate mainly through its omissions, and one would expect Laȝamon to have retained Wace's fuller, Vulgate-based account.

(b) Laȝamon used the Vulgate.

As Wace's *Roman de Brut* is indebted to the Vulgate after Merlin's prophecy only, the first part of the English *Brut* should show traces of the influence of the Vulgate, but not from the prophecies of Merlin onwards.

---

[21] *Romania* 98 (1977): 1–14.
[22] See the introduction to Neil Wright's edition of the Variant Version.

(c) Laȝamon used a composite text.

Jacob Hammer's introduction shows that the extant composite manuscripts tend, like Wace's *Roman*, to start with the Variant Version, and end with the Vulgate version. If Laȝamon used one such manuscript, the influence of Geoffrey's *Historia* on the English poet would be virtually impossible to trace.

The list of agreements between Laȝamon and the two versions of the *Historia* against Wace is of little help in this matter. In addition to the six points of possible relevance noted by Visser, one may mention a number of further elements of varying importance:[23]

(1) *Brut*, 584–5. Brutus is told about Diana's shrine by his seamen. Wace (651–4) offers no explanation for Brutus' consultation of Diana, but both the Vulgate and the Variant mention that Brutus visited the shrine on the suggestion of his followers.

(2) *Brut*, 605–7. Brutus promises to build temples to Diana in his new land before his vision, as in both the Vulgate and the Variant. In Wace, this promise comes later.

(3) *Brut*, 1287. Laȝamon mentions Ebrauc at the beginning of his passage on the sodomy of Membriz, as in both the Vulgate and the Variant. Wace (1493) only mentions Ebrauc after Membriz's death.

(4) *Brut*, 2142. We are told that Belin and Brennes were reconciled before the division of Britain between them. Both the Vulgate and the Variant versions (ch.35)[24] imply that there had been strife among the brothers before the division of Britain: 'cum inter se de regno contenderent' (Variant); 'maxima contriti sunt discordia' (Vulgate). Wace suggests nothing of the sort.

(5) *Brut* 3995–4015, Cassibelaune laments at the news of Caesar's escape, yet rejoices in the destruction of the Roman fleet. These feelings correspond to those mentioned in the Vulgate slightly earlier in the narrative, in a scene not included by Wace, where the king surveys the sinking Roman ships (ch.60): 'gaudet propter periculum submersorum sed tristatur ob salutem ceterorum'. Wace (4311), like the Variant, only mentions Cassibelaune's later rejoicing at his victory.

(6) *Brut*, 5077–81. The destruction of the pagan idols. Laȝamon's account

---

[23] Points 4, 5 and 6 of this list also feature in Herbert Pilch's list of major discrepancies between Laȝamon and Wace.
[24] References are to Neil Wright's chapter divisions of both the Vulgate and Variant versions.

is very similar, even in wording, to the Variant Version (ch. 72), though in a slightly expanded form. Wace (5245–48) only mentions the purification of the pagan temples (as does the Vulgate).

(7) *Brut*, 5827. Maximien leaves Britain after five years (as in the Vulgate and the Variant); Wace (5887), after three years.

(8) *Brut*, 6097–8: Maximien is killed at Rome, as in the Vulgate (ch. 88): 'interfectus fuit Maximianus Rome'. The Variant retains this, but also mentions (ch. 86) that Maximianus died at Aquilea, a contradictory detail derived from Bede. Wace 6121–2 chooses to follow the Bedan account, and his Maximien slain 'en Aquilee'.

(9) *Brut*, 10256–7: Arthur welcomes Hoel affectionately: 'custen & clupten & cuðliche speken', as in the Vulgate (ch. 144): 'Excepit illum ... mutuos amplexus sepissime innectens'. This goes against Wace (9163–4): 'Ne firent ... plai de lunc acuintement'.

(10) *Brut*, 10791. Childric is slain by Cador. The detail may have been suggested by the Variant or the Vulgate, which read: 'Nec requieuit donec perempto Cheldrico' ('and he did not rest until Childric was slain'; *Historia*, ch. 148). Wace (9393–4) just states that Childric was killed.

(11) *Brut*, 12816–7. The giant of Mt St Michel eats men as well as animals (as in the Vulgate version, ch. 165). Wace (11296–11316) just mentions the terror he inspires.

(12) *Brut*, 13400–9. The Roman prisoners are taken to Paris by four earls and 300 knights. Variant and Vulgate versions (ch. 166): by four earls and their personal retinue. Wace 12167–72 only mentions four head leaders at the Roman ambush, when the Britons divide their forces in four under four main chiefs (a detail deleted by Laȝamon).

(13) *Brut*, 15247. Cadwallan has to stay at Gernemuðe because of contrary winds. The Vulgate version (ch. 193) likewise explains the delay through 'ex inprouiso tempestates'. Wace (14193–6) implies he has to stay there because of his illness.

(14) *Brut*, 15271–2. It is explicitly stated that Cadwallan ate Brian's 'venison', as in the Vulgate (ch. 193). Wace (14221): 'ne sai ...'

One may notice that, irrespective of the relative importance of these points, half (7 out of 14) agree with both the Vulgate *and* the Variant versions, while of the passages pointed out by Visser, only one instance – Laȝamon's 'grickisce fure' (316) – suggests the Vulgate 'Greco igno' (ch. 11) rather than the Variant's 'sulphureis taedis'. Moreover, most of these 'indiscriminate' parallels fail to provide convincing evidence that the English poet made use of the *Historia*. The first point of the list – the advice of seamen to Brutus, as motivation for his consulting her shrine – is thus a variation of Laȝamon's favoured 'messenger' theme. The tenth point is too slight to be truly relevant. Points 2, 3 and 12, which merely shift information around, are sufficiently general to allow the possibility of coincidence; whilst the seventh point of the list may perhaps be due to a flaw in manuscript tradition, for numerals are notoriously prone to corruption in the scribal process.

This winnowing leaves us with the fourth and eighth points of my list, and the five cases brought up by Visser in the Arthurian section. The agreement between Laȝamon 11082–3 and both versions of the *Historia* (ch. 152) in mentioning that Lot had two sons, Gawain and Modred, where Wace 9639 only mentions Gawain, could possibly be explained away by a gloss in Laȝamon's Wace manuscript; in any case, one would expect such a detail to have been widely known. The fourth point of Visser's list, however, requires more attention. As noted above, the agreement between the English *Brut* and the *Historia* in having Merlin's mother mention the maidens in her bower, and describe the beauty of the apparition which fathered Merlin upon her, could conceivably be the result of coincidence. The chamber of a young princess would obviously have housed other maidens, and the beauty of Merlin's father could possibly have been inferred from his supernatural nature. But the fact remains that Wace's text does not provide any hint which could have been developed in this way; and though the detail is not of major significance, it may corroborate further evidence.

Such evidence may be found in points 6, 9 and 11 of Visser's list. While Laȝamon was quite capable of making Aurelius' messengers search far and wide for Merlin as a delaying device, there is no doubt that this detail, linked as it is with more specific information concerning Merlin's habits, implies an influence other than Wace. As for the prophecies concerning Arthur, his future successes against Rome, his 'messianic' stature for the poets and minstrels of generations to come, and the fate of Winchester, the link with Geoffrey's work is clear. To this, one may add Laȝamon's mention on line 2024 of his poem that Belin and Brennes were reconciled – thereby implying some sort of prior contention – before their inheritance was divided between them. It would of course be possible to postulate a gloss; in this case however, one would expect a gloss to be a little more explicit than just a bare word, and one would equally have expected Laȝamon to have included more incidental information on the conflict, if he had any. The parallel with the *Historia* is difficult to explain in its present form otherwise than through direct borrowing. Similarly, Laȝamon's following of the *Historia* (ch. 88) rather than Wace 6121–2 as to the death place of Maximien would seem to indicate indebtedness to

Geoffrey, especially as this comes shortly after another agreement with the *Historia*, on the number of years Maximianus stays in Britain.

There remains to establish which version of the *Historia* was used. Of the seven cases which point towards either the Vulgate or the Variant, one agrees with the Variant, and six with the Vulgate; but, taken in isolation, only very few of these may be considered as significant. The theme of the destruction of pagan idols, linked with that of conversion to Christianity, could have been found elsewhere than in the Variant Version of the *Historia*. To quote but one possible source, Bede, in his *Ecclesiastical History* (chapter 13, book 2), describes a similar scene at the conversion of the English to Christianity, where the high priest Coifi desecrates the pagan temples and destroys their idols himself. The taste for human flesh of the giant of Mt St Michel (point number 10) in both the *Brut* and the Vulgate may be due to coincidence: this giant clearly belongs to the ogre category, and such a detail would be an obvious addition to a passage stressing the monstrosity of the creature.[25] The parallel between Arthur's welcome of Hoel in the *Brut* and the Vulgate is undermined by the fact that Laȝamon's 'custe & clepte' is an alliterative phrase which is found elsewhere in the English poem (see especially *Brut* lines 2500 and 9386), in similar scenes. As for the twelfth point – the reasons for Cadwallan's delay at Gernemuðe – it may be noticed that good or bad winds are a regular feature of Laȝamon's descriptions of sea-journeys, and that adverse winds occur elsewhere in the *Brut* (notably in the Arthurian section, 14091–4, where Arthur is forced to wait a fortnight before being able to make the crossing to Britain to avenge himself on Modred). Finally, Laȝamon's statement that Cadwallan *did* eat Brian's meat loses its significance when one knows that all of Wace's 'ne sai' passages are replaced by positive statements. A good example of this may be found at lines 4483–4 of the *Brut*, where we are told that Cassibelaune died childless, where Wace (4838) states his ignorance as to whether the king had any children. The two versions of the *Historia* just record Cassibelaune's death, without any mention of offspring.

It thus appears that the single agreement with the Variant does not carry much weight; though, as noted above, the chances of finding significant evidence in favour of Laȝamon's use of the Variant were virtually nil. The case in favour of the Vulgate, however, is strong, for the two remaining parallels – the 'grickisce fure' and Cassibelaune's lament at Caesar's safe departure – point firmly in that direction. It could perhaps be objected that the 'grickisce fure' parallel between the *Brut* and the Vulgate version of the *Historia* may be due to a gloss in Laȝamon's copy of

[25] See Fontenrose, *Python. A Study of Delphic Myth and its Origins*, esp. pp. 9–10. One may add moreover that the specific details furnished by the *Historia* (the giant's eating of the knights sent to rescue Helen, for example) are not to be found in the *Brut*.

the *Roman de Brut*, and that Cassibelaune's speech occurs at a slightly different point to the passage to which it is compared in the Vulgate. However, there seems to be nothing to support the former suggestion, while in the latter case, the insertion of this psychological touch at an earlier stage of the narrative would have caused some difficulty, for only at the Roman retreat does Wace mention Cassibelaune's feelings, thereby giving the English poet scope for expansion.

It is therefore reasonable to conclude that Laȝamon must have known at least the Vulgate *Historia*. The evidence does not suggest a systematic use of the work, though; there is no indication that Laȝamon bothered to check the *Roman* against the *Historia*. The sum of these different agreements does however indicate that the English poet had read the *Historia* at some time or another, and remembered enough of it to be able to 'complete' Wace in parts, as well as being more or less consciously influenced by it in his own, independent expansions.

This need not come as a surprise; indeed, considering the fame of Geoffrey's *Historia Regum Britanniae*, one would be tempted to think in terms of finding specific reasons for the English poet *not* to have known of it, rather than the contrary.

In such conditions, to postulate that Laȝamon may have known of the Merlin material through a separate manuscript comprising only the seventh book of the *Historia* (i.e., the Prophecies of Merlin) seems an unnecessary complication; for if such a hypothesis may account for the two references to Merlin's prophecies in the English *Brut*, it leaves unexplained, or unsatisfactorily explained, the two passages referring to Merlin's conception and habits (Visser's points 4 and 6), which show indebtedness to books VI and VIII of the *Historia*.

One may raise R.H. Fletcher's objection: why didn't Laȝamon acknowledge the *Historia* in his Prologue?[26] There are many answers to this. Wace's *Roman de Brut* respects the *Historia* scrupulously. Apart from the obvious modifications of language, metre, and what one may call cultural adaptation, the *Roman de Brut* sticks to the facts as related in the *Historia*, and there is no mistaking that we are dealing with the same material, treated *grosso modo* in a similar manner. Why quote the *Historia* when the basis of your work is clearly the newer edition of that same book? For the same reason, Laȝamon would presumably not have felt it necessary to keep a copy of the *Historia* for reference during the composing of his poem. Moreover, one fails to see why a medieval poet should have been expected to turn his prologue into a long and tedious bibliography, acknowledging all the works which he had found interesting or useful.

It is therefore most probable that, even though Geoffrey of Monmouth is nowhere mentioned by name in the English *Brut*, the *Historia Regum*

26 R.H. Fletcher, 'Arthurian Fragments', p.91.

Britanniae, the 'best-seller' of the Middle Ages, should have been known by Laȝamon. The extreme closeness of Wace to his main source makes it difficult to detect specific areas of indebtedness to the *Historia*; but it may be considered as certain that Laȝamon knew the seventh book of Geoffrey's work, while incidental agreements between the English *Brut* and the rest of the *Historia* strongly suggest that this knowledge was not restricted to the *Prophetia Merlini*.

Vita Merlini

The probability of Laȝamon having been familiar with the *Historia Regum Britanniae* is all the greater as the *Brut* shows definite signs of indebtedness to Geoffrey's lesser-known *Vita Merlini*.

The *Vita Merlini* was written some twelve years after the *Historia Regum Britanniae*, towards the end of Geoffrey's life. It comprises two parts: first, a narrative part, in which Merlin is the wild man of the woods of Welsh (and North British) tradition; then come the prophecies, and Geoffrey's attempt to merge the 'wild man' with the enchanter of the Arthurian section of the *Historia*. The prophet/bard Taliesin also makes his appearance, and the poem ends with Merlin, his sister Ganieda, Taliesin and Maeldin (a former madman) deciding to devote the rest of their lives to mystic contemplation, while Ganieda receives the gift of prophecy forsaken by her brother. As Basil Clarke stresses in the introduction to his edition of the *Vita Merlini*, Geoffrey's Merlin is a composite figure, inspired by different wild men of Celtic literature: Lailoken, whose story is told in the life of St Kentigern, Suibhne Geilt, and of course Myrddin.[27]

Parallels between Geoffrey's *Vita Merlini* and some of Laȝamon's expansions have been noticed by several scholars, but the exact relationship between both texts was not given a thorough investigation, for the *Vita* was considered a less likely source than other works. For example, R. H. Fletcher, in his *Arthurian Material*, states:

> The mention of Merlin's life in the forest is altogether coincident with the idea in Geoffrey's *Vita Merlini*, and it is impossible not to suppose that Laȝamon was influenced by Welsh tales about Merlinus Silvestris.[28]

Such also is the opinion of Herbert Pilch, who postulates that Laȝamon

---

[27] On the tradition of the 'wild man', see Basil Clarke, *Life of Merlin. Geoffrey of Monmouth, Vita Merlini*, Introduction, ch. 4, pp. 22–25.

[28] R. H. Fletcher, *Arthurian Material*, p. 163.

knew of the Welsh poems about the *llallogan* Myrddin, which Geoffrey had used for his *Vita Merlini*. However, the exact nature of the legend surrounding Myrddin in medieval Wales is somewhat uncertain; what material remains is in the form of lyrical poems, the interpretation of which is not always easy.[29] Moreover, even though the extant manuscripts of Geoffrey's *Vita Merlini* are few, and only one of these complete (almost), the stemma suggested by Clarke postulates at least two 'generations' of complete copies by the late thirteenth century.[30] The poem was therefore circulating to a limited extent, and more readily understandable for a thirteenth-century English priest than oral Welsh tales. Laȝamon could indeed have been told of the existence of a legend of Myrddin by a Welsh friend or informant; however, one would assume that a poet who shows such interest in the character of Merlin would also have been curious about whatever Latin works on the subject came his way.

The possibility that the English *Brut* may be indebted to the *Vita Merlini* is supported by a number of similarities between both poems:

(1) A first parallel may be found in the *Brut*, 3547–50, where we read:

> Seoððen comen Normans   mid heore nið-craften
> and nemneden heo Lundres   þeos leodes heo amærden
> Swa is al þis lond iuaren   for uncuðe leoden
> þeo þis londe hæbbeð bi-wunnen   and ef[t] beoð idriuen
> hennene.[31]

Herbert Pilch quotes this passage as a possible indication of indebtedness to certain Welsh prophecies which also state that the French will be expelled from Britain. The English poet, however, does not really announce the end of the Norman rule as such; it is more akin to the anti-Norman animosity found in the *Vita Merlini* (1511–3):

> Iteque Neustrenses, cessate diutius arma
> ferre per ingenuum violento milite regnum!
> Non est unde gulam valeatis pascere vestram.[32]

The *Vita* and the *Brut* agree in stating the negative aspect of the Norman conquest ('this people they destroyed'; 'there is nothing left'), whilst the *Brut*'s stress on the cyclic nature of history does indeed imply that the

---

[29] See A.O.H.Jarman, 'The Welsh Myrddin Poems', in *ALMA*, pp.20–30.

[30] See the introduction to Basil Clarke's edition of the *Vita Merlini*, pp.43–54.

[31] For the translation of this passage, see above, chapter 4, note 77.

[32] 'Normans – go! No longer take your armies of violent soldiery through our native kingdom. There is nothing left to fill your maw.' All quotations from Basil Clarke's edition and translation of the *Vita Merlini*. Here, pp.134–5.

Normans are doomed to the same fate as the Britons and the English. The similarity between the *Brut* and the *Vita* is undeniable, but the feelings expressed are too widespread in the writings of the time for the passage to be accepted as indicative of a definite link between the texts.[33]

(2) *Brut*, 4767. Arviragus and Claudius conquer Orcanie and a total of 32 islands. Wace (5057–60): they conquer Orchenie and the surrounding islands, the name of which he does not know. The *Vita* (878–9) states that there are 33 islands in the Orkneys. If Laȝamon's source of information is indeed the *Vita*, the number 32 would naturally arise from the distinction between a mainland 'Orcanie' and its surrounding islands. The reading of the *Historia* (ch. 68), 'Orcadas et prouinciales insulas' would make such a misunderstanding easy, despite J. S. P. Tatlock's astonishment at such a distinction.[34] This statement that there were 32 Orkney islands and one mainland is repeated in Laȝamon, where the distinction between mainland and minor islands is made even clearer when Arthur conquers 'al Orcaneies lond / and twa and þritti æit-lond þe þider in liggeð' (*Brut*, 11246–7).[35] However, as noted by Tatlock, the *Vita Merlini* agrees in this respect with Isidore of Seville, and it is possible that Laȝamon's 32 islands may be due to a reminiscence of Isidore, or the result of a gloss inspired by Isidore's work.

(3) The mention in the *Brut* (12112–5) that Caerleon seems bewitched may be a reminiscence of the *Vita* (624–5):

> inque tuo, Sabrina, sinu cadet urbs Legionum
> amittetque suos cives per tempora longa.[36]

The fact that a definite extant parallel may be found for this passage, which does *not* appear in the Prophecies of Merlin, is all the more interesting as Laȝamon explicitly refers to books at this point.

(4) *Brut*, 7434–90. Rouwenne poisons Vortimer herself. This is found neither in the *Historia*, which explicitly states that Ronwen had the poison given to Vortimer by one of his servants whom she had bribed ('per quendam familiarem', ch. 102), nor in Wace's *Roman de Brut*, which merely mentions that 'Ronwen ... Fist envenimer sun fillastre Vortimer'

---

[33] The passage in the *Vita* is thus understood as a reference to the French troops of the invasions of Stephen's reign. See Clarke, *Life of Merlin*, p. 154. Feelings of impatience at the supremacy of Normandy over England are also expressed by Henry of Huntingdon and William of Malmesbury.

[34] J. S. P. Tatlock, *Legendary History*, p. 500.

[35] Wace just mentions the submission of Gonvais, 'ki ert reis d'Orchenie', at this point (*Roman de Brut*, 9708). In so doing, he follows the *Historia*.

[36] 'The City of Legions will fall into your bosom, Sabrina. It will lose its citizens for a long age'. Clarke, pp. 84–5.

(7157–9: 'Ronwen had her stepson Vortimer poisoned'). Herbert Pilch notes that the Welsh translation of the *Historia* MS Llanstephan 1 agrees to some extent with Laȝamon's reading:

> or dywed esef ekauas eny kyghor gwnevthvr gwenwyn ... a rody hvnnv ydav – She finally decided to make poison ... and give it to him.[37]

This passage, however, describes Ronwen's intentions, not the actual carrying out of her plan; moreover, even if the parallel had been of more significance, the Llanstephan 1 version of the *Historia* is posterior to the *Vita Merlini*, and could therefore have been influenced by it.[38] The corresponding passage in the *Vita* reads as follows:

> Set soror Hengisti successus Renua tales
> indignando ferens protectaque fraude venenum
> miscuit, existens pro fratre maligna noverca,
> et dedit ut biberet fecitque perire bibentem.[39]

The similarity with Laȝamon's account is striking. First, we have the 'protectaque fraude', 'under the cover of deceit', which may be considered as the starting point of Ronwen's feigned conversion in the *Brut* (7447–54), an element found neither in the *Historia* nor in Wace, but used by Laȝamon to motivate the feast which provides Ronwen with the opportunity for poisoning Vortimer. The following scene (up to line 7482) is among the most memorable of the *Brut*; and while the credit for its effectiveness goes entirely to the English poet, the general layout of the episode clearly follows the lines indicated by the *Vita Merlini*.

(4) Both the *Vita* and the *Brut* mention that Arthur's wounds are tended by a queen: Morgen, the ruler of the Isle of Apples, in the *Vita* (908–940), and Argante, in the *Brut* (11511–2 and 14278).[40] Neither Wace nor the *Historia* mention this detail; the corresponding passage in Wace simply reads (13277–8):

---

[37] MS Llanstephan 1, p.123. Quoted from Pilch, *Literarische Studie*, p.46. An alternative translation for the latter part of Pilch's quotation could be 'and have it given to him'.

[38] The parallel under discussion does not seem to warrant such a supposition, though.

[39] 'But Hengist's sister Renua could not accept his success, and burned with indignation. Concern for her brother turned her into a vindictive stepmother. She concocted a poison under cover of deceit, gave it to Vortimer to drink and so caused his death'. *Vita* 1033–6, Clarke pp.108–9.

[40] Argante and Morgen are certainly the same names. G.J.Visser (see below, chapter 6, p.127) notes several cases, in different languages, of the loss of the initial M of Morgen's name, and of the addition of a more 'regular' ending in -e. These modifications, due to copying errors or 'improvements', must already have been present in Laȝamon's source; the name Argante is twice repeated in the *Brut*, and in lines where internal alliteration would require that form of the name.

> En Avalon se fist porter
> Pur ses plaies mediciner.[41]

The resemblance between Geoffrey's Morgen and Laȝamon's Argante is striking. The *Vita Merlini* describes a blessed isle governed by nine sisters,

> quarum que prior est fit doctior arte medendi
> exceditque suas forma prestante sorores.
> Morgen ei nomen didicitque quid utilitatis
> gramina cuncta ferant ut languida corpora curet.
> Ars quoque nota sibi qua scit mutare figuram
> et resecare novis quasi Dedalus aera pennis.[42]

The main features of this portrait recur in the *Brut*. Argante's beauty is stressed three times ('Argante þere hende', 11512, and 'uairest alre maidene', 14277, 'aluen swiðe sceone', 14278); her supremacy over the island is implied by her being called a queen (14278); her skill at healing and her knowledge of medicines is given special emphasis by the repeated use of the word 'haleweiȝe' (ointment, balsam).[43] As for the more supernatural attributes of Morgen, they are suggested by Laȝamon's 'aluen swiðe sceone', 'elf most fair'. These similarities point either to a direct borrowing from the *Vita*, or to Laȝamon's knowledge of Geoffrey's (oral?) source.

(5) The other parallels are all more or less connected with the character of Merlin and his prophecies:

Merlin lives in a wild forest, as in the *Vita Merlini*.

Laȝamon's geographical indications place this forest in the North-West of Britain,[44] a location implicit in the *Vita* 26–27, which opens with the war between Peredurus 'dux Venedotorum' and Guennolous 'Scocie qui regna regebat'.

There is a certain similarity of pattern between Laȝamon's account of Uther's search for Merlin and Ganieda's search for Myrddin. In itself, this

---

[41] 'He had himself borne to Avalon to have his wounds tended'.

[42] *Vita*, lines 918–23. 'The one who is first among them has greater skill in healing, as her beauty surpasses that of her sisters. Her name is Morgen, and she has learned the uses of all plants in curing the ills of the body. She knows, too, the art of changing her shape, of flying through the air, like Daedalus, on strange wings.' (Clarke, pp. 100–1).

[43] *Brut*, 11513: 'for heo sculde mid haleweie helen his wunden' ('for she would heal his wounds with balms') and 14279–80: '& heo s[c]al mine wunden makien alle isunde / al hal me makien mid haleweiȝe drenchen' ('and she will heal my wounds entirely, make me completely well with health-giving medicines').

[44] *Brut*, 9378 and 9431: the forest is 'in þene west ænde', and Merlin goes 'riht suð' to see Uther. However, Laȝamon does not mention the name of the forest – an indication perhaps that the poet was not entirely conscious of the influence of the *Vita* when he was writing.

is of little significance, as the inclusion of a messenger-type figure is a recurrent device in the *Brut*; however, it is worth mentioning, as in both cases we have royal messengers unable to find the 'wild man' until they meet a traveller (a hermit, in the *Brut*) who can guide them.

Merlin refuses all gifts from Aurelius or Uther (*Brut*, 8509–11 and 9444–6), an attitude also found in the *Vita*, where Merlin rejects Rodarch's gifts, saying:

> Munus avarus amat cupidusque laborat habere.
> Hii faciles animos flectunt quocunque jubentur.
> Munere corrupti quod habent non sufficit illis.
> At michi sufficiunt glandes Calidonis amene
> Et nitidi fontes per olentia prata fluentes.
> Munere non capior, sua munera tollat avarus.[45]

The parallel with Merlin's response to Aurelius's envoys is striking:

> Ne recche ich noht his londes   his seoluer no his goldes
> no his claðes no his hors   miseolf ich habbe inowe.[46]

Merlin is friendly with a hermit, while in the *Vita* Merlin becomes a hermit himself, with Telgesinus, Ganieda and Maeldinus.

Herbert Pilch, in accordance with his theory that Laȝamon had direct access to a number of Welsh sources, suggests that these elements may be due to indebtedness to the story of Lailoken, the wild man of the woods, and certain poems attributed to Myrddin, such as the *Afallennau*.[47] However, one may note:

(a) that the poems postulated as possible sources for Laȝamon are precisely those which may have inspired Geoffrey's *Vita Merlini*;

(b) that in none of these Welsh Myrddin poems or in the Lailoken stories do we find the theme of the madman's rejection of riches as such;

---

45 'A gift is what a miser loves and a grasping man works hard to get. Such men are corruptible by presents and will turn their shallow minds whichever way they are told, because what they have is not enough for them. But for me the acorns of pleasant Calidon are enough, and the sparkling streams that run through fragrant meadows. Let the miser take his gifts: gifts do not buy me.' *Vita* 272–7, Clarke, pp. 66–7. The same idea is also found on lines 239–45.
46 *Brut*, 8510–1. 'I care nothing for his land, his silver or his gold, or his clothes, or his horses; I have enough myself'. The idea that the gift of prophecy is incompatible with graspingness and riches in general is further expressed in the *Brut* at line 9446: 'ȝif ich wilne æhte þenne wursede ich on crafte', 'If I wished for possessions, then would I deteriorate in skill'. This last instance is paralleled to some extent in Wace, where Merlin also refuses gifts – but in a very deferential way (*Roman*, 8639–4).
47 Herbert Pilch, *Literarische Studie*, p. 47.

(c) that the hypothesis of Laȝamon having collated a number of Welsh sources leaves unresolved those parallels between the *Vita* and the *Brut* which do not concern Merlin directly, such as the account of Vortimer's poisoning by Ronwen, or the mention of Arthur's healing by Argante/ Morgane;

(d) that the reversal of rôles between the madman (Merlin/Lailoken) and the saintly man (hermit/Kentigern) presented by Geoffrey is also present in the *Brut*, with the difference however that Merlin does not act as a foil for the hermit, as in the saint's life; on the contrary, the hermit in the English *Brut* becomes an indicator of Merlin's moral qualities.[48]

In such conditions, it is difficult to sustain the postulation that Laȝamon, having studied a similar sample of Welsh legends, coincides with Geoffrey's adapted conflation by mere chance.[49] The evidence points towards Laȝamon's knowledge of the *Vita Merlini*; and while the poem is clearly not a major source for the *Brut*, it is likely that it contributed to the portrayal of Merlin, and may have provided the starting-point for such scenes as the poisoning of Vortimer and the finding of Merlin by the hermit in the forest.

To sum up, Geoffrey's works appear to have had more influence on Laȝamon than has generally been accepted. Considering the complex relationship between the two versions of the *Historia* and Wace's *Roman de Brut*, the chances of finding any traces of the *Historia* in the English *Brut* were scarce; yet a number of parallels between the *Historia* and the *Brut* not to be found in Wace do appear at a close scrutiny. Most significant are the similarities between both texts of the speech of Merlin's mother to Vortigern; the agreement between the *Historia* and the *Brut* in suggesting that there had been strife between Belin and Brennes immediately after their father's death; Cassibelaune's regret at Caesar's safe escape; the resemblances between Geoffrey's Morgen and Laȝamon's Argante; and, to a lesser extent, the death of Maximien at Rome rather than Aquilea, and the explicit statement that both Gawain and Modred were Lot's sons. These details confirm the intuitive feeling that a thirteenth-century educated man who was interested in the

[48] Alexandre Micha, in his *Etudes sur le 'Merlin' de Robert de Boron*, suggests (pp. 34–5) that the hermit is a mere 'décalque' of Blaise, the father-figure / spiritual guide / confidante / secretary of Merlin, and putative author of the work. In fact, the parallels between both characters are so tenuous that they may be disregarded; moreover, as the original poem of Robert de Boron has come down to us in a very fragmentary form, and its contents only survive in a thirteenth-century prose 'translation', indebtedness to it on Laȝamon's part would be difficult to sustain.

[49] This is especially the case as the *Vita* shares to some extent the *Brut*'s outlook on the Angles and the Saxons, in that references to the Angles appear as either positive, or at least not negative (*Vita* 632–3; 654–7; 1053–5), whereas Saxons are depicted as savage oppressors (*Vita* 625–6; 630–1; 948–50; 1001 sqq.; etc.).

Arthurian legend could hardly have failed to come into contact with such a seminal and popular work.

Geoffrey's *Prophetia Merlini*, which circulated both as part of the *Historia Regum Britanniae* (of which it is the seventh book) and separately, has long been recognized as one of Laȝamon's sources. There are three passages which support this view:

(a) *Historia*, ch. 112: 'Tremebit Romulea domus', the prophecy of Arthur's victory over Rome;

(b) *Historia*, ch. 116: the prophecy of the destruction of Winchester;

(c) *Historia*, ch. 115: Arthur's deeds will be food and drink to minstrels and poets (reference twice repeated in the *Brut*).

Whilst the first two of these passages are of general enough a nature to accommodate the hypothesis of oral transmission, the third passage is too strikingly similar to the Latin text not to suggest direct indebtedness. If the hypothesis that Laȝamon was acquainted with the entire *Historia* is correct, the poet may have found the prophecies within the *Historia*, as the seventh book Wace decided not to use.

Geoffrey of Monmouth's third 'Arthurian' work, the *Vita Merlini*, was less well-known than either the *Historia* or the *Prophetia*; but considering Laȝamon's overriding interest in the character of Merlin, if the *Vita* was at all available to him, one would expect him to have consulted it. A handful of parallels between the *Brut* and the *Vita* betray some indebtedness of the English poet to the Latin work, in an adapted form. Laȝamon's additions concerning the character of Merlin could to a limited extent be explained away by Welsh tales about Myrddin or Lailoken told by a Welsh informant; but the outlook on Merlin is closer to that of the *Vita* than of the Welsh legends or saints' lives. Moreover, two passages not directly related to the prophet also point towards a use of the *Vita*: Vortimer's poisoning by Rouwenne, and the curse on Caerleon.

The influence of Geoffrey of Monmouth's works on Laȝamon cannot therefore be ignored. Considering the status of the *Historia* throughout the Middle Ages, it is probable that Laȝamon's first written encounter with the Arthurian legend was through Geoffrey's Latin 'chronicle', which he endeavoured to complete by additional readings; and, having inwardly digested his material, he proceeded to translate into English the most skilful rendering of it available at the time: the French version of the *Historia*, written in verse by a clerc named Wace.

6

The Welsh Sources

The discussion of Laȝamon's potential Welsh sources is closely linked with a number of issues, partly political, partly cultural, partly scholarly, which far exceed the restricted importance of an isolated English translator-poet.

First of all, the opinion of different generations of critics has been deeply influenced by the prevalent attitude towards the Celtic peoples in general, and the Welsh in particular. Basically, as minority cultures within a dominant political unit, they were looked down upon, and even, in some cases, actively fought against. Historians will remember France's grisly, systematic repression of the use of Breton (*inter alia*) among schoolchildren.[1] On the other hand, the romantic movement had put Celtic tradition on a pedestal, with its fascination for Ossianic poetry and Breton folk-songs, and the resulting Celtomania.

When Madden published his edition of Laȝamon's *Brut*, in 1847, these conflicting forces were in full swing; and while Madden can in no way be termed a 'Celtomaniac', or even a 'philocelt', as Matthew Arnold puts it, his attitude is one of quiet acceptance of the existence of an independent body of literature and learning in Wales:

> That Layamon was indebted for some of these legends to Welsh traditions not recorded in Geoffrey of Monmouth or Wace is scarcely to be questioned ... Many circumstances incidentally mentioned by Laȝamon, are to be traced to a British origin.[2]

This statement is made on very shaky evidence: a few proper names, a number of expansions seemingly of 'British origin', and the fact that Laȝamon's parish, Areley Kings, is on the borders of Wales. This lack of solidity was unavoidable: the Welsh material which could have lent some authority – perhaps – to Madden's hypothesis was unedited and

---

[1] On the origins of this phenomenon, see Michel de Certeau, Dominique Julia, Jacques Revel, *Une Politique de la Langue. La Révolution française et les patois: l'enquête de l'abbé Grégoire*.
[2] Madden, p.xvi.

untranslated. The field of Celtic Studies, born as a result of the romantic interest, was striving to provide solid ground to learned speculations; but the language barrier prevented most scholars from acquiring knowledge of the work done. As the discussion was shifting from hazy presumptions to hard facts (albeit often at second hand, through very few translations), so the blindly enthusiastic Celtomania became a thing of the past. This new situation was perceptively described by Lord Strangford, in March 1866:

> Till thirty years ago it was usual to attribute a mysterious and unfathomable antiquity to the two Celtic main languages [i.e., Welsh and Irish]. Their history was uninvestigated; nobody knew or thought of asking whether or not they had any recorded stages of development; on their surface they were utterly unlike anything else in the world; and this halo of age and mystery pleased their speakers and compensated them for the loss of political power. But the result of recent inquiry ... has broken down the charmed circle and dissipated the obscuring and magnifying halo. These languages are no granitic or protozoic formation of the elder world; they are, broadly speaking, the mere detritus of an older speech, just as French or English is a detritus.[3]

In the field of Arthurian studies, this new, critical outlook resulted in the well-known Tysilio controversy. At the origin of this heated debate was a massive effort of text-editing by a team of Welsh scholars, Owen Jones, Edward Williams and William Owen-Pughe, whose *Myvyrian Archaiology of Wales*, first printed in 1801, was republished in 1870. The *Myvyrian Archaiology* is not used to a great extent nowadays, mainly because modern editions are now available for most texts, but also because the editors freely used material transmitted by Iolo Morganwg, a notorious eighteenth-century forger. This however does not concern the two texts around which the controversy arose: *Brut Tysilio* and *Brut Gruffudd ap Arthur*, two Welsh versions of Geoffrey of Monmouth's *Historia Regum Britanniae*.

Brut Gruffudd ap Arthur is a composite text, the oldest component of which is the thirteenth-century Llanstephan 1 version of the *Historia*; *Brut Tysilio* is a shorter version of the *Historia*, with some additional material and minor divergences. 'Gruffudd ap Arthur' (G. son of Arthur) refers to Geoffrey of Monmouth, while Tysilio is a legendary saint, thought to have been a poet and a historian. The titles are of no significance as to the authorship of the two Bruts. A Note of Warning to the

---

[3] 'Mr Arnold on Celtic Literature' in Matthew Arnold, *On the Study of Celtic Literature and Other Essays*, Appendix I, p. 228.

Reader specifies that these names were assigned to the Bruts for the sake of distinction only.[4] But the Note of Warning passed unawares, as scholars excitedly discovered that several manuscripts of *Brut Tysilio* comprised a note declaring that Walter of Oxford had translated the work from Welsh into Latin, and then once again into Welsh. *Brut Tysylio* thus came to be regarded as Geoffrey's 'liber vetustissimus'; it was translated into English in 1811, and this English translation was in turn the basis of a German translation, in 1854, by San Marte, who included it in his edition of the *Historia*. As the text of *Brut Tysilio* became accessible to non-specialists, there started heated discussions as to its position as regards the *Historia*. I do not intend to describe the Tysylio debate at length: suffice it to say that *Brut Tysilio* is no longer considered as Geoffrey's source, and is generally accepted as a late version of the *Historia*.[5] However, behind the polemic was another issue – that of the birth-place of the Arthurian legend, which opposed the partisans of an insular origin to those of a continental origin. In favour of the continental theory was a supposed pro-Breton bias in the *Historia*, and the fact that Geoffrey of Monmouth may have been of Breton extraction.[6] Against it is the fact that Brittany's stormy history has left us very few documents in Middle Breton, and certainly nothing relevant to this matter.[7] The 'insular' camp suggested two possible origins: either Cornwall, where John of Cornwall claims to have found his *Prophecies of Merlin* (though, as in the case of Brittany, we have no manuscript evidence to support this view), or Wales. The Welsh claims are supported by some proper names (Gwrgint Barbtruc, Dunvallo Molmutius) in the *Historia*, which seem to be taken from a written source,[8] and lists of names which strongly suggest that Geoffrey may have used Welsh genealogies.[9] But this is a far cry from Geoffrey's 'old British book written in a fair style', and in any case, the link with the Welsh genealogies has only been demonstrated of fairly recent years, and did not enter the Tysilio-debate.

To add to the confusion, Geoffrey's 'liber vetustissimus britannici sermonis' is defined in highly ambiguous terms, as 'britannici sermonis'

[4] *The Myvyrian Archaiology of Wales*, 784a.

[5] On the subject, see B. F. Roberts, *Brut Tysylio*. A good summary of the Tysylio dispute may be found in Edmund Reiss, 'The Welsh Versions of Geoffrey of Monmouth's *Historia*', *Welsh History Review* 4 (1968–9): 97–128, and Walter Schirmer, *Die frühen Darstellungen des Arthurstoffes*, pp. 36–7.

[6] See E. M. R. Ditmas, 'Geoffrey of Monmouth and the Breton Families in Cornwall', *Welsh Historical Review* 6 (1972–3): 451–61.

[7] Gwenaël Le Duc, 'L'*Historia Britannica* avant Geoffroy de Monmouth', shows however that much is still to be done in that field, and suggests that one may expect interesting developments in the future.

[8] This hypothetical source could in fact have been written in any of the Brythonic languages, as the orthography of Old Welsh, Breton and Cornish was the same.

[9] See Stuart Piggott, 'The Sources of Geoffrey of Monmouth'. Geoffrey seems to have put several genealogies on end, in an unbroken sequence.

may be understood as Welsh, Cornish or Breton indifferently, and each possibility has been advocated in its time.[10] As a result, the origins debate often boils down to nationalistic sympathies, in what may be seen as a product of Anglo-French rivalry.

Denying or accepting the idea of Laȝamon's indebtedness to Welsh sources was therefore far from being an innocent matter, and partook more of prejudice than of research, especially as most of the relevant Welsh sources were long to remain untranslated, sometimes even un-edited. Consequently, when Richard Wülcker and A. C. L. Brown tried to give firmer foundations to Madden's postulation of Welsh sources, oral and written, for the *Brut*, they found themselves unable to add new evidence to the argumentation. Moreover, as these scholars were not specialists in the field of Celtic Studies, they became somewhat confused in their terminology, using the terms 'Celtic' and 'Welsh' inter-changeably. A. C. L. Brown's use of *Irish* tales and Posidonius's descrip-tion of the *continental* Celts as proof of the *Welsh* origin of certain of Laȝamon's expansions was thus ultimately to provide Rudolf Imelmann with additional arguments for his rejection of Madden's hypothesis.[11]

The link between Laȝamon's sources and the wider polemic on the origins of the Arthurian legend is stated explicitly by A. C. L. Brown, in his 'Welsh Traditions in Layamon's *Brut*'. Stressing once again the Welsh origin of certain proper names, and noting, as Madden and Wülcker had done before him, that 'most of the noteworthy additions made by Laȝamon are connected with Wales and the Welsh tradition' (p. 96), he postulates that this information would have been

> either heard directly from [Laȝamon's] Welsh-speaking neighbours
> or got second-hand from his English parishioners, among whom
> the legends were doubtless popular,

a sure sign that the Welsh also had 'a romantic Arthur' (p. 101).

The great dissenting voice on this issue is that of Rudolf Imelmann, whose *Layamon. Versuch über seine Quellen* (Berlin, 1906), marks the beginning of an epoch which lasted for almost thirty years. In his intro-duction, Imelmann explains that he started his research on the assump-tion that Laȝamon had used Welsh sources; but that he had reached the conclusion that these sources were just a *fable convenue*. Imelmann bases his argumentation on two *a-priori* postulations: first, that the English and

---

10 See Léon Fleuriot, 'Sur quatre textes bretons en latin, le "liber vetustissimus" de Geoffroy de Monmouth et le séjour de Taliesin en Bretagne'; P. Zumthor, *Merlin le Prophète*; R. Taylor, *Political Prophecy in England*. The problem of the language of the 'liber vetustissi-mus' (providing it ever existed) remains unsolved to this day.

11 See A. C. L. Brown, 'Welsh Traditions in Layamon's *Brut*', and 'The Round Table before Wace'.

the Welsh did not mix enough in Laȝamon's day for Welsh traditions to have much impact on the poet; and secondly, that it was not the habit for medieval writers to use more than one manuscript at a time. All the important expansions in the *Brut* must therefore have been present in Laȝamon's only source, identified by Imelmann as a (lost) compilation of Wace's *Roman de Brut* and Geffrei Gaimar's (lost) *Estorie des Bretons*.

To list all the textual arguments brought forth by Imelmann in support of his hypothesis would be tedious, and unnecessary, for G. J. Visser's brilliant refutation has proved them to be either mistaken or irrelevant. What is striking, however, is that Imelmann's entire theory is based on hypothesis. Whilst acknowledging that Areley Kings was on the commercial route between London and Wales, and that Welsh influence had spread well beyond Areley, Imelmann rejects the very idea of Welsh contacts for Laȝamon, mainly on the grounds that the Welsh 'literarisch jedenfalls um 1200 nicht existierten'.[12] The Arthurian material must have come through the Breton troops of William of Normandy; and those elements of the *Brut* which may be of Welsh origin could only have been known through Laȝamon's Norman source:

> Wir wissen ja, dass zwischen Normannen und Kymren in jener Zeit enge Beziehungen bestanden haben.[13]

This argumentation is fraught with contradictions. Not only does Imelmann betray a preposterous ignorance of medieval Welsh literature and history, but, as Visser points out, he has no qualms in making the redactor of his hypothetical Norman source use a variety of manuscripts, while the whole credibility of his argumentation lies in the assumption that medieval writers rarely, if ever, used more than one.

The flaws of Imelmann's theory are evident. A hypothetical source is postulated on grounds that are inconsistent with the argumentation. It is therefore a matter of no small wonder for the modern mind that this theory should have been so unanimously accepted, and for so long, by men of such undoubted scholarly acumen as J. D. Bruce, E. K. Chambers, or R. S. Loomis. Such uncritical acceptance was due to some extent to 'dislike of the once prevalent Celtomania', as noted by Visser (p. 24); but the main reason is certainly that diagnosed by Herbert Pilch – a mental anachronism, by men so steeped in the cultural imperialism of their time that they could not conceive of Wales as of a land of internationally recognised prestige. In that respect at least, Imelmann's theory may be

---

[12] '... had no literary existence around 1200 anyway'. Imelmann, p. 6.
[13] 'For we know that there were close relations between the Normans and the Welsh at the time'. Imelmann, p. 8.

considered as a true reflexion of the socio-political mentality of his day.

The result, from our point of view, is that from 1906 to 1935, Laȝamon-research no longer claims to deal with *Laȝamon*'s Welsh sources, but with those of the lost Wace/Gaimar compilation; while those studies concerned primarily with the English version of this compilation tend either to avoid the issue altogether, or endeavour to prove Laȝamon's lack of acquaintance with the Welsh language.

There seemed indeed to be good grounds for such doubts. In 1911, J. D. Bruce, in 'Some Proper Names in Layamon's *Brut* Not Represented in Wace or Geoffrey of Monmouth', comes to the following conclusion:

> If I am right in my identification, the name [Oriene] ... would furnish striking evidence that Layamon was wholly dependent on his French sources, and did not recognize a Welsh name in the form he had before him.[14]

Two years later, in his study on the 'Mort Arthur Theme in Medieval Romance', he adds: 'Layamon's so-called expansions are, doubtless, all due to his French original'.[15] Similar views were repeated in 1921 by Katherine Schreiner, who considered the Celtic material in the *Brut* to be due to indirect Breton influence, rather than direct, Welsh influence. Such was also the opinion of E. K. Chambers in his *Arthur of Britain*.

The alternative approach – that of avoiding the question of sources as much as possible – was adopted by Frances Lytle Gillespy, in her article entitled 'Layamon's *Brut*: a Comparative Study in Narrative Art'. Gillespy chooses to stress the Germanic inheritance of the poet, whilst rejecting both Imelmann's expanded Wace and Wülcker's theory of Celtic sympathies in the *Brut*; her conclusion is that

> from the point of view of narrative technique, the French *Brut* must be considered as solely representative of the Old French line of influence. Many of the differences ... can be explained by the higher poetic and dramatic power of the English writer.[16]

F. L. Gillespy's voice was long to remain isolated; yet her study betrays a clear consciousness of the implications of Imelmann's theories in assessing the literary value of the *Brut*. Her rejection of a major bone of contention, in favour of a renewed stress on the poetic talent and cultural identity of Laȝamon, was necessary (in that context) in order to focus on the poem as a work of art, rather than as a piece of a defective puzzle. For

---

14 *Modern Language Notes* 26 (1911): 65–69.
15 *Romanic Review* 4 (1913): 452.
16 Gillespy, p. 407.

if every expansion was to be traced back to a hypothetical source, could one still call the *Brut* Laȝamon's? Could he still be called a poet, if all he did was slavishly transliterate a French source of outstanding literary merit? In fact, in those conditions, could the *Brut* be considered an English poem at all?

This thought prompted Henry Cecil Wyld to write his 'Layamon as an English poet',[17] in which he so openly adheres to Madden's views, in terms both of English and Welsh sources, that R.S. Loomis felt it necessary to chastise him:

> The cumulative effect of writing on the subject since 1906 has been to show that Layamon's Celtic additions to Wace are derived only remotely from Wales. Their immediate source must have been either that expanded MS of Wace for which Imelmann and Bruce argued, or else those Breton 'conteurs' to whom Wace alludes, and whose share in the promulgation of Arthurian romance has been so generally underestimated.[18]

At the same time, the issue was gaining in complexity with J.S.P. Tatlock's suggestion that Laȝamon may have been personally familiar with Ireland, on the grounds that the accuracy of Irish costume in the *Brut* hinted at a fairly good knowledge of the country by the poet.[19] The rejection of *Welsh* sources had resulted in a broadening of the field of research to *Celtic* sources in general.

The post-Imelmann confusion was clarified in 1935, with Gerard J. Visser's *Laȝamon: an Attempt at Vindication*. This study, remarkable for its dispassionate common-sense, provides a full survey of Laȝamon's possible sources in Latin, Welsh and French; and in so doing, Visser meticulously demolishes Imelmann's theory, point by point. Imelmann's arguments thus prove to be irrelevant, insignificant, or mistaken. Whatever remains may be accounted for by Geoffrey's *Historia*, which Visser counts among Laȝamon's written sources. The third chapter of his study, 'Laȝamon's Welsh Sources', provides us with the first systematic and reasonably impartial assessment of the arguments brought up since Madden for or against Welsh influence. It therefore deserves to be presented in some detail.

Visser first dismisses Imelmann's *a-priori* postulation that Anglo-Welsh contact was improbable in Laȝamon's day: 'Can Welsh influence at all have been operative in an English author, in view of the hatred between the Welsh and the English nation?' Indeed, yes. As far back as the Anglo-Saxon period, there seems to have been some intermarriage

---

[17] *Review of English Studies* 6 (1930): 1–30.
[18] 'Notes on Layamon', p.79.
[19] See 'Irish Costume in Lawman'.

between the English and the Welsh; moreover, notes Visser, once the Saxons were Christians, there was no obstacle to a peaceful mingling of the populations. The Welsh place-names found alongside English ones in Flintshire and Denbighshire would suggest that this must indeed have happened, while J. Loth traces 'British' communities in Somerset up to the VII–VIIIth century. Visser therefore concludes: 'A-priori Welsh influence cannot be considered impossible, or even improbable'.

He then proceeds to assess the three main arguments advanced by Richard Wülcker in favour of Welsh influence on the *Brut*:

(1) Laȝamon often gives a better form of Celtic names than Wace.

(2) Laȝamon gives some episodes and names in connection with Wales not found in Geoffrey or Wace.

(3) Laȝamon sometimes changes the aspect of the story in favour of the Britons and against the Saxons.

Visser agrees with Imelmann that the first argument is 'on slippery ground': the first critical edition of Wace's *Roman de Brut* was still to be published at the time (Ivor Arnold's edition only came out in 1940) and there is no knowing what Laȝamon's Wace-MS read, as proper names are notorious for varying from one copy to another. Moreover, though it is a fact that Laȝamon keeps very close to the Welsh forms of certain names, Visser remarks that 'this is practically confined to a few well-known names', like Gwenayfer and Kai; in the majority of cases, Laȝamon follows Wace. Which leads to the conclusion that:

> As no Wace MS has yet provided us with perfect equivalents of the first-mentioned Welsh names, it would appear most likely that Laȝamon was acquainted with the Welsh names of the principal characters figuring in the Arthurian stories, because he had probably heard tales about them. Not knowing Welsh, he would only remember the names of those characters that stood out conspicuously, while he forgot or never heard the name of the rest, and so followed Wace there.[20]

In this respect, therefore, Visser agrees with A. C. L. Brown's implicit postulation of an oral transmission of the Welsh material to Laȝamon, whilst accepting J. D. Bruce's conclusion that the English poet did not know the Welsh language.

The discussion then turns to the 'Welsh additions' in the *Brut*. Richard Wülcker had grouped them under three headings: (a) the satirical songs

---

[20] Visser, *Vindication*, p. 29.

on the Welsh king Carric by his own subjects, at lines 14400–6 of the *Brut*; (b) the satirical songs on Octa and Ebissa by the soldiers of Uther Pendragon, *Brut* 9766–9772; and (c) the additions to the story of Arthur.

A. C. L. Brown had suggested that Carric's nickname, Cinric, was an English corruption of 'Cymraeg', i.e., Welsh (language); Visser agrees with Imelmann that this is linguistically impossible. However, he rejects Imelmann's hypothesis that Cinric was not a Welsh king at all, but the result of a misunderstanding by Laƶamon of lines 819–823 of Geffrei Gaimar's *Estorie des Engles*:

> Certiz od son navire
> Ariva a Certesare
> ...
> La ariva il e son fiz
> Engleis lapelerent Chenriz,[21]

for Certiz and Chenriz are explicitly shown to be two different persons a few lines later.

> Either Laƶamon must have invented the whole, or he must draw upon Welsh tradition ... and as invention seems out of the question, Welsh influence remains,

considers Visser, who thereupon notes that even if Welsh history does not know of a king called Caredig (the prototype suggested by previous scholars), the names Ceredig and Caradog occur frequently, and a Welsh triad mentions a certain 'Kerric y Gwyddyl', while the *Annales Cambriae* have for the year 616 the entry 'Ceretic obiit'. Visser therefore equates, convincingly, Laƶamon's Carric with Geoffrey's Careticus, the prototype of Wace's Charic, and derives – less convincingly – the nickname Cinric from the Welsh 'cynnhrig', 'aboriginal':

> As this Careticus was a lover of civil war and therefore hateful to God and the Britons, it is by no means impossible that there existed mocking songs about him, and even a nick-name ... may have been applied to him derisively by the Saxon part of the population.[22]

The mention of satirical songs by Uther's soldiers on Octa and Ebissa, which appears neither in Wace, nor in Geoffrey, nor in the Welsh Bruts *Tysilio* and *Gruffudd ap Arthur*, Visser considers to be an independent

---

[21] 'Certiz with his ship arrived to Certesare ... There he arrived with his son, whom the English called Chenriz'.

[22] *Vindication*, p. 33. Why the Saxons should have given a Welsh nickname to King Carric, Visser does not attempt to explain.

expansion, by a Laȝamon 'with an eye for dramatic effect'.[23]

Previous research had noted six main additions in Laȝamon to the story of Arthur:

(1) The elves at Arthur's birth, bestowing gifts upon him, were considered by Imelmann as a Breton element, and by B. Ten Brink, in his *Geschichte der Englischen Literatur*, as a Germanic trait. Visser ascribes the detail to Welsh tradition, on the grounds that 'the imaginative Welsh are not and never have been without fairy-tales' (p. 34).

(2) The name Argante (the queen of Avalon) was derived by Imelmann from the Celtic stem *arganto. Visser follows J. D. Bruce in seeing the name as a corruption of Geoffrey's Morgen, in the *Vita Merlini*. The final, French -e he explains through 'a copyist changing an original -e-less form into a more normal-looking form with -e', whilst pointing out a similar loss of the initial m in Spanish (Urganda), in the Dutch *Merlin* (Organie), and in the French *Roman de Troie*. The phenomenon therefore seems to have been widespread, and could equally have occurred in Welsh, English or Latin.[24]

(3) Laȝamon's account of Arthur's translation to Avalon, suggests Bruce, was probably drawn directly from Celtic tradition;[25] though he does not rule out the possibility that it may be derived from the *Vita Merlini*. Visser vindicates a Welsh origin for this passage: 'immediately after Geoffrey's work became known, the Welsh literary activity increased tremendously', and with it, the chances for Laȝamon to have come across Welsh material. This argument of the availability of Welsh legends is repeated in connection with

(4) The institution of the Round Table.[26] Visser notes, with Fletcher, that in this episode Laȝamon explicitly refers to a *tale*, not a book; a tale which must have been 'Welsh or anglicized Welsh', because of

> the rough-and-tumble spirit in which it is written. The courteous manners of a later age are absent in this vulgar brawl ... in which the relentless, cruel punishments suggest an earlier and more barbarous age than that of the medieval French Bruts or the court romances.[27]

[23] *Vindication*, p. 34. Another reference to songs occurs in the *Brut* 7308, where 'loft-songe', 'songs of praise', are sung at Vortimer's coronation. However, this may be part of the ceremonial rather than morale-boosting songs.

[24] See above, chapter 5, the discussion of the *Vita Merlini*.

[25] By the hypothetical author of the hypothetical expanded Wace, of course, in Bruce's mind.

[26] The Round Table is mentioned by name in Wace (9747–60 and 10285), but no account of its founding is provided.

[27] Visser, *Vindication*, p. 39.

Visser thus rejects J. D. Bruce's opinion that the story was ultimately of Armorican origin; it is 'a Welsh tale in English garb'.

The last two points discussed by Visser occur in the description of Arthur's armour. Arthur's helm is called Goswhit, a name which is only found in the *Brut*. Madden, Wülcker and Brown understand the name as 'goose-white' – many other names connected with Arthur are composed with 'gwen', 'white'. Visser advocates with Imelmann the possibility of it being a corruption of the Welsh adjective 'gospeith'; the argumentation is however based on a misunderstanding.[28]

Griffin, the smith of Carmarthen who made Arthur's spear, is another source of contention. A. C. L. Brown had suggested that the name may be a corruption of Gofan, the divine smith of Celtic mythology; but Imelmann convincingly demonstrated that this was impossible, on philological grounds. Visser further recognizes in Griffin a Latin or Anglo-Saxon corruption of Gruffudd: both the *Descriptio Kambriae* of Giraldus Cambrensis, and the *Anglo-Saxon Chronicle*, testify of similar forms (Griphinus, Griffin) for Gruffudd.

Having summed up the different arguments brought up for or against Welsh influence on the *Brut*, Visser concludes:

> Though probably unacquainted with the Welsh language, [Laȝamon] must have collected stray bits and names of Welsh tradition from bi-lingual natives ... the reflection of which we find in his elaborations. Dependence on written Welsh tradition may be deemed out of the question in Laȝamon's case.[29]

However, Visser provides no specific reason for his rejection of Laȝamon's knowledge of the Welsh language, or his use of written sources. The air is cleared of Imelmann's hypothetical compilation, but the question of Welsh sources is still hazy. Apart from a few proper names, the 'Welshness' of the additions in the *Brut* remains uncertain. The barbaric overtones of the scene of the founding of the Round Table, for example, certainly preclude transmission through 'classical' French literary forms, but as the Welsh and Breton languages were mutually understandable at the time, and both countries were in close contact, one fails to see why one should have been less 'barbaric' than the other.[30] The more positive aspect of Visser's argumentation is based on probability and common sense: geographical proximity and normal human exchange. But it lacks historical documentation and inner evidence,

---

[28] Imelmann and Visser understood 'gospeith' as meaning 'glittering, polished'; in fact, it means 'honoured'. In his discussion of the name, Herbert Pilch postulates a translation of a Welsh *gwydd-wen.

[29] Visser, p. 95.

[30] See Léon Fleuriot, *Les Origines de la Bretagne: l'émigration*.

hence the implicit criticism in J.R.Seal's remark that Visser 'tends to emphasize his view that Laȝamon may have drawn on various Welsh sources',[31] and the general lack of impact of Visser's view on the subject.

We have to wait till 1950 for the question of Welsh sources to crop up again, in J.S.P.Tatlock's *Legendary History of Britain*. Tatlock's research on Laȝamon is remarkable for its careful use of historical records in trying to assess the different possible influences on the poet. Tatlock thus undertakes an investigation of the practical means of contact between Wales and Worcestershire, looking for early references to ferries in the area of Areley Kings. He finds a mention of a ferry at Redstone, in the seventeenth century, and of two others, one six miles north of Areley, at Upper Areley, and another three miles north, at Bewdley, in the years 1333–7. He also notes the presence of a bridge over the Severn at the city of Worcester, ten miles south. However, stresses Tatlock, this need not involve intense contact with Welsh people; on the contrary, Areley Kings

> was not a suitable place for through traffic, not being on a line between important places, and the country westward being broken.[32]

Moreover, the place-names west of Areley between the Severn and the Wye are English. As for the internal evidence in the *Brut* suggesting Welsh influence, it amounts to 'mere detail', and a few proper names 'guessed to be of Welsh origin'.[33]

Yet, suggests Tatlock, the *Brut* does betray Celtic influence – but from Ireland, not Wales. Laȝamon appears to be familiar with Irish costume, equipment and warfare habits; he knows the three major Irish saints, whose names he gives in a form got 'by hearing, not reading': Patrick, Bride and Columkille. Further familiarity with things Gaelic is apparent in Laȝamon's personal names beginning with 'Gill-', 'young man' in Irish: Gille Caor, Gille Callaet, Gillemaur, Gille Patric, etc.

Laȝamon is also aware of the kinship between Scots and Irish, whilst the 'imaginative ferocity' of the *Brut* is typically Celtic, considers Tatlock, who gives examples of the 'ferocity and barbarity' of the Welsh and the Irish, as attested in their historical and hagiographical writings. As for the 'avowed appearance of the faery' in the *Brut* (the elves at Arthur's birth, his magic equipment, the wondrous lakes of Scotland), it has numerous analogues in the Irish saga.

---

[31] Jonathan Seal, *Kings and Fated Folk: A Study of Lawman's Brut*, p.110.
[32] Tatlock, *Legendary History*, p.510.
[33] Tatlock, *Legendary History*, p.492.

The degree to which Lawman seems to have appropriated Irish temperament and reactions suggests that he was young when first exposed to them, perhaps even born in Ireland

considers Tatlock, who continues (p. 528):

We know the antiquity and closeness of the relations of Ireland to England ..., enormously intensified by the Norman conquest of it beginning in 1169 ..., with various later expeditions and many colonists within the generation. The invaders come largely and naturally from west Britain and Worcester and its vicinity contributed much more than their share of fresh population.

The study of a twelfth-century list of some 1500 citizens of Dublin shows that there were more people from the city of Worcester than of any other British place, and twice as many as from Bristol. Moreover, the archbishop of Dublin and the chief executive official of Ireland in the 1180s were both connected with Worcester. Tatlock therefore imagines a reconstruction of Laȝamon's life: his father Leovenað may have gone over to Ireland from Worcestershire, with the early invaders, in 1169 or later. There, he may have married a Scandinavian Irishwoman, whence Laȝamon's puzzling Scandinavian name. Leovenað would of course have spoken his own dialect of English to his son – which would explain the fact that the *Brut* shows signs of the Worcestershire dialect. After some time in Ireland, Laȝamon would then have 'returned to the region whose dialect he seemingly spoke, and where his family may have originated'.[34]

Laȝamon's fairly good knowledge of the geography of south Wales, and his accurate description of the once marshy area of St Davids lends further support to this hypothesis, suggests Tatlock: the poet knew 'the south-west of Great Britain, seaports, and the route to southern Ireland', whilst his nautical scenes show he was 'much at home with the sea', to an extent astonishing for an inland Worcester man.[35] This Irish experience, considers Tatlock, was personal, not learned or literary; therefore, he does not postulate any specific Irish sources for the *Brut*, which he sees as a thoroughly English poem, written for English people, and born almost exclusively 'from Wace and Lawman's inspiration' (p. 487).

Tatlock may thus be said to represent the opposite extreme to Imelmann. Whilst Imelmann considered that virtually none of the additions in the *Brut* were due to Laȝamon's imagination, Tatlock suggests that they nearly all are. This attitude probably explains the flaw in Tatlock's

[34] Tatlock, *Legendary History*, p. 529.
[35] Tatlock, *Legendary History*, pp. 502 and 489.

reasoning, as he summarily dismisses the idea of Welsh influence on Laȝamon whilst postulating that the poet may have travelled through the country on the borders of which he lived. Tatlock's Irish theory, and his remarks on Laȝamon's geographical knowledge, makes some amount of contact with Wales and the Welsh people more than probable.

This reconstruction of Laȝamon's life, however, is entirely hypothetical; and indeed, not necessary, states R. S. Loomis:

> Surely an English priest with any curiosity would have known of SS. Columkille, Brendan and Bride, and would not have had to be born in Ireland to know that the natives when summoned in battle removed their breeches, for, after the Norman conquest of Ireland ... Irish fighting habits, especially one so bizarre, would have been common topics for conversation in England.[36]

As for the ferocity in the *Brut*, Loomis notes that it is not an exclusively Irish trait, and suggests that it is somewhat more akin to the *chanson de geste* than to the Irish narrative. He therefore dismisses the whole matter, and proceeds to defending his own theory of a continental origin for Laȝamon's three major expansions to Wace's Arthurian episode, i.e., the elves at Arthur's birth, the origin of the Round Table, and Arthur's departure to Avalon with Argante:

> The evidence regarding these passages is consistent and plain: their sources were not in the poet's own brain but in Breton stories related in French, either orally or in manuscript.[37]

As proof of this, Loomis quotes from the Didot-Perceval, which contains a close parallel to Laȝamon's account of Arthur's translation to Avalon, and the fact that the name given in the *Brut* to one of Modred's sons, Melyon, matches the name Melehan given to him in the Vulgate *Mort Artu*, and also appears in a Breton lay. As for the fairies at Arthur's birth, the same theme recurs in the second continuation of *Perceval*, in *Floriant* and in *Ogier le Danoys*:

> Since three French poets knew this tradition and could not have got it from Layamon, evidently it was a French legend.[38]

The fact that none of the French works in question is significantly older than Laȝamon's *Brut* does not trouble Loomis, whose theory presupposes, on the one hand, that Welsh and Breton tradition were totally different from one another, and on the other that it was easier for french-

---

[36] Loomis, 'Layamon's *Brut*', in *ALMA*, p. 105.
[37] Loomis, p. 109.
[38] Loomis, p. 108.

ified Breton material to cross the Channel than for Welsh material to cross the Severn. A highly debatable assumption.

Herbert Pilch's *Layamons Brut. Eine literarische Studie*, may be considered as a reaction against such an attitude. With as great a preconception as Imelmann or Loomis had had against the idea of Welsh sources, Pilch enthusiastically advocates the case in favour of them, even to the point of methodological error. It must be said from the outset that Herbert Pilch's study is most remarkable, whatever its shortcomings otherwise, for the enormous number of sources, many of them unpublished, which the scholar examined in gruelling detail. No less than forty Welsh sources are mentioned in Pilch's bibliography, most of which are used as complementary documentation, or as evidence of the impact of certain (medieval) works on the Welsh learned tradition (and/or vice-versa). For the first time in Laȝamon studies, the Welsh material is canvassed systematically, thereby making a scientific approach to the problem of Welsh sources possible.

The avowed aim of Herbert Pilch was to produce a full-scale study on Laȝamon, similar in scope to that of Madden. Laȝamon's Celtic relations, he declares (p. 26) is to be but one issue among others: his first and foremost concern is literary criticism. In practice, however, we find references to Welsh material on virtually every page, and Welsh tradition is made to appear as one of the deepest influences on the *Brut*.

Pilch first proves the historical plausibility of cultural exchange between Wales and Worcestershire. He gives instances of Welsh-speaking communities in Herefordshire and south-west Shropshire in the twelfth and thirteenth centuries, and notes that the Severn was considered a frontier river, where Welsh and English rulers could meet without loss of prestige. Moreover, Pilch stresses that in Laȝamon's day, English was at its lowest, the language of the ruling classes being French, whilst Welsh was in a strong position, being the language of the princes whose support rival English factions strove to secure. One way of so doing was by marriage, and Pilch notes that the offspring of such unions usually spoke Welsh. The twelfth century was therefore a period of expansion for the Welsh, both politically and culturally. Welshmen such as the latimer Bleddri mentioned by Thomas and Giraldus Cambrensis brought their native culture to the courts of France and England;[39] there is evidence of some contact between at least the court of Powys and such centres of learning as the rhetorical school of Wolverhampton; and Anglo-Welsh exchange on the borderlands is attested by Walter Map. Pilch therefore concludes (p. 24) that a poet living on the political border, and probably in a bilingual area, must certainly have taken an interest in the Welsh people, whose history he was writing: there is no obstacle to Laȝamon's

---

[39] See C. Bullock-Davies, 'Marie de France and South Wales', pp. 440–1.

having been in close contact with the Welsh language and literature. Pilch consequently proceeds to extensive comparisons between Welsh literature, poetry and historical writing, and the *Brut*. Though he assumes that Laȝamon was also familiar with the English, French and Latin literatures of his time, Pilch's argumentation revolves in effect around the Welsh evidence.

His conclusions are startling. On the grounds of a number of word-for-word agreements between the English *Brut* and the Welsh Bruts, Pilch first postulates that Laȝamon supplemented his Wace-text with a Welsh translation of Geoffrey's *Historia Regum Britanniae*. This Welsh work is identified as 'a version close to MS Llanstephan 1' (p. 83); Llanstephan 1 being a thirteenth-century translation of the *Historia*, the manuscript of which is dated 1225–1270. Pilch finds further agreements between the English poem and other, later Welsh Bruts, which he attributes to common sources such as 'older Welsh or Latin annals'. He also stresses the importance of native sources of information, such as the 'beird' (bards) and the 'kyvarwydeyt' (story-tellers), whose existence is attested by the older Bruts. Pilch therefore understands Laȝamon's references to unspecified books and 'writen' as Welsh poems, triads, or narratives similar to the *Mabinogion*. From these, Laȝamon drew a number of themes and symbols, and adapted the intricacies of the Welsh 'cynghanedd', a complex sort of alliteration, to his own medium of expression.

Pilch's theory implies a new outlook upon Laȝamon. From Tatlock's patronizing attitude towards the poet, we are now faced with the image of an immensely cultured man, familiar with French, English and Latin, perhaps even knowing the Irish narrative, with a complete mastery of the Welsh language, and well versed in all aspects of Welsh culture, be it oral or written. From Imelmann's denial and Loomis's scepticism that Wales could have had any impact at all on the English *Brut*, Pilch's hypothesis makes Welsh a major influence in Laȝamon's attempt to readapt the obsolescent traditional English versification to his everyday language; the poet's very way of thinking in triads betrays the mark of Welsh culture.

It is tempting – and, I think, legitimate – to see this reversal of attitudes as a symptom of a more widespread current towards the recognition of previously despised or ignored minority cultures, which found its political expression in an upsurge of the claims to recognition of many European minorities. It was no longer aberrant or heretical to think of medieval Wales as culturally active, and Herbert Pilch could therefore look at Welsh history and literature in a positive way without ridicule: and he did so in a remarkably efficient way, researching extensively all the relevant (and sometimes not so relevant) material in the National Library of Wales. He is, to my knowledge, the first Laȝamon-critic to have systematically gone directly to the sources, rather than remaining content with what was available in translation, as had tended to be the case before him.

However, Pilch's methodology was not up to his erudition; or, to put things differently, the unexpected wealth of Welsh material led him astray. Where earlier scholars had questioned the use of Geoffrey's *Historia* (with the exception, of course, of the seventh book) because of insufficient evidence, Pilch claims to see traces not only of the *Historia*, but of the very translation used. Yet the early Welsh translations of the *Historia* are extremely faithful to their original, and the only significant interpolation in the Llanstephan 1 version – the *Cyfranc Lludd a Llefelys* – is not to be found in the English *Brut*. Pilch suggests that Laȝamon retraced Geoffrey's steps, going back to Welsh legends for material already brought to fame by the *Historia*. This implies, on the one hand, that he believes Geoffrey to have been a fairly accurate transmitter of Welsh material; and on the other, that Welsh tradition remained strangely uninfluenced by Geoffrey's work. In fact, what little evidence we have tends to contradict both these assumptions, and Pilch's quest for parallels to certain expansions of the *Brut* in inappropriate works further undermines his position. As for the possible influence of the Welsh 'cynghanedd' on Laȝamon's versification, Pilch himself notes that 'cynghanedd' did not yet have a fixed, standardized form in Laȝamon's day, stating moreover that, due to the passage to English, Laȝamon cannot have borrowed more than the formal principle of 'cynghanedd'.[40] In these conditions, 'cynghanedd' is merely a convenient way of denoting a metrical pattern not found in classical poetical terminology – a name-tag of no real significance. Nevertheless, Pilch makes a number of thought-provoking remarks. He notes (p. 220) that Laȝamon's stylistic art has a few interesting parallels in Old Welsh poetry (notably the poems of Taliesin), and he points out word-for-word agreements between certain passages of the *Brut* and two Welsh poems attributed to the poet-prophet Myrddin, the *Afallennau* and *Armes Prydein*.

Pilch's arguments in favour of indebtedness to the *Afallennau* fail to convince: most of the correspondences between the poem and the *Brut* may be explained by Laȝamon's use of the *Vita Merlini*, while the most specific element of the *Afallennau*, Myrddin's apple-tree, remains unmentioned by Laȝamon. One cannot deny, however, a certain similarity between the two passages analysed by Pilch (*Brut* 16026–9, and the last stanza of the *Afallennau*). This is best explained by a similar vein of inspiration, which culminates in the passage which Pilch considers a direct borrowing from *Armes Prydein*. Like the *Afallennau*, *Armes Prydein* is linked to the name of Myrddin.[41] Both poems prophesy future victories

---

[40] Pilch, *Literarische Studie*, p. 170: 'Keinesfalls kann Layamon jedoch der kymrischen Dichtung mehr entnommen haben als die formalen Prinzipien des cynghanedd'.
[41] In the case of *Armes Prydein*, this link is totally spurious. The reference to Myrddin at line

for the Welsh people, and sing them in the traditional heroic manner. The general mood is therefore one of elation, as the poems are, in effect, celebrating in advance victories to come. In other respects, however, the *Afallennau* and *Armes Prydein* are quite different. The date of composition of the *Afallennau* is hazy: the datable references within the 'prophecies' point to late twelfth or early thirteenth century, but the original core of the poem is much older; Myrddin's vaticinatory poems enjoyed a great prestige, and stanzas were added on at different periods to suit the moment. On the other hand, *Armes Prydein* points back to a specific date – 937, and the battle of Brunanburh: the poem appears to have been written to urge the Welsh princes to join the coalition against Æthelstan (presumably around 930).[42] *Armes Prydein* thus provides fairly precise contextual reference, which makes it that more specific, and ought to make it that more detectable in certain lines or expressions in the *Brut*. Pilch's claim that lines 10374–98 of the *Brut* are 'unverkennbar angeregt' from *Armes Prydein* (especially 63–76) must therefore be the object of close examination.

Both passages describe the sad situation of the Saxons after a major defeat. In Laȝamon, the Saxon messengers present their plight to Arthur after the battle of Lincoln, begging for mercy and permission to take their boats back to their own land, which Arthur disparagingly grants. In *Armes Prydein*, the poet is gloating over the desperate state of the Saxons after their final defeat. Of the six close agreements between the two passages discussed by Pilch, two are mistaken, and another two of little significance.[43] The last two, however, raise a number of questions, and may safely be said to be the most conclusive evidence found in the *Brut* in favour of Laȝamon's knowledge of at least some aspects of Welsh poetry. First, we have the Saxons beseeching Arthur

> ȝif heo moten liðe   heonene mid liue
> into heore leoden   & lað-spæl bringen,[44]

---

17 of the poem – 'Dysgogan Myrdin kyueryd hyn', 'Myrddin foretells that they will meet' – is generally accepted as an interpolation. The text of the *Afallennau* may be found in *Llyfr Du Caerfyrddin*, A. O. H. Jarman ed., pp. 27–8. I quote both the text and the translation of *Armes* from *Armes Prydein*, Ifor Williams ed., English version by R. Bromwich.

42 This is the date suggested by Ifor Williams, in his preface to *Armes Prydein* (pp. xii–xxiv). However, David N. Dumville, in his 'Brittany and *Armes Prydein*', advocates a slightly later date of composition – some years *after* Brunanburh, rather than before.

43 The opposition between the riches expected by the enemy and the death received is not explicitly present in the Welsh text, and the statement that Childric is *sad*, i.e., *sated* of the land is not an exact translation of 'trwy law gyghor', which means 'in sad counsel'. Moreover, the fact that in both cases the Saxons retreat to their ships vowing never to return cannot be considered as significant, for such features are dictated by the circumstances. For a detailed discussion of this passage, see F. Le Saux, 'Laȝamon's Welsh Sources. A Critical Review of Herbert Pilch's Thesis', pp. 92–97.

44 *Brut*, 10381–2. 'If they may set out alive from here to go to their country, and bring the disastrous news'.

which Pilch puts in parallel with 'dyhed eu gwraged y dywedant', 'they will tell the disastrous tale to their wives' (75). In both cases we have an agreement in theme – the defeated Saxons are the messengers of their own destruction – which is further enhanced by a similar construction. The English 'laŏ-spæl' is very close to the Welsh 'dyhed', 'disaster', while in both cases the recipients of this news are specified in strongly marked terms: 'leoden', 'gwraged', which both emphasize the closeness between the messengers and their hearers, and give the expression considerable emotional impact. This agreement is all the more striking as neither Geoffrey nor Wace include this vision of the defeated enemy returning to their homeland with their tale of woe, nor does the extant English litera-ture before Laȝamon provide us with anything comparable. In Welsh heroic poetry, however, the poet frequently gloats over the affliction of the enemy, revelling in the streams of Saxon blood flowing from their heaped corpses, and gleefully anticipating the sorrow of the Saxon womenfolk, as in Aneirin's famous

> o gyvryssed gwraged gwyth a wnaethant
> llawer mam oe deigr ar y hamrant,

'In battle they made women widows, and many a mother with tears in her eyelids'.[45] The savage irony of *Armes Prydein*, which has those same Saxons wash their blood-stained shirts after having announced their own defeat to their wives, may therefore be placed within a tradition, whereas Laȝamon stands isolated.

The theme of the self-announced defeat recurs elsewhere in the *Brut*, notes Pilch, on lines 9768–772, where Uther's victorious soldiers also anticipate the dirges the vanquished Saxons will compose in their country. The (conventional) stress of Welsh poetry on the impact of a defeat on the surviving enemies may therefore be said to have been assimilated to a degree by Laȝamon, who felt sufficiently at ease with the concept to re-use it. On the other hand, we may notice a certain distance of the English poet in using the theme. In one case, it appears in the mouth of Saxon envoys whose speech is determined by the expectation of the listener – Arthur – and their own aims. They wish to get away alive, and in order to obtain their life, they must stress their own debasement, in those terms most acceptable to the Britons. The whole of their message may therefore be said to be a reflexion of Briton rather than Saxon speech. This is confirmed by the preceding passage, put entirely in the mouth of Uther's Briton soldiers. The Saxons are echoing Briton words, and as the themes have been introduced in a preceding episode, the reader rec-

---

[45] *Canu Aneirin*, Ifor Williams ed., no. LVIII, lines 672–3. English translation by Kenneth Jackson, *The Gododdin*, p. 139.

ognises them as such: as if Laȝamon wished to stress the 'Britonness' of a theme amply attested in Middle Welsh literature.

The second parallel detected by Pilch occurs from line 10398 onwards of the *Brut* and *Armes Prydein* 66:

Ah of him bið iwurðen   swa bið of þan voxe[46]

Trwy uwrch y dinas ffoxas ffohyn – Through ramparts of the fortress the 'foxes' will flee.

Pilch's argumentation is marred by a faulty quotation which makes the correspondence look closer than it really is.[47] It boils down, ultimately, to the term 'fox', placed in a similar context. But the agreement remains puzzling. Laȝamon's choice of a fox for his famous simile is unexpected: the fox is not associated with warriors in the Old English heroic tradition, nor has the passage any parallel in either the *Roman de Brut* or the *Historia*.[48] The foxes in *Armes* Gwyn Thomas convincingly derives from Jeremiah (Lamentations 5.18); but this cannot be said of Laȝamon's passage. It is therefore tempting to see the *Brut*'s fox as an adaptation of the 'ffoxas' of *Armes Prydein*.

But the adaptation is great. The blunt insult of *Armes* has been expanded by Laȝamon into an intricate simile – one of the most famous passages of the *Brut* – while the explicitly offensive nature of the Welsh 'ffoxas' is as it were rubbed out. Laȝamon's simile does bear offensive overtones, but they are restricted by a narrowing of the focus from the indiscriminate rabble of the Saxons to their leader, Childric. Pilch attributes this to Laȝamon's poetic instinct, and considers that, despite the obvious differences, the simile is conclusive proof of the poet's indebtedness to *Armes Prydein*. A somewhat hasty conclusion, for it must be admitted that this single word is very tenuous evidence. Yet, the presence of the fox, of all animals of prey, within such a context, is altogether too unexpected for one to rule it out as mere coincidence, linked as it is to a specific situation, and treated in the specific tone of poems prophesying Welsh victories. The accumulation of correspondences between *Armes* and lines 10398 sqq. of the *Brut* makes the probability of Laȝamon having used the Welsh poem high enough for the connection to be taken seriously.[49] The question therefore arises: why

---

[46] 'But it has happened of him as it does of the fox'.

[47] Pilch's 'ffoxas ffohyn ... rei y dyffryn y bryn' ('the foxes flee ... some in valley and hill') is a collage from two different stanzas; the parallel with *Brut* 10418 ('þene vox driveð ȝeond dales and ȝeond dunes') is reduced to the fox element, once the Welsh lines are put into context again. The second part of Pilch's Welsh quotation then reads: 'rei y dyffryn a bryn nys dirwadant', 'some in valley and hill do not deny it'.

[48] The use of an English word ('ffoxas') by a Welsh poet is of no particular significance, as Welsh from an early time has unmarked borrowings from English.

[49] For a more detailed analysis of these passages, see F. Le Saux, 'Laȝamon's Welsh

Armes Prydein, and through what channels could Laȝamon have got to know it? One may rule out from the outset the hypothesis of Laȝamon's first-hand experience of Welsh literature in general, and of *Armes* in particular: whatever evidence we may glean from the *Brut* confirms that the English poet did not know Welsh. The three Welsh translation-loans pointed out by Pilch prove to be inexact, or so trite as to be useless; neither do his other arguments (the nickname Kinric, and a scribal error) in favour of Laȝamon's proficiency in the Welsh language carry much weight.[50] G. J. Visser had moreover noted that even though Laȝamon's Welsh names are more correct than those of Wace, they are few in number, and tend to be the names of major characters of the Arthurian legend, such as Kei or Gwenayfer; while J. D. Bruce, after a study of proper names in the *Brut*, felt entitled to state that Laȝamon was not capable of recognizing a Welsh name when he saw one. H. Pilch's remarks confirm that such names as Ridwathlan must have been transcribed from an oral source. This would suggest a limited amount of familiarity with Welsh (especially Welsh Arthurian) tradition, but no intimate knowledge of it. Laȝamon obviously had sufficient contact with his Welsh neighbours to be able to transcribe the most famous Welsh names correctly, and had access to specific information: but in an incomplete form. In other words, he knew Welsh people, who were prepared to provide him with whatever information he required, within certain limits.

The limits set by the Welsh informant(s) are readily perceived. The highly antagonistic feelings towards the English pervading Welsh literature would have to be underplayed, for example, and it is legitimate to

Sources', *English Studies* 67 (1986): 385–93.

50 The three translation-loans postulated by Pilch are:
(a) 'funde on his ræde' (*Brut*, 885, 7176, 10945), which Pilch derives from 'cauas yny gyghor', a common expression in Middle Welsh, meaning 'he obtained in counsel'. In Middle English, the expression appears to be limited to Laȝamon, though Toller's supplement to the Old English Dictionary attests similar expressions for the Old English period ('in hige funde', and 'on his mode findan', meaning 'to find resolution, courage, heart'; cf. p. 219, 'findan', meaning 2b). It is therefore highly probable that 'funde on his ræde' is of Anglo-Saxon formation; moreover, there is a substantial difference in meaning between the Welsh and the English expression, for while the English refers to a personal decision, the Welsh evokes formal deliberation between a king or chieftain and his counsellors.
(b) 'þa wes he swa bliðe swa he nes næuer ær an liue' (*Brut*, 916, 1122, 2334, 5572, 6408, etc.) – 'then was he so happy as he was never before in his life' – is compared to 'Ac eissyoes ny buassei lauenach ynteu eiryoet o uym noc oed yna', 'And never was he happier than he was then'. These two expressions are too trite for the similarity in meaning to be significant, while on the formal level the parallel is not exact.
(c) 'Hit com him on mode & on his mern þonke' ('It came to him in mind and in his main thought', *Brut* 6). The Welsh phrase advanced by Pilch as a possible model for this line – 'a dyuot yn y uryt ac yn y uedwl', 'it came to his mind and thought' – is not attested with such frequency as to be considered as typically Welsh; moreover, Laȝamon's phrase appears to be a straightforward variation on 'mode', 'it came to his mind'.

expect some amount of euphemism and tactful glossing over, in dealing with a kindly disposed, and possibly admiring English scholar.

The exact nature of Laȝamon's requests may at first glance seem difficult to determine; yet both the poem and what we know of the general cultural background of the late twelfth century agree in directing us firmly towards the Welsh Arthurian tradition, and more specifically, the Welsh prophetical tradition. The influence of the prophecies of Merlin is especially prominent. The indebtedness of the *Brut* to Book VII of the *Historia* was accepted even by those critics who rejected the idea of a direct influence of the *Historia* on Laȝamon. Merlin's Arthurian prophecy is repeated at each of the turning-points in Arthur's life, to the extent that it may be considered a major artistic device in the episode, providing stress, rhythm, and a general feeling of inevitability, tainted towards the end with fatality. No less than seven references to Merlin's prophecies are thus added in the *Brut*, and Laȝamon's attitude towards prophecies in general, and Merlin's prophecies in particular, is markedly different to that professed by Wace. Not only does he delete Wace's mention that Merlin's prophecies were not included in his work because he could not understand them (*Roman de Brut*, 7535–42), but he turns the Arthurian prophecy into a leitmotiv, recurring throughout 5000-odd lines (i.e., 8031–13968). Of Merlin's prophetic utterances, we are told that 'his quiðes weren soð', and this open respect is accompanied by frequent expansions and elaborations of those scenes involving the prophet, such as his first appearance in the Vortigern episode, the moving of the Stonehenge circle, or the conceiving of Arthur. The character of Merlin is given a fuller treatment in the English poem than in Wace, stressing for example his disinterestedness,[51] and he is the object of two new scenes: the description of a prophetic trance (8935–40), and the account of Uther's search for him, to find him finally thanks to a hermit who lived in the same forest (9363–9430). This points to a vivid interest of Laȝamon in Merlin and his prophecies, and makes it extremely probable that the English poet looked for additional information concerning the famous prophet. There are signs of his having consulted Geoffrey's *Vita Merlini* (see above), and considering the proximity of Wales, it is to be expected that he made use of Welsh tradition.

In favour of such an hypothesis, we find both internal and external evidence. That Laȝamon made some amount of enquiry on the subject is attested by his description of Merlin's trance:

[51] Merlin repeatedly refuses the riches offered to him by Aurelius' envoys (*Brut*, 8502–26) and Uther (*Brut*, 9441–6), in scenes not to be found in Wace (these passages are quoted above, chapter 5, p.32). The link between madness, poverty and the gift of prophecy is traditional.

> Mærlin sæt him stille   longe ane stunde
> swulc he mid sweuene   swunke ful swiðe
> Heo seiden þe hit iseȝen   mid heore aȝen æȝen
> þat ofte he hine wende   swulc hit a wurem weore
> Late he gan awakien   þa gon he to quakien
> & þas word seide   Merlin þa witeȝe.[52]

This reference to eye-witnesses is all the more striking as the scene depicted by Laȝamon tallies remarkably well with the testimony of another thirteenth-century writer, Giraldus Cambrensis. In his *Descriptio Cambriae*, Book 1, chapter 14, Giraldus mentions disapprovingly the existence in Wales of poets who 'composed' in a trance-like state:

> Among the Welsh there are certain individuals called 'awenyddion' who behave as if they are possessed by devils ... When you consult them about some problem, they immediately go into a trance and lose control over their senses, as if they were possessed. They do not answer the question put to them in any logical way. Words stream out of their mouths, incoherently and apparently meaningless and without any sense at all, but all the same well-expressed: and if you listen carefully to what they say you will receive the solution to your problem.[53]

It is scarcely doubtful, therefore, that Laȝamon looked towards Wales in his quest for further information concerning Merlin; and in so doing, he was following a trend. The works of Geoffrey of Monmouth and John of Cornwall had led to widespread interest in the prophecies of Merlin, which were now the object of commentaries. Giraldus Cambrensis tells us that Henry II was so eager to know the 'real' prophecies of Merlin that he (Giraldus) set off to Wales to procure them.[54] No literate person could have been unaware of the existence of a Welsh prophetic tradition, least of all a man who had spent years of his life working on the early history of Britain.

However, Merlin's 'genuine' prophecies were delicate material to present to a well-disposed Englishman, as Welsh prophetical poetry is aggressively – indeed, savagely – offensive towards the hereditary enemy, the 'Saesson', literally the Saxons, but in fact a generic term for the English as a whole, be they Angles, Saxons or Jutes.[55] Laȝamon's

---

[52] *Brut*, 8935–40. 'Merlin sat still for a long time, as if he were deeply immersed in a dream. They said, those who saw it with their own eyes, that he often writhed like a worm. Finally, he awoke; then he started to tremble, and Merlin the wise said these words'.
[53] Translation by Lewis Thorpe, *Gerald of Wales, The Journey Through Wales and the Description of Wales*, pp. 246–7.
[54] Giraldus Cambrensis, *Opera* VI, J. S. Brewer ed., p. 402.
[55] This is not to say, of course, that in a very specific context the term 'Saesson' could not

apparent distinction between Angles and Saxons, suggested by an ambiguity in his Wace text, it would seem,[56] becomes especially interesting in this connection. As I.J. Kirby notes, there is in the *Brut*

> a deliberate attributing of the Germanic heathendom and cruelty to Gurmund and the Saxons, and a deliberate avoidance of attributing anything of the sort to the Angles;

Angles who, moreover, 'as far as the story is concerned, have come from nowhere', appearing only in the final section of the poem, with the anecdote of Pope Gregory and the English slaves at the market place at Rome.[57] It is to these Angles that Gurmund grants overlordship over Britain – not to his Saxon allies – and from the first appearance of the Angles, Laȝamon's attention and sympathies shift from the Britons to the Angles, whom Cadwalader's vision further confirms as the rightful possessors of England/Britain. Whatever the reasons that encouraged Laȝamon to make such a distinction,[58] there is no doubt that this dichotomy between Angles and Saxons would have considerably attenuated the sting of the Welsh prophecies for a non Welsh-speaking Englishman. From the moment the English are recognized as good Angles, as opposed to the villainous Saxons of the past, the curses directed against the 'Saesson' lose their emotional impact, provided one remains unaware that 'Saesson' means 'English'. Assuming, therefore, as the poem leads us to believe, that Laȝamon did not know the generic value of the word 'Saesson', and that his informant encouraged him in dissociating Angles and Saxons, there was little danger of the English poet losing his equanimity in reading – or rather hearing a loose translation of – Welsh prophetical poetry. And within the Welsh prophetical corpus, *Armes Prydein* is particularly appropriate to both the outlook of the *Brut* and what can be deduced of Laȝamon himself. For *Armes* is somewhat different from most of the other Welsh prophetical poems in that it explicitly admits non-Celtic peoples in the final anti-Saxon coalition that was to restore the overlordship of Britain to the Britons. The first stanza of *Armes Prydein* reads:

> Gwaethyl gwyr hyt Gaer Weir gwasgarawt allmyn
> gwnahawnt goruoled gwedy gwehyn

have referred to 'Saxons' as opposed to 'Angles'.

56 Robert Mannyng of Brunne, who seems to have used a Wace-manuscript very similar to that of Laȝamon, also makes this distinction between Angles and Saxons. See Madden, vol. III, pp. 416–7 (note to lines 29391–421).

57 See I.J. Kirby, 'Angles and Saxons in Layamon's *Brut*', p. 59.

58 W.R.J. Barron, 'Arthurian Romance: Traces of an English Tradition', suggests that Laȝamon ignored the Saxon origins of the English 'inspired ... by social tensions in his own society some century and a half after the Norman Conquest' (pp. 6–7). This hypothesis seems highly probable.

A chymot Kymry a gwyr Dulyn
Gwydyl Iwerdon Mon a Phrydyn
Cornyw a Chludwyd eu kennwys genhyn.[59]

The interesting element here is the 'gwyr Dulyn', the men of Dublin, who, as is well known, were Scandinavians. The reasons for their inclusion in the poem are to be found in the historical circumstances surrounding the poem: Ifor Williams points out that the coalition which opposed King Æthelstan at Brunanburh in 937 included Olaf of Dublin. But a later reader of what, on the face of things, was an as-yet-unaccomplished prophecy, would presumably not have been aware that these men of Dublin referred to tenth-century historical fact; taken from its context, *Armes Prydein* could easily be interpreted as meaning that the Celtic peoples required outside help to overcome the invader, thereby implying the legitimacy of non-Celtic, or at least of shared sovereignty over Britain. A reading singularly in keeping with the *Brut*, which blurs the ethnic issues of British history to promote a 'national' outlook, as noted by W. R. J. Barron:

> [Laƺamon] turns [the Saxons'] conquest of Britain into a British triumph, one of many in the history of an ancient and honourable people.[60]

In the specific case of Laƺamon, one may venture that *Armes Prydein* was all the more convenient for a Welsh informant, as the non-Celtic people with whom the Britons were to share their victory are Scandinavians, as Laƺamon may have been himself. A tactful commentator would thus have had no difficulty in masking the aggressivity of the poem; not only would Laƺamon have felt unconcerned by the abuse against the Saxons (as opposed to the Angles), but he may even have felt some identity with the people through whom the final deliverance is to come. Moreover, Ifor Williams suggests that Geoffrey of Monmouth may have been influenced by *Armes* in the writing of his *Vita Merlini*:[61] in both poems, the promised deliverers of the Britons are Cynan and Cadwalader, and Geoffrey's list of the peoples who will participate in the liberating of Britain 'are named in the Prophecy, except for the Danes of Dublin'. This omission is important: the men of Dublin are precisely the element by which *Armes* may be recognized as a specific, political statement, rather than the traditional expression of a myth. However, the fact that *Armes Prydein*, as the *Vita*

---

[59] 'The warriors will scatter the foreigners as far as Caer Weir, they will rejoice after the devastation, and there will be reconciliation between the Cymry and the men of Dublin, and the Irish of Ireland and Anglesey (?) and Scotland, the men of Cornwall and of Strathclyde will be made welcome among us'. *Armes Prydein*, 5–11.

[60] Barron, 'Arthurian Romance', pp. 6–7.

[61] See Ifor Williams, *Armes Prydein*, pp. xxx–xxxiv.

Merlini, draws upon the conventions of the prophetical genre as a means of legitimization, would presumably have made a potential medieval Welsh informant invest the 'prophecy' with enough authority for him to take it into account.[62]

The hypothesis of an informant rather than of an unknown source already containing a number of allusions to *Armes Prydein* is further supported by the extensive research of Constance Bullock-Davies, who establishes the importance of multi-lingual translators, or 'latimers', throughout the eleventh and twelfth centuries in Wales and on the Welsh borderlands.[63] She notes that in the lordships of William of Gloucester,

> From Wareham, in Dorset, to Cardiff and Caerleon in Glamorgan and Gwent, at least four languages were daily spoken: French, English, Welsh and Cornish; we cannot tell, but that there may have been some pockets in which Breton, too, was heard.[64]

Every court or baronial household in which a knowledge of languages was imperative thus appears to have had its 'demeine latimer', the role of whom C. Bullock-Davies considers far exceeded that of mere business matters:

> The 'demeine latimer' was a member of a king's or a baron's household; he was permanently resident, necessarily a personal attendant upon his lord, and, by inference, well-known to everyone, including domestic minstrels, clerks, heralds and, of course, the ladies; in other words, he was known to all who enjoyed and created literary and musical entertainment in the hall. As a master of many tongues he was, no doubt, much in demand and of great service during his leisure hours, for his knowledge of other literatures could enlarge the minstrel's répertoire.[65]

One such household translator could certainly account for Laȝamon's remarkably correct Welsh names, and may also be the source of those additions to the *Roman de Brut* concerning the birth of Arthur, his creating the Round Table, and his translation to Avalon; the household

---

[62] How this informant could have had access to the poem in the first place is a difficult question, as *Armes* has come down to us in one manuscript only, the *Book of Taliesin,* which is dated to the first half of the fourteenth century. If one accepts that the *Armes* poet was a monk of south Wales (see introduction to the edition, p. xxvi), one would also expect any early manuscript(s) to be preserved in south Wales, which would imply that Laȝamon's hypothetical informant was a south-Welsh cleric.

[63] Constance Bullock-Davies, 'Marie de France and South Wales', 1963; p. 436. A useful summary of part of the conclusions of this unpublished dissertation may be found in print, in C. Bullock-Davies, *Professional Interpreters and the Matter of Britain,* Cardiff: Univ. of Wales Press, 1966. A latimer is mentioned by both Wace (6958) and Laȝamon (7146).

[64] C. Bullock-Davies, 'Marie de France', p. 436.

[65] C. Bullock-Davies, 'Marie de France', p. 453.

latimer may also be one of the eye-witnesses referred to in connexion
with Merlin's trance. And even if the lord of the Areley district did not
maintain a latimer on the spot, the work of Melville Richards has established that bilingual individuals were not rare along the Welsh borders.
The accuracy in the representation of Welsh names in the family papers
of the border estates thus leads Richards to state:

> The attorneys or their clerks or whoever was responsible for draw-
> ing up the documents could do three things: speak, read and write
> Welsh. One does not wish to exaggerate this, but I think we must
> admit a state of real bilingualism along the Border during the
> Middle Ages.[66]

Laȝamon would thus have had no trouble in finding an informant.
Lines 16088–90 of the *Brut* suggest moreover that this informant was
Welsh, well-educated, and enjoyed a good social status:

> þæs Bruttes on ælc ende   foren to Walisce londe.
> and heore laȝen leofeden   & heore leodene þæuwen
> and ȝet wunie[ð] þære   swa heo doð auere-mære.[67]

Herbert Pilch notes the assertiveness of these lines, which betray,
according to him, a personal knowledge of Welsh customs and the Welsh
legal system. Indeed, this assertiveness is significant, in that Laȝamon is
taking full responsibility for his statement, which was not the case at
lines 8937–8 of the *Brut*, where the poet makes it clear that the un-
dignified comparison of Merlin to a worm is not his, but that he is merely
reporting what he was told. These lines are all the more significant as
Laȝamon contradicts his source, Wace, which reads at the corresponding
passage:

> Tuit sunt mué e tuit changié
> Tuit sunt divers e forslignié
> De noblesce, d'onur, de murs
> E de la vie as anceisurs.[68]

The contrast is striking. On the one hand, the Welsh are presented as
an old and respectable people who have maintained their venerable
customs against all odds; on the other, an image of total degeneracy. This

---

[66] Melville Richards, 'The Population of the Welsh Border', pp. 90–1.
[67] 'These Britons on each side went to the Welsh land, and observed their laws and the
customs of their nation; and they still dwell there, as they shall do evermore'.
[68] 'They are all changed and different, they have completely deviated and degenerated
from the nobility, the honour, the customs and the life of their ancestors'. Wace,
14851–4.

begs the question: who else but a Welshman could have instilled this positive outlook on Wales? And who but a man of undoubted learning and status could have inspired Laȝamon with such respect as to put his word before the testimony of written authority? Herbert Pilch and (by implication) J. S. P. Tatlock explain this feature by a first-hand experience of Wales. Tatlock considers that Laȝamon may have travelled through Wales:

> He knows better the geography of south Wales and generally the south and south-west of England

than of the north and north-east of Britain; he knows the exact locations of Bath and Exeter, and 'that the region between the Severn and the Wye had been but was no longer part of Wales'; he shows an awareness of the insignificance of Caerleon in his day, and possibly of the existence of skilled armourers in Carmarthen, the center of royal power in south Wales. Moreover, 'he seems to show knowledge of the topography around St Davids (Menevia) in south-west Wales', mentioning 'waters and fens' in this area. Tatlock connects this knowledge to Laȝamon's hypothetical links with Ireland:

> Since St Davids was one of the most used ports for travel to Ireland, and is remote, this points to personal knowledge. Such acquaintance as the poet shows with south Wales may well be due to a limited traveling through it. We are justified in inferring that when the poet says 'Laȝamon gon liðen wide ȝond þas leode', he used merely a manner of speaking. But he did know the south-west of Great Britain, seaports, and the route to southern Ireland.[69]

Whether or not one accepts Tatlock's highly imaginative reconstruction of Laȝamon's life, his conclusions as to the poet's knowledge of British geography remain valid. The evidence in favour of Laȝamon's 'limited traveling' through south Wales is of restricted enough a nature to allow the hypothesis of second-hand information, for example through travellers' accounts. However, if one accepts the statement in the Prologue that Laȝamon 'gon liðen ȝond þas leode' in search of books, it would appear quite normal for the poet to have gone to Wales, which he knew to be the birthplace of his material. A direct, if limited, experience of the Welsh ways and customs would certainly explain the poet's readiness to believe in the continuing prowess and worthiness of the Welsh people, while a trip to Wales could not have failed to provide Laȝamon with an adequate informant. For if we can only assume the presence of a

---

[69] Tatlock, *Legendary History*, pp. 501–2.

latimer at Areley Regis (or, failing that, at Worcester), the existence not only of interpreters, but also of numerous high-ranking multilingual persons in the south of Wales is established: Constance Bullock-Davies notes a number of Welshmen bearing the cognomen 'Sais', among the witnesses to several charters in the Margam collection. This epithet was apparently given to those who could speak English; one example of these is Hywel Sais, son of Lord Rhys, who was a hostage at the court of Henry II from 1158–1171, and apparently knew Latin, English and French as well as Welsh.

It is therefore clear that Laȝamon did not need to know Welsh to make himself understood in south Wales, and that he would have had no problem in finding a learned Welshman to guide him through those Welsh manuscripts that were available (presumably by translating them aloud), and explain certain features of Welsh tradition to him. One of these appears to be the Welsh triads.

A predilection for triple groupings is discernible among the Celtic peoples from the time of their earliest records, notes Rachel Bromwich;[70] this tendency is apparent in the works of Gildas and 'Nennius', for example, while later Welsh works show that the triadic form was used as 'a means of cataloguing a variety of technical information'. Triads are used extensively in legal codes as well as in poetical treatises; they may also deal with general moral, gnomic or proverbial statements, and are frequently used as a literary device. The body of triads which would have been of interest to the author of a Brut belong to a specific mass of triadic literature called the Triads of the Isle of Britain, 'Trioedd Ynys Prydein' (= TYP). Rachel Bromwich sums up the dominant themes forming the oldest nucleus of the TYP as follows:

> It becomes evident that the stories referred to in the triads were focused: (a) upon figures of the early Welsh semi-mythological tradition, who belong to the milieu of the *Mabinogi*; (b) upon what may be described as the medieval Welsh view of the country's history in pre-Saxon times, and in the period of the arrival of the Saxons, i.e., the traditions centred upon Caswallawn, Maxen Wledig and Gwrtheyrn (= Vortigern), and (c) upon characters and events of the British Heroic Age of the sixth and seventh centuries, who belonged both to Wales and to North Britain.[71]

The oldest version of the TYP is in MS Peniarth 16, a fifteenth-century manuscript, but which preserves traces of an older system of orthography, indicating an early thirteenth-century copy. There is no doubt,

---

[70] *Trioedd Ynys Prydein. The Welsh Triads*, Rachel Bromwich ed. and transl. (= *TYP*).
[71] Bromwich, *TYP*, p.lxvii.

therefore, that the material was available in Laȝamon's day; and several passages in the *Brut* suggest indebtedness to this area of Welsh tradition.

We may first consider a passage which shares none of the stylistic peculiarities of the triadic form: Laȝamon's account of Vortimer's reign, where we find the English *Brut*'s only addition of the Crusade theme. Vortimer is consistently presented as the ideal Christian king, as opposed to his father Vortigern; in his zeal for the spread of the Gospel among his people, he takes on a saint-like stature, while the Britons themselves appear in a black-and-white contrast with their Saxon enemies. They are Christians against pagans, and nothing else:

> þe king hehte ælcne mon   þe luuede þene Cristindom
> þat heo þa hæðene   hatien scolden
> & þa hæfden bringen   to Vortimer þan kinge
> & twalf panewes habben to mede   for his wel-dede.[72]

This state of affairs, which recurs nowhere else in the *Brut*, suggests external influence: for the straightforward equation between Christianity and ethnic identity is carefully eschewed in other parts of the poem.[73] It is therefore interesting to note that this apparent contradiction occurs at a crucial point in the history of Britain, as seen by Welsh tradition. Vortimer's struggle is the first Briton upsurge against the Saxons; and the whole episode, starting with Vortigern's treacherous befriending of the Saxons and ending with the massacre of Stonehenge, is a leitmotiv in the Welsh historical and prophetical writings. As for Vortimer himself, the triads allude to him as 'Gvertheuyr Vendigeit', Gwrthefyr the Blessed.[74]

Whilst the explicit sanctity of Vortimer in the Welsh triads may be the origin of Laȝamon's treatment of the character, one must stress that the linking of the cause of the Cymry/Britons with that of God is recurrent in Welsh prophetical poetry. *Armes Prydein* (to restrict our considerations to a poem Laȝamon may have known of) thus reads:

> Yr amser Gwrtheyrn genhyn y sathrant.
> ny cheffir o wir rantir an karant.
> Neu vreint an seint pyr y saghyssant.
> neu reitheu Dewi pyr y torrassant.[75]

---

[72] *Brut*, lines 7325–8. 'The king commanded that every man who loved the Christian faith should hate the heathens, and bring their heads to Vortimer the king. And he would have twelve pennies as reward for his good deed'.
[73] See below chapter 7, p. 159 sqq.
[74] See Bromwich, *TYP*, no. 37 (pp. 88–96): 'Tri Chud a Thri Datcud Enys Prydein', 'The Three Concealments and Three Disclosures of the Island of Britain'.
[75] 'Since the time of Gwrtheyrn they have oppressed us: not rightfully will the inheritance

The monastic author of *Armes* depicts the struggle between the Saxons and the Britons (more specifically, the Cymry) in terms both of moral and political antagonism; and the reference to Gwrtheyrn (*alias* Vortigern) clearly anchors the origin of the troubles to the very time LaƷamon chose to expand in so uncharacteristic a way. The massacre at Stonehenge, which follows close on Vortimer's poisoning, is referred to in the Welsh poem as 'rin dilein', 'secret slaughter' (l.34), which now allows the scavengers of Gwrtheyrn Gwynedd to wear a crown. As in all Welsh prophetical poems, *Armes* predicts that the ultimate outcome will be favourable to the Britons: but not so much because of the justice of their claims as of the innumerable crimes the Saxons have committed against God and His saints, especially Dewi Sant, Saint David, patron of Wales.[76] LaƷamon's handling of the Vortimer episode certainly suggests the influence of a strong historical tradition, and the cumulated evidence of the Welsh prophetical genre and of the Triads build up a remarkably similar image to that offered by the *Brut*.

There are four passages in the *Brut* which display triple groupings or divisions, and may therefore be suspected of having been derived from triads:[77]

> 3594–595: Julius Caesar is said to have conquered a third of the world.

> 14380–1: Maelgwn is the fairest man with Adam and Absalon, 'swa alse þe boc us suggeð', 'as the book tells us'.

> 14263–5: only Arthur and two of his knights survive Camlan.

> 13716–7: Arthur's battle with Luces is 'þat þridde mæste uiht þe auere wes here idiht', 'the third greatest fight to have ever taken place here', 'swa al swa suggeð writen þæ witeʒen idihten', 'as the writings by the wise men say'.

None of these passages have exact counterparts in the extant Welsh triads.

In the first case, Herbert Pilch considers (p. 37) that the division of the world in three is derivative of the tripartite division of Britain in Welsh tradition. But this need not be the case, as medieval geography also divides the world in three – Asia, Africa, and Europe; a fact noted by

---

of our kinsmen be won. Or why have they trampled upon the privileges of our saints? Why have they destroyed the rights of Dewi?' *Armes Prydein*, lines 137–140.

[76] See *Armes*, 98 and 105: the Cymry count among their allies the Trinity as well as Dewi and the saints of Britain.

[77] Herbert Pilch, *Literarische Studie*, sees five triadic passages in the *Brut*; one of these, however, is not in triadic form (*Brut*, 5839, Maximian's departure never to return).

Pilch himself. It would therefore be unwise to lay too much stress on this particular instance. Equally dubious is the reference to Camlan, which does indeed number three survivors, but where the stress is on the number two, as may be seen with a fuller quotation:

þa nas þer na-mare   i þan fehte to laue
of twa hundred þusend monnen   þa þer leien to-hauwen
buten Arður þe king ane   & of his cnihtes tweien.[78]

The opposition between 'twa hundred þusend' and 'tweien' is a device to highlight the extent of the massacre, and has little to do with the triadic technique. Moreover, as Arthur is not mentioned in the Welsh triads among the survivors of Camlan, it follows that this passage would not have been derived from Welsh tradition.

The two remaining passages are more interesting; first, because both betray a marked formulaic nature and have parallels (albeit imperfect) with extant triads; and secondly, because in both cases, we have an appeal to authority which suggests more than mere convention. As H. Pilch points out, the statement that Maelgwn was the fairest man ever with Adam and Absalom is very similar to the triad 'Tri dyn a gauas pryd Adaf', 'The three men who had Adam's beauty' (TYP 48). The Welsh triad mentions Absalom, Jason and Paris, with Adam being the ultimate in manly beauty. The 'triad', as presented in the Brut, betrays a strong biblical bias: two of the three handsome men have a scriptural basis to their reputation, Adam, the first man, being closest to God's image, and therefore most perfect, and Absalom, David's outstandingly handsome son. An adaptation for the sake of the priest Laʒamon, perhaps? The obvious discrepancy with the extant Welsh triad could suggest an oral gloss (despite the mention of a 'boc'); or, alternatively, this may only be an instance of the general Indo-European attraction to the number three.

The authority referred to in lines 13716–7 of the Brut is more significant. 'þat þridde mæste uiht þe auere wes here idiht' is typical of the Welsh triadic tradition, both in its formulation and in its use as a literary device.[79] Pilch (p. 55) puts the passage in parallel with the triad 'Trywyr Gvarth', 'The three dishonoured men of the Isle of Britain' (i.e. Androgeus, Vortigern and Modred; TYP 51), and postulates a lost triad, 'The

---

[78] 'Then, of two hundred thousand men that lay there slain, there were none who survived the fight, except only Arthur the king, and two of his knights'.
[79] See for example in Branwen Uerch Lyr (Derick Thomson ed., p. 18), the reference to a now lost triad as a literary device: 'A llyny ual y teruyna y geing honn o'r Mabinyogi, o achaws Paluawt Branwen, yr honn a uu tryded anuat palawt yn yr ynys honn', 'And like this ends this branch of the Mabinogi, concerning Branwen's Blow, and this was the third unfortunate blow in this island'. The similarity with the wording in the Brut is striking.

three great battles of Britain'. The 'here', which apparently means 'in Britain', seems to point to a confusion with Camlan; a very gross error, at a first glance, but which may be explained as 'Trywyr Gvarth' devotes a few lines to the reason of the dishonour of the three men; and in the case of Medrawd, 'the third and the worse', the account of Camlan is preceded by a long introduction on Arthur's battle with 'Lles, emperor of Rome', finishing with these words:

> Ac yn y diwed y kyuaruu Arthur a'r amheravdyr, ac Arthur a'e lladawd. Ac yno y llas goreugwyr Arthur. A phan gigleu Vedravd...
> – And in the end Arthur encountered the emperor, and Arthur slew him. And Arthur's best men were slain there. When Medrawd heard that Arthur's host was dispersed ... (*TYP*, p.133)

A causal link is thus established between Medrawd's treason (which leads to Camlan) and Arthur's battle with Lucius; this could well explain a statement such as Laƺamon's, especially if, as I suggest, the English poet had no direct access to Welsh sources, whether oral or written, and had to depend on a translator who may sometimes have been a little confusing.

Whatever the medium of transmission of triadic lore to Laƺamon, there remains in the *Brut* a distinct awareness of some form of authority behind statements in triadic form. This awareness is expressed by referring to 'bocs' or 'writen', the authors of which are the 'witeʒen', the 'wise men'. This apparently trite statement takes on more significance when set beside what we know of the Welsh learned tradition. For parallel to, and sometimes in conflict with, the bookish, latinate tradition was a native learned tradition, preserved and dispensed by the 'kyuarwydyt'. This dual source of learning, and the equal credit given to both, appears clearly in the *Cyfranc Lludd a Llefelys*, a legendary tale inserted in a number of Welsh versions of Geoffrey's *Historia*, including the Llanstephan-1 MS version. The *Cyfranc* starts in this way:

> Y Beli Uawr vab Manogan y bu tri meib, Llud a Chaswallawn a Nynhyaw. A herwyd y kyuarwydyt, petweryd mab idaw uu Lleuelis.[80]

The first sentence, 'Beli Mawr son of Manogan had three sons', follows the *Historia*; the second then quotes another authority: 'according to the *kyvarwydyt*, he had a fourth son'. This alternative authority is considered

---

[80] 'Beli Mawr son of Manogan had three sons, Lludd and Caswallawn and Nynhyaw. And according to the *kyfarwyddyd*, he had a fourth son, Llefelys'. *Cyfranc Lludd a Llefelys*, ed. B.F.Roberts, p.1. On the versions of the tale in Welsh translations of the *Historia*, see the Preface, pp.xx–xxvii.

serious enough for its teaching to be interpolated in the text of the original Latin *Historia*. The translation for 'kyuarwydyt' is generally 'tale'; the 'kyuarwyddyaid', the people who told 'kyuarwyddyd', are usually termed 'story-tellers'. The original meaning of 'kyuarwyddyd' had a much wider scope, though, as established by Proinsias MacCana, in his *Learned Tales of Medieval Ireland* (p.139):

> The basic form is the adjective 'cyfarwydd', which derives evidently from the root *veid-, 'to see', and comprises the meanings 'well-informed, learned, expert, skilful, skilled in magic' ...; as a noun it has the corresponding meanings 'guide, well-informed person, expert', as well as, in the laws, 'witness, spectator (of a crime)', while the derivative 'cyfarwyddyd' normally denotes 'guidance, direction, instruction, information, knowledge, skill, art', etc. There can be little doubt that the meanings 'storyteller' and 'storytelling' are secondary to these.

The *cyfarwydd*'s interest in traditional narrative must have been of a similar nature to that of the Irish *fili*, suggests P. MacCana:

> his primary concern would have been not so much to recite the old tales as to be capable of interpreting them in terms of history and genealogy.

In such conditions, one wonders if 'witezen' may not be a gloss for 'cyfarwyddiaid', especially considering the close links between the triads and the *cyfarwyddiai*. Rachel Bromwich considers that the triads were composed by the *cyfarwyddiaid*, and inserted by them as an integral part of their narrative, at the time when the telling of *chwedlau* (tales) constituted a flourishing oral literature:

> The Triads added emphasis to the *cyfarwydd*'s tale – and the utilisation of Triads for this purpose is well exemplified in the *Pedeir Kainc* – and at the same time acted as a mnemonic device. During the eleventh century the flower of this narrative art began to decline, at the same time as the *cyfarwydd* began to commit his works to writing ... As an accompaniment of the antiquarian movement which led to the permanent recording of a part of the saga material of the past, the Triads ... were assembled and committed to writing. They provided the key to a body of rapidly dissolving oral literature. Thus these collections soon assumed an independent importance, and, in the case of the Triads a certain vicarious significance, which may almost be called mystic – the bards did not wish the key epithets to be readily intelligible since they provided them not only

with a useful and much drawn-upon repository of names but also with an easily assumed veneer of traditional learning.[81]

The linking of 'wise men' to material in triadic form in Laƹamon is strikingly similar to the situation described by R. Bromwich. Whether or not we give credit to 'writen' and 'bocs' is another matter; that the triads were available in written form at the beginning of the thirteenth century is virtually certain, though Laƹamon would presumably not have been able to recognize such a manuscript had he seen it, for lack of knowledge of the Welsh language. What seems assured, however, is that the poet's informant provided him with those triads which seemed most congenial to the material of the *Brut*, either translating directly from a manuscript (a word-for-word translation could perhaps account for the readings of the *Brut*), or from memory, but stressing that this material went back to an ancient tradition, codified in manuscripts, and written down by the *cyfarwyddiaid*, the 'well-informed persons', to quote P. MacCana.

There remains to be considered the possible influence of oral tales (Welsh or Celtic) on the *Brut*. It is a complex issue. First, because of the difficulty in assigning an exact birthplace to any tale which appears to have influenced Laƹamon. Assuming a tale is of Celtic origin, is it an Irish, a Welsh, a Breton, or a Cornish story? Irish influence upon the material of the *Brut* seems unlikely. J. S. P. Tatlock points out that Laƹamon knew the names of the major Irish saints, and was aware of Irish fighting habits, and of the kinship between the Irish and the Picts; but this knowledge does not seem to have extended to Irish literary tradition. Those Celtic tales which earlier critics detected in certain expansions of the *Brut* appear to have been *brythonic* tales, from Wales, Brittany or Cornwall. But it so happens that in the twelfth century, Welsh, Breton and Cornish were very similar – Breton and Cornish still are intercomprehensible, to some extent – and all three were designated as 'lingua britannica', the Briton/Breton language. This linguistic kinship was moreover strengthened by the close relations between these countries. Not only was trade flourishing, but the Norman invasion brought to Britain a great number of Bretons, who must have kept some contact with their original homeland. The best known of these Breton/British is probably Geoffrey of Monmouth himself.[82] To this, one may add a constant cultural exchange due to the itinerant Breton and Welsh minstrels touring the courts of Europe in general, and of Britain in particular.

In such conditions, the Brythonic countries must have shared their main myths, tales and literary developments to a very great extent. A Welsh story-teller could tell a Breton story in Welsh, just as a Breton story-teller could tell a Welsh tale in Breton; and, one assumes, either

---

81 Rachel Bromwich, 'The Character of the Early Welsh Tradition', pp. 117–8.
82 See Ditmas, note 6 supra.

could have told those same tales in French, thereby adding to the confusion.

The 'Celtic tales' incorporated by Laȝamon in h's *Brut* illustrate this
situation very well. On the one hand, the proper names within those
passages – Gwenhayfer, Pridwen, Kei, Ridwathlan – certainly seem to
indicate that the minstrel, or whoever recited the tales, was Welsh rather
than Breton; but as Areley is on the borderlands of Wales, these names
may just have been adapted to conform to the expectations of the local
audience. Moreover, the mention that Arthur was taken to *Brittany* as a
baby (a detail found neither in Wace nor in Geoffrey) suggests some
amount of Breton influence; though it could be objected that it is fitting
for the saviour of the Britons to come from the land of Cynan, founder of
Brittany, whose glorious return with Cadwallader is to mark the beginning of a new Briton Golden Age, according to Welsh tradition. The issue
is further complicated by the fact that, whatever the origins of the
minstrel (or informant), such tales would probably have reached
Laȝamon through the medium of French or English. Attempts to claim a
continental origin (as opposed to an insular origin) for Laȝamon's additional material, in the Arthurian section especially, are therefore
doomed to be unsatisfactory.

The question of non-Celtic influence on these same tales is another
matter. For if the lack of sources forbids us from postulating an English
influence over Celtic tales recited in English, we have ample evidence
regarding those tales recited in French. The complexity of the relationship between Brythonic Celtic and French literary material lies in the fact
that, as French literature borrowed Celtic themes and stories, there must
needs be some amount of identity between a given French work and its
Celtic analogue. And as the French work is usually preserved in written
form, while the Celtic tale is more often than not a second-hand hint,
such as in Laȝamon's *Brut*, or else contained in a relatively recent Welsh
manuscript, the odds are that a French origin will be assigned to the
story, through Brittany, whose specifically Celtic Brythonic identity is
underplayed in view of its contemporary status (or non-status) within
France. Thus arises the quaint idea expressed by Visser, for example, that
if a tale shows traces of courtly behaviour, it must have been Breton; yet
the three romances in the *Mabinogion* amply show that the courtly conventions could also be exploited in Welsh. Specifically French cultural
adjuncts are attributed to Breton culture, which is thus considered as
significantly different to Welsh culture. Yet, as noted above, the evidence
tends to show that such was not the case. Moreover, why should a Breton
minstrel be more capable of adapting his material to a French audience
than a Welsh one? The political background of such a debate is of course
an aggravating factor, and as long as nationalistic rivalries complicate the
issue, the matter will remain confused.

Taking all these elements into consideration, the probability is that Laȝamon heard a number of tales, of various origins, from a number of minstrels. His special interest in the history of pre-Saxon Britain, and in particular in the reign of Arthur, would have led him to enquire further on the subject. The authority with which the English poet speaks of the Welsh people and customs suggests that he found himself an informant whom he regarded highly, and from whom he gathered some knowledge of Welsh prophetical poetry, especially those prophecies attributed to Myrddin/Merlin, among which one may postulate a direct influence of *Armes Prydein*. Laȝamon also gathered elements of the native learned tradition, in the form of triads, which however are badly corrupted in the *Brut*, and obviously misunderstood. The Welsh influence, though not as great as suggested by Herbert Pilch, cannot therefore be said to be absent from the *Brut*.

7

'An preost wes on leoden'

Laȝamon defines himself from the very first line of his poem as 'an preost'; more so than a poet, it is as a cleric that the reader is invited to comprehend him, with all the social and intellectual implications that this suggests. More specifically, it leads to the assumption that the *Brut* must bear the mark of the calling of its author in its moral and religious stances, and betray reminiscences of patristic, biblical or hagiographical works. Thus, when G. J. Visser attempts to explain Laȝamon's 'unnatural' pro-Briton bias at the beginning of the *Brut*, his main argument is: 'Obviously, he was guided by his religious faith, his sense of justice and charity rather than by the dictate of kinship.'[1] This expectation of a greater mark of religion on the English *Brut* than on Wace's *Roman de Brut* or Geoffrey's *Historia* is not really justified: Wace and Geoffrey were also clerics, Wace being a 'clerc lisant' and Geoffrey ending his life as bishop of St Asaph's.[2]

Yet there is no doubt that Laȝamon's moral consciousness comes through more forcibly than that of Wace, his immediate source; to quote F. L. Gillespy, 'the later writer is far more intense'.[3] The poem as a whole is framed by a request for prayers (Prologue) and a proverbial statement on the power of God; the reader is offered numerous judgements on the character or actions of given kings, stressing for example Vortigern's unchristian behaviour, condemning Malgo's homosexuality, or reviling the incestuous murderer Conan as

þe for-cuðeste mon þet sunne here scean on.[4]

---

[1] G. J. Visser, *Vindication*, p. 91.
[2] Wace's description of himself as 'clerc lisant' is to be found in the third part of his *Roman de Rou* (line 180: vol. 1, p. 168 of *Le Roman de Rou de Wace*, Anthony John Holden ed.). The exact meaning of 'clerc lisant' has been a matter of some debate; it probably means that Wace was a teacher (as well as being a cleric). See Urban Tigner Holmes Jr., 'Norman Literature and Wace', pp. 55–7. Concerning Geoffrey's bishopric, see Lewis Thorpe, 'The Last Years of Geoffrey of Monmouth', pp. 663–72.
[3] F. L. Gillespy, 'Layamon's *Brut*: a Comparative Study in Narrative Art', p. 477.
[4] *Brut*, 14358. 'The wickedest man that sun here shone on' (Madden III, 151). This comment is not in Wace.

This moral dimension is felt to be so characteristic of the English *Brut* by some critics that it leads them to hasty conclusions. For example, C. V. Friedlander states that 'habitually Layamon characterizes an event which was morally neutral in his source', on the basis of three examples only, one of which may be said to be erroneous.[5] It is a fact that, as noted by F. L. Gillespy, the English poem mentions Christianity as a condition of peace more often than the French *Roman de Brut*, and that the kings Laȝamon approves of are shown to be more religious than Wace's; an observation echoed by A. C. Gibbs:

> One can say that Laȝamon's poem is more obviously Christian than its French original, with some confidence, for the references to Christianity are there to be collected.[6]

However, Gibbs hastens to add:

> The poem is not Christian in any profound sense. It *is* unflinchingly moral, according to the lights of its author ... [but] the moral drive of the poem is not generated by Christianity.[7]

Laȝamon's moral standards are essentially heroic, and hinge on the principle of 'retributive reaction', notes Gibbs.[8] Moreover, suggests Gillespy, the moral judgements in the *Brut*, though striking, may not be as significant as they seem:

> Layamon's own remarks are usually conventional or drawn rather obviously from the facts of the case, as when a tag such as 'his hap

---

[5] Friedlander, 'Early Middle English Accentual Verse', p. 226. Friedlander's discussion centres on the concepts of 'good king', 'traitor', 'Christian' and 'heathen hounds', which she claims are virtually foreign to Wace. The erroneous example is that involving Archbishop Guencelin's quest for help against the pirates (*Brut*, 6308–55). Friedlander founds her case on the clerical setting at the beginning of the embassy, and the twice repeated mention that it was feared that the pirates would destroy Christendom in Britain. This theme, however, is already present in Wace 6316–8; and as I demonstrate below, the 'crusade' theme is actually toned down through Laȝamon's deleting of Guencelin's final 'Christus vincit ...'. Friedlander's two other examples are instances of wars of conquest presented as contests between right and wrong: the Roman campaign of Belin and Brennes is thus given a motivation (like all the military expeditions of the *Brut*), and the Romans are presented as deceitful traitors, in a scene added by the English poet; Arthur's Roman campaign likewise takes place against explicitly heathen opponents.
[6] Gibbs, 'Literary Relationships', p. 224. Instances of these 'references to Christianity' are Laȝamon's expansions on the birth of Christ, his interest in the history of the early Church and his denunciation of heathendom. One may note however that among the few accounts of strictly religious ceremonies in the *Brut*, the more memorable – Brutus' ceremonial at Diana's shrine, and especially Cassibelaune's sacrifice to Apollo – are instances of heathen worship.
[7] Gibbs, pp. 225–6.
[8] This aspect of Laȝamon's poem is also discussed by Jonathan Roger Seal in the first chapter of his *Kings and Fated Folk*, 'The Ethos of Laȝamon's *Brut*', pp. 12–57.

(or value) was the worse' is added after the mention of some decided flaw of character or morals ... When comment is given not by the author but by one of his characters, it is appropriate to the person speaking and cannot always be accepted as Layamon's opinion ... On all questions of undoubted right and wrong one may say without undue generalization that the poet sides with the right ... When there is a conflict of two rights, however, it is often difficult, sometimes impossible, to tell which side the poet favors. And, on the other hand, when two wrong motives are present it is sometimes quite impossible to tell exactly where the author's condemnation lies.[9]

It would seem that Laȝamon took it for granted that his audience had the same set of ethical standards as himself, and therefore did not think it necessary to give many explicit moral judgements; one may notice, though, a tendency to make the 'correct' response clearer, by adding reprehensible traits to a given character (Conan's incest, unmentioned by Wace), or aggravating circumstances to an evil action (Constantine's defiling St Amphibalus' altar with Meleon's blood).

Closely related to the issue of moral attitude and religious outlook is the theme of the Christian crusade, which Herbert Pilch (followed by Friedlander, Gibbs, Donahue and others) considers as one of the main unifying devices of the poem.[10] All the examples provided by Pilch of this 'Holy War' theme (expressed through the systematic underlining of the heathenness of the Britons' adversaries) ultimately go back to Laȝamon's main source, Wace's *Roman de Brut*. This is scarcely astonishing, as the 'crusade' aspect is already an essential component of Geoffrey's *Historia*, especially in its Arthurian part. Wace tends to underplay this element of his source, deleting for example the speech of Dubricius, but it remains prominent enough for even a slight elaboration by Laȝamon to be noticeable. Moreover, Laȝamon's independent additions and expansions often underline the actively Christian, rather than the negative pagan element. This may be seen from the expansions concerning the birth of Christ, followed by Telghesinus/Taliesin's prophecy to King Kinbelin: Wace's 27 lines (4850–4876) become 53 long lines (4521–4573). The Christianizing of Britain is also extensively reworked, to include a vivid image of the bishops Dunian and Fagan preaching to the Britons, their idols being destroyed, and King Luces having those who refuse baptism slain.[11] Wace (5229–5264) relates the event from a purely technical point of view, describing the founding and providing of monasteries, churches, bishoprics, archbishoprics, etc.

[9] Gillespy, pp. 469–70.
[10] Pilch, *Literarische Studie*, pp. 173–182.
[11] *Brut*, 5067–94.

Contrary to what may be assumed, however, these expansions on the Christianizing of the Britons do not turn them into a chosen people, even at this early stage of their history. If Laƶamon follows Wace in stating that Telghesinus' prophecy made the Britons accept Christianity readily, he also stresses, in connection with the passage dealing with the Christianization proper:

> Naþeles heo weoren soðden   swiðe awæmmed
> ladliche iniþered   þurh niðfulne craft
> & eft heo weoren irihte   swa hit weolde Drihten
> ...
> þ[u]s heo gunnen driuen   & forƶeten to swiðe
> þat heom tæhte þe hehƶe mon   þe gode biscop Dunian
> & Fagan his i-uære   þe while þe heo weoren here.[12]

This passage, which has no parallel in Wace, is revealing. First, by adding elements that are not strictly necessary for the narrative, Laƶamon appears as a moral historian, giving greater priority to his message than to its medium. On the other hand, the Celtic inhabitants of Britain are shown to be spiritually flawed from the outset: their faith and religious institutions are corrupt before even the death of the king who introduced Christianity to the island. This propensity towards corruption reminds one strongly of Gildas, but the way in which it is expressed, and its general function in the poem, is very close to Bede. As in Bede, it reaches its culmination with the refusal of the Briton bishops to recognize St Augustine's authority; Laƶamon explicitly turns this episode into a confrontation between God's servant and those who hate him for doing his duty:

> For no scal hit nauere iwurðen   a þissere worlde-richen
> þat we auere buƶen   Austine þan uncuðen
> for he is ure fulle ifa   & his iferen al-swa
> For Austin is iboƶen hidere   in-to þissen londe
> and haveð i-fulleƶed þene king   Cantuaren aþeling
> Aðelbert ihaten   heh inne Anglene
> and he hafueð ifunden here   hundes heðene
> þa comen of Sexlonde   mid Gurmu[n]de þan kinge
> þeo he alle fullehteð   and to Gode fuseoð
> þeo haldeoð ure kinelond   mid unrihte on heore hond

---

[12] *Brut*, 5095–7 and 5106–8. 'Nevertheless they were afterwards greatly corrupted, badly debased through evil ways, and afterwards they were corrected; such was the will of the Lord'; 'Thus they went on, and forgot too quickly what the high man had taught them, the good bishop Dunian, and Fagan, his companion, while they were here'. This view of a 'bad' people periodically redeemed by the virtues of their kings is not unlike what we find in the Book of Judges.

Cristine we beoð alle   and of Cristine cunne
and ure elderne swa weoren   agan is þreo hundred ȝeren
& heo beoð neowene icumen   and Cristindom habbeoð
                                                under-numen
and Austin heom fullehteð   and to Gode fuseoð
For ðan we hine hatiȝen uulleð   <& heren [h>ine nulleð]
nauere to ure liue   no scullen we him wurðen liðe.[13]

This passage diverges from Wace mainly in the twice-repeated lament
that the Anglo-Saxons are now reconciled with God. Whereas in Wace
the main argument of the bishops is that they refuse to recognise the
authority of someone who has no right over them either in terms of
ecclesiastical hierarchy or antiquity of seat, the implicit message in
Laȝamon is that now the pagan invaders are converted, the Britons have
lost their moral justification in repulsing them – and that they are aware
of it. The issue is diverted from its purely historical or legal aspect (the
claims of the Celtic church to independence from Augustine), to concentrate on the moral shortcomings of a people who take pride in their
Christian identity, but are incapable of maintaining their religious
inheritance and are totally devoid of charity towards their benighted
enemies – the Britons refuse to help Augustine preach to the Angles.

To claim any intrinsic superiority of the Britons in the English *Brut*
would therefore be an error; Laȝamon actually gives us a darker spiritual
image of them than Wace. Where the 'crusade' aspect appears, it is always linked with one specific king, whose personal virtues keep his
people in the right path. This is especially so in the Arthurian episode,
where Laȝamon consistently adds a reference to God in Arthur's
speeches, thereby reinforcing his 'crusader' image in front of enemies
whose heathen beliefs are equally stressed.[14] Arthur's observance of
church festivals and Lenten fasting is also supplied by Laȝamon: the
Irish expedition only takes place after Easter, when men have fasted
(11133); Arthur enforces church-peace in Ireland (11138); and before his
fight with Frolle, he has psalms sung all night (11842–6 and 11853–5).
Such realistic touches, which are found neither in Wace nor in Geoffrey,
could be due to the pastoral outlook of a parish priest.

13 *Brut*, 14849–64. 'For never in this world shall it be, that ever we bow to Austin the
stranger; for he is a full enemy to us, and his companions also. For Austin has come hither to
this land, and has baptised the king named Æthelbert, lord of the men of Kent, high among
the Angles. And he has found here the heathen hounds who came from Saxlond with
Gurmund the king: he is baptizing and converting to God all those who unjustly hold our
kingdom in their hand. We are all Christians and of Christian kin, and our elders have been
so for the past three hundred years; and they are newcomers, and have taken on the
Christian faith, and Austin is baptizing them and converting them to God. We will for that
reason hate him, and we will not obey him; never in our lives shall we be favourable to
him'.
14 Luces thus invokes Mahoun (*Brut*, 13673), and his allies are explicitly pagan peoples.

There is however one instance where the crusade-element attains greater complexity than elsewhere in the *Brut*. This is in Laȝamon's largely unnoticed expansion connected with Vortimer, whose Christian faith is explicitly and repeatedly opposed to his father's pagan sympathies, and whose savage persecution of the Saxons goes far beyond either Wace or Geoffrey. The equation between the fight against heathendom, the crushing of outlawry and the fight for survival reaches a peak with Vortimer's putting a reward on every Saxon head (*Brut* 7325-8). Here, and here only, does Christianity become the genetic attribute of the Britons, presented as justifying the eradication of the alien ethnic group.[15] Vortimer is consistently presented as the king of the Christians, as opposed to his father Vortigern, king of the heathen. Thus, Wace's

> Li reis creï plus les paiens
> E ama que les crestïens,
> E li crestïen l'en haïrent
> E sun cunseil e lui guerpirent[16]

becomes a vivid statement in direct speech:

> Nulle we nauere-mare   þine iboden here
> ne to þine hirede cumen   ne þe uor king halden
> ah hatien we wulleð   mid hæhȝere strengðe
> alle þine hæðene wines   & hærme igreten
> bidden us to fultume   þat is Crist Godes sune.[17]

Then follows a highly rhetoricized passage, featuring anaphora and repetition, which gives the scene particular dignity:

> Forð iwenden eorles   forð iwenden beornes
> forð iwenden biscopes   & þa boc-ilæred men
> forð iwenden þæines   forð iwenden sweines
> alle Brutleoden   þat heo comen to Lundene.[18]

---

15 Possibly as a result of Welsh influence; see above, chapter 6, pp.147-8.
16 Wace, 7019-22. 'The king trusted the pagans and loved them more than the Christians; and the Christians hated him for it, and abandoned him and his counsel'.
17 *Brut*, 7292-6. 'We will never again obey your command, nor join your retinue, nor recognize you as king, but we will hate with all our might all your heathen friends, and greet them with harm. Let us pray for assistance Christ, who is God's son!'
18 *Brut*, 7297-300. 'Forth went the earls, forth went the lords, forth went the bishops, and the book-learned men, forth went the thanes, forth went the swains, all the British people, until they arrived at London'. This passage expands Wace 7077-9:
> Dunc se sunt Bretun assemblé,
> A Lundres sunt ensemble alé;
> Vortimer unt a rei levé.
'Then the Britons assembled; they went together to London; they raised Vortimer to kingship'.

The Briton rebels therefore comprise bishops and learned men, and the whole passage is stamped with the seal of religious fervour – an element lacking in Wace. Vortimer is made king by 'Al þat folc ... þat luueden þene Cristten-dom' (l.7305); Laȝamon portrays him as an explicit 'miles Christi':

> þa wes Vortimer   Cristine king þer
> & Uortiger his fader   fulede þan hæðenen.[19]

Whilst such a treatment of the figure of Vortimer may have been suggested by the contrast between him and his father, one may note that Vortimer almost takes on the stature of a first Arthur; he shares with Arthur the epithet of 'young',[20] like Arthur he is a successful defender of the Britons against the heathen Saxons, like Arthur he dies through treachery. Rather than merely anticipating the figure of Arthur, though, Laȝamon's portrayal seems to be influenced by the image of a saintly Vortimer, the crusader who reinstated Christianity in Britain, and died a martyr of heathen duplicity. Thus, Laȝamon puts Vortimer at the heart of the re-Christianizing of Britain, replacing Wace's flat statement that St Germain and St Louis of Treies came from Rome by an elaborate scene where Vortimer is shown greeting the papal envoys bare-foot, and presenting the situation to them in direct speech. Vortimer is presented as an evangeliser himself:

> he wes milde ælche cnafe   & tahte þan folke Godes læȝe
> þan ȝungen & þan ælden   hu heo Cristindom sculden
> halden.[21]

The king's saintly nature is clearly expressed through St German's answer to his words:

> Ich þonkie mine Drihte   þe scop þes daȝes lihte
> þet he swulce mildce   sent to moncunne.[22]

Laȝamon's reshaping of the character of Vortimer thus takes on definite

---

19 *Brut*, 7309–10. 'Then Vortimer was made a Christian king there, and Vortiger, his father, followed the heathens'.
20 Gillespie notes (p. 429): 'He <i.e., Arthur> is conceived as a young man throughout. At the time of his father's death he is fifteen years old and is called Arthur the young (19929). The same epithet is applied later after a considerable time has elapsed (23014)'. (Gillespy's line numbers refer to Madden's edition). In fact, the usual epithets for Arthur in the *Brut* are 'noble', 'keen' or 'bold', though 'young' is applied to him at lines 9944, 10011, 11484.
21 *Brut*, 7387–8. 'He was kind to everyone, and taught the law of God to the people, to the young and to the old, how they should hold the Christian faith'.
22 *Brut*, 7423–4. 'I thank my Lord, who created the light of day, that he sent such grace to mankind'.

hagiographical overtones, even though the king is never actually called a saint.

This case of mistaken hagiography reveals a more widespread taste for saints' lives in the *Brut*, exemplified by Laȝamon's minor expansions on the works and miracles of St Augustine of Canterbury, his mention of St Milburga, and his divergent ending to his account of the life of St Oswald, which betrays considerable research and interest on the poet's part.[23]

Laȝamon's account of Augustine's mission among the English, whilst following Wace quite closely, has the overall effect of a closer focus on Augustine/Austin as a central agent. Where Wace merely states that king Aldebert of Kent

> ... ad saint Augustin oï,
> Baptisiez fu, en Deu creï,[24]

Laȝamon provides a glimpse of Austin giving Athelbert instruction and arousing his desire to be converted before mentioning the baptism proper:

> Aðelberde he talde tidende   of þan heoueneliche kinge
> he seide him þat godd-spel   and þe king him luste swiðe wel
> wel he þat lar-spel unde<r>-nom   an-eouste he ȝirnde
>   Cristindom.[25]

Augustine the teacher is given the overtones of a potential martyr in the episode relating his rejection by the inhabitants of Dorchester. Where Wace has them mock Augustine, Laȝamon also has them stone him. Where Wace has God say to Augustine, in the ensuing vision, 'tu iés mis serfs' ('you are my servant', 13761) in the English version, he is 'þu leof min', 'my beloved' (14784); and Wace's tepid:

> tu me pleis
> E bien me plaist ço que tu fais.[26]

---

[23] To these major instances, one may add the mention of the relics of saints Bride, Brendan and Columba (11178–82) in the Arthurian part of the work. The only instance of omitted hagiography in the English *Brut* – Ursele's martyrdom in Cologne is replaced by the statement that she was killed by Wanis and Melga – must certainly be explained by a lacuna in Laȝamon's Wace-text. Ivor Arnold's edition shows that a group of early manuscripts of the *Roman de Brut* (MSS D L J T) do not include the two lines referring to the martyrdom of Ursule and her companions (6073–4; a piece of information added to Geoffrey's *Historia*).
[24] Wace, 13695–6. He 'heard St Augustine, was baptized, believed in God'.
[25] *Brut*, 14734–6. 'To Æthelbert he told the news of the King of heaven; he preached the Gospel to him, and the king listened to him very intently; he received the teaching favourably, quickly desired to become a Christian'.
[26] Wace, 13761–2. 'I am pleased with you, and what you are doing pleases me well'.

becomes a more emphatic 'þu ært swiðe leof me', 'you are very dear to me' (14787). After this vision, Laʒamon's Austin prays for grace, and tells his companions of 'þa sæʒen of ure Drihten';[27] he takes his staff which he had fixed on the spot of the vision, whereupon a stream surges up from the ground. The order of events in Wace is somewhat different. First, there is no explicit prayer of Augustine's after the vision, but more importantly, the stream surges up as soon as he plants his staff on the holy spot, *before* his thanking the Lord and addressing his companions. The miracle of water in the desert is therefore linked to the quality of the vision rather than to the virtue of the saint. Laʒamon's stress on the spiritual dimension of Augustine prepares the way for another expansion, which completes the hagiographical nature of this episode:

> Sone uolc gadere[de]   to Austin þan gode
> and al bi his læuen   þider gunnen liðen
> and bi-gunnen þer to bulden   bi þan watere þa was hende.
> Moni mon þer uætte hele   [28]

The magnetism of the saint and the miracles performed by the holy stream are regular features in saints' lives. It is noteworthy that, in parallel with these additional elements, we have a substantial reduction of learned details, such as the explanation of the name 'Cernel': Wace's 24 lines (13789–12) shrink to 9 in the English *Brut* (14809–17), whilst the following scene – Austin's baptizing the English – displays in the English poem a wealth of rhetorical adornment, with the repetition, five times, of 'he fullehtede' ('he baptized') + Object, thereby giving a triumphant conclusion to the episode. In Wace, the baptizing of the pagan Anglo-Saxons merely serves as introduction to Augustine's problems with the Celtic church, with no apparent link to the Cernel episode.

The differences between Laʒamon's rewriting of Augustine's early difficulties and Wace's version are not such as to warrant an extra source for the English poet; though the detail of the stones thrown at Austin and the cures effected by his miraculous stream suggests that the English priest knew of the legend of Augustine of Canterbury through other channels than just Wace – as is indeed to be expected with a saint of such stature.[29] What is striking, though, is that the reshaping of the episode

---

27 'The sayings of our Lord'; *Brut*, 14801.
28 *Brut*, 14806–9. 'Soon people gathered around Austin the good; and with his permission, all came there and began there to build by the water that was fair. Many a man obtained health there'.
29 Another version of the miracle of the stream is mentioned by William of Malmesbury, in his *Gesta Pontificum Anglorum*, N. E. S. A. Hamilton ed., p. 185: 'Nam et ibidem cum ab baptismum deesset aqua, ad jussum pontificis ex occultis meatibus fons eripuit, qui hodie-que et Augustini merito et usus sui commodo incolis clarus habetur'. 'For as there was no water there for baptism, at the order of the prelate, a spring surged up from hidden parts

results in a greater emotional impact on the reader. Augustine is no longer an angry, self-righteous man (albeit of God) who gets his own back on the city of Dorchester: he is a saint who risks bodily harm as well as shame, whose miracles are positive (the cure-working stream) as well as negative (the fish-tails), and who is humble enough to pray for grace, even when it is obvious to all that he is well endowed with it. As such, he conforms better with the model expected by the non-clerical listener whom Laȝamon seems to have had in mind when pruning Wace's philological considerations about Cernel, to concentrate on the virtues of the place. Moreover, one may notice that during the unsavoury episode opposing Augustine and the Briton bishops, the saint is pushed determinedly to the background; whereas in the conversion phase he was both the starting-point and the centre of action, he now appears almost exclusively through the words of the Briton bishops. Only four verbs of action are applied directly to Austin: he got in touch ('funde', 14828) with the bishops and archbishop of the Britons; he sent letters to the seven bishops (14836); then, after their answer, he rushed to Athelbert, and 'complained' to him.[30] These are the only intrusions of Austin Laȝamon allows us to see in the action: from then on the saint disappears from the narrative. His responsibility in the ensuing conflict, which leads to the massacre of the monks of Bangor, is correspondingly diminished. The monks of Bangor thus appear as the victims of the ruthless king Ælfric, whom Laȝamon calls 'fur-cuðest alre kinge', 'most wicked of all kings', rather than of Augustine's vindictiveness. Similarly, the horror of the massacre itself is toned down. Wace's exclamation 'Deus, quel dolur! Deus, quel pechié!' is omitted,[31] as also his simile of the ravenous wolf and the sheep, and his likening of the Briton victims to martyrs.[32] The only explicit sign of disapprobation in the English *Brut* is the remark that the monks were slain '[mid] unrihtes', 'unjustly'.[33]

The part of the *Brut* dealing with Augustine therefore betrays a tendency towards a systematic reappraisal of the saint, by emphasizing his responsibility in the christianizing of the pagan Saxons, and by underplaying his role in the less saintly aspects of his mission. In other words, Augustine is here an idealized rather than a historical character, and the episode bears the obvious mark of the hagiographical genre.

By contrast, the reference to St Milburga is extremely terse and cryptic.

---

which today still, through the merit of the prelate, is well-known by the inhabitants for its properties'.

[30] *Brut*, 14868–71: '[he] fuse him gon sone and ferde to þan kinge and mænde to [Aðel]berte'.

[31] Wace, 13917. 'Lord, how terrible! Lord, what a sin!'

[32] Wace, 13924: 'Martirs firent des cumfessors'; 'they made martyrs of the confessors'.

[33] *Brut*, 14919. It may be, however, that the crime was so heinous that the English poet felt that the facts spoke for themselves.

Indeed, we are not even told she is a saint; line 15478 merely reads (talking about Penda):

he wes Mærwales fader   Mildburʒe alde-uader.[34]

This Mildburʒe was obviously a well-known character to Laʒamon's first audience, and the reason for inserting this remark 'quite irrelevantly' (to quote Tatlock) in the middle of the story of Penda was presumably to spur on interest in the narrative through a local reference. One may notice moreover that this 'backward' pedigree occurs just before Penda is about to gain in stature – and wickedness – by allying himself to Cadwalan: Penda is justified by his fruits, so to speak. Milburga is known to us through William of Malmesbury, *inter alia*; she founded a convent in 680 at Wenlock, in Shropshire, some twenty miles from Areley, became an abbess and attained sainthood. Her house was revived in 1080 by Cluniac monks, and her relics are said to have performed many miracles of healing. But Milburga's fame did not spread very wide, to judge from the location of the six churches dedicated to her;[35] except for one in Wales, all of them are in Shropshire or in neighbouring counties; and there was one in Worcestershire, not far from Areley, at Offenham. Milburga was therefore very much a local saint, and the simple fact that Laʒamon did not need to explain who Milburga was points towards his having written for a local audience.

Penda, the ancestor of St Milburga, is also connected with another saint: he is the slayer of St Oswald, whose life-story in the *Brut* diverges strongly from Wace, Geoffrey, and Bede. Laʒamon's introductory lines on Oswald underline the legitimacy of his claim to the throne of Northumberland. Where Wace merely states that Oswald inherited the kingdom and was noble (the stress being put more on his Christianity), the English poem repeats three times that Oswald was of Edwine's kin, the only one left after Cadwalan's persecution of the family. Cadwalan and Penda's hounding of Oswald therefore appears as totally unjust, and Cadwalan's speech (an addition of Laʒamon's) shows him up as a megalomaniac, unwilling to accept the existence of any other king but himself.[36] When they come to battle, Oswald is 'þas heʒes Godes icorne', 'the chosen one of the high God';[37] and if Cadwalan delivers the care of

---

[34] 'He was the father of Mærwal, the grandfather of Milburga'.
[35] See F. Arnold-Forster, *Studies in Church Dedications: or England's Patron Saints*, vol. II: 379–81 and vol. III: 21, 429. Arnold-Forster gives no precise indication as to the period these dedications go back to, except that four of them are pre-Reformation. She does not cite any specific source or justification.
[36] *Brut*, 15625–32. This speech is interesting also in that it contains a series of vows strongly reminiscent of the Anglo-Saxon 'beot'.
[37] *Brut*, 15635. This expression recurs at line 15665: 'he wes to Godes hond icoren', 'he was chosen to God's hand'.

pursuing the retreating Oswald to Penda, it is not due to weariness and
unwillingness to tire his men, as in Wace, but out of fear, because of all
the evil he has done to the northern folk. The cowardice of Cadwalan is
explicitly opposed to Oswald's reluctance (in the English poem) to forsake this first encounter with his enemy. Oswald thus appears as a perfect epic hero, noble and dauntless, as well as a man favoured by God;
and Laȝamon gives him a heroic death, like that of Vortimer, Uther or
Arthur: through treason. The English *Brut* has Penda suggest a compact
to Oswald; they meet at Heavenfield to make amity, not to make battle, as
in Wace and other sources. There, Oswald erects a great cross and bids
his army pray, not in anticipation of a forthcoming fight, but in order
that the Lord should avenge them should Penda break the peace. Penda
arrives, addresses Oswald in direct speech, advising him to send a
number of expensive gifts to Cadwalan with a greeting, in order to effect
reconciliation, and suggests a counsel between the two of them, accompanied by just two of their men. Oswald thus rides on, unarmed, and is
slain by Penda. Only then does Laȝamon specify the saintly nature of the
king:

> þis wes Seint Oswald   þe amurðered wes aquald.[38]

Oswald's knights react immediately, and Penda escapes with difficulty:

> and neoðeles he at-ræd   þe Seint Oswald biswac.[39]

The episode ends in Cadwalan's rejoicing, though not without some
uneasiness.[40] By comparison, both Wace and Geoffrey state that Oswald
won the battle of Heavenfield, but was finally killed by the joint forces of
Penda and Cadwalan.

The reason for such a version of Oswald's death being more congenial
to Laȝamon's global conception of the history of Britain is readily perceived. It completes the reversal of sympathies effected in the Augustine
episode; the Christian Britons fighting against the pagan Saxons have
turned into the saint-killing persecutors of the righteous Angles. Though
both parties are now Christian, the linking of the Britons with the
treacherous Penda puts them in the same moral position as the Roman
emperor allied to the heathens, in the Arthurian episode. This is clearly
demonstrated in Laȝamon's reworking of the Oswi episode, the overall
effect of which is totally different to that of his source. Where Oswi, in
Wace, begins his reign by submitting to Cadwalan, Laȝamon states that

---

[38] *Brut*, 15688. 'This was Saint Oswald, who was put to death, murdered'.
[39] *Brut*, 15694. 'And nevertheless he escaped, he who deceived Saint Oswald'.
[40] *Brut*, 15698: 'hit of-þuhte him ful sone for þan swikedome'.

the northern chiefs made him king, thereby suggesting some degree of independence from the British king. Where Penda merely answers the Northumbrian rebels that he must have Cadwalan's permission before attacking their new king, Laȝamon has him express personal enmity, in direct speech, and his fear that Oswi may avenge Oswald's death; whilst his condition before helping them is not Cadwalan's permission as much as an allowance in money and men. Penda's motivation thus appears to be fear of the consequences of his past actions, and his relationship with Cadwalan, one of interest rather than of loyalty. Laȝamon further underlines Penda's deviousness by having him prepare the way, by sending Oswi's opponents to Cadwalan 'mid falsæn dome'.[41]

The dichotomy between the Christian outer image of the Britons and their actions is stressed in the Whitsun crown-wearing scene. The setting is similar to the Whitsun gatherings of the Arthurian section: first, messengers bearing a summons, then an enumeration of the different estates assembled, including bishops and 'book-learned men', culminating in the statement that the king was 'man most true, his truth he well held'.[42] However, the similarity ends there: for where Arthurian Whitsuntides lead to rejoicing and prospects of glorious victories, here, we have Penda with 'false his spellen'[43] expanded into a full direct speech, wanting to punish Oswi for his absence at the gathering. Whereupon Cadwalan, after feebly suggesting that Oswi may have been taken ill, takes counsel. It must be admitted that the scene in Wace is far more convincing: Penda first remarks on Oswi's absence; Cadwalan replies that Oswi is ill; at which Penda accuses Oswi of raising troops in Saxony to wage war on the king, and offers his service to destroy the traitor; whereupon Cadwalan decides to take counsel with his men on the matter. Laȝamon's modification has the double effect, however, of focusing the attention on Penda as an agent (through the usual device of direct speech), whilst underlining his influence over the king. He needs to be far less convincing to obtain what he wants. The mention of troops coming from Saxony is also deleted, and any suggestion that Oswi could be other than perfectly innocent is carefully avoided. The speech of Margadud, which follows Cadwalan's suggestion that he send Oswi a second summons (a detail not in Wace) is deliberately rendered ineffective to the reader by its virtual absence of rhetorical figures: by contrast, in Wace, it is a striking passage, with a four-times repeated anaphora of 'membre vus', 'remember', (*Roman*, 14583–6). The English *Brut* thus gives more weight to the hatred within the speech rather than to the grounds for this hatred; the stress is on the cynicism of the Britons, who clearly

41 'with calumny'. *Brut*, 15734.
42 *Brut*, 15746: 'for þe king wes swiðe treowe mon his treouþe wel he iheold'.
43 'His false speech'. Brut, 15749.

have no more respect for their ally Penda than for their putative enemy. The assent given to Margadud's words is further enhanced by the addition of a man expressing his approval, in direct speech, in words directed to Cadwalan himself. Cadwalan 'the most true' is therefore at the head of *untrue* men, who out of ethnic hatred are prepared to endorse a murderous expedition against a loyal man; and the wholesale mortality which occurs in the following reign – that of Cadwalader, leading to the final loss of Britain for the Britons – may be seen as divine retribution.

Laȝamon's modification of the account of St Oswald's death is therefore amply justified on artistic grounds, for it provides both a foil to the massacre of the monks of Bangor, and a decisive impulse in the blackening of Cadwalan's reign, through the medium of Penda. The treacherous slaying of Oswald is a turning-point, where the negative image given by the Briton clergy in the Augustine episode is extended to the whole of the Briton nation, to be confirmed in the Oswi incident.[44]

But such a significant change, however convenient its effects, is difficult to justify on merely artistic or ideological grounds: for, as is stressed in the Prologue of the *Brut*, the poem is supposed to be 'soðere word'; and indeed, Laȝamon's additions are all minor, or are based on clues provided by the Wace-text, or proceed from additional information which the poet wished to merge into his material. A case in point would be the reference to eye-witnesses to Merlin's trance, or the addition of tales relating to Arthur. Such an important divergence from the Wace-text, on a matter, moreover, of national history, strongly suggests that Laȝamon chose here to echo an alternative tradition about St Oswald, where Oswald's death would have been made to conform better to the canons of saintliness and martyrdom. This alternative version of the life and death of Oswald is not represented in any of the major historians of Laȝamon's time, while Wace, Geoffrey and Bede all agree that the saint was killed in battle. Pilch notes that 'Nennius' suggests that Penda killed Oswald by unfair means: 'per dolum', 'per diabolicam artem'.[45] This could indeed be the starting point for a tradition of death by treachery. More revealing than 'Nennius', however, is the analogue with the *Chronicon* of Helinandus de Frigidi Montis (Hélinant de Froidmont) pointed out by Pilch. This Cistercian monk, who is known mainly for his poem *Les Vers de la Mort*, wrote under the 643 entry of his *Chronicon*:

---

[44] On this reversal of the role of the Britons, see also C. V. Friedlander, 'The Structure and Themes of Layamon's *Brut*'.

[45] Pilch, p. 69. The reference is to 'Nennius', paragraph 65. See *Nennius. British History and The Welsh Annals*, John Morris ed. and transl., p. 39. The *Historia Brittonum* first mentions that Penda killed Anna king of the East Angles and St Oswald, king of the Northerners by treachery ('per dolum'); we are then told that Penda's victory was due to the 'arts of the Devil', for he was never baptized.

643. Oswaldus rex a Penda Merciorum rege perimitur. Hujus dex-
tera multarum eleemosynarum largitrix cum brachio et cute et
nervis incorrupta jacet, tot reliquo corpore in cineres dissoluto.
Excitata rebellione a Penda rege Merciorum, ipse Oswaldus fraternam salutem in pectore gerens, pro animabus fidelium suorum Deo
supplicabat. Hujus defaucti brachia cum manibus et capite insatia-
bilis victoris ira desecta, et stipiti appensa sunt; brachium cum
manibus, adhuc inviolata durant.[46]

Helinandus' vignette is a more promising starting-point for the sort of
tradition echoed by Laȝamon than the vague suggestion of foul play in
'Nennius': 'fraternam salutem in pectore gerens' implies (albeit in an
ambiguous way) that Oswald was killed unawares, out of the formal
battle context. The probability of Laȝamon's indebtedness to Helinandus, however, is slight. The *Chronicon* covers the period between 635 and
1202; it was therefore composed roughly at the same time as the *Brut*.
Even assuming a late *terminus ad quem* for Laȝamon's poem, the chances
for a manuscript of the *Chronicon* to have crossed the Channel are scarce:
Vincent de Beauvais attests that by 1208 already, Helinandus' work was
extremely difficult to find.[47] We must therefore assume that somehow,
Helinandus and Laȝamon had access to a common source; and one may
notice that the passage from Helinandus bears a great resemblance to
William of Malmesbury's account of the reign of Oswald, in his *Gesta
Regum Anglorum*, in particular in the statement that Oswald's right hand
was preserved from corruption due to his liberality, which corresponds
almost word for word with the *Chronicon*:

dextra ille regalis, tantarum eleemosinarum largitrix, hodieque cum
brachio, cute et nervis, incorrupta viget; totum vero corpus reli-
quum, praeter ossa, in cineres dissolutum, communiorem mortali-
tatis non evasit.[48]

---

46 *Helinandi Frigidi Montis Monachi necnon Guntheri Cisterciensis Opera Omnia*, J. P. Migne,
Patrologia Latina vol. 212, col. 775: '643. King Oswald is killed by Penda king of the Mercians.
His right hand, which donated so many alms, remains incorrupt with its arm and skin and
tendons, whilst all the rest of the body has gone to ashes. Rebellion having been fostered by
Penda king of the Mercians, the same Oswald prayed God for the souls of his faithful
(followers), bearing in his heart a brotherly greeting. His arms with his hands were torn
away, and his head cut off, and empaled in the insatiable fury of victory; an arm remains
inviolate to this day, with the hands'.
47 See Migne, *Patrologia Latina*, vol. 212, cols. 477–82.
48 *Willelmi Malmesbiriensis Monachi. De Gestis Regum Anglorum Libri quinque; Historiae
Novellae, Libri tres*, William Stubbs ed., vol. 1, book 1, paragraph 49, pp. 50–54. 'This royal
right hand, which gave so many alms, remains incorrupt to this day with its arm, skin and
sinews; but all the rest of the body except the bones dissolved into ashes, and did not escape
the more common lot of mortality'. Oswald's generosity and the preservation of his right
hand is mentioned also in Bede III, 6, and in Ælfric.

The mention in Helinandus of Oswald's persistence in prayer, even at the approach of death, also coincides with the *Gesta Regum*. The hint at treachery while Oswald was 'fraternam salutem in pectore gerens', however, is nowhere found in William's work,[49] and points in its very ambiguity towards a non-historical tradition connected with the saint; a possibility supported by Malmesbury's 'vulgatum quoque est', 'it is said that', introducing this 'hagiographical' part of his account.

This hypothesis is confirmed to some extent by Oswald's legend in the *South English Legendary*, which reads:

> Atte toune of Marsfeld hy smite togadere faste
> Ac seint Oswold þis holyman aslawe was attelaste
> And imartired of þis luþer men for oure Louerdes loue.[50]

The 'imartired' indicates more than mere death in battle, and suggests an alternative tradition as to the exact way Oswald was killed. Moreover, the mention by Helinandus and William of Malmesbury of the surviving parts of the body of the saint implies the existence of centres where the relics of Oswald were venerated, and which would presumably have fostered a number of saintly anecdotes concerning him. It is therefore reasonable to assume that Laȝamon's version of the death of Oswald is derived from some legend (presumably oral) which arose in one of these shrines. The probability that this was so is reinforced by William of Malmesbury's account of what happened to Oswald's relics. Whilst expressing strong doubts as to whether they were really still in existence, William mentions that Oswald's head was said to be at Durham, and that the bones of his body were first kept in Bardney, not far from Lincoln, then transferred to Gloucester. It therefore appears that Oswald's relics were preserved in a neighbouring county to Worcestershire, and that Laȝamon was well placed to hear of the more or less spurious legends circulating about the saint. One may add, moreover, tnat the proximity of such a shrine to Worcestershire probably meant that the local audience of

---

[49] The corresponding passage in Malmesbury's *Gesta Regum* reads: 'rebellione per Pendam regem Merciorum excitata, cum stipatoribus fusis ipse quoque ferratam silvam in pectore gereret, nec atrocitate vulnerum, nec mortis confinio, potuit argui quin pro animabus fidelium suorum Domino Deo supplicaret' (Stubbs, vol. 1, p. 52). 'Rebellion having been fomented by Penda king of the Mercians, as his escort had been dispersed and he himself was bearing in his breast a forest of iron, neither the atrocity of his wounds nor imminent death could prevent him from interceding to the Lord God for the souls of his followers'. It is clear, in this text, that Oswald dies praying for the souls of his followers, without this indicating in the least that he was slain by treachery or unexpectedly.
[50] *The South English Legendary, Edited from Corpus Christi College Cambridge MS 145 and British Museum MS Harley 2277 with Variants from Bodley MS Ashmole 43 and British Museum MS Cotton Julius D IX*, Charlotte D'Evelyn and Anna J. Mills eds., Corpus Christi version, vol. II, p. 358; lines 33–35. 'At the town of Marsfeld they fought together stoutly; but St Oswald this holy man was finally slain and was martyred by these evil men, for the love of our Lord'.

the *Brut* also knew these legends, and expected to hear the familiar version of the story, rather than the official one.

This would not be an isolated instance of Laʒamon's use of oral saints' legends. P.J.Frankis suggests that the *Brut*'s expanded version of the episode of Gregory and the English slaves may have been derived from a Life of Gregory which was later written down in the *South English Legendary*.[51] The basis for this hypothesis is limited to the agreement on the number of slaves at the market-place (both the *Legendary* and the *Brut* mention three); however, it offers some confirmation that the English poet took an interest in the stories told about certain saints. Indeed, the case of St Oswald suggests that Laʒamon actually gave more credence to traditions heard at a saint's shrine than to his written authorities. Because the English poet's departures from Wace are not 'in the direction of historical fact', A.C.Gibbs considers that 'Laʒamon, even by the standards of Wace and Geoffrey of Monmouth, is not a responsible historian'.[52] This, however, is an overstatement: Laʒamon does not disregard historical fact, but looks for it in different quarters. Whether this is due to the fact that the poet was also a priest engaged, it would seem, in a pastoral activity, is difficult to say: but the conventions of hagiography seem to have influenced him strongly, and he obviously considered that saints' lives carried more weight than chronicles, even those written by Bede himself.

What is striking in considering Laʒamon's hagiographical expansions is that with the exception of Vortimer (who is never actually called a saint anyway), all the cases occur in what may be termed the 'pro-English' section of the *Brut*, and are either connected with the actual Christianizing of the Angles (Gregory, Augustine), or deal with English saints (Milburga, Oswald). Of the Briton saints (or saintly figures) mentioned at one point or another of the *Brut*, none is the object of any elaboration, with the exception perhaps of Helen, for whom Laʒamon provides a description of her arrival at Jerusalem with a rich retinue, and obtaining the Holy Rood by promising money to the Jews.[53] Laʒamon's account of

---

51 See P.J.Frankis, 'Laʒamon's English Sources', pp.70–1. If one accepts Frankis's suggestion that the account of the death of Gratian may be derived from the legend of St Kenelm, and the name of his slayers taken from Felix's life of St Guthlac, Laʒamon's debt to hagiography would seem even greater.

52 Gibbs, *Literary Relations*, p.206.

53 Laʒamon (5565–73) expands Wace's four lines into nine. Wace 5721–4 reads:

> En Jerusalem trespassa,
> Tuz les vielz Judeus assembla,
> Si fu par li la croiz trovee
> Ki lunges out esté celee.

'She went over to Jerusalem, assembled all the old Jews, and the Cross was found by her, which had long been hidden'. This isolation of Helen among the Briton saints is all the more striking as there is no lack of saintly figures in the first part of the *Brut*.

Archbishop Guencelin's embassy to Brittany for help apparently provides another counter-example; Wace's

> Par le conseil de ses evesques
> En Armoriche trespassa [54]

is indeed expanded into a vivid scene, where Guencelin summons all the clerics of Britain to him, and addresses them in direct speech, exposing the necessity for him to seek help, and enjoining them to pray for him while he is away. However, the English poet inserts in the middle of this scene a mention of St Augustine, with all the negative connotations this retrospectively entails for the Briton clergy.[55] Moreover, Laȝamon deletes the 'Christus vincit, Christus regnat, Christus vincit et imperat' with which Wace (6415–6) has Guencelin greet Aldroën's decision to grant help to the afflicted Britons. This may be explained to some extent by Laȝamon's desire to make his work more intelligible to a lay audience; but as he did not hesitate to *add* Latin earlier in the scene (*Brut* 6313–4: the archbishop greets the Briton clergy with 'Pax vobis', and they answer 'Et cum spiritu tuo'), this explanation fails to convince entirely.[56] The poet could have given an English paraphrase for the 'Christus' passage, as he did for the 'Pax vobis' passage. An alternative – a more probable one – is that Laȝamon did not wish to delay the account of Constantin's campaign. As a result, the archbishop is reduced to the position of a mere envoy, rather than a man of God seeking help against a heathen enemy: a sure sign that Laȝamon was not much concerned with that aspect of things at this point in the narrative.

The 'Crusade' theme detected by a number of critics in the *Brut* cannot therefore be ascribed to any especial stress on the worthiness or saintliness of the Britons, but rather to the obviously heathen nature of their opponents. The obstinate heathendom of the Saxons is expressed repeatedly, be it in Rouwenne's pretence at wanting to become a Christian, or the feigned conversion of Octa and his men. The Saxon apostasy is further underlined in the English poem through the explicit statement that Octa and his companions were baptized, thereby preparing the reader for the crusade-like quality of the reigns of Aurelius and Arthur.

---

[54] Wace, 6330–1. 'He went over to Brittany on the advice of his bishops'.
[55] Wace mentions the change of the seat of the archbishopric from London to Canterbury, but modestly says 'ne sai par quel achaisun' (6327) 'I know not for what reason'.
[56] One may object that the Latin words introduced by Laȝamon are more familiar than those in Wace, and therefore easier to understand for a lay audience; and that it was more logical to have an ecclesiastic speak to fellow priests in Latin than to a king. However, the 'Christus vincit' passage is eminently relevant, addressed to a king who is about to launch a 'crusade'; moreover, the relative difficulty of the two Latin passages in question is somewhat secondary, as Laȝamon found it necessary to paraphrase even his 'easy' Latin.

But the 'crusade' aspect itself is barely elaborated by Laȝamon.[57] Even his characteristic 'heathen hounds' (for the Saxons) has a parallel in Wace, who calls the Saxons 'dogs' on a couple of occasions. As for the virulent statement repeated throughout the *Brut* that the Saxon souls sink to Hell, and the prayers the Britons make for their eternal damnation, they may be considered as the expression of the popular belief that only Christians could hope to attain the bliss of heaven; and one may note that the idea occurs well before the Saxon section, with Laȝamon's deploring that such a man as Julius Caesar should have been doomed to Hell. What the English poet *does* tend to elaborate upon, however, are the descriptions of the atrocities perpetrated by the Saxons on the defenceless members of the Briton society, and especially the clerics and the women.[58] Rape and blood-lust is a recurrent characteristic of Laȝamon's heathen villains, be they the pirates Wanis and Melga or the Mt St Michel giant. The Saxons thus have all the attributes of the arch-enemy. They are heathen through choice, having consciously rejected the chance offered to them by Aurelius, and their only wish is to destroy Christendom on the island, and reduce the Britons to their level. This threat is clearly expressed in the Gurmund episode:

> And þe king hehte   al þa[t] hine lufede
> þat whar-swa heo mihten finde   Bruttes i þissen londe
> þat h<i>ne anan sloȝen   oðer mid horsen to-droȝen
> buten he libben wolden   his lif in þral-dome
> and for-saken Godes mæsse   and luuien hæ[ð]enesse
> þenne moste he libben   þeou a þisse londe.[59]

This episode, which culminates in the destruction of the Briton power and the breaking down of the Christian faith, recalls the undercurrent theme within the *Brut* that the Britons lack spiritual determination and fortitude, expressed in a parenthesis in the very account of the Christian-ization of Britain under Luces. They are a flawed people, capable of

---

[57] C. V. Friedlander, 'Accentual Verse', p. 226, and 'The Structure and Themes of Layamon's *Brut*'; or, to a lesser extent, Pilch, *Literarische Studie*, 173–182.

[58] The *Brut* has two main expansions on such passages: 7671–3, after the massacre at Amesbury:

> Mete heo ferden   al þat heo funden
> heo for-læiȝen þa wif   & Godes laȝen breken
> heo duden i þan londe   al þat heo wolden

'The food they took away, all that they found; they raped the women and broke God's law; they did in the land all that they wanted'; and in the Gurmund episode, 14537–43 and 14651–3, where we are told that monks were tortured, noble women turned into whores, priests slain, churches destroyed, clerics killed, children slain and knights hanged.

[59] *Brut*, 14662–7. 'And the king commanded to all who loved him, that wherever they might find a Briton in this land, that they should immediately slay him or quarter him with horses, unless he accepted to live his life in slavery, and forsake God's mass, and love the heathen ways; then he would be allowed to live as a slave in this land'.

producing a Vortimer, an Aurelius or an Arthur, yet prone to following
fiends like Vortigern, whose contempt for the Church is apparent from
the outset through Laȝamon's elaborate expansion of the scene where
Constantine's abbot is forced to unhood him, even before Vortigern has
cast in his lot with the Saxons.[60]

The struggle throughout the Saxon period cannot therefore be defined
in terms of pure Good against pure Evil. The cause of the earlier Briton
kings is just, because they are Christians confronted with the servants of
the devil; but that they are unworthy of the grace bestowed upon them is
intimated from the reign of Luces onwards. The reader is thus prepared
for the reversal of sympathies which occurs immediately after the statement that Christianity was wiped out in England for a hundred years
(implying that the Britons have accepted Gurmund's heathen thral-
dom).

At this point, where Wace goes on directly to relating the mission of St
Augustine, Laȝamon makes a clear break, introducing a new element:

> Bisiden Allemaine is a lond   Angles ihaten.[61]

A new element – yet not so new. What is happening is that the Germanic
invaders are being re-introduced to the reader; but not as Saxons. As
Angles. That is, as the people who gave England its name. This ono-
mastic anecdote is also in Wace (13643–52), but in the *Roman*, it remains
firmly connected with the 'Sednes'. Though the narrative states clearly
that Gurmund had promised the kingdom to the Saxons, we are now told
that it is in fact held by the Angles: as though, suddenly, we were confronted with another people. On a formal level, indeed we are: I. J. Kirby
notes that the Saxons virtually disappear from the poem from this point
onwards, and there is reason to believe that Laȝamon himself thought of
Angles and Saxons as two related, yet somehow different peoples.[62] The
situation is therefore changed. We no longer have God's enemies versus
God's soldiers, but God's chosen people, the angelic Angles, opposed by
the erring Britons.[63] And as such, it is fitting that Laȝamon should have

---

60 One may also mention Modred, who does not hesitate to seek heathen allies to support
his unjust cause; this detail, however, is also to be found in Wace.

61 *Brut*, 14668. 'Beside Alemaine is a land named Angles'.

62 See I. J. Kirby, 'Angles and Saxons', and A. C. Gibbs, 'Literary Relations', p. 200. Madden
notes a similar distinction between Angles and Saxons in Robert Manning of Brunne's
paraphrase of Wace's *Roman de Brut* (see Madden III, 416–8). The origin of this misconception may be due to an ambiguity in Laȝamon's Wace-text, which we know to have been
close to that used by Manning.

63 It is striking that of the eight Briton kings mentioned after Arthur's death, only two are
depicted in an altogether positive way. Constantine, Arthur's successor, kills Modred's two
sons in churches, thereby spurning the protection of the Church. Though Laȝamon does
not explicitly condemn this double murder (whereas Wace does), he aggravates Constantine's position by stating that Meleon's blood covered the altar of St Amphibalus – the

reworked the last part of the *Brut* to read as political hagiography: the insuperable ascension of the people chosen by God, whose abundant grace is perceptible from its saintliness, which culminates on the worldly level with the successes of the reign of Æthelstan and the institution of Peter's Pence.[64]

Moreover, this first mention of Æthelstan, well before his reign, places him in direct relationship with the reader. He is not just the king of England, like Cadwalan; he is the king *of this people*, 'of þissere leode' (14940), thereby suggesting an emotional continuity from his reign that we do not find with his predecessors. This feeling that Æthelstan belongs to a different epoch than all the kings presented up to that point in the *Brut* is confirmed by Laȝamon's account of Æthelstan's coming to the throne, while Cadwalader is in Brittany, seeking refuge from the plague. Laȝamon deletes Wace's lengthy exposition of the meaning of different words in Welsh and English: Britons and Welsh disappear, swallowed up in the great mortality inexorably described over eight lines where the verb 'quelen' is repeated no less than ten times. Æthelstan is a new king in a new land, and Laȝamon admits of no limits in expressing his power.[65] In supplying a scene where Æthelstan himself goes to Rome to renew the vow of his ancestor Inne (while in Wace, it is Edward who renews Peter's Pence), this first English king is also legitimized as a Christian king whose reign, firmly grounded in faith and in respect of the Church, is made to last.[66]

Hagiography may therefore be considered as a powerful influence on the *Brut* as a whole, and an important source of information in the latter

---

abomination is such that no words are needed. Constantine's successor, Conan, is not only an incestuous and bad king, but obtains his crown by betrayal and poisoning (Wace mentions neither incest nor poisoning). The homosexuality of Malgus is extended in the English *Brut* to the whole of Britain; and Cadwalan is a puppet in the hands of bad counsellors who cause his enmity with Edwine and the slaying of St Oswald. Of the remaining kings, Vortiporus is a mere name. Margadud and Cadwan are presented as *Welsh* kings. Carric, of whom Laȝamon says a lot of good, fails to fulfill his royal duties and lacks authority. As for Cadwalader, his main virtue is his renunciation of his birthright.

[64] The 'predestined' nature of the English is also hinted at by Bede, in the first book of his *Historia Ecclesiastica*. This may perhaps have contributed to the outlook of the *Brut*. On the importance of this episode of British history for different historiographers, see Leckie, *The Passage of Dominion*.

[65] This impression is reinforced by the absence of Wace 14759–80:

> ... ot tute l'Angleterre en baille
>
> Fors sul Guales e Cornuaille.

'He held sway over all England, with the sole exception of Wales and Cornwall'. This however may be due to a lacuna in the Wace-MS; the two lines in question are missing in MS H.

[66] The 'sanctifying' function of the anecdote suggests that Laȝamon's controversial 'Drihten wat hu longe þeo laȝen scullen ilæste', 'God knows how long the law will last' (15964) may express the poet's sense of social rupture following the Norman invasion, and his pessimism as to the moral steadfastness (and legitimacy!) of the Norman rule, rather than irritation at the tax.

part of the poem. Other genres of religious writing are more difficult to trace. Though a priest, Laȝamon shows little sign of knowing his Scriptures. Not a single element of his expansion of Bishop Eldad's speech urging the execution of Hengest is of biblical origin, despite the fact that Eldad's argumentation refers directly to the death of King Agag, in I Samuel 15, 31–33. Laȝamon actually goes *against* the Scriptures in stating that the execution of Agag took place at the market-place of Jerusalem. The only addition made by Laȝamon which may be called openly biblical occurs in the passage mentioning the birth of Christ, and Teleisin's prophecy to King Kinbelin about the Salvation of mankind.

Wace's mention of the birth of Christ covers five lines (4850–4):

> En sun tens fu nez li Salvere,
> Fiz Deu Jesu, ki del ciel vint,
> Deus ert, mais pur nus huem devint,
> E pur nostre redemptiun
> Suffri en la croiz passiun.[67]

Laȝamon turns the passage into a highly lyrical piece of catechism:

> On Kinbelines dæie   þe king wes inne Bruttene
> com a þissen middel-ærde   anes maidenes sune
> iboren wes in Beðleem   of bezste alre burden
> He is ihaten Iesu Crist   þurh þene Halie Gost
> alre worulde wunne   walden englenne
> Fæder he is on heuenen   froure moncunnes
> Sune he is on eorðen   of sele þon mæidene
> & þene Halie Gost   halded mid him-seoluen
> þene gast he wel daleð   to þan þe him beoð leoue
> al-swa he dude Peture   þe wes a wræche fiscære
> þe makede hine an mancunne   hehst of alre manne.[68]

Laȝamon has added three elements to Wace: the importance of the Virgin, the place of Christ in the Trinity, and the exalted position of Peter. The source for Mary's virginal conception of Christ, the naming of the future child by the archangel Gabriel, Christ's birth at Bethlehem and the

---

[67] 'In his time was the Saviour born, Jesus Son of God, who came from heaven; He is God, but became man for us, and for our redemption He suffered the Passion on the Cross'.
[68] *Brut*, 4521–31. 'In the days of Kinbelin, who was king in Britain, came on this middle-earth the son of a maiden. He was born in Bethlehem, of the best of all maidens: he is named Jesus Christ, through the Holy Ghost, the joy of the whole world, the lord of angels! In heaven he is the Father, the comfort of mankind; on earth he is the Son, of the good maiden; and he holds with himself the Holy Ghost: this Spirit he imparts generously to those who are dear to him, as he did to Peter, who was a poor fisherman, whom among mankind he made highest of all men'.

appointing of Peter as shepherd of the Church is obviously the Gospels. The description of the Trinity, however, betrays a strange conception of the relationship between the Father and the Son, and could be indicative of faulty theology. This distinction between the persons of the Trinity according to their 'locus' reminds one somewhat of Origen's hierarchy within the Trinity according to their function, though too remotely for Origen to have influenced the passage. J. S. P. Tatlock considers this may be an echo of Sabellianism. It is more likely, however, that it is just a case of awkward wording. The passage reveals, though, that Laȝamon was no theologian, for all that he was a priest, and that he was somewhat lacking in perception regarding the finer points of doctrine.

On the narrative level, the inclusion of Peter – and therefore, of the Church – in this passage may be considered as a hint, providing the reader with a key as to how he should react to the incident between the Briton bishops and St Augustine, special envoy of the successor of Peter. It also betrays the poet's interest in such issues as the practical manifestations of the authority of Rome, an interest which reappears in the twice-repeated reference to Peter's Pence.

Teleisin's prophecy takes on much more dramatic lines in Laȝamon. It is placed within a definite framework of cause and effect, being sollicited in order to explain 'strange marvels': because of the birth of a little child in Bethlehem, 'tacnen þer beoð on sterren an monen & on seonnen', 'tokens there are in the stars, in the moon and in the sun'.[69] Kinbelin's request is not due to mere curiosity, as in Wace 4861–3:

> Li preia li reis e requist
> Qu'alcune chose li deïst
> Del tens qui veneit en avant,

but is the result of fear: 'muchele is & stor þe eiȝe'; 'eie is on mon-cunnen'; 'for her-fore is alches londes folc læd-liche afered'.[70]

This particular expansion is doubtless inspired by circumstances surrounding the visit of the Magi to the infant Jesus; the signs in the stars and moon and sun probably refer to the star mentioned in the second chapter of the Gospel of Matthew, and the apocrypha.

Wace's prophecy of Teleusin (five lines, 4844–9, enjoining men not to be sad, for the long-awaited Saviour Jesus Christ has come on earth) is expanded in the English Brut with a reference to sayings 'of yore said',[71]

---

[69] Brut, 4552–3.
[70] Wace, 4861–3: 'The king prayed and requested of him that he tell him something about the time to come'. Brut, 4552–3 and 4557: 'Great and strong the fear'; 'dread is upon mankind'; 'for that reason is the people of each land horribly frightened'.
[71] Brut, 4559. This is implicit in Wace's 'atendu avum nuit e jur', 'We have waited night and day' (4866).

and an impressive list of patriarchs and pre-Revelation men, for whom this advent means the release from 'læðe heore bendes', their hateful bonds in Hell. As noted by Pilch (pp. 39–41), the general tone of this passage is strongly reminiscent of the account of Christ's Harrowing of Hell, such as may be found in the apocryphal *Gospel of Nichodemus*.[72] It also bears a great resemblance to the Old English *Descent Into Hell*.

All these elements, with the exception of Laȝamon's unorthodox conception of the Trinity, were part of general medieval knowledge. More revealing, perhaps, is the omission of Christ's Passion, to dwell on His victory, an attitude akin to that of earlier English poets. The history of the Redemption of mankind is told very much in the tradition of Old English religious poetry, both in the treatment of the subject and the vocabulary: I shall return to this point in the chapter devoted to the English influence on the *Brut*. The image we get is that of a priest who was far from being a mystic, and seemingly did not take an overwhelming interest in such things as biblical exegesis, patristic writings or homiletic material, though one assumes he regarded them with the highest respect, and probably made some use of such material in his clerical duties. Religion in the *Brut* is a practical matter, and it is noteworthy that most of Laȝamon's 'religious' expansions touch the external signs of the Christian faith: fasting at Lent, praying before major crises for help, praising the Lord after victories, and attending mass. Rarely do we have a glimpse of true spiritual life, with the exception of Oswald and, to a lesser extent, Augustine and Cadwalader. It is therefore improbable that the *Brut* should present more than reminiscences of specialised, learned religious writings, and where they do (or may) occur, one would expect them to be of a very general sort, and too vague to be ascribed with certainty to any given source.

Such indeed is the drawback encountered by P. J. Frankis in his study on the influence of Ælfric's homilies on Laȝamon.[73] Frankis notes a number of verbal and syntactical parallels between Ælfric's *De Falsis Diis* and *De Auguriis*, and the passages of the *Brut* dealing with the Christianization of Britain under Luces, the references to divination in the Diana section, and when Vortigern tries to build his tower.

Frankis first suggests that *Brut* 5079–81 betrays the influence of Ælfric's *De Falsis Diis*, 556–9. Both passages thus describe idols (one specific idol, in the case of the sermon) being dragged, then burned. In the *Brut*, the idols are dragged out of their temples to be consumed in a black fire; in Ælfric, the idol's head is dragged through the town and its limbs burned.

However, the burning theme cannot be considered as significant. Bede

---

[72] Also known as the Acts of Pilate. See *New Testament Apocrypha*, E. Hennecke and W. Schneemelcher eds (R. M. Wilson transl.), pp. 444–84.
[73] See Frankis, 'Laȝamon's English Sources'.

himself mentions in his *Ecclesiastical History* that the Saxon idols and heathen enclosures were destroyed by fire under Edwin;[74] Herbert Pilch notes that Bede's *Sibyllinorum Verborum Interpretatio* presents a very close parallel to the passage as a whole, with the mention of the destruction of the pagan idols, their replacement by the Cross, and the killing of those who refused Christianity.[75] Moreover, the Old Testament has a number of instances of idols being destroyed. In Exodus xxxii, 20, Moses takes the Golden Calf, and burns it; the book of Deuteronomy vii, 5 reads:

> Ye shall destroy their altars, and break down their images, and cut down their groves, and burn their graven images with fire;

and other examples may be found in I Kings 13 and II, 14 and 15.[76] The scene could therefore have been suggested to Laȝamon through other sources than Ælfric, and one may suspect that he was drawing on a common fund of imagery.

In the Diana section, Frankis notes five parallels between the *Brut* and Ælfric's *De Auguriis*:

(1) *Brut* 575: 'þe Deouel heo luuede', 'the Devil loved her'; Ælfric 162: 'þe þa leahtras lufodan, þe liciað þam deofle', 'who loved the sins that please the Devil'. The parallel here is limited to the word 'devil', which (as pointed out by Frankis) is also used by Wace in this context (*Roman* 636–7: 'Diane ... diables esteit'). Moreover, the mention that the Devil loved or helped some iniquitous character is not restricted to Diana in the *Brut*.

(2) *Brut* 578: 'a þon heðene lawen me heold heo for hehne godd', 'by the heathen laws she was considered to be a high deity'; 4030, 'heo heolden hine for hæhne godd', 'they held him for a high god'; Ælfric 114: 'Iuno, swiðe healic gyden', 'Juno, a very high goddess'; 128: 'þisne wurðodan ða hæðenan for healicne god', 'the heathens honoured him as a high god'; 136: 'þone macodan þa hæþenan him to mæran gode', 'the heathens made him into a famous god'.

In one case, we have a double parallel with, first, the statement of the heathendom of the worshippers of the idols, and last, the juxtaposition of 'heah' and 'godd'. The first element is commonplace. Laȝamon reminds the reader of the non-Christian status of the early Britons (and later on, of the Saxons) in other passages, such as the description of the festivities after Caesar's initial defeat (8074). The translation of 'deuesse' or 'Deus'

---

[74] *Ecclesiastical History*, II, 13.
[75] Pilch, p. 43. He quotes from Bede, *Opera* I, 1185.
[76] The Bible is quoted from the King James translation.

as 'high/ great god' is also recurrent in the *Brut*. In the example given by Frankis, one may even consider it a straightforward rendering of the *Roman* 644–5:

> Ert l'image bien coltivee
> E tenue ert en grant enur.[77]

Put in its context, the second passage of the *Brut* quoted by Frankis reads:

> þer stoden in þere temple   ten þusend monnen
> þet wes þe bezste cure   of al Brut-londe
> biforen heore mahun   þe heom þuhte mære
> Apolin wes ihaten   heo heolden hine for hæhne godd.[78]

This Frankis further puts in parallel with *De Falsis Diis* 582, 'þe wæs gehaten Apollo', 'who was named Apollo'.

This passage raises two questions: the relevance, once again, of the juxtaposition of the adjective 'high' before the noun 'godd', and the origin of the names Laȝamon gives to his pagan gods. As regards the first point, it may be interesting to examine Laȝamon's list of the Saxon gods. The first thing one may note is a marked tendency for the English poet to qualify 'godd' with an epithet: 'we habbeð godes gode'; Woden, 'ðat is an weoli godd'; Appollin, 'þat is a godd wel idon'; Tervagant, 'an hæh godd in ure lon[d]'; 'ure goden deore'.[79] These epithets denote, on the one hand, faith in the gods; and, on the other, might, power and lofti-ness. The power aspect is further stressed in such lines as 'Mercurius þat [i]s þe hæhste ouer us', 'Mercury, who is highest over us', or

> ȝet we habbeð anne læuedi   þe hæh is & mæhti
> heh heo is & hali   hired-men heo luuieð for þi.[80]

These elements are already in Wace, though to a lesser extent. The attachment of the Saxons to their gods is thus expressed in the *Roman* at line 6783: 'Pur Woden, lur Deu qu'il amerent' ('For Woden, the god whom they loved'); Mercury is called Woden 'par grant religiun' ('with

---

[77] 'The image was much venerated and was held in great honour'.

[78] *Brut*, 4027–30. 'There stood in the temple ten thousand men, the best of all Britain, before their idol, that they considered mighty; he was named Apolin. They believed him to be a great god'. Wace merely states (4317–8):
> Pramist as Deus comunement
> Feste a faire mult haltement
'He promised all the gods that he would hold a celebration with great solemnity'.

[79] *Brut*, 6935–54. 'We have good gods'; Woden, 'who is a mighty god'; Apolin, 'who is a brave god'; Tervagant 'a high god in our land'.

[80] *Brut*, 6943–4. 'We also have a lady, who is noble and powerful; she is noble and holy: retainers love her for that reason'.

great devotion', 6780), and Frea, 'Ki par tut est mult enuree' ('who is greatly honoured everywhere', 6788) has the sixth day of the week devoted to her 'par grant auctorité' ('by great authority', 6791). The juxtaposition of 'heah' and 'god' cannot therefore be considered as a new concept added by Laȝamon; and while his predilection for this construction may possibly be due to some literary influence, it is hardly enough to justify the naming of any specific source.

The same may be said of the pagan gods introduced by Laȝamon in his poem. Apolin, as noted above, is already present in Wace. Only three idols are not to be found in the *Roman de Brut*: Tervagant, Mamilon and Dagon. I do not include Mahoun in my list, as Laȝamon uses it as a generic term meaning 'pagan god', following in that respect medieval French usage. Dagon is also present in Ælfric's *De Falsis Diis*, notes Frankis, who suggests that Laȝamon may have borrowed the name from Ælfric 'rather than the apparently more obvious biblical source'.[81] This hypothesis, however, still leaves us with Tervagant and Mamilon to account for, and is convincing only inasmuch as one accepts the idea that Ælfric had more influence on, or was better known by Laȝamon than the Scriptures.

(3) *Brut* 582: 'þe wile þeo on þan eit-londe wes folc woniende', 'at the time when people were living on the island'; *De Falsis Diis* 104: 'An man wæs eardiende on þam ilande', 'a man was dwelling on that island'. Laȝamon has taken this directly from Wace 643: 'Kant cele terre esteit poplee', 'when that land was inhabited'. 'Cele terre' refers here to Leogice, Diana's island, which is explicitly called an 'ille' at the beginning of the passage (621).

(4) *Brut* 583: 'heo wurðeden þat anlicnes', 'they worshipped the image', is also the exact translation of Wace 644: 'Ert l'image bien coltivee', 'the image was well honoured'.

(5) *Brut* 635–6: Brutus' promise to Diana to make her a temple and an image of red gold ('wrchen hire ane temple and on licnesse of ræde golde') translates Wace 697: 'Temple e image li fereit' ('He would make her a temple and an image'). The only relevant parallel with *De Falsis Diis* 190–4: 'Hi worhtan eac anlicnyssa þam arwurþum godum, sume of smætum golde ... and him hus arærdon þæt hi heton tempel' ('they also made images for the honoured gods, some of pure gold ... and built a house for them that they called temple') is therefore the mention of gold, a detail often added by Laȝamon in descriptive passages, to denote quality and richness. To give but a few examples, the 'vaissel / Plein de vin et de leit novel' (Wace, 657–8; 'vessel full of wine and fresh milk') held by

---

81 Frankis, p. 68. Dagon appears in *De Falsis Diis*, 224–33.

Brutus before his dream, becomes in Laȝamon 'ana scale ... al of reade golde' ('a vessel ... all of red gold', 592); Wace's

> Aveir lur tolirent mult grant,
> Dunt il furent riche e manant [82]

brings about Laȝamon's comment:

> Nefde Brutus nenne swa wreche man   þat gold & pal ne dude
> him on.[83]

Brutus' celebrations, once in the island of Britain, take place 'mid seoluer and mid golde (914, 'with silver and with gold'; unmentioned by Wace); Æstrild in her cellar has 'goldene ponewæs', golden pennies (?), and the coffins of kings are regularly said to have been made of gold (Belin), or inlaid with gold (Nennius). One cannot therefore accept this detail as evidence in favour of the influence of *De Falsis Diis*.

There remains the case of *De Auguriis*. Frankis points out the verbal parallels 'leoten weorpen' (*Brut* 7734, 7740)/ 'hleotað', 'hleotan' (Ælfric 80, 84) and 'wigeling' (*Brut* 7880)/ 'wiglung' (Ælfric 70, 87, 79, 100), meaning 'to cast lots' and 'divination, sorcery', respectively; and a more extensive parallel between *Brut* 7739:

> summe heo wenden to þan wude   summe to weien læten

and *De Auguriis* 129–30: 'Sume men synd swa ablende þæt hi bringað heora lac ... to treowum'; 'Eac sume gewitlease wif farað to wega gelætum'.[84]

As regards the first parallel, 'leoten weorpen' is the exact translation of Wace 7347: 'Cil unt deviné e sorti', 'they have divined and cast lots'. The case of 'wigeling' is more delicate; but to consider it as significant would amount to postulating that the word was exclusively Ælfric's, and that consequently, Laȝamon was using words that his audience did not know. As for line 7739 of the *Brut*, it shows no structural parallel with *De Auguriis*, and the agreement is limited to the fact that both Ælfric and Laȝamon knew that pagan rituals took place in forests and at crossroads.

The evidence brought forth by Frankis therefore fails to convince, partly, as he himself notes, because 'the correspondences are not exact',

---

[82] Wace, 717–8. 'They took very great possessions from them, from which they became wealthy and rich'.
[83] *Brut*, 650. 'Brutus had no man so poor that he did not wear gold and silk'.
[84] 'Some went to the wood, some to the crossroads'; 'Some people are so blind that they take their offerings ... to trees', 'also some stupid women go to crossroads' (Frankis, 'Laȝamon's English Sources', pp. 66–7).

but mainly because most of these passages follow Wace closely, or are recurrent features of the *Brut*, or are of so general a nature that they could be explained by a number of sources, such as the Scriptures.

The overall impression is therefore that Laȝamon's calling did not have as great an influence on his poem as was once thought. The passages which betray scriptural influences are few and far between; the poem's indebtedness to homilies is unlikely; and Laȝamon's attempt to 'explain' the Trinity is a failure. The only religious genre that has left its stamp on the *Brut* is hagiography, which was widely accepted as history in Laȝamon's day, but is now recognized for what it is – literature. More than 'an preost wes on leoden', the Prologue should have read 'an scop wes on leoden'.

8

An Intensely English Poet

The 'Englishry' of Laȝamon (to quote Gwyn Jones)[1] is a commonplace among the critics of the *Brut*. The idea goes back to Sir Frederic Madden, who in his introduction to the poem wrote the very first words on the subject:

> It is a remarkable circumstance, that we find preserved in many passages of Laȝamon's poem the spirit and style of the earlier Anglo-Saxon writers. No one can read his descriptions of battles and scenes of strife, without being reminded of the Ode on Æthelstan's victory at Brunanburgh. The ancient mythological genders of the sun and moon are still unchanged; the memory of the *witenagemot* has not yet become extinct, and the neigh of the *hængest* still seems to resound in our ears. Very many phrases are purely Anglo-Saxon, and with slight change, might well have been used in Cædmon or Ælfric.[2]

One may notice that at no point does Madden suggest indebtedness to any specific Anglo-Saxon source: in effect, he is merely noting Laȝamon's conservative language, his knowledge of pre-Conquest institutions, and the similarity of his treatment of certain themes with that of the older poetry. Moreover, even though Madden calls Laȝamon 'our English Ennius' (p. vii), he firmly places him within *Anglo-Saxon* tradition, a neutral term which has the effect of defusing the modern, nationalistic overtones of 'English'.

Richard Wülcker, in 1876, first made an attempt to find a specific Anglo-Saxon 'model' for Laȝamon's poem, hinting at some influence of *Beowulf*.[3] The result, however, was not very conclusive; to most critics, the 'Englishness' of the *Brut* appeared nebulous, not to say totally subjective. Rudolf Imelmann, in his epoch-making dissertation, dismisses

---

[1] Gwyn Jones, p. xi of his introduction to *Wace and Layamon. Arthurian Chronicles* (Eugene Mason transl.). The title of this section is also quoted from Gwyn Jones, p. xi.
[2] Madden, Introduction, p. xxiii.
[3] Richard Wülcker, 'Über die Quellen Laȝamons', pp. 524–55.

the 'germanischen (englischen) Elemente bei Laȝamon' as having 'keine besondere Bedeutung'.[4] He acknowledges that the smith Wygar may be identical to 'unserem Wieland', that the account of the foundation of Gloucester could go back to a local, English tradition, or that Laȝamon may have been acquainted with *Beowulf*; however,

> es ist kein Zweifel, dass solche Züge ganz vereinzelt sind und den Anteil englischen Überlieferung an dem Werk unseres Dichters als minimal erscheinen lassen.[5]

The issue of English material – which, interestingly enough, has become *Germanic* material under Imelmann's pen – is therefore totally ignored in his discussion. In so doing, Imelmann is subtly rejecting the poem as a whole: it is a refusal to recognize that the English *Brut* may partake to any extent of his own, native culture, the identity of which is emotionally expressed in his *'our* Wieland'. And indeed, Imelmann's dissertation as a whole proceeds from some obscure urge to destruction, systematically negating the *Brut* as a living work of art, to see it only as the reflexion of something else. There is no point in spending much time in presenting Imelmann's arguments in favour of an expanded Wace which Laȝamon slavishly reproduced. G. J. Visser has amply demonstrated that Imelmann's methodology was unscientific, his working assumptions mistaken, and his conclusions incorrect. What is important, though, is the shift which at the turn of the century brings Laȝamon within the realm of Germanic rather than merely English tradition: a shift which, in the socio-cultural background of pre-world-war I Europe, is pregnant with political implications. The main consequence of this for Laȝamon-studies is that the poem will tend either to be defined in antagonistic terms with non-Germanic (i.e., Romance) culture, or else be merged with the 'alien' culture. Imelmann's position partakes of the latter option, and the *Brut* is consequently reduced to its French source.

These two strains run throughout the history of Laȝamon research, gradually blending into a more realistic view of things, but still recognizable as a sort of Anglo-French rivalry, expressing itself on the one side in terms of nationalistic pride, and on the other, through the underlining of the prestige of France and French literature throughout the ages. Imelmann's theory was all the more acceptable at the time as, indeed, French was the dominant culture in Britain even in Laȝamon's day, and English was the language of a vanquished – and therefore, in the political ideo-

---

4 'The Germanic (English) elements in Laȝamon [have] no particular meaning'. Imelmann, *Laȝamon. Versuch über seine Quellen*, p. 2.
5 'There is no doubt that such traits are quite isolated, and the part of the work of our poet derived from English tradition appears to be minimal'. Imelmann, p. 2.

logy of early twentieth-century Europe, an inferior – people. As noted by
A. C. Gibbs:

> Supporters of the 'expanded Wace' theory are ... influenced less by
> textual evidence than by a conviction that it was impossible for an
> English poet, at this time, to do anything more than translate.[6]

The absurdity of such a view is amply demonstrated by the very
existence of *The Owl and the Nightingale*.

That Gibbs should have felt compelled to re-state this 26 years after
Visser's meticulous refutation of Imelmann's theory is an indication of
the vigour of certain preconceptions in academic circles. Indeed, the
'expanded Wace' hypothesis had the support of such prestigious names
as R. H. Fletcher, J. D. Bruce, and even, for a time, R. S. Loomis.[7]

An early representative of an English, (timidly) nationalistic outlook,
F. L. Gillespy, raised a dissenting voice in 1916. Gillespy, comparing the
narrative techniques of Wace and Laȝamon, stressed the Germanic inheritance of the English poet, going as far as to state that:

> Many of the most valuable elements in his work come from the
> Germanic side. He appears to have profited both by English en-
> vironment and by English literary inheritance.[8]

Significantly, Gillespy rejects both Imelmann's expanded Wace and
Richard Wülcker's suggestion of Celtic sympathies in the *Brut*. She
considers that Laȝamon was 'well read in Old English literature', but
prudently abstains from getting involved in any discussion about
sources, to concentrate on the poem itself. As was to be expected,
Gillespy tends to underrate the French element in the poem, and
expresses the relationship between the English *Brut* and the *Roman de
Brut* in terms of relative inferiority or superiority:

> From the point of view of narrative technique, the French *Brut* must
> be considered as solely representative of the Old French line of
> influence. Many of the differences ... can be explained by the
> higher poetic and dramatic power of the English writer, by his
> keener sense of imaginative probability, and his epic tendency.[9]

Gillespy's arguments – the presence in the *Brut* of certain Old English

[6] A. C. Gibbs, 'Literary Relations', p. 1.
[7] The crux of the argumentation for these critics, however, was the origins of the Arthurian legend (insular, i.e. 'British', or continental, i.e. 'French'), rather than the *Brut*'s possible roots in Anglo-Saxon tradition.
[8] Gillespy, p. 510.
[9] Gillespy, pp. 497–8.

concepts as 'wyrd', or the recurrence of formulas such as 'þe fæie feollen'
– are however of a very general nature, and her argumentation lacked
system.

National enthusiasm meets with its most emphatic expression in
Henry Cecil Wyld's 'Laȝamon as an English poet' (1930). Wyld is wildly
hyperbolic in his appreciation of the *Brut*:

> Laȝamon's language is not merely the ancient speech of English-
> men, almost free ... from foreign elements, it is the language of their
> old poetry, as Madden well says; 'at every moment reminding us of
> the splendid phraseology of Anglo-Saxon verse'. Laȝamon is thus
> in the true line of succession to the old poets of his land. His vo-
> cabulary and his spirit are theirs. His poetry has its roots, not
> merely in the old literary tradition, but also ... in the essential
> genius of the race. The intensity of feeling, the wealth of imagery,
> the tender humanity, the love of nature, the chivalric and romantic
> spirit, which distinguish the poetry of Laȝamon would give him a
> high place among the English poets of any age ... The more we read
> the *Brut*, the more we are impressed by the versatility of the author.
> Laȝamon is gifted with an inexhaustible flow of poetical language, a
> tender and graceful fancy, a never-failing vigour and gusto, a wide
> sympathy with, and enjoyment of, every phase of life and action.
> He never fails to interest the reader, whether his theme be drawn
> from his rich stores of legendary lore, from his own observation of
> nature, or whether it be a battle or a banquet.[10]

One may notice the total absence of argumentation. Wyld grossly under-
estimates the importance of Wace's *Roman de Brut*, both as source of the
English *Brut* and as a piece of literature, with statements such as:

> Instead of the matter-of-fact humming and hawing of 'Maistre
> Gasse', Laȝamon contrives to create ... an atmosphere of wonder
> and mystery ... The English version transcends the French in pic-
> turesqueness and human interest ... Laȝamon visualizes a scene
> and a situation ... with a glowing imagination ... quite beyond
> Wace.[11]

Wyld met with a mild rebuke from R. S. Loomis (though not on the
grounds one would have expected), and having made no real contribution on the subject, had relatively little impact.[12]

---

[10] Wyld, pp. 2 and 29.
[11] Wyld, pp. 7 and 10.
[12] See Loomis, 'Notes on Laȝamon's *Brut*'.

G. J. Visser's dissertation, entitled *Laȝamon: An Attempt at Vindication*, was published within five years of Wyld's article; and though Visser does not discuss the problem of Laȝamon's 'Englishness', his outlook is favourable to the poem in that he considers the *Brut* for its own sake; as indeed all subsequent critics were forced to do, following the discredit brought upon Imelmann's theory. As a result, the polarization around the poem, of which Wyld and Imelmann represent the extremes, also tends to recede. Tatlock, Loomis, Schirmer, Gibbs, Pilch – in short, all modern critics acknowledge the influence of Laȝamon's native culture on his poem, as well as his indebtedness to Wace.

To discuss the elements within the *Brut* of an English or Anglo-Saxon origin, or to suggest the influence of an English tradition, presents some difficulties. First, because 'English' and 'Anglo-Saxon' are not strictly synonymous. Laȝamon's 'English' society was the result of a considerable amount of cultural mixture, between the Celtic peoples on its immediate borders, centuries of exchange, peaceful or otherwise, with the Scandinavians, and over a hundred years of French overlordship.[13] Twelfth- or thirteenth-century English tradition was no longer that of the tenth century, and a post-Conquest 'Anglo-Saxon' was 'Germanic' (to take over the terminology of Imelmann or Gillespy) in part only. The restriction of Laȝamon's 'Englishness' to those traits, concepts or literary devices also found in the Old English period is therefore artificial, though necessary, considering the dearth of evidence and the difficulty in interpreting what little has come down to us. Moreover, as the *Brut* is written in English, we find 'Anglo-Saxon' influence on the most basic level – that of language – and language carries with itself its own connotations and cultural specificities. To quote F. L. Gillespy, the 'Germanic' elements in Laȝamon present a very considerable array. For the sake of convenience we shall first examine the areas of general influence, such as

---

[13] The possibility of Scandinavian influence on the *Brut* has been hinted at by a number of scholars: Madden (vol. 3, p. 376) suggests that *Brut*, 10473–80, where Childric's men boast they will make a bridge of Arthur's back and tie his bones with gold thread to hang them on Childric's door, may be slightly reminiscent of the fate of King Ella at the hands of the sons of Ragnar, in *Ragnars Saga Loðbrokar*. Roland Blenner-Hassett ('Two Old Norse Motifs in Lawman's *Brut*') considers that the episode of Locrin and Æstrild betrays echoes of the *Volsunga Saga*, and that of Bladud, of the *Volundarkviða*; and A. C. Gibbs notes in *Ragnars Saga Loðbrokar* a similar device as that used in the *Brut* for the building of Thwoncaster. However, none of these passages, except that pointed out by Madden, make any significant addition of material to Wace's account; while the episode of *Ragnars Saga* referred to by Madden is quite different from the boasting of the *Brut* – Ivar has the blood-eagle cut on Ella's back. See *Volsunga Saga ok Ragnars Saga Loðbrokar*, ed. Magnus Olsen, pp. 167–8. The quest for Scandinavian influence on the *Brut* thus leads to a dead end: a disappointing conclusion, especially as the work of C. E. Wright (*The Cultivation of Saga in Anglo-Saxon England*) and R. M. Wilson (*The Lost Literature of Medieval England*) suggests that some form of *Ragnars Saga* circulated in England in Laȝamon's day.

lexis, to widen our scope to versification and rhetorics, then to recurrent themes ascribed to Laȝamon's Anglo-Saxon (i.e. Old English) heritage. Only then will specific areas of indebtedness which may (or may not) be traced back to a given source, be considered.

A. Vocabulary

It is to be expected that a poem written in a given language, using current words, should evoke for the reader other works in the same language, using similar words. In the case of Laȝamon, this means that the medievalist is bound to hear echoes of Old English literature in the *Brut*, because Laȝamon's English is closer to that of the Anglo-Saxon Chronicle, for example, than to that of Shakespeare. A certain amount of lexical overlap between the *Brut* and the older poetry is thus inevitable. Walter Schirmer notes in particular Laȝamon's 'predilection for those compounds so appreciated in Old English poetry'.[14] It is these compound nouns, continues Schirmer, which account for the Anglo-Saxon aura of the *Brut*. The question therefore arises: were compound nouns a natural part of Laȝamon's style, or do they proceed from a deliberate attempt on the poet's part to re-create the effect of Old English poetry?

J.P.Oakden, in his *Alliterative Poetry in the Middle Ages*, investigates the problem in an extensive study of the nominal compounds in the *Brut*. Oakden's list comprises 411 nominal compounds,[15] a number which remains small in comparison to Old English practice. Of these compounds, 135 occur more than once; 318 are poetic compounds. The majority of Laȝamon's compounds, notes Oakden, 'are of the type which consists of a simple word followed by a descriptive adjective or noun', such as 'dæþsið', 'eorðhus', 'fæiesið', 'feðerhome', etc. Moreover, Oakden points out a number of 'hackneyed compounds' (six compounds with 'burh-', nine with 'here-', eight with 'hired-', eleven with 'kine-', fifteen with 'leod-', six with 'lond-', nine with 'mon-', fourteen with 'sæ-', seven with 'weorld-', eleven with 'wiðer-' and eleven with 'wunder-'), a phenomenon also noted by F.P.Magoun in *Beowulf*, where he found nineteen compounds with 'sæ-', fourteen with 'here-', thirty with 'grið-' and twenty-four with 'wæl-'.[16] It would thus seem, considers Oakden, that

---

[14] 'Vorliebe für die im Germanischen möglichen und in der altenglischen Poesie so beliebten Kompositabildungen'. Walter Schirmer, *Die frühen Darstellungen des Arthurstoffes*, p.65.
[15] This list does not include 'those which were no longer recognized as compounds in any real sense of the term' (J.P.Oakden, *Alliterative Poetry*, vol.2, p.130).
[16] F.P.Magoun Jr., 'Recurring First Elements in Different Nominal Compounds in *Beowulf* and the Elder *Edda*'.

'Laȝamon was in the direct succession of the English and Germanic alliterative poets'.

Of Laȝamon's 411 compounds, 183 are found in both Old English poetry and prose; only 52 were exclusively poetic in the Old English period. However, stresses Oakden, by Laȝamon's time a great many of the Old English prose words had become poetic.

Apart from these 'inherited' compounds, Laȝamon uses 228 compounds not found in Old English, of which six were Old Norse words, and five contained an Old Norse element. This leaves us with 217 entirely English compounds unattested in the older literature; however, 17 of these compounds at least must have existed also in the Old English period, as they have parallels in other Germanic languages.[17] On the other hand, considers Oakden,

> It is not likely that Laȝamon used 200 compounds (the majority of them poetic) which existed in Old English, but which were never recorded.[18]

Laȝamon must therefore have created some himself. A confirmation of this hypothesis may be found in the fact that 261 of Laȝamon's compounds are not used by any other Middle English writer, nor is the majority of them to be found in Old English poetry either. 'The alliterative tradition must have been very much alive', concludes Oakden.

The matter was further examined by A. C. Gibbs in an appendix to his dissertation.[19] From the outset, Gibbs questions Oakden's criteria in establishing his list of compounds. How, for example, did he distinguish the 'real' compounds from those 'which were no longer recognized as compounds in any real sense of the word'? Moreover, Oakden does not analyze these compounds or draw any conclusions from their nature or occurrence, beyond the mention that some had become colourless or fossilized, whilst others are genuinely poetic and original: Gibbs' discussion therefore concentrates on the semantic fields covered by the compound nouns. He notes two major groups of compounds: touching on war and warfare, and on the concept of 'leod'. Of the 'warfare' compounds, ten are based on 'here-', four of which are recorded in Old English; seven are based on 'hired-', two of which are recorded in Old English; three are based on 'duȝeðe', and seven on 'cniht'. The compounds based on 'leod' (fifteen compounds)[20] or 'land' (six compounds)

---

[17] These 17 cases are: 'furbrond', 'heorteblod', 'ifurndaȝen', 'leodfolc', 'nute-scalen', 'onfreond', 'richedom', 'stangraffen', 'sweordbroþen', 'tæuelbrede', 'wadæi', 'wilspel', 'winschence', 'wiðerlaȝen', 'wunderteole', 'wundergod', 'wunderkene'.
[18] Oakden, vol. 2, p. 132.
[19] Gibbs, 'Literary Relations', pp. 270–277.
[20] Gibbs provided slightly different figures, due to his different standards in recognizing a compound.

Gibbs feels are especially important; most of them convey the idea of national feeling.[21] Only six of these compounds are found in extant Old English texts, but a number of parallel compounds may be found in the older literature; for example, the two compounds 'leodscome' and 'lond-sorȝe' recall similar compounds in *Beowulf* ('leod-bealo' and 'leod-hyre'), which also denote a specifically national catastrophe. Gibbs therefore considers these compounds as 'genuinely meaningful', and suggests they underline 'one of Laȝamon's main preoccupations, national unity'.[22]

In terms of distribution, Gibbs shows that compound nouns tend to occur more frequently in passages which bear a strong mark of Anglo-Saxon culture, such as those dealing with the concept of 'wyrd';[23] as may be expected from the semantic fields covered by Laȝamon's compounds, they tend to be especially present in battle-scenes or accounts of military campaigns. The ratio of compounds in the particularly martial Arthurian section is rather higher than average (252 occurrences, 112 distinct nominal compounds); but on the whole, the overall pattern is one of homogeneity. Gibbs stresses the absence of sizeable clusters of compounds in passages not inspired by Wace, and concludes by saying that the style of Laȝamon's finer passages 'does not reveal him as being heavily in debt to the Old English poetic tradition'.[24]

What comes clearly through the works of both Oakden and Gibbs is that Laȝamon's use of compound nouns is fully conscious. They appear in order to produce a given effect, rather than being triggered off by the reminiscence of a similar situation in an old poem. In other words, they are part of a *living* vocabulary for the poet, who used them according to the context and according to their meaning. One must assume, moreover, that compounds were also part of the vocabulary of Laȝamon's initial audience. Oakden's remarkable study shows that about a third of Laȝamon's compounds, though not used by later Middle English poets, are found in other Early Middle English works. Oakden mentions more particularly in that connection the *Ancrene Riwle*, a most interesting fact since the *Ancrene Riwle* is what may be termed 'utilitarian literature' (therefore, with a vested interest in being easily understood) and totally unconnected in theme and in treatment to the *Brut*. A further proof that Laȝamon's compounds must have been widely intelligible is that even

---

21 Gibbs records only two exceptions: 'londgauel', land-tax, and 'lond-tilie', labourer.
22 Gibbs, p. 274. The problem of national unity thus seems to recur on most levels of the *Brut*.
23 Gibbs notes in that connection that compounds based on '-sið' are all used to convey the idea of fate and mortality, and tend to appear when Wace, in the corresponding passage, discusses the idea of the wheel of Fortune (systematically deleted from the English *Brut*).
24 Gibbs, p. 280.

some fifty years later, the Otho scribe retains 203 of them in his modernized version.[25]

As a result, any attempt to demonstrate the indebtedness of the *Brut* to an Old English work on the basis of vocabulary only is bound to be inconclusive, even if the parallels happen to be compound nouns. Laȝamon used compounds, and possibly sometimes created them, in his own independent way, as part of the lexical fund provided by his mother-tongue.

B. Versification

Laȝamon's verse is a descendant of the Old English long line; but critics have had some problems in ascertaining its exact parentage. Madden describes the *Brut* as being composed of

> lines in which the alliterative system of the Anglo-Saxons is preserved, and partly of couplets of unequal length rhiming together.[26]

In other words, the *Brut* is metrically a hybrid. A first bone of contention in academic circles was where Laȝamon's rhyme came from. Certain critics assumed that it was due to the influence of French; others, to the number of which Madden belongs, pointed out:

> rhime was known and practised to some extent before the Conquest, although it is probable, that it was seldom or never used in compositions of a higher or graver cast.[27]

This observation was confirmed by the research of J. S. P. Tatlock, who supported the view that French rhyme merely encouraged English poetry in a pre-existing tendency: Laȝamon's rhyme would thus appear as a native trait. A third school of thought, following Moritz Trautmann,[28] argued that the *Brut* was written in the rhythmic acatalectic iambic dimeter of Otfrid's *Krist*, a meter descended from Ambrosian poetry, in which every half-line consists of four metrical stresses. To be effective in the *Brut*, however, this system had to be very accommodating. This situation led a number of critics to see the poem as a mixture of metres, a

---

[25] Laȝamon's 'antiquizing' of the poem, suggested by E. G. Stanley in 'Laȝamon's Antiquarian Sentiments', is restricted to the *visual* level, with the use of archaistic spellings.
[26] Madden, p. xxiv.
[27] Madden, p. xxii. These 'couplets' refer to long lines linked by internal rhyme.
[28] Moritz Trautmann, 'Über den Vers Layamons'. A representative of this school of thought is Ewald Standop ('Der Rhythmus des Layamon-Verses').

representative of a transitional stage in English versification: such is the opinion which is now prevalent.[29]

In such conditions, the principles of scansion of the poem were bound to lead to heated discussion. It was obvious that Old English metrics had taken some battering in the *Brut*, and the reluctance to envisage an original prosody for the poem led to a long debate, involving such questions as whether Laȝamon's verse was based on musical rhythm (Karl Luick), rhythmic speech (Wilfried Hilker), or something different yet (Dorothy Everett).[30] One thing, however, was undeniable: Laȝamon's free verse preserves the half-line structure of Old English verse. R.S.Loomis describes it in the following way:

> The basic verse form is still the alliterative line with four accents and a slight pause in the middle, but the alliteration is quite irregular, in many lines absent, and the lines are longer. Moreover, the hemistichs are often linked by assonance or rhyme.[31]

Loomis is here following Jakob Schipper, in placing the *Brut* in the tradition of four-stress Germanic accentual verse; such a vision of the poem naturally results in attempts to apply Sievers' Five Types to Laȝamon's verse.[32] This procedure, on the whole, comes to negative conclusions. Karl Luick, the first to investigate in that direction, ends up questioning the nature of Laȝamon's verse, because of the high frequency of secondary stresses in the poem. Schipper resorts to foreign (French) influence to explain Laȝamon's expanded (hypermetric) lines. Max Kaluza then tried to apply the four-beat theory of Old English Verse to Laȝamon's *half-line*:[33] the result, to quote A.W.Glowka, is that his model 'flattens out the contrasts that give Layamon's verse its special

---

29 See Edwin Guest, *A History of English Rhythms*, ed. W.W.Skeat; Sarah J.McNary, *Studies in Layamon's Verse*; George Saintsbury, *Historical Manual of English Prosody*; C.S.Lewis, introduction to G.L.Brook's *Selections from Laȝamon's Brut*. Most recent is A.W.Glowka ('Rhyme and Rhythm in Layamon's *Brut*: A Study in Prosodic Decorum'), who summarizes the situation in the following way (p.123–4):

> From Anglo-Saxon tradition [Layamon] inherited alliteration and some freedom in rhythms. Latin accentual poetry gave him models of verse with the regular alternation of stressed and unstressed syllables, a dignified free verse in the liturgical sequence, and a fully developed system of rhyme and assonance. French verse reinforced his motivation to use rhyme and longer line lengths, while Welsh poetic practice encouraged his use of multiple alliteration and internal rhyme and lent him certain types of consonontal rhymes. Laȝamon drew from all these traditions.

30 Luick, 'Geschichte der Heimischen Metra'; Hilker, 'Der Vers in Layamons *Brut*: Untersuchungen zu seiner Struktur und Herkunft'; Everett, 'Laȝamon and the Earliest Middle English Alliterative Verse'.

31 Loomis, 'Layamon's *Brut*', p.105.

32 See Schipper, *Englische Metrik in historischer und systematischer Entwicklung*, vol.I, pp.146–62, and *Grundriss der Englischen Metrik*, pp.57–70.

33 Kaluza, *A Short History of English Versification*.

rhythmic quality'.[34] Next comes Herbert Pilch, who sees the metre of the *Brut* as essentially Anglo-Saxon, with four metrical stresses per long line (two per half-line), to which he applies musical scansion;[35] and later, N. F. Blake argues that the *Brut* is not derived from Old English alliterative verse, but from the alliterative rhythmical *prose* of the period.[36] Glowka summarizes the problems as follows:

> Scholars who see Layamon's verse as a form of Old English meter point to the limits of their view when they see the shadows of syllable stress meters in the *Brut*. Many of Layamon's lines are just too long to fit the ideal four-stress model proposed for Old English, and indeed Old English verse itself often breaks into lines longer than the four-stress or four-member model will hold. The demotion of stresses to secondary levels, the reduction of words to fit 'members' and the hasty or slow pronunciation of words in order to make the lines fit the meter are means too artificial to be introduced into any kind of imaginable performance. These models are too clumsy for dealing with the alternating patterns of rhythm that Layamon used in his poem.[37]

It appears that whatever traditions Laȝamon had at his disposal gave him no ready-made answer to his problem, namely, that the language he was using to write his poem had changed so much since the classical Old English period that an adequate prosody had to be created for it. The relative failure of 'classical' prosodic theories to account for the versification of the *Brut* has led critics to consider the relation between prosodic form and sense. Glowka thus notes that Laȝamon uses vowel and consonant rhyme, assonance and shifts in line-length to close episodes and mark notable events, and that he controls the focus on the narrative through patterns of rhythm. This achievement, however, is personal to the poet, and cannot be put down to any specific tradition; moreover, the change in language that made it necessary for Laȝamon to elaborate his new prosody would have made it equally necessary for him to re-model any Old English material he wished to integrate within his poem. If Laȝamon was indebted to Old English poetry, it is therefore doubtful whether the metrics of the *Brut* would betray the fact to any great extent.

---

[34] Glowka, p. 17.
[35] Pilch, *Literarische Studie*, pp. 135–147.
[36] See Blake, 'Rhythmical Alliteration', *Modern Philology* 67 (1969): 118–24.
[37] Glowka, p. 19.

C. Epic Formulas

Referred to by Gwyn Jones as 'remembrancers of the Germanic past' and considered by J. S. P. Tatlock as 'the most characteristic trait of Laȝamon's poetic style', the epic formulas of the *Brut* have been the object of considerable attention. Tatlock's 'Laȝamon's Poetic Style and its Relations', in 1923, was the first systematic approach to what had been mooted since Madden, namely, that the *Brut* betrayed a composition technique similar to that of Old English poetry; and it was accompanied the same year by a study specifically on the so-called epic formulas of the *Brut*. These formulas Tatlock describes (p. 3) as similar phrases, used repeatedly, and as a rule in similar circumstances. Tatlock numbers 128 such formulas in the *Brut*, each of which is found three times or more in the poem, and a couple 'on an average once in every ten lines'. Some of the formulas have definite parallels in Old English literature, such as 'feollen þæ fæie'; others merely sound Anglo-Saxon, such as 'balu wes on folke', but have no exact parallel in the older literature.[38] There is not much point reproducing Tatlock's list of formulas here: suffice it to note that very few have Old English analogues, and that Laȝamon's use of them, which Tatlock qualifies as 'slapdash', has more in common with later works such as the late thirteenth-century *Amis and Amiloun* than with the older poetry. Moreover, epic formulas are not typically Anglo-Saxon, nor are they exclusively Germanic:

> They are normal in early epic, as is shown by the frequency of epic formulas in Homer, the *Chanson de Roland*, the *Cantar del mio Cid* and other early poems.[39]

In fact, the epic formula is nearly (but not quite) as characteristic of the *Niebelungenlied* as of the *Brut*, notes Tatlock, who stresses moreover that Old English poetry, being based on variation, avoids such formulas:[40]

> Not a great many of his formulas are found in the extant Anglo-Saxon or twelfth century Middle English poetry. Most of the parallels are idiomatic or colloquial expressions, or riming or alliterating

---

[38] It is such formulas that underlie Gillespy's and Schirmer's remark that Laȝamon tends to favour concrete expressions, or to personify abstract concepts such as joy, sorrow or strife.

[39] Tatlock, 'Laȝamon's Poetic Style and its Relations', p. 3.

[40] James Noble ('Variation in Laȝamon's *Brut*') points out that variation *does* occur in the *Brut*, though in a less sophisticated form than in the extended passages of variation which occur in Old English poetry. He thus notes the frequency of chiastic structures in a number of short passages of variation; this chiastic pattern he suggests is derived from Old English tradition, which also makes use of this device. There is no doubt, however, that it is a very minor feature in the *Brut*.

phrases sometimes found in prose as well as verse. None is likely to
have been handed down only by poetic tradition, have consciously
passed from one poet to another, unless the formula *fæȝe feollon*. It
is safe to say that the formulas in Laȝamon were not traditional in
Anglo-Saxon poetry.[41]

Laȝamon's use of epic formulas does not therefore go back to classical
Old English poetry; Tatlock suggests it may be more in the tradition of
Old English *popular* poetry, but as so little of it is extant, it is difficult to
express a valid opinion on the matter. Epic formulas, which were among
the main arguments of the early supporters of a strong Anglo-Saxon
influence on the *Brut*, thus prove to be disappointing. There is no reason
to believe that Laȝamon could not have understood any Old English texts
or written poems that came his way (especially as he claims to have
consulted the English Bede); but his knowledge of the older poetry
would appear to be limited to what popular memory retained of it.

D. General knowledge, literary analogues and written sources

In dealing with the additions in the *Brut* which are likely to be of English
origin, it is necessary to make a distinction between those elements
which were probably part of the 'general culture' of a twelfth- or
thirteenth-century Englishman, and those which the poet may have
derived from written sources. On a practical level, this means that
mythological references and literary echoes which are too vague to be
traced back to any extant work are best distinguished from those reminiscences for which specific sources or analogues can be found.

1. Mythological references and literary echoes

Myth – more precisely, Germanic myth – makes its first avowed appearance in the *Brut* in the description of Arthur's weapons, before the battle
of Bath: he puts on his coat of mail

he wes ihaten Wygar   þe witeȝe wurhte;

he hangs by his side the sword Calibeorne,

iworht in Aualun   mi[d] wiȝele-fulle craften;

41 Tatlock, 'Epic Formulas', p.515.

on his head, his helm named Goswhit, adorned with

moni ȝim-ston   al mid golde bi-gon.[42]

Fixed around his neck is his shield engraved in red gold with a likeness of the Virgin, and named 'on Bruttisc' Pridwen; and in his hand, his spear, named Ron.

This passage is remarkable for its curious admixture of Celtic and Germanic names. Calibeorne, Pridwen, Ron are the traditional names for Arthur's sword, shield and spear; as underlined by Laȝamon himself, these names are 'Bruttisc'.[43] On the other hand, Wygar, Witeȝe (?) and Goswhit, decidedly non-Celtic names, are nowhere else connected with Arthur. The tendency among earlier critics was therefore to explain them away. This attitude was reinforced to some extent by Madden's understanding of line 10545 as 'he was named Wygar, the witty wright' (II, 643): Wygar being in Madden's mind the name of the 'aluisc smið' who made the coat of mail. Wygar was thus generally considered to be a corruption for Weland, and the critics' efforts were mainly devoted to trying to explain the reason for the Germanic name of Arthur's helm. Madden, Wülcker and Brown understood 'Goswhit' as meaning 'goose-white', a straightforward calque on some unspecified Welsh name comprising as second element '-gwen', 'white'. This hypothesis was rejected by Imelmann, who suggested a Welsh origin for the name: 'gospeith', 'glittering, polished', which would have been corrupted through oral transmission. Visser agrees with this derivation, considering Imelmann's hypothesis as

> extremely probable, in fact, much more so than the theory of a translation from the Welsh, as the name Goswhit would then be a unicum among all the others that have remained untranslated.[44]

However, R.S. Loomis imposed a different interpretation in his 1934 'Notes on Laȝamon', following an informal suggestion made by Kittredge to A.C.L. Brown: if the masculine pronoun 'he' on line 10542 was a scribal error for a feminine 'heo', Wygar would be the name of the mail coat, not of the smith.[45] Such an error would be understandable, for

[42] *Brut*, 10543–57. 'It was named Wygar, which Witeȝe made'; or 'He was named Wygar, who skilfully worked'; see below. Calibeorne is 'made in Avalun with skilful work'; Goswhit has 'many a precious stone, all encompassed with gold'.
[43] These names are also in Wace.
[44] Visser, p.39. Imelmann's suggestion was based on a mistranslation (see above, chapter 6, p.128), and can no longer be considered; however, the reason given by Visser for accepting it remains interesting.
[45] See A.C.L. Brown, 'Welsh Traditions in Layamon's *Brut*', p.99, note 4.

the passage occurs in a list of Arthur's arms and throughout Laȝamon follows a regular formula of mentioning an object and then referring to it again by the personal (or relative) pronoun ... When, accordingly, we read after the mention of Arthur's 'burne', 'he wes ihaten Wygar', there can be little doubt that the reference was to the burny, despite the incorrect gender.[46]

Wygar, suggests Loomis, is a corruption of 'Wig-hard', Mercian for 'battle-hard': 'a most appropriate epithet for a corselet'. Moreover, 'witeȝe' could not mean 'witty', 'as words of this kind end in -i'. Loomis therefore suggests that it should be translated 'which a wise man wrought',

> or, better still, if we capitalize 'witeȝe' and understand it as a substitution for the name of Weland's famous son, Wudga, Widia or Wittich, we may translate: 'which Widia wrought'.

This, considers Loomis,

> makes of the lines complete sense, and offers astonishing illustration of the longevity of English heroic tradition and of Laȝamon's effort to convert Arthur into an English hero. If Beowulf had a white helm and a burny the work of Weland, Arthur had to possess a helm called 'Goosewhite' and a burny wrought by Weland's son.[47]

So attractive is the hypothesis, and so great was Loomis's authority, that this interpretation of the lines in question is now generally accepted, to the extent that the Brook and Leslie edition capitalizes Witeȝe. There are however flaws in Loomis's argumentation. On the one hand, the statement that throughout the passage recurs a pattern of mentioning an object, then referring to it by the personal or relative pronoun, does not take into account the fact that for all the other items of Arthur's equipment, the personal or relative pronoun immediately follows the mention of a given piece of armour, or its description. Between the coat of mail and the name 'Wygar', we have the elaborated mention of the 'elfish smith': a strict application of the syntactical principle implicitly postulated by Loomis would lead one to see the relative as referring to the smith rather than the burny. Loomis's half-formulated suggestion that this may be a *Beowulf*-reminiscence adds nothing to the question, while his statement that this converts Arthur into an English hero is excessive. And the major weakness of Loomis's hypothesis is that it depends on emendation.[48]

[46] Loomis, Notes on Laȝamon', pp. 83–4.
[47] Loomis, 'Notes', p. 84.
[48] This emendation is moreover difficult to justify; not only because the line makes good

The rejection of this emendation led Herbert Pilch to reconsider the question.[49] Pilch accepts that 'wite3e' could not be an adjective, but suggests that it should be understood as meaning 'the wise one'. 'wite3e' would then be the English paraphrase of a Welsh 'gwydd-gar' ('lover of wisdom'), from which Pilch derives the name Wygar.[50] The line would thus read: 'he was named Wygar; the wise one created (or: worked)'. The weakness of this hypothesis, however, is that it demands an implicit object, such as 'weapons'.

An alternative possibility, which would avoid emendation and meet the demands of syntax more satisfactorily, is to consider the -e of 'wite3e' as an adverbial ending. Rather than a noun, we would then have an adverb ('skilfully') modifying the verb 'to create'; and the lines would read: 'He put on his burny, woven of steel, which an elvish smith made with his noble art: he was named Wygar, who worked with skill'. Emendation is therefore not necessary to make sense of the passage. Moreover, one may note that the first reader of the Brut to have left his trace – the person(s) who designed the layout of the Caligula text, checked any scribal errors, integrated the black-ink historical glosses in the margins and pointed out which names were to be highlighted by their being inscribed in red in the margins – this first reader obviously did not feel that 'wite3e' was a personal name. All proper nouns appear in the margins in red ink when they occur for the first time in the text: Wygar, Calibur, Goswhit, Prid (sic), Ron, are duly present in the margins at this point (ff. 123v–124r); 'wite3e' is not, nor is it called to our attention within the text (no capital letter, no red ink stroke).[51]

One cannot therefore say that the ambiguity of line 10545 of the Brut has been resolved. Pilch, for whom La3amon was an early-day Celtic scholar, favours a Welsh derivation of Wygar; Loomis, Gibbs, and those for whom La3amon was an English patriot, opt for the alternative which inflates the poet's 'Germanicity', replacing a difficult but plausible Weland/Wygar by a highly dubious Widia. Wygar is far from Weland,

---

sense without, but also because the sort of error this would imply seems to go against what we can see in the Caligula manuscript. There are a number of instances where the scribe has written a feminine 'heo' for a masculine 'he' (they are usually corrected: see lines 468, 1750, 3092, 3499, 14565): but as far as I can see, this would be the only case of the inverse error.
[49] Literarische Studie, p.78.
[50] The hypothesis of a Welsh origin of the name Wygar may to some extent be supported by the fact that the other smith mentioned in the Brut, Griffin, (line 11869: Arthur's spear was made in Carmarthen, by a smith named Griffin) is firmly placed in Wales, and has a Welsh name. Griffin is a widely attested English form of the Welsh name Gruffudd (see Visser, Vindication, pp. 40–1).
[51] A possible objection to this reading is that Arthur's coat of mail would then be the only piece of his equipment not to be given a name. To this, one may answer that perhaps the English poet simply did not know of one; moreover, the coat of mail is the first piece of armour to be mentioned in the list, and could therefore be understood as an introductory 'pedigree' for Arthur's weapons.

and 'gwydd-gar' is not a personal name: the problems are different, but they are of equal difficulty, and the interpretation of this passage in terms of ethnicity and cultural transmission will necessarily be heavily influenced by the reader's vision of the *Brut* as a whole.

Similar ambiguity characterizes the two other passages which critics have put forth as possibly containing Germanic mythological elements: the fairies at Arthur's birth, and the monsters of Loch Lomond.

The account of Arthur's birth is analogous to that of a number of medieval heroes:

> Sone swa he com an eorðe   aluen hine iuengen
> heo bigolen þat child   mid galdere swiðe stronge
> heo ȝeuen him mihte   to beon bezst alre cnihten
> heo ȝeuen him an-oðer þing   þat he scolde beon riche king
> heo ȝiuen him þat þridde   þat he scolde longe libben
> heo ȝifen him þat kine-bern   custen swiðe gode
> þat he wes mete-custi   of alle quike monnen
> þis þe alue him ȝef   and al swa þat child iþæh.[52]

These elves were first considered to be a Germanic trait.[53] The word 'elven' is indeed of Germanic origin, and the Old Norse *Helgakviða Hundingsbana* offers an analogue to this scene. On the other hand, Rudolf Imelmann, and later R. S. Loomis, considered them a French tradition, possibly of Breton origin. And it is a fact that the account of the birth of Ogier le Danois is remarkably similar to that of Arthur. Visser ascribes the elves to Welsh tradition, on the grounds that 'the imaginative Welsh are not and never have been without fairy-tales'.[54] To this, one may add that Stith Thompson's *Motif Index of Folk Literature* attests to the popularity throughout the world of supernatural creatures endowing the newborn child with qualities which will determine his fate. It is therefore safer to conclude that these 'fairy godmothers', whatever their exact origin, were part of general medieval culture. To quote Seal,

> They and other supernatural beings were clearly objects of considerable interest in many lands, and seem to have been part of an old and varied folklore which caught Laȝamon's imagination and, apparently, that of his audience.[55]

[52] *Brut*, 9608–15. 'As soon as he came on earth, elves took him; they enchanted the child with very powerful magic; they gave him strength, to be the best of all knights; they gave him as second gift that he would be a powerful king; they gave him as third gift that he would live long; they gave to that prince very good qualities, so that he was most generous of all men alive. This the elves gave him, and so did the child thrive'.
[53] Gillespy, p. 497, and earlier, B. ten Brink in his *Geschichte der Englischen Literatur*, vol. I, p. 223.
[54] Visser, *Vindication*, p. 34.
[55] J. R. Seal, 'Kings and Fated Folk: A Study of Laȝamon's *Brut*', p. 85.

The passage describing the marvels of Loch Lomond has repeatedly been compared to the description of Grendel's mere in *Beowulf*:[56]

> þat is a seolcuð mere   iset a middel-ærde
> mid fenne & mid ræode   mid watere swiðe bræde
> mid fiscen & mid feoȝelen   mid uniuele þingen
> þat water is unimete   brade nikeres þer ba[ð]ieð inne
> þer is æluene ploȝe   in atteliche pole.[57]

The 'reedy mere' image may be due to Wace's calling the lake an 'estanc'; the rest of the description, the evil creatures, the 'nikeres' and the elves, is an entirely independent expansion of Laȝamon's. 'Nennius''s *Historia Britonum*, in the 'Wonders of Britain' section (the ultimate source of this passage) mentions no supernatural creatures in his Loch Leven. It is possible that the mention of the numerous streams flowing into the lake suggested to Laȝamon treacherous, therefore evil waters: an equation made in his description of the (unrecognized) Severn tides, of which the poet exclaims (through Arthur) 'þat water is un-fæle', 'that water is evil'.[58] On the other hand, the persistence of such legends as the Loch Ness monster makes it quite possible that similar stories were being rumoured about Loch Lomond at Laȝamon's time.

This passage was compared with the description of Grendel's mere by A. C. Gibbs, who came to the conclusion that the resemblance is only slight. Two features only give this part of the *Brut* an Old English colouring, notes Gibbs: the (factually wrong) marshy setting, and the 'nikeres'.

> The rest is supplied by the reader from his knowledge of the older literature ... It is hard to say whether the faint similarity between the two passages points to a tradition of such descriptions, but stronger evidence than Laȝamon exists in a passage from one of the Blickling Homilies, 'To Sanctae Michahelis Mæssan', a translation from the Latin of the Greek 'Vision of St Paul'... Even so, we cannot say with assurance that it was influenced by it, or, for that matter, that it influenced the 'Beowulf' poet in its Latin form.[59]

Other reminiscences of Anglo-Saxon culture are claimed to be seen in the *Brut*'s repeated reference to the 'fæie', those doomed to die, and to the

---

56 See R. Wülcker, p. 549; F. L. Gillespy, p. 489; H. C. Wyld, p. 14; R. S. Loomis, 'Laȝamon's *Brut*', p. 110.
57 *Brut*, 10848–52. 'It is a strange lake, situated in middle-earth: with marshland and with reeds, with a broad expanse of waters, with fish and with birds, with evil things. The lake is enormously wide; water-monsters bathe in it; elves play in the sinister pool'.
58 *Brut*, 10987.
59 Gibbs, pp. 123–4.

related concept of destiny, 'wyrd'.[60] Walter Schirmer (p. 68) notes that the formula 'feollen þæ fæie' recurs over thirty times in the *Brut*, usually in battle-passages; Gillespy (p. 455) links this insistence on the 'fæie' with a more general tendency to predict the outcome of things:

> This device of warning the reader in some fashion or other of the denouement becomes at times almost a mannerism in the English writer.

Seal (pp. 141–2) concurs:

> The way in which Laȝamon's characters respond to setbacks and reversals is revealing, for it demonstrates both a stoic fatalism and a determination to couch his version in archaic terms that are more resonant of the English past than of the popular view of man as subject to the whims of the goddess Fortuna and her wheel.

However, such comments assume that the words 'wela' or 'fæie' had the same connotations for a late-twelfth century priest as they had for the Anglo-Saxon poets; and we cannot be certain that such was the case. That 'wela', good fortune, is used to translate the allegory of Fortuna, proceeds from cultural transposition, and the fatalism implicit in this passage is also present in Wace – it is inherent to the idea of Fortune. The recurrence of the formula in battle-scenes certainly indicates that it was linked in the poet's mind to a heroic context, but we have no way of ascertaining whether he was aware of the implications the concept conveyed in the older language.[61] In a number of cases, 'fæie' is just a poetic synonym for 'dead', and on one occasion (l.8000) it means little more than 'unfortunate'.[62]

The influence of the Old English poetic tradition on the *Brut* is more diffuse. As underlined by F. P. Magoun, the language change following the Norman Conquest meant that the Old English method of composition could only be used in an indirect way, in congenial matters, such as battles, sea-descriptions or religious material;[63] and it is in such areas that the 'Englishness' of the *Brut* is most apparent. This is implicitly confirmed by Gwyn Jones' remark:

---

[60] The actual word 'wyrd' is not attested in the *Brut*, though Gibbs (p. 48) and Seal (p. 13) argue that Laȝamon expresses a very similar concept in those passages replacing Wace's references to Fortune and her wheel (see *Brut* lines 1704–5 and 1726).

[61] Even for Old English texts, it is not certain that the 'pagan' colouring of certain words or concepts was still felt by the poets, though the survival of the 'fey' concept into modern times makes some awareness probable. See E. G. Stanley, *The Search for Anglo-Saxon Paganism*.

[62] Madden devotes a glossarial remark to Laȝamon's use of the word (vol. III, p. 442); see also Kurath and Kuhn, 'fei(e)'.

[63] Magoun, 'The Oral Formulaic Character of Anglo-Saxon Narrative Poetry'.

We are in a world of feasts and vaunting speeches, flytings and lusty battles, fierce deeds and bloody humour, with the Fiend, the Adversary of Man, always around the next corner.[64]

The relationship of such passages with the Old English tradition was investigated more especially by A. C. Gibbs.[65] He first notes (p. 101) that 'Laȝamon's stylized pictures are a form of poetic decoration', in the sense that they are not pieces of military history as, say, *The Battle of Maldon* or *Brunanburh*. They are successful in creating an atmosphere of noise, colour and confusion: but they are not truly epic. All these scenes are made up of a small number of basic motifs, but not many of Laȝamon's phrases go back directly to Old English poetry, with the exception of 'feollen þe fæie' ('the doomed/ mortally wounded/ dead fell'; also found in *Maldon* and *Brunanburh*), 'helmes þer gullen' ('helms there resounded'; also found in *Andreas*, 127), or such commonplace phrases as 'breken brade speren', 'broad spears broke' or 'burstleden sceldes', 'shields burst'. But most cannot be traced. Moreover, notes Gibbs, Old English battle-descriptions are far more elaborate; they have a much wider range of synonyms for instruments of war and warriors, and a richness of parallel phrases unknown to the *Brut*. The prose-content of Old English verse can be quite small:

> By comparison, Laȝamon's narrative is fast-moving, his descriptions are not meant to attract so much attention.[66]

The battle-scenes of the *Brut* are thus devoid of kennings (with the sole exception of 'gras-bedde'), and the conventional Old English beasts of battle are 'conspicuously absent'. The descriptive technique of the *Brut* is also quite different from that of Old English poetry in that in *Beowulf* or the *Battle of Maldon*, for example, we are presented with a series of individual exploits, rather than a general picture – a method Laȝamon never uses, unless it is already present in Wace. As for sea-pieces, Gibbs notes that they are not very common in the extant Old English poetry. The realistic, personal experience of *The Wanderer* or *The Seafarer* has no parallel in the *Brut*, while the celebrated sea-pieces of Cynewulf's *Christ* and *Andreas* ultimately go back to Latin sources. Moreover, sea-voyages are often to be found in Wace, and

> some of Laȝamon's paraphrases are a good deal less spirited and elaborate than the original.[67]

64 Gwyn Jones, introduction to *Wace and Layamon. Arthurian Chronicles*, E. Mason transl., p. xi.
65 The depiction of feasts and battle-scenes has already been discussed from the point of view of narrative technique, in chapter 3.
66 Gibbs, p. 108.
67 Gibbs, p. 110.

Laȝamon seems to have a rather wider choice of formulae for his sea-pieces than for his battle-scenes: but once again, there is a striking lack of kennings, and very few compound nouns for the sea and ships.[68] A few traditional phrases remain ('ploȝede þe wil<d>e fisc', 'the wild fish played', *Brut* 892, *Andreas* 350), while the storm scene in *Andreas* (370–4) 'bears some sort of resemblance' to Laȝamon (973–4); but the parallels are slight, and Gibbs concludes that

> Laȝamon's sea-pieces bear rather less testimony to the survival of
> the Old English literary tradition than the battles.[69]

Laȝamon's feasts appear to have more elements in common with Old English poetical tradition. Most of these passages are quite different to Wace's:

> Even when both do give a detailed account, the features selected by
> Laȝamon are different, and conform fairly closely ... to what we
> consider ... Old English custom to have been.

However, whilst feasts offer the English poet one of his most frequent opportunities for expanding Wace, they do not show him at his most inventive, notes Gibbs; only few formulas are used, which appear with 'more than usual regularity'.[70] Where parallels with the older literature are to be found, moreover, they come from the late Old English writings.

It is in the last area mentioned by Magoun as harbouring remnants of the Old English literary tradition – religious terminology – that the *Brut* shows the closest affinity with Old English verse; though, as Gibbs stresses, its importance in the poem as a whole is marginal. Almost all of Laȝamon's kennings are religious; and though no exact parallels for these kennings may be found in Old English poetry, nearly all the components appear in very similar older kennings.[71] In addition to these authentic kennings, one may find a few epithetical phrases applied to God, which may be translations or expansions of kennings, such as 'þe alle domes waldeð', 'who wields all dooms', which occurs five times and recalls the

---

[68] Gibbs notes what may be an instance of a kenning 'translated' into a more modern form (*Brut*, 11547: the ships fly as if they had wings), but adds that the simile is an obvious one anyway (pp. 114–6).

[69] Gibbs, p. 116.

[70] For Gibbs' analysis of the 'feast' formulas, see pp. 116–121.

[71] 'domes waldend', 'ruler of destiny' and 'froure moncunnes', 'comfort of mankind', thus appear three times; 'walden anglenne', 'ruler of the angels' and 'middelærdes mund', 'guardian of middle-earth', occur twice; and 'worulde wunne' and 'waldende hæfnen' appear once. In one case only ('domes walden', applied to the emperor Luces, 12369) is a kenning not applied to the Deity. For the passages in which these kennings appear, see below, in the section on echoes of religious poetry.

older 'domes waldend'. Another case may be Laȝamon's 'þe scop þes daȝes liht'.[72] Simple synonyms for God, however, are not numerous – the most frequent is 'Drihten', Lord, followed by 'Hælend', Saviour. The powers of Evil are referred to as 'þe Wrse' or 'þe scucke', which also appears in *Beowulf* and the Old English Homilies.[73]

Gibbs is thus led to agree with J. S. P. Tatlock that the *Brut* is descended from popular rather than classical Old English poetry, and he therefore examines the poems of the *Old English Chronicle* which constitute our only extant examples of this popular tradition. His results are meagre. *The Battle of Brunanburh* still follows in many ways a conventional pattern, while the other poems resemble Laȝamon only in that they are 'less highly wrought and metrically regular' than classical poetry, and sometimes use rhyme, or neither rhyme nor alliteration. Their movement remains the traditional one: 'thick with kennings'.[74] The entry for 1036, relating the death of the atheling Ælfred, does indeed display 'the rhyme, the speed of movement, and the repetition of construction characteristic of Laȝamon's style';[75] however, as Gibbs stresses, this is not typical of Old English poetry, and seen in isolation, the other passages do show considerable traces of the classical tradition. Moreover, in a total view of the *Brut*, the 'Old English' elements take a fairly minor place. The 'Englishness' of the *Brut* cannot be pinned down to anything specific; a fact already noted by Dorothy Everett:

> While all authorities are agreed on the specifically 'English' atmosphere of the work, it is now felt that too close connexions have been made between it and Old English poetry, and that the atmosphere is produced by something more vague and tenuous than direct recollection of earlier literature.[76]

In other words, the *Brut* sounds English mainly because it is written in English, by a man whose mother-tongue was English, and whose cultural background was English.

2. Written sources

References to unspecified written sources occur some six times in the *Brut*: twice in so-called 'triadic' passages; once as origin of the rumour

---

[72] 'Who created daylight'. Gibbs (p. 122) notes eleven instances of this phrase in the *Brut*.
[73] The most frequent of these in the *Brut* is 'þe Wrse', which appears a dozen times, followed by 'þe scucke' (five occurrences). 'Feond' is twice used to refer to the devil, and 'deovel' once.
[74] Gibbs, p. 125.
[75] Gibbs, p. 125. See *The Anglo-Saxon Minor Poems*, ed. Elliott Van Kirk Dobbie, pp. 6–12.
[76] Dorothy Everett, p. 37.

that Caerleon was bewitched (12114); once as proof of a dependable, historical tradition about Arthur (as opposed to the stories of the minstrels, 11468); as testimony of the widespread usage of Carric's nickname Cinric (14406); referring to the fame of Dunwallo Molmutius (2120); and most relevant to our immediate concern, on line 5407, a reference to an English book as authority for the name of the brook into which Livius Gallus was cast:

> & a þere Ænglisce boc   he is ihaten Wale-broc.[77]

Such references cannot of course be automatically taken at face value: they are a recurrent element of the conventional appeal to authority. In the case of line 5407, however, we are given a specific piece of information, the credibility of which would in no way have been impaired had this additional authority been omitted. The 'book' cannot have been the Anglo-Saxon Bede acknowledged in the Preface, or the *Anglo-Saxon Chronicle*, as neither mention the story of Wall-brook; Madden therefore suggests (p. xvii) that it must have been one of those works 'extant in the time of Laȝamon, but which are not now to be recognized'.

Recognition of an additional English source is all the more difficult in this case as the passage seems to have been derived directly from Wace:

> Del nom Galli sun nun reçut,
> Nentgallin l'apelent Bretun,
> Gualebroc Engleis e Seissun.[78]

The reference to an English book may just be due to Laȝamon's impression that Wace consulted English sources at this point. The reference to Wall-brook therefore leads nowhere; but its very presence nourished the feeling that since Laȝamon mentioned an *English* book at this point, he must certainly have supplemented Wace with English sources, probably of a historical nature, and which might be revealed by a careful combing through the poem. Hence the generally favourable reception of H. S. Davies' hypothesis of a lost English source for the Arthurian section.

3. The 'Battle of Bath' source

At the basis of this theory we have Davies' impression that Laȝamon's

---

[77] 'And in the English book it is named Wal-brook'.
[78] Wace, 5564–6. 'It took its name from the name of Gallus; the Britons call it Nentgallin, the English and Saxons, Gualebroc'. One of the Wace manuscripts moreover has the name in the same form as Laȝamon ('Wallebroc', MS. F).

long-tailed similes are unevenly distributed in the poem. Even though one-line similes occur fairly evenly throughout the poem, Davies notes that longer similes are concentrated within about 1700 (short) lines; after which, they disappear in an 'almost startling' way, as suddenly as they had arrived. This, suggests Davies, indicates a particular source, rather than a literary model (such, for example, as Vergil). This source must have dealt specifically with Arthur's campaign against the Saxons, and more precisely with the battle of Bath, the account of which differs in many respects from that of Wace or Geoffrey.

In all three accounts this battle takes place in two phases: in the first phase, the Saxons are driven from their positions around Bath, and take refuge on a hill; in the second phase, the hill is stormed and the Saxons slain. However, where the Saxon leader Childric flees at the end of the second phase only in Wace and Geoffrey (after the death of his two chief lieutenants), in the *Brut* he flees at the end of the first phase. This, admits Davies, could be due to Laȝamon's 'sense of dramatic effect'; but the content of the speeches which accompany the battle are also modified. In Geoffrey, the speech is made by St Dubricius, who presents the coming battle as a Christian crusade. Wace deletes Dubricius, and turns Arthur's short opening address before the battle (i.e., phase 1) into a speech on the theme of vengeance, delivered before the storming of the hill (i.e., phase 2). Laȝamon, in turn, has Arthur speak about vengeance and broken faith, but at the beginning of the *first* phase, while as a prelude to the second phase, the English *Brut* has a long exultation by Arthur over his enemies: an addition which would not have been possible, stresses Davies, if Childric had not been made to flee during the first stage of the battle. Moreover,

> Arthur's exultations on this occasion are quite unlike his conduct towards his other enemies.[79]

There is no such vaunting in the campaign against Modred, for example; these 'barbaric exultations' are restricted to Arthur's first campaign, and are closely linked to the longest of the similes of the *Brut*: 'indeed, their main substance is precisely these similes'. Davies therefore concludes that it was very probable that Laȝamon had a source other than Wace for this episode: a source, moreover, which must have been known to Geoffrey of Monmouth, since the general pattern of campaign is the same in all three chronicles. This source Davies suggests was 'presumably derived from local tales',[80] which would explain Geoffrey's equation of Bath with the Badon of Gildas and 'Nennius', in an 'attempt

[79] Davies, 'Laȝamon's Similes', p. 134.
[80] Davies, p. 137–8.

to reconcile two rather different sources of information bearing on what he took to be the same matter'. As Laȝamon's long similes are 'quite untypical' of the poetic styles of Old English, Latin or French, the 'most likely' language for this source must have been (Middle?) English, and it was presumably in poetry. Its pro-Celtic bias would suggest Wessex, where 'British traditions' are thought to have survived longer than elsewhere, and more specifically Somerset, where the series of Arthurian battles attains its climax and its most realistic setting, whilst being a region 'readily accessible to Geoffrey' in Oxford, and to Laȝamon himself.

This hypothesis was discussed two years later by A.C.Gibbs. Whilst admitting the possibility of an additional source responsible for the long-tailed similes, Gibbs notes, first, the importance of the *short* similes in the *Brut*, and the fact that the 'extended' similes differ from the shorter ones 'not in kind, but in scale'.[81] He thus challenges Davies' statement that the longer similes are 'quite uncharacteristic' of Laȝamon's style, and points out two concentrations of similes (albeit short ones), covering the career of Vortigern and the arrival of the Saxons, and the campaigns of Aurelius and Uther. This Gibbs explains by the fact that

> Laȝamon finds the theme of defence of the homeland more congenial than that of imperial conquest. In this, he follows in the old Anglo-Saxon tradition.[82]

As to the savagery in Arthur's speech, it is typical throughout the *Brut*, though it is not usually expressed in the same form. If Laȝamon had a source for this passage, remarks Gibbs, 'he incorporated it into his work fairly thoroughly'. Concerning the *language* of this hypothetical source, the style of the similes is unlikely in an Old French work, and as we know nothing about the poet's skill at translating Latin, 'we are left with Old English'. The question is therefore whether Laȝamon would have incorporated the source into the *Brut* as it stood, or whether he would have felt the need to adapt it and 'bring the language up to date'. Gibbs inclines towards the former alternative. He notes that the few passages where Laȝamon seems to be quoting older poetry are 'immediately recognizable as extremely archaic',[83] and quite unlike the Saxon passage in style: the long-tailed simile passage is no more archaic than the rest of the *Brut* as far as construction, vocabulary and diction go. This opinion is supported by E.G.Stanley, who states:

---

[81] A.C.Gibbs, 'Literary Relationships'. The discussion of Davies' theory is on pages 93–6.

[82] Gibbs, p.93.

[83] These passages are *Brut* 12759–63 and 14077–8. They are discussed below.

Even though elaborate similes were by no means rare in Old English poetry, it is hard to believe that Laȝamon drew on an Old or early Middle English poem for this part; it has far too much in common linguistically and stylistically with the rest of the poem for it to be at all likely that Laȝamon was here following a different method of composition.[84]

This argumentation was further elaborated by D. P. Donahue and J. R. Seal.[85] The main subject of Donahue's thesis is the concept of formulaic composition in the *Brut*, following the tracks of Gibbs and, to a lesser extent, Ringbom. The issue of a separate source for Laȝamon's long-tailed similes first appears in Donahue's discussion of the Feast-theme:

An understanding of how Lawman used themes, of how he freely adapted and expanded these devices, leads us to argue that Lawman's expanded similes and metaphors were also part of his own creation ... Extended or long-tailed similes are found in all parts of the poem. They appear where Lawman expanded the whole of the matter in which the particular simile or metaphor would normally appear.[86]

Donahue's chief example – the image of Arthur being food and drink to poets – is somewhat unconvincing as a totally independent expansion, for the image is altogether too similar to that in Geoffrey's *Prophetia Merlini*;[87] of more interest, though, is his remark that several of Laȝamon's longer similes appear within the Single Combat theme, where a warrior may frequently be compared to an animal (wolf, lion, fox, boar ...). The technique used by Laȝamon in the famous simile of *Brut* 10628–36 is no different to that in other parts of the poem.

J. R. Seal's argumentation also bears on Davies' statement that long similes are uncharacteristic of Laȝamon's style:

There are some notable similes in the *Brut* both before and after the passage in question, there are obvious and compelling reasons why the defeat of the Saxons should be rendered in a heightened style, and, in Laȝamon's version especially, the Saxons seem richly to deserve the unrestrained destruction and vaunting contempt they receive from Arthur.[88]

84 E. G. Stanley, 'Laȝamon's Antiquarian Sentiments', p. 24.
85 Donahue, 'Thematic and Formulaic Composition in Lawman's *Brut*' and Seal, 'Kings and Fated Folk'.
86 Donahue, pp. 140–1.
87 See above, chapter 5, pp. 98–9.
88 Seal, p. 104.

The stylistic reasons advanced by Davies in favour of a hypothetical source cannot therefore convince. It remains true, though, that the English account of the battle of Bath does not tally with that of Wace. That Laȝamon should have inserted Arthur's speech in response to Childric's flight is one thing; that he should have made Childric flee *in order* to make Arthur speak, however, implies his taking greater liberties with his source than the rest of the poem would warrant. This discrepancy is of the sort to suggest either that the poet misread the passage, or that his copy of Wace was corrupt at this point.

The notes in Ivor Arnold's edition of the *Roman de Brut* support this hypothesis to some extent, for Wace's account of the battle is not as clear as Davies' summary would suggest. In the French poem, Arthur comes down from Scotland to Bade; he makes his men get prepared in a great plain, by a wood; he also equips himself. The battle has not even started properly but the Saxons have to retreat to a hill: the whole of the first 'phase' covers only four lines, one of which (line 9306, the only direct reference to the battle-clash) is missing in at least one of the extant manuscripts.[89] The impression, therefore, is that the battle is defensive from the start for the Saxons: that they retreated as soon as they saw the Briton army approaching. Arthur's speech consequently seems to be at the *beginning* of the hostilities, rather than in the middle of them: it certainly introduces the first actual battle-scene of the passage. Moreover, it is striking that the only reference made to Childric in the French poem is

> E Cheldric s'en ala fuiant,
> Il e altre ...[90]

At no moment do we see Childric fighting; the assumption that he did not actually take part in the battle would therefore be an understandable one, and a tempting one as well, for a poet intent on magnifying his hero. What Laȝamon appears to have done is to provide a battle-scene motivating both the Saxon retreat to the hill and the non-participation of Childric in the fight, which, in turn, brings about Arthur's speech. One may further note that Wace's laconic

> Mort fu Baldulf, morz fu Colgrin [91]

is expanded into some fifty lines describing the brothers' vigorous defence, Arthur's despatching of them and his ensuing speech, which contains no similes, and is therefore not suspect of having been derived

---

[89] Wace, 9306: 'Mais cil nes pourent sustenir', 'But they could not withstand it'. This line is missing from MS R, a late thirteenth or early fourteenth century manuscript.
[90] Wace, 9359–60. 'And Childric ran away, he and others'.
[91] Wace, 9358. 'Killed was Baldulf, killed was Colgrim'.

from some additional source. Davies' theory may thus be dismissed on all grounds, as being unnecessary as well as unverifiable.

4. The 'Northumbrian' source

More rigorous is the attempt of A. C. Gibbs to trace back to an extant, English historical source Laȝamon's divergences from Wace in the part of the *Brut* from Oswald to Æthelstan. Gibbs singles out the following points:[92]

– the Brut supplies the relationship between Edwine and Oswald. But this information could have been taken from Bede.

– long passages of the campaign against Oswald are either greatly amplified from Wace (as a result of 'natural' amplification), or wholly independent of him. The additional information they contain, notes Gibbs, does not agree with the Old English annalists: Laȝamon seems to have confused two distinct battles, Heavenfield (635 AD) and Maserfield (642 AD). Oswald won the first and was killed in the second.

– in the Oswi section, Laȝamon omits to mention Oswi's submission to Caswallawn (Wace, 14499–516) and Penda's accusation that he was mustering troops in Saxony (Wace, 14555–60).[93] His narrative is erroneous again in the final battle between Penda and Oswi, where he has Oswi killed and Penda victorious (though wounded).

In this case, I suggest straightforward mistranslation. Wace reads for this passage:

> Oswi ot en Deu grant fiance,
> Mult ot en lui ferme creance,
> E Peanda mult s'orguilla
> Es granz meisnees se fia;
> Mes descunfit fud e ocis,
> Od lui plusurs de ses amis.[94]

As this follows the account of another king who put his confidence in God and ended up being slaughtered by Penda (St Oswald), it would be understandable that in a moment of flagging attention Laȝamon should

---

[92] See Gibbs, chapter 1, pp. 19–20.
[93] Gibbs does not attempt to discuss this omission.
[94] Wace, 14629–34. 'Oswi had great confidence in God, he had a very firm faith in Him, and Penda grew very proud and put his confidence in his great hosts; but he was defeated and killed, and with him many of his friends'.

have taken this 'mes descunfit fud' as referring to Oswi:[95] previous experience had shown that on battlefields 'granz meisnees' are of more help than 'en Deu grant fiance'. One may note, moreover, an alternative manuscript reading where instead of 'E Penda mult s'orguilla',[96] we find 'Molt refu fel Peanda', 'Penda was very treacherous again': a suggestion of foul play that emphasizes the parallel with the Oswald episode, and makes the reader expect a similar *dénouement*.

– Osric was Penda's son, not Oswi's, as stated by Laꝝamon, and he was granted his father's lands. This error is the direct consequence of the previous one, as Wace does not explicitly say who Osric's father was. The only thing that is clear from the Wace-text is that he is the son of the king who was killed.

– further confusion is found in the *Brut*'s reworking of Wace's account of Æthelstan's reign. First, it places Æthelstan in the seventh century, and secondly, the *Brut* shows a 'curious deviation' in the story of the renewal of Peter's Pence.[97]

On the whole, considers Gibbs, most of these non-Arthurian expansions can be credited to Laꝝamon, rather than to some hypothetical intermediate source:

> There is scarcely a trace of his having been under the influence of a serious historical writer, or of his having altered his material with a view to historical probability.[98]

However, in the divergences from Wace of the last 2000 lines of the *Brut*, 'there are not the usual indications of Laꝝamon's invention'. Gibbs therefore postulates either a corrupt Wace-text (a possibility strengthened by the fact that Robert Mannyng of Brunne, after a very close translation of Wace, starts drawing upon other sources at this point); or else an independent English historical or poetic account of these battles. The very inaccuracy of Laꝝamon's traditions would tend to go against such a hypothesis; on the other hand, R. M. Wilson *does* adduce some evidence of the existence of such poems about the campaign between Oswy and Penda.[99] Henry of Huntingdon, in his *Historia Anglorum*, thus has an appropriate quotation for many important battles, introduced by some such phrase as 'unde dicitur'; and these quotations, suggests Wilson

---

[95] Especially, one may add, in the absence in a manuscript of all punctuation which could have made the true subject of the clause clearer.

[96] Wace, 14631, MS F. One MS (MS G) omits lines 14631–2 altogether.

[97] I have already suggested that these modifications partake of the overall ideology of the *Brut*. See above, chapter 7, pp.174–5.

[98] Gibbs, p.21.

[99] R. M. Wilson, *The Lost Literature of Medieval England*, pp.28ff.

(pp. 32–4), seem to fall in alliterative verse when translated into Old English. Among these battles are those of Heathfield, Maserfeld and 'In Winwed', the battle where Oswi finally defeated Penda. As Henry of Huntingdon was interested in Old English poetry, to the extent of including a paraphrase of *Brunanburgh* in his work, Gibbs thinks it 'quite likely' that he was quoting from vernacular poems on the subject, and that if these poems were accessible to Henry of Huntingdon, they must have been also to Laȝamon:

> A vague reminiscence of [such poems] would account for Laȝamon's deviations from his text better than the previous explanations given.[100]

This, however, is unverifiable. The existence of alternative traditions to that of Wace would certainly have encouraged Laȝamon to take more liberties with his source than he would have otherwise; but on the whole, the divergences and expansions of the last two thousand lines of the *Brut* are more easily explained by a misreading of the Wace-text (Oswi), the interference of a hagiographical legend (Oswald), and the poet's own vision of the history of his people (Æthelstan).

5. Religious poetry

That Laȝamon's religious passages are more archaic in tone than the rest of the poem has been noted by many a critic. F. L. Gillespy, for example, remarks that

> the lists of appellatives for God, frequent in Layamon, can be paralleled from the *Beowulf*, although the beginning of Cædmon's hymn furnishes a better illustration.[101]

Gibbs further points out that almost all of Laȝamon's 'small store' of kennings are religious, and refer to the Deity; that on two occasions three kennings come into juxtaposition, and in one case, we find four kennings: and that two of these three passages are prayers. This echoes Tatlock, who in his 'Poetic Style' points out the three same passages as having 'the true antique ring':

> In his lyric and hymnic mood, who knows what religious poem of his childhood may have come to his mind? It is natural that this

---

[100] Gibbs, p. 23.
[101] Gillespy, p. 501.

traditional embellishment should survive chiefly in that chief refuge of traditional usage, the world of religion.[102]

This open invitation to examine Laʒamon's relationship with Old English religious (rather than heroic) poetry was not taken up by subsequent Laʒamon critics, and therefore needs to be discussed at this point.

The first passage singled out by Tatlock and Gibbs is connected with Laʒamon's expansion on the Nativity of Christ, and Taliesin's subsequent prophecy, at the beginning of the poem:

> On Kinbelines dæie   þe king wes inne Bruttene
> com a þissen middel-ærde   anes maidenes sune
> iboren wes in Beðleem   of bezste alre burden.
> He is ihaten Iesu Crist   þurh þene Halie Gost
> alre worulde wunne   walden englenne.
> Fæder he is on heuenen   froure moncunnes
> Sune he is on eorðen   of sele þon mæidene
> & þene Halie Gost   haldeð mid him-seoluen
> þene gast he wel daleð   to þan þe him beoð leoue.[103]

> Hit wes ʒare iqueðen   þa quides beoð nu soðe
> þat scolden beon a child iboren   of alle folke icoren
> & þat scolde beon ihaten Hælend   and helpen his freondes
> alesen his leofue wines   of læðe heore bendes
> of helle bringen Adam   Noe & Abraham
> Sadoc & Samiel   & Symeon þene alde
> Iosep an Beniamin   & alle his broðeres mid him
> Iohel & Eliseon   Asor & Naason
> Ysaac & his broðer   & monienne oðer
> moni hundred þusend   þe iþud beoð to hellen
> & for swulchere neode   he is icumen to þere þeoden.[104]

Whilst the first part of this passage is too general to direct us towards a specific Old English text, the second part dealing with the Harrowing of Hell has an Old English analogue in a fragment of the Exeter Book (fol. 119b–121b) known as 'The Descent into Hell'.[105]

---

[102] Tatlock, 'Poetic Style', p.6.

[103] *Brut*, 4521–9. This passage is translated above, chapter 7, note 68.

[104] *Brut*, 4559–69. 'It was said in former days – the sayings are now accomplished – that a child would be born, chosen among all nations, and that he would be called Saviour, and help his friends, release his beloved friends from their hateful bonds, bring out of Hell Adam, Noah and Abraham, Sadoc and Samuel and Symeon the old, Joseph and Benjamin and all his brothers with him, Johel and Eliseon, Asor and Naason, Isaac and his brother, and many others: many a hundred thousand who have been thrust into Hell. And because of such need has he come to the people'.

[105] 'The Descent into Hell' is quoted from *The Exeter Book*, G. P. Krapp and Elliott Van Kirk Dobbie eds., pp. 219–223. Translation by S. A. J. Bradley, *Anglo-Saxon Poetry*.

The most striking similarity between both poems, at a first reading, is the presence of a list of the patriarchs and prophets released from the bondage of Hell, an element implicit, but undeveloped, in the apocryphal *Acts of Pilate*, from which the theme of the Harrowing of Hell is ultimately derived:

> Wræccan þrungon
> hwylc hyra þæt sygebearn   geseon moste,
> Adam ond Abraham,   Isac ond Iacob,
> monig modig eorl,   Moyses ond Dauid,
> Esaias ond Sacharias,
> heahfædra fela, swylce eac hæleþa gemot,
> witgena weorod, wifmonna þreat,
> fela fæmnena,   folces unrim.[106]

Of the thirteen patriarchs mentioned by name in the *Brut*, only three (Adam, Abraham and Isaac) coincide with the 'Descent'; Laȝamon clearly chose his names for the alliterative effects he could produce (see especially the alliteration of 's' at line 4544). In both cases, we have a 'crowding' effect due to the accumulation of names, linked with the idea of release from bondage, and the stress on the Nativity, the necessary condition for this release. This convergence in theme and treatment need not however indicate indebtedness to the 'Descent', as the theme was a very popular one, and is treated in a somewhat similar way in the 'Ordo Prophetarum' which closes the Anglo-Norman *Jeu d'Adam*.

The other two passages are very short, and occur in the Arthurian section of the poem. They consist in oaths uttered by Arthur and Gawain:

> Lauerd Drihten Crist   domes waldende
> midelarde mund   monnen froure
> þurh þine að-mode wil   walden ænglen ...

> Ældrihten Godd   domes waldend
> al middel-ærdes mund   whi is hit iwurðen ...[107]

These two passages, with their rhetorical accumulation of kennings, are reminiscent of certain high-style passages of Old English religious

---

106 'The Descent into Hell', 42–49; Bradley, p. 393: 'The exiles came crowding, trying which of them might see the victorious Son – Adam and Abraham, Isaac and Jacob, many a dauntless man, Moses and David, Isaiah and Zacharias, many patriarchs, likewise too a concourse of men, a host of prophets, a throng of women and many virgins, a numberless tally of people'.
107 *Brut*, 12760–3 and 14077–8. 'Lord Christ, ruler of destiny, protector of middle-earth, comforter of men, through your merciful will, ruler of angels ...' and 'Almighty God, ruler of destiny, guardian of all middle-earth! Why has it happened ...'.

poetry. As pointed out by Gillespy, this is one of the striking features of Cædmon's hymn; but it may also be found in a number of other poems, amongst which we may mention 'The Descent into Hell' 115–122, where the patriarchs address Christ:

> þu meaht ymbfon   eal folca gesetu,
> swylce þu meaht geriman, rice drihten,
> sæs sondgrotu, selast ealra cyninga.
> Swylce ic þe halsige, hælend user,
> for [.]inum cildhade, cynynga selast,
> ond fore þære wunde, weoruda dry[...
> ...] þinum æriste, æþelinga wyn.[108]

On the whole, however, the lexical parallels between the religious passages of the *Brut* and the 'Descent' are few. Most obvious are those referring to Christ, who in both texts is called 'Hælend' ('Descent' 26, 118; *Brut* 4561); 'frea moncynnes' ('Descent' 33, similar second element as *Brut* 4525, 'froure mancunnes');[109] 'dryhten Crist' ('Descent' 108; *Brut*, 'Lauerd drihten Crist'); 'þeoda waldend' ('Descent' 112, same second element as *Brut* 12759 and 14077, 'domes waldende'); or 'waldende ænglen' (4525 and 12761 'walden englenne'); 'æþelinga wyn' (same final element as in 'alre worulde wunne', *Brut* 4525); or finally a more extended parallel between the 'Descent', 86–88:

> We þæs beofiende
> under helle dorum   hearde sceoldon
> bidan in bendum.

and *Brut* 4562, 'læðe heore bendes', 4568 'moni hundred þusend þe iþud beoð to hellen'.

None of these parallels are conclusive evidence that Laȝamon was acquainted with 'The Descent into Hell'; however, they are sufficient to confirm Tatlock's hypothesis that the English poet was influenced by Old English religious poetical writing. It is therefore permissible to search among Old English religious poems for the origin of Laȝamon's odd definition of the Trinity, noted in chapter 7.

---

[108] 'You are able to embrace all the habitations of the peoples; likewise, mighty Lord, you are able to count the sands of the sea, Best of all kings. Likewise I entreat you, our Redeemer, by your infancy, Best of kings, and by your wounding, Lord of hosts and by your resurrection, Joy of princes ...' (Bradley, p. 393). Other instances may be found at the beginning of *Genesis A*; in *Elene* 79–85, 670–82, 1073–86; *Exodus* 8 sqq., 427 sqq.; Daniel 8 sqq., 188 sqq.; *Andreas* 76–88, 118–122; 225–230; *Beowulf* 170–189, *inter alia*. They tend to be found in contexts of invocations, oaths, prayers, etc.

[109] In Old English religious poetry, one may note that 'froure', 'Comforter', was used to refer to the Holy Spirit (Paraclete), not Christ. See the Old English 'Christ', 197. A similar kenning recurs in *Brut* 12761, 'monnen froure'.

The authority with which Laȝamon makes his statement that the difference between the first and second Persons of the Trinity is one of locus suggests a written source; or if not actually written, so well known that it carried the same weight. This source, moreover, must have been orthodox, even though Laȝamon's formulation is not: one fails to see how Sabellianist texts could have found their way to a late-twelfth century Worcestershire poet, and one would have expected the Church authorities to redress that specific passage of the *Brut* had it really been redolent of heresy. The most satisfying explanation is that somehow, Laȝamon got the wording of a well-known text wrong.

A possible candidate for such a text is the Benedictine Office Creed, to be found in MS Junius 121, where the Latin 'Credo in Deum patrem omnipotentem et in Jesum Christum filium ejus unicum' is paraphrased as

> Ælmihtig fæder up on rodore,
> ...
> þu eart lifes frea,
> engla ordfruma, eorðan wealdend,
> and ðu garsecges grundas geworhtest,
> and þu ða menegu canst mærra tungla.
> Ic on sunu þinne soðne gelyfe,
> hælendne cyning, hider asendne
> of ðam uplican engla rice
> ...
> and ymbe Bethleem bodedan englas
> þæt acenned wæs Crist on eorðan.[110]

It is readily apparent that Laȝamon's questionable passage reads remarkably like a summary of this expanded paraphrase of the Creed. While it could not have been derived from the Latin version, it has in common with the Old English Creed its beginning and its end; and it is most probable that Laȝamon thought he was merely summarizing the formulation of a familiar version of the Creed – hence, his assurance in this passage. The influence of such a prominent part of the Christian liturgy on a priest is hardly surprising, and if the version of the Creed which Laȝamon misformulated was not exactly the same as that of the Old English Benedictine Mass, it cannot have been considerably different.

---

110 *The Anglo-Saxon Minor Poems*, ed. Elliott VanKirk Dobbie, pp.78–9, 1, 5–12 and 23–4. 'Almighty Father in heaven on high ... you are the Lord of life, the Author of angels, the Ruler of earth, and you wrought the depths of ocean, and you know the myriads of the illustrious stars. I believe in your righteous Son, the Saviour-King, sent hither from the realm of angels on high ... And round about Bethlehem angels proclaimed that Christ was born upon earth' (Bradley, p.541).

6. Other English Religious Sources

The probability of a late-twelfth century priest having made use of books of homilies is such that the hypothesis advanced by P. J. Frankis cannot be dismissed altogether. As noted above, the internal arguments brought forth in favour of Laȝamon's indebtedness to Ælfric's homilies are restricted to agreements over isolated words: 'wigeling', 'feðerhome', 'monqualm'. Only one passage agrees with Ælfric both in lexis and in theme; but even there, Frankis has to piece together two sentences some 18 lines apart in Ælfric, to produce something quite dissimilar both in context and in phrasing to what is found in the *Brut*.[111] Frankis also notes the presence in Felix's *Life of St Guthlac* of the names Æthelbald and Ælfwald, given by Laȝamon to the twin churls who kill Gratian. But, once again, the contexts do not agree, and these two names occur in other works as well:[112] C. S. Lewis's suggestion of a lost Anglo-Saxon legend at the origin of this expansion remains as likely as ever.[113] Frankis's hypothesis is thus entirely dependent on external elements, most important of which is availability. N. R. Ker's *Catalogue* shows that among the manuscripts known to have been in Laȝamon's part of the world in the thirteenth century, there were a number of copies of Ælfric's homilies: as stressed by Frankis, the material was readily at hand for our poet. However, as mentioned above, Laȝamon's interest in theology appears to have been minimal; in fact, if we had not been told in the Prologue that the poet was a priest, we could not have guessed it. Moreover, the credibility of Frankis' theory hinges on his identification of the Latin book by Albin and Austin (mentioned in the Prologue) as a (now lost) English book 'with pieces derived from Alcuin and St Augustine of Canterbury'.[114] One can readily accept that Albin, Alcuin and Ælfric were considered as variants of the same name; but it is more difficult to understand why a book which Laȝamon specifies is in Latin should turn out to be in English, when in terms of availability composite manuscripts of this type were more common in Latin than in English anyway. Whilst Frankis is indisputably right in calling our attention to the possibility that Laȝamon may have been familiar with Old English homilies, it must be admitted that they have left no recognizable mark on the *Brut*, and cannot therefore be counted among Laȝamon's sources of inspiration.

---

[111] i.e. *Brut*, 1739, 'summe heo wenden to þan wude, summe to weien-læten'. See above, chapter 7, pp. 178–82.
[112] Frankis (p. 70, note 20) mentions the *Anglo-Saxon Chronicle* (778 entry) and the Letters of St. Boniface.
[113] See C. S. Lewis's introduction to the *Selections from Laȝamon's 'Brut'*, p. xi.
[114] Frankis, p. 74.

7. The Proverbs of Alfred

A limited amount of proverbial material is integrated by Laȝamon into his *Brut*; thus, in an authorial comment following the description of Leir's distress (l.116):

> After vuele cumeð god   wel is him þe hit habbe mot;[115]

in a speech by Cassibelaune, lamenting the fact that Caesar has managed to get away:

> Ful soh seide þe seg   þe þeos saȝe talde
> ȝif þu ileuest ælcne mon   selde þu sælt wel don;[116]

and most dramatically, as the closing line of the poem:

> i-wurðe þet iwurðe   i-wurðe Godes wille.[117]

The resemblance between these passages and certain sections of the Middle English *Proverbs of Alfred* was first noted in 1907 by Skeat, in the introduction to his edition of the *Proverbs*. As the accepted date of composition of the *Brut* in Skeat's day was late twelfth to early thirteenth century, he took the passage as a reference to Laȝamon's 'chronicle'. However, the gradual shifting of the *terminus ad quem* of the *Brut* within the thirteenth century, and O. Arngart's establishing of the date of composition of the *Proverbs of Alfred* 'towards the middle of the [twelfth] century' resulted in a reversal of the relationship of the two works, and Laȝamon was considered to have borrowed either from the *Proverbs* or from a common source.[118] The proverbs which Laȝamon was thought to have quoted from were

> god after vuele
> weole after wowe
> wel is him þat hit ischapen is;[119]
>
> Gin þu nefre leuen
> alle mannes speche
> ne alle þe þinges

---

115 *Brut*, 1802. 'After evil comes good: fortunate is he who may experience it'.
116 *Brut*, 3997–8. 'Very truly spoke the man who said this proverb: if you believe everyone, you will seldom do well'.
117 'Happen what may happen, may the will of God be accomplished'.
118 Arngart, p.57 of his edition of the *Proverbs of Alfred*. Arngart suggests (p.44) that this common source may have been the *Distichs of Cato*, as this particular section of the *Proverbs* is derived from the *Distichs of Cato*, iii, 11.
119 'Good after evil, weal after woe, well it is for him to whom it befalls'. *Proverbs of Alfred*, Jesus College MS version, 119–121 (Arngart, p.85).

> þat tu herest singe
> For mani haueþ fikel muþ
> & he is manne for-cuþ
> Scal he þe neuere cuþen
> hwanne he þe [wule] bi-sweken[120]

and

> wurþe þat i-wurþe
> wurþe godes wille.[121]

The verbal overlap between the first two of these proverbs and the corresponding proverbial passages of the *Brut* is minimal, to the extent that one may confidently say that Laȝamon's source, in those specific instances, was almost certainly not the *Proverbs of Alfred*. The only striking case of agreement in wording as well as in contents is that of the closing line of the *Brut* with lines 504–5 of the *Proverbs*. However, even that one remarkable agreement becomes less significant after a survey of the manuscript tradition of the *Proverbs of Alfred*, for Arngart's reconstruction of the stemma of the *Proverbs* demonstrates that the manuscript whose reading is closest to what we find in the *Brut* – Maidstone Museum A 13 – belongs to a later textual tradition. The best extant manuscript – MS Jesus College, Oxford 323 – does not have the proverb in question.[122] This would suggest that this particular proverb was added to the corpus at a given moment, due, one assumes, to its popularity.

Arngart's survey of the manuscripts of the *Proverbs of Alfred* shows quite clearly that we are dealing with a living tradition, which at given times integrated new material into the corpus. *The Owl and the Nightingale*'s use of the name of Alfred confirms this: Atkins, in his study of the poem, points out eighteen proverbial utterances, eleven of which are ascribed to King Alfred. Only very few correspond to those in the extant *Proverbs of Alfred*, and among those, two are not referred to as being Alfred's.[123] Helen South advances the hypothesis that the author of *The*

---

[120] 'Never believe the speech of all men, nor all the things that you hear sing; for many have fickle mouths and are of a wicked disposition. They will never warn you when they deceive you'. *Proverbs*, no. 19, Maidstone MS version, 325–332 (Arngart, pp. 106–109).
[121] 'Happen what may happen, may the will of God be accomplished'. *Proverbs*, lines 504–5.
[122] See Arngart, pp. 11–55. The *Proverbs* are found in four manuscripts, which all date from the early to the late thirteenth century. The best extant text is considered to be MS Jesus College, Oxford 29. MS Cotton Galba A xix, the oldest of the four, was badly damaged in the 1731 fire; its text is known to us through transcripts. And finally, we have MS Trinity College, Oxford 323 and MS Maidstone Museum A 13, which Arngart considers are derived from the same, later original.
[123] See J. W. H. Atkins, *The Owl and the Nightingale*. The 'clear' parallels are between *Owl* 2933–7, *Proverbs* 450–3 (Jesus MS); *Owl* 1269–74 and *Proverbs* 138–41 (Trinity MS). Two

Owl and the Nightingale used a different collection of Alfred's proverbs, similar in part to the extant versions, but containing additional material.[124] This seems an unnecessary complication, as the chief reason for ascribing the proverbs to Alfred is that (to quote E.G. Stanley) 'his name will lend authority to what the birds assert'.[125] It is thus reasonable to assume that both Laȝamon and his audience connected King Alfred with proverbial material; but this is not sufficient to postulate indebtedness to the specific, written corpus known as the *Proverbs of Alfred*.

Gibbs notes a number of lexical parallels between the *Brut* and the *Proverbs*, such as the kenning 'domis-lauerd', and the compounds 'bale-siþes' and 'soðcweðes';[126] but this cannot be considered as conclusive evidence, for proverbs are known for preserving archaic words and phrases well after they have disappeared from everyday speech. Moreover, at no moment is the name of Alfred linked specifically with proverbial material in the *Brut*, unlike *The Owl and the Nightingale*, for example.[127] The only time King Alfred appears in the *Brut* is as translator of the Mercian laws; a passing remark also found in Wace. The epithet given to Alfred in this passage ('Engelelondes deorling') is not derived from Wace, and H. South points out that the traditional epithets used for Alfred ('englene herde', 'Englene derling', 'englene frowere')[128] are all to be found in the *Proverbs*, most sections of which begin with the words 'þus cwað Alured'. One may note however that similar formulae are used in the *Brut* for characters other than Alfred: Arthur, for example, is repeatedly called 'Bruttenes deorling'.

It would therefore appear as probable that the proverbial passages in the *Brut* are taken from oral tradition; the similarity between the two 'i-wurðe þet iwurðe i-wurðe Godes wille' passages may readily be explained by the fact that the rhythm of this line is catching enough to have been preserved, and eventually fossilized, in common usage. This hypothesis seems to be confirmed by the presence in the *Anglo-Saxon Chronicle* of a very similar utterance at the end of the 1066 entry as Laȝamon's at the end of his poem: 'wurðe <gòd> se ende þonne God wylle'.[129] The similarity is not as striking as with the Maidstone version of

passages are 'adapted', *Owl* 458–60, *Proverbs* 325–8 (Jesus MS); and *Owl* 1039–40, *Proverbs* 78–9. Arngart points out another two, dismissed by H. South as being too different: *Owl* 325–8, *Proverbs* 563–70 and *Owl* 761–2, *Proverbs* 605–6 (Trinity MS). The two parallels in sayings not ascribed to Alfred are *Owl* 769–72 and 787–8, *Proverbs* 190–201 (Jesus MS).

124 See Helen P. South, *The Proverbs of Alfred Studied in the Light of the Recently Discovered Maidstone Manuscript*; esp. pp. 56–63, on Laȝamon's *Brut*.
125 E.G. Stanley, *The Owl and the Nightingale*, p. 34.
126 See Gibbs, pp. 221–2.
127 The obvious explanation for this, of course, is that Laȝamon could hardly have attributed to Alfred a proverb quoted by Cassibelaune, or made in connection with Leir.
128 Guardian, darling, comforter of the English.
129 1066 entry of MS Cotton Tiberius B iv (i.e., the Worcester Chronicle), in the Plummer and Earle edition (*Two of the Saxon Chronicles Parallel*, vol. 1, p. 200). 'gòd' is interlined, perhaps by a later hand.

the *Proverbs*; however, one may note that the statement is made against the background of the Norman invasion, as are, implicitly, the final lines of the *Brut*.

Laȝamon shows no indebtedness to the *Anglo-Saxon Chronicle* in his poem; one therefore comes to the conclusion that the presence of the proverb in three apparently unconnected works must be due to the similarity of the situations described. The context in both the *Chronicle* and the *Proverbs of Alfred* is one of helplessness, as may be seen by at quotation *in extenso* of section 28:

> if þu in þin elde
> best wele bidelest (*sic*)
> & tu ne cunne þe leden
> mid none kinne liste
> Ne þu miht mid strengþe
> þe selue steren
> þanne þonke þu þi louerd
> of alle hise lone
> & of þin oȝen lif
> & of þe daies liht
> & of alle þe murhþe
> þat he þe for man makede
> & hwider so þu wende
> sai þu atten-ende
> wurþe þat i-wurþe
> wurþe godes wille.[130]

Within the *Proverbs*, Laȝamon's closing line is the motto of the defenceless old man who has nothing left but life; in the *Anglo-Saxon Chronicle*, it is the cry of a defeated people for whom all is lost. That the *Brut*, more than a century after the Conquest, should end on such a note puts the whole poem in a new perspective. The *Brut* becomes a bid to survive, like the helpless old man, waiting for God's will; hoping for the renewal of strength promised by the coming of a second Arthur, who will reinstate the age of justice.[131]

---

[130] 'If you in your old age are deprived of wealth and cannot lead yourself, nor can steer yourself with strength for all your good-will, then thank you the Lord for all his goodness, and for your own life, and for the daylight, and for all the pleasing things that he made for man, and as you so go on, say finally: Happen what will happen, be accomplished God's will'. Maidstone MS version, 490–505 (Arngart, pp. 123–5).

[131] The poem would thus take on a subversive dimension, if one accepts my suggestion that the 'sanctification' of the 'English' Angles, linked with the explicit condemnation of the 'nið-craften' of the Normans, makes the Norman Conquest morally incomprehensible where the former transferral of sovereignty had appeared just. This reading, if correct, would imply that Laȝamon wrote before the separation of England and Normandy: after the separation, such bitterness would have been pointless, as the Normans would have been 'sent back' already, in a way.

8. The question of nationalism

As an Englishman, there are a number of things Laȝamon was better placed to know than Wace. One of those is his own country. F. L. Gillespy, in her discussion of Laȝamon's patriotism, notes that 'the descriptions of England in Layamon are fuller and of a more enthusiastically complimentary turn' than Wace's.[132] However, none of these passages go beyond the conventions of the 'locus amoenus' topos, and reveal little of the poet's personal knowledge. Indeed, J. S. P. Tatlock's investigation on the matter shows that Laȝamon was somewhat ignorant of the geography of Britain:

> Of the north and east he shows only such special knowledge as might be due to hearsay, and sometimes shows striking ignorance.[133]

The only areas which he seems to have known are south Wales, and 'generally the south and south-west of England': the spatial indications in the *Brut* for those regions are roughly correct. Laȝamon's more specific geographical indications concern Wales, notes Tatlock, who suggests that the poet must have had personal experience of the country. Considering where the poet was living, that would scarcely be astonishing.

More interesting is Laȝamon's information about the history of the Welsh borderlands. Tatlock points out two passages in the *Brut* where Laȝamon, he suggests, shows greater knowledge on the subject than Wace. Laȝamon first corrects Wace 1271–2:

> E Kamber ad la terre prise
> Ke Saverne vers north devise

'And Kamber took the land that extends north of the Severn' into: 'Camber hefde al him-sulf bi westen Sæuarne' – 'Camber held the territories west of the Severn' (1068). He also mentions, at the end of the poem (14942–4) that Æthelstan moved the boundaries of Wales westwards.

This point, however, loses some of its significance at a reading of the Wace-text; for contrary to what Tatlock seems to have thought, Laȝamon has added nothing to his source. Wace 13941–6 reads:

> Chatwan esteit reis de Northwales
> E Margadud reis de Suthwales;
> Tut esteit lur jesqu'en Saverne
> Ki lez le munt curt de Malverne;

---

[132] Gillespy, p. 475.
[133] Tatlock, p. 500.

> Mais Aedelstan tant les destreinst
> Que ultre Weie les enpeinst.[134]

The only element of personal knowledge displayed by Laȝamon is therefore that Wales extended to the west as well as to the north of the Severn,
and that Menevia was marshy.

English customs and institutions are better represented. The wassail
scenes (both linked to the character of Rouwenne) are depicted in more
detail than in the French *Roman*. H.C.Wyld notes in particular the richness of Rouwenne's clothing, in her first appearance, and her kneeling in
front of Vortigern; more interesting than these elements of *mise en scène*,
however, is the fact that Laȝamon corrects Wace in two points. Where
Wace states:

> Dunc beit cil tut u la meitied
> E pur joie e pur amistied
> Al hanap receivé et baillier
> Est custume d'entrebaisier [135]

the English poem specifies that the person offering the cup drinks it up
completely, and that *another* cupful is served to his companion; they then
exchange *three* kisses. This may be understood as reflecting local usage,
especially as Wace repeats twice (6967 and 6979) that the cup-bearer may
drink 'plein u demi'. In the scene of the poisoning of Vortimer,
Rouwenne does indeed drink 'half', but Laȝamon finds it necessary to
specify: 'after þes kinges dom' (7479), at the order of the king. The drinking of only half of the cupful therefore appears as a breach of tradition,
enforced by Vortimer's will – possibly as an ineffectual precaution
against poisoning.[136]

Madden and Gillespy suggest that the description of Locrin's betrothal
to Gwendoleine, 'i hond fæst', that is, by the ceremony of joining of
hands, may also reflect custom.[137]

On an institutional level, Laȝamon makes numerous mentions of hustings – what Madden calls 'the memory of the *witenagemot*' – to decide on
important matters such as the election of a king, the punishment to inflict
on evil-doers (Hengest), or the attitude to adopt in the face of foreign

---

[134] 'Chatwan was king of North Wales, and Margadud king of South Wales; all was theirs
up to the Severn, which flows along the mount of Malvern. But Æthelstan pressed them so
that he pushed them beyond the Wye'. This passage is the source of Laȝamon's anachronism in placing Æthelstan before his time.
[135] Wace, 6967–70. 'Then he drinks all or half, and for joy and for friendship, when receiving and giving the cup , it is the custom to give each other a kiss'.
[136] This is what seems to be suggested at lines 7485–6 of the *Brut*.
[137] Gillespy, p. 407; Madden, vol. III, p. 312, notes that this form of betrothal was practised
in the north of England at one time.

pretensions (Rome). The importance of these 'democratic' counsels, as opposed to Wace's aristocratic deliberations, is underlined by F. L. Gillespy. The proclamation of the hustings, the social classes summoned, in one instance even the penalty for those who refuse to come; the wise men rising to deliver speeches on the matter under debate, the final decision and preparation for action: these scenes are visualized in the English poem with an immediacy suggesting more than antiquarian reminiscences.[138] A possible explanation for this would be that Laȝamon appears to have transposed certain aspects of the judicial procedure of medieval law-courts to the hustings situation. Similarly, Queen Judon's death by drowning may possibly reflect some superseded punishment for infanticide (though I have no proof on this matter); whilst Arthur's condemning the trouble-makers at his court to death in fens (*Brut* 11406), M.-C. Blanchet suggests may be a reminiscence of the Germanic custom related by Tacitus.[139]

On the whole, however, the *Brut* does not reflect contemporary customs or institutions to any great extent, a fact which may be due to the historian-poet's reluctance to introduce too many recognizably thirteenth-century elements in a narrative dealing with the Celtic civilization which preceded that of the Anglo-Saxons. However, the sense of anachronism was not particularly strong in the Middle Ages, and one may advance the hypothesis that Laȝamon's relative lack of additional 'contemporary' references may be due to other reasons.

That Laȝamon had no compunction in mixing cultural references is obvious from his giving Gratian's two slayers Germanic names, long before the Saxons make their appearance. This phenomenon reaches its climax in the Arthurian section: as noted above, Arthur's helm is apparently given an English name, 'Goswhit', as also (perhaps) the maker of his corslet, 'Wygar'; but we also find a curious assimilating of the Anglo-Saxon *beot* with 'Bruttisce speche' (see 13248 and 13393; the underlying idea being that 'Bruttisc' *beots* always lead to successful acts).[140] The great tragedy of Camlan, suggests Laȝamon (13923–5), is precisely that it prevented Arthur from fulfilling his *beot* that he would destroy Rome. The English poet appears to have wished to blend Anglo-Saxon references into his Celtic material: to blur the distinctions, as it

---

138 See Gillespy, pp. 398–401; 410.
139 Blanchet, 'Le double visage d'Arthur', p. 82. In Scandinavian mythology, it is more especially the punishment of cowards and sorcerers.
140 This does not mean, of course, that boasting was unique to Old English tradition – the *beot* is quite close to the Old French *gab*. However, it corresponds to nothing precise in Welsh heroic poetry, and this is clearly an extension of an English cultural factor to the Celtic heroes of Britain. The importance of fulfilling your *beot* is explicitly stated on 13252–4, and the boasting of an enemy is a frequent incentive to start a campaign, or gather strength in a battle (see for example 2891–6, or 10814–7).

were. This tendency to underline the essential similarity between his own, native culture and that of his Welsh neighbours is explicit on lines 3147–53 of the *Brut*:

> Seo[ð]ðen þer-æfter   monie hundred wintre
> com Alfred þe king   Englelondes deorling
> and wrat þa laȝen on Englis   ase heo wes ær on Bruttisc
> and whærfde hire nome on his dæȝe   and cleopede heo
>   Mærcene laȝe
> Ah þet I þe sugge þurh alle þing   ne makede heo noh[t] ærst
>   Ælured king
> ah heo makede þa quene   þe me Mærcie cleopede
> and Ælured heo seide on Englisc   þis is seoð ful iwis.[141]

This stressing that the Mercian laws were *not* made by Alfred suggests that Laȝamon was going against the common knowledge of his audience: Worcestershire was part of Old English Mercia, and local tradition had certainly never heard of the eponymic Marcie, who probably owes her spurious existence to Geoffrey of Monmouth's imagination. Whilst he adds nothing new to the Wace-text, the English poet's insistence on assimilating of the laws of the Celtic queen Marcia with those of the English king Alfred is striking. The repeated linking of Marcie and Alfred lends a double source of prestige to the Mercian laws. On the one hand, they are shown to be of considerable antiquity, with all the prestige this entails; on the other, their outstanding value is underlined by King Alfred's seal of approval. On a broader level, Laȝamon is subtly negating the difference between Briton and English – and he uses the full weight of his authority to make his audience accept the fact. This explicit bond between Mercia's cultural heritage and the Briton, non-English past of the island, makes the history of Britain appear as an uninterrupted flow, until the Norman break. Laȝamon's readiness to contradict Wace, at the end of the poem, precisely on the question of laws and customs in Wales, is consistent with this implicit merging together of Briton and English identity: if Mercian laws were originally Briton laws, then they must be akin to the Welsh customs, which are also explicitly said to be those of the ancient Britons. How, then, could the Welsh be degenerate? The link between English and Welsh is further suggested, in the Æthelstan passage, by Laȝamon's omission of Wace's:

---

[141] 'Subsequently, many hundreds of winters after that, came King Alfred, England's darling; and he wrote the law in English, as it was before in British, and in his day he changed its name and called it Mercian law. But I absolutely maintain to you that it was not King Alfred who first made it, but the queen who is called Marcie made it, and Alfred translated it into English. This is the plain truth'.

... ot tute l'Angleterre en baille
Fors sul Guales e Cornuaille.[142]

As noted above, Laȝamon admits of no limits in expressing the power of Æthelstan, founder of the English nation, and the Welsh are implicitly gathered under him as well. It seems as though the English poet was trying to rub out the dividing line between Welsh and English, through a general mixing of cultural referents (especially proper names), the stressing of institutional similarities (the Mercian laws), their common past since Æthelstan, the legitimate heir to the Briton kings. This (apparently) harmonious passage from Briton to English rule contrasts strongly with the antagonism Laȝamon expresses towards the Normans; and to that extent, the *Brut* may read as an attempt to kindle a spirit of solidarity between the Welsh and the English, the legitimate inhabitants of Britain, against the invaders. To call this attitude 'patriotism' or 'nationalism' is dangerous, for these words have connotations which do not tally with the ideological background of the twelfth or thirteenth century; yet this *is* national feeling of a sort. The Welsh and the English have become natural allies, in such an outlook: both are shown to partake of the Briton past, and the Arthur whom the Welsh await legitimately becomes the saviour of the English as well. Whatever may be said about the 'Englishness' of Laȝamon, the poet's loyalties are not expressed in ethnic terms, but proceed from a sense of institutional continuity, and the acceptance of cultural admixture. More than Germanic, English or Anglo-Saxon, Laȝamon's outlook is already British, in the modern sense of the word.

---

[142] 'He held sway over all England, except Wales and Cornwall'. Wace, 14759–60. However, these lines are missing in one Wace-manuscript (MS H).

Conclusion

It appears from this study that Laʒamon was far from writing in a vacuum. His interests went far afield, though not always in the direction one would have expected.

The Prologue announces the historical and religious readings of the poet: Bede is the uncontested authority for the early history of the English, and the mysterious manuscript containing the works of Albin and St Augustine suggests a blend of patristics and history. But no trace has been found in the *Brut* of additional chronicles or annals, and the religious instruction provided by the poet is both limited in scope and popular in nature, being derived from the apocrypha and an Old English paraphrase of the Creed.

The *Brut* is almost entirely inspired by literary sources: hagiography, Geoffrey of Monmouth's *Historia Regum Britanniae*, his *Vita Merlini*, the Welsh triads, *Armes Prydein* (or, at the least, Welsh prophetical poetry), and of course, the *Roman de Brut* itself. Yet, most of these works which are now dismissed as spurious or unhistorical would have been true history to a medieval audience. Hagiographical writings were accepted as serious sources by historians until quite recently; the Welsh material was surrounded by an aura of antiquity and authenticity which endowed it with considerable authority; as for Geoffrey's work, it was widely accepted as genuine, though admittedly the 'serious' historians of his day denounced him as a stranger to the truth. Laʒamon's poem is therefore a piece of literature nurtured by other literary works, by a poet under the misconception that his *Brut* was a piece of historical writing based on dependable, historical sources.

This misconception has as immediate consequence that the influence of overtly literary sources is difficult to detect, because it touches not the contents but the narrative technique, and the handling of certain themes. Thomas's *Tristan* is thus the only *roman* to have left a recognizable mark on the *Brut*. However, Laʒamon must also have been familiar with other genres; the Brutus section contains what seems to be a hint at the *chanson de geste*. Moreover, a number of the poet's additions can only be explained by oral tales, be they Welsh or Breton, and the style and narrative technique of the *Brut* suggests that Laȝamon's ear was tuned to the older English poetry, though possibly of a more popular sort than that now extant.

There is no unity of genre in the works which Laȝamon integrated within his poem, but there is unity of matter. All his major additions revolve around the figures of Arthur and Merlin: all the sources which have left some trace on the *Brut* are related in some way to the great king and his prophet. The long recognized emphasis given by Laȝamon to the Arthurian section of his poem is thus reinforced by his having consistently looked towards Arthurian sources for additional information.

It has been said that the *Brut*'s ending is a half-hearted postscript to Arthur's adventures; that the poet had expended his enthusiasm on the great hero, and plodded on uninspiredly to the end of his material. Such a view betrays a basic misunderstanding of the structure of Laȝamon's poem in general, and the function of the Arthurian part in particular. The investigation of the relationship of the English *Brut* to its French source has shown that despite an almost perfect agreement in contents, the *Brut* has a different internal structure to the *Roman de Brut*, through the rearranging of the relative weight given to different incidents or episodes. The main consequence of this is that the central theme of both Geoffrey's *Historia* and Wace's *Roman* – the dealings of the Britons with Rome – becomes a secondary issue in the English *Brut*.[1] The Roman campaigns of Belin and Brennes and of Arthur are considerably pruned down by the English poet. As noted by A. C. Gibbs, Laȝamon expands those episodes which take place on English soil instead; the central theme is no longer Britain and Rome, but Britain and the outsiders – whatever their origin. And the capital issue of the end of the poem is, I suggest, the 'naturalization' of the Angles to the status of legitimate inhabitants and rulers of what is to become England. The whole point is to prove, first, that the Angles were worthy of such a favour (hence, the extensive use of hagiography); and second, that they hold the land by right of succession rather than conquest. In other words, that there is no institutional or spiritual gap between the rule of the first kings of Britain, whose emanation is Arthur, and that of the English, whose emanation is Æthelstan. This does not turn the Britons into English, or vice-versa, but it is a statement of kinship, based not on ethnic grounds, but ultimately on a common insularity.

Such a discourse places Laȝamon in an ambiguous position regarding the Welsh of his day, who considered themselves the true heirs to the

1 See Brynley F. Roberts, 'Geoffrey of Monmouth and Welsh Historical Tradition', p. 36: 'The theme of Wales and Rome is a recurrent one in the *Historia*, and structurally it is the one which gives cohesion to the work'. This was obviously felt by Wace, who expands the passages where the theme appears, especially in the Arthurian section.

ancient Britons, and the English those of the Saxon arch-enemy. The *Brut* has the ancient Britons all but wiped out; they all die in the great mortality under Cadwalader, and the Welsh remnant is confined to Wales by divine decree – Yvor and Yuni have no right over Britain as a whole. The Welsh, one assumes, partake of the promised release by Arthur, in that they have remained true to the institutions and customs of their forebears: but the English have as many rights to claim Arthur as theirs, in the view of the *Brut*. More so, in fact: the Welsh feature nowhere in Cadwalader's vision. Such a view of the history of Britain had little chance of being accepted by the Welsh people, and even though the English poet obviously had a great respect for his Welsh neighbours, his interest in them was only skin deep. The outlook of the poem is strongly divergent from Welsh tradition, and even though the initial audience of the *Brut* probably included Welshmen (if only Laȝamon's informant), it is clear that the work was not composed for a Welsh audience.

Laȝamon's attitude towards the Normans is also characterized by ambiguity, of another sort. Where the Welsh are accepted but culturally ill-defined, the Normans are explicitly rejected, whilst Laȝamon displays a firm grasp of their language, and betrays some knowledge of their literature. The Normans are *de facto* integrated within the narrative fabric of the *Brut* as the Welsh are not – though the poem is obviously not directed towards the Normans.

The poem is focused on the English people, written in the English language, eschewing excessively learned detail, making use of proverbs and local references (such as Milburga). Laȝamon gives them a more prestigious pedigree than 'standard' histories, and provides them with an answer to the problem of legitimacy posed by the Normans, in distinguishing them from those mere conquerors by the force of weapons, but also with regard to the Welsh, whose prior claims are subtly denied. Laȝamon's *Brut* reads as an attempt to create a new foundation myth, that could give his countrymen both moral justification and the incentive to survive. The Otho-scribe, in replacing Laȝamon's statement that an Arthur would come 'Anglen to fulste' by 'Bruttes ... for to healpe' (14297) thus betrays his lack of comprehension of the work he was revising. The history of the kings of Britain was not alien matter to Laȝamon. It was the very foundation of English rule over a God-given land.

Select Bibliography

Abbreviations

ALMA   *Arthurian Literature in the Middle Ages*, ed. R.S. Loomis, London: Oxford U.P., 1959.

BBIAS   *Bibliographical Bulletin of the International Arthurian Society.*

DAI   *Dissertation Abstracts International.*

PMLA   *Publications of the Modern Language Association of America.*

A. Sources

Ælfric's Catholic Homilies. The Second Series text, ed. Malcolm Godden, London/New York/Toronto: Oxford U.P., 1979 (EETS suppl. series 5).

The Homilies of Ælfric, ed. J.C.Pope, London: Univ. Press, 1967–8; 2 vols. (EETS 259–60).

The Sermones Catholici or Homilies of Ælfric, ed. B.Thorpe, London: Ælfric Society, 1844–6; 2 vols.

Afallennau, in *Llyfr Du Caerfyrddin*, ed. A.O.H.Jarman, Caerdydd: Univ. Wales Press, 1982, pp.27–28.

Two of the Saxon Chronicles Parallel with Supplementary Extracts from the Others, ed. C.Plummer, J.Earle, revised by D.Whitelock, Oxford: Clarendon, 1952 (repr. 1980).

The Anglo-Saxon Minor Poems, ed. Elliott VanKirk Dobbie, New York: Columbia U.P.; London: Routledge & Kegan Paul, 1942 (ASPR VI).

Canu Aneirin, ed. Ifor Williams, Cardiff: Univ. Wales Press, 1938.

Armes Prydein. The Prophecy of Britain. From the Book of Taliesin, ed. Ifor Williams, English version by Rachel Bromwich, Dublin: Dublin Institute for Advanced Studies, 1972.

Early Welsh Genealogical Tracts, ed. Peter C.Bartrum, Cardiff: Univ. Wales Press, 1966.

Beda, Opera Historica, ed. C. Plummer, Oxford: Clarendon Press, 1896; 2 vols.

The Old English Version of Bede's Ecclesiastical History, ed. J. Miller, London: Oxford U.P., 1890–1898; 2 vols.

Branwen Uerch Lyr. The Second of the Four Branches of the Mabinogi, ed. Derick S. Thomson, Dublin: Dublin Institute for Advanced Studies, 1976.

Brut y Brenhinedd: Cotton Cleopatra Version, ed. and transl. J. J. Parry, Cambridge Mass.: The Medieval Academy of America, 1937.

Brut y Brenhinedd, Llanstephan MS 1 Version, ed. B. F. Roberts, Dublin: Dublin Institute for Advanced Studies, 1971.

Brut Dingestow, ed. Henry Lewis, Cardiff: Univ. Wales Press, 1942.

The Text of the Bruts from the Red Book of Hergest, ed. John Rhys and J. Gwenogvryn Evans, Oxford: J. G. Evans, 1890.

Chardry's Josaphaz, Set Dormanz und Petit Plet. Dichtungen in der anglonormannischen Mundart des XIII. Jahrhunderts, ed. John Koch, Wiesbaden: Sändig, 1968 (repr. of 1879 ed.).

Cyfranc Lludd a Llefelys, ed. B. F. Roberts, Dublin: Dublin Institute for Advanced Studies, 1975.

La Vie des Set Dormanz by Chardri, ed. Brian S. Merrilees, London: Anglo-Norman Text Society, 1977.

The Exeter Book, ed. E. V. K. Dobbie and G. P. Krapp, New York: Columbia U.P.; London: Routledge and Kegan Paul, 1936 (ASPR III).

Geffrei Gaimar, *Lestoire des Engles*, ed. T. D. Hardy and Charles Price, London: Eyre and Spottiswood, 1888.

Geoffrey of Monmouth, *Historia Regum Britanniae*, ed. Acton Griscom, London: Longmans & Green, 1929 (repr. Genève: Slatkine, 1975).

La Légende Arthurienne, ed. Edmond Faral, Paris: Champion, 1929 (vol. 3).

The Historia Regum Britanniae of Geoffrey of Monmouth, I Bern, Burgerbibliothek MS 568, ed. Neil Wright, Cambridge: Brewer, 1985.

The Historia Regum Britanniae: a Variant Version, ed. Jacob Hammer, Cambridge Mass.: Mediaeval Academy of America, 1951. Review by J. Frappier, *Romania* 74 (1953): 125–8.

The Historia Regum Britannie II: First Variant Version, ed. Neil Wright, Cambridge: Brewer, 1987.

Life of Merlin. Geoffrey of Monmouth: Vita Merlini, ed. and transl. Basil Clarke, Cardiff: Univ. Wales Press, 1973.

Gildas. The Ruin of Britain and Other Works, ed. and transl. Michael Winterbottom, London and Chichester: Phillimore, 1978.

Giraldus Cambrensis, *Opera*, ed. J. S. Brewer, J. F. Dimock, G. F. Warner, London: Rolls series, 1861–1891; 8 vols.

Gottfried von Strassburg, *Tristan*, ed. Friedrich Ranke, modern German transl. R. Krohn, Stuttgart: Reclam, 1980.

Helinandi Frigidi Montis Monachi necnon Guntheri Cisterciensis Opera Omnia, Paris: Migne, 1855 (Patrologia Cursus Completus ... series Latina, vol. 212).

Curley, Michael J. ed., 'A new edition of John of Cornwall's *Prophetia Merlini*', *Speculum* 57 (1982): 217–249.

Lancelot. Roman en prose du XIIIe siècle, ed. Alexandre Micha, Genève: Droz, 1978–83, 9 vols.

Laȝamon's Brut, or Chronicle of Britain; a Poetical semi-saxon Paraphrase of the Brut of Wace, now first published from the Cottonian Manuscripts in the British Museum, accompanied by a Literal Translation, Notes and a Grammatical Glossary, ed. Frederick Madden, Osnabrück: Otto Zeller, 1967 (repr. of the 1847 ed.); 3 vols.

Laȝamon: Brut. Edited from British Museum MS Cotton Caligula A ix and British Museum MS Cotton Otho C xiii, ed. G. L. Brook and R. F. Leslie, London/New York/Toronto: Oxford U.P., 1963–1978; 2 vols.

Laȝamon's Brut, ed. Joseph Hall, Oxford: Oxford U.P., 1920.

Selections from Laȝamon's Brut, ed. G. L. Brook, revised by J. Levitt, Exeter: Exeter University, 1971. Review of the first ed. by I. J. Kirby, *Studia Neophilologica* 36 (1964): 183–9.

Llawysgrif Hendregadredd, ed. John Morris-Jones and T. H. Parry-Williams, Cardiff: Univ. Wales Press, 1933.

Robert Manning of Brunne. The Story of England, ed. Frederick J. Furnivall, London: Eyre and Spottiswood, 1887; 2 vols.

The Myvyrian Archaiology of Wales, ed. Owen Jones, Edward Williams, William Owen-Pughe, Denbigh: T. Gee, 1870.

Nennius. British History and the Welsh Annals, ed. and transl. John Morris, London and Chichester: Phillimore, 1980.

The Owl and the Nightingale. Reproduced in Facsimile from the surviving manuscripts Jesus College 29 and British Museum Cotton Caligula A ix, ed. N. R. Ker, London/Toronto/New York: Oxford U.P., 1963 (for 1962).

The Owl and the Nightingale, ed. E. G. Stanley, New York: Barnes and Noble; Manchester: Manchester U.P., 1972 (first publ. 1960).

The Proverbs of Alfred, ed. O. Arngart, Lund: Gleerup, 1955; 2 vols.

The Proverbs of Alfred Studied in the Light of the Recently Discovered Maidstone Manuscript, ed. Helen P. South, New York: Haskell House, 1970 (repr. of the 1931 ed.).

Volsunga Saga ok Ragnars Saga Loðbrokar, ed. Magnus Olsen, Copenhagen: S. L. Möller, 1906–8.

The South English Legendary, Edited from Corpus Christi College Cambridge MS 145 and British Museum MS Harley 2277 with Variants from Bodley MS Ashmole 43 and British Museum MS Cotton Julius D IX, Charlotte d'Evelyn and Anna J. Mills eds., London: Oxford U.P., 1956.

Thomas, Les Fragments du Roman de Tristan, ed. B. H. Wind, Genève: Droz; Paris: Minard, 1960.

Le Roman de Tristan par Thomas, ed. Joseph Bédier, Paris: F.Didot, 1902–1905; 2 vols.

Trioedd Ynys Prydein, ed. and transl. Rachel Bromwich, Cardiff: Univ. Wales Press, 1978.

Le Roman de Brut de Wace, ed. Ivor Arnold, Paris: Société des Anciens Textes Français, 1938 and 1940; 2 vols.

La Partie Arthurienne du Roman de Brut de Wace, ed. Ivor Arnold and Margaret Pelan, Paris: C.Klincksieck, 1962.

Le Roman de Rou de Wace, ed. A.J.Holden, Paris: Picard, 1970.

Willelmi Malmesbiriensis Monachi. De Gestis Regum Anglorum Libri quinque; Historiae Novellae, Libri tres, ed. William Stubbs, London: Eyre and Spottiswood, 1887–9; 2 vols.

Willelmi Malmesbiriensis Monachi. Gesta Pontificum Anglorum, ed. N.E.S.A.Hamilton, London: Longman; Cambridge: Macmillan; Oxford: Parker, 1870.

B. Translations

Anglo-Saxon Poetry, S.A.J.Bradley transl., London/Melbourne/Toronto: Dent, 1982.

New Testament Apocrypha, ed. Edgar Henneke, Wilhelm Schneemelcher, English transl. and ed. by R.McC.Wilson, Philadelphia: Westminster Press, 1963.

The Earliest Welsh Poetry, Joseph P.Clancy transl., London: Macmillan, 1970.

Bede. A History of the English Church and People, Leo Sherley-Price transl., Harmondsworth: Penguin, 1955.

Geoffrey of Monmouth. The History of the Kings of Britain, Lewis Thorpe transl., Harmondsworth: Penguin, 1966.

Gerald of Wales. The Journey Through Wales and The Description of Wales, Lewis Thorpe transl., Harmondsworth: Penguin, 1978.

The Gododdin. The Earliest Scottish Poem, Kenneth H.Jackson transl., Edinburgh: Edinburgh U.P., 1969.

Wace and Layamon, Arthurian Chronicles, Eugene Mason transl., introd. by Gwyn Jones, London: Dent; New York: Dutton (Everyman), 1976.

C. Dictionaries, etc.

Bosworth, J. and T.N.Toller, *An Anglo-Saxon Dictionary* (1882–98); Supplement by T.N.Toller (1891). Revised ed. London, 1972.

Flutre, Louis Ferdinand, *Table des Noms Propres avec toutes leurs variantes figurant dans les Romans du Moyen Age écrits en Français ou en Provençal*

et actuellement publiés ou analysés, Poitiers: Centre d'études supérieures de civilisation médiévale, 1962.
Geiriadur Prifysgol Cymru. A Dictionary of the Welsh Language, ed. R.J. Thomas, Caerdydd: Gwasg Prifysgol Cymru, 1950–.
Keller, Hans-Erich, *Etude Descriptive sur le Vocabulaire de Wace*, Berlin: Akademie-Verlag, 1948.
Middle English Dictionary, ed. H. Kurath and S.M. Kuhn, London: Oxford U.P., 1956–.
Stratman, F. M., *A Middle English Dictionary*. Revised by H. Bradley, London: Clarendon Press, 1891.
Thomson, Stith, *Motif Index of Folk Literature*, Helsinki: Suomalainen Tiedeakatemia, 1932–36; Folklore Fellows Communications 39–42, 46, 47.
Von Wartburg, W., *Französisches Etymologisches Wörterbuch: eine Darstellung des galloromanisches Sprachschatzes*, Bonn: F. Klopp, then Basel: Helbing & Lichtenhahn, then Basel: Zbinden, 1928–.

D. Studies on Laȝamon

Ackerman, R. W., 'Sir Frederic Madden and Medieval Scholarship', *Neuphilologische Mitteilungen* 73 (1972): 1–15.
Barron, W.R.J., 'Arthurian Romance: Traces of an English Tradition', *English Studies* 61 (1980): 2–23.
Baumann, W., 'Pound and Layamon's *Brut*', *Journal of English and Germanic Philology* 68 (1969): 265–276.
Berger, Sydney Elliot , 'A Concordance to Layamon's *Brut*. Part I, A–F', Ph.D. Univ. Iowa, abstract in *DAI* 32 (1971): 2631A.
Blake, N.F., 'Rhythmical Alliteration', *Modern Philology* 67 (1969): 118–24.
Blanchet, Marie-Claude, 'Arthur chez Wace et Lawman', *BBIAS* 6 (1954): 108.
Blanchet, Marie-Claude, 'Layamon et l'Ecosse', *BBIAS* 15 (1963): 97–107.
Blanchet, Marie-Claude, 'L'Argante de Layamon', *BBIAS* 18 (1966): 164–165.
Blanchet, Marie-Claude, 'Le Double Visage d'Arthur chez Layamon', in *Studi in Onore di Italo Siciliano* (Archivum romicum Biblioteca, series 1, vol. 86), Florence: L.S. Olschki, 1968; pp. 71–84.
Blanchet, Marie-Claude, 'Encore le "sadisme" de Layamon', in *Mélanges offerts à Rita Lejeune, Professeur à l'Université de Liège*, Gembloux: Duculot, 1969; vol. II, pp. 957–69.
Blenner-Hassett, Roland, 'The English river names in Lawman's *Brut*', *Modern Language Notes* 55 (1940): 373–377.

Blenner-Hassett, Roland, 'Gernemuðe: a place-name puzzle in Lawman's Brut', Modern Language Notes 57 (1942): 179–181.

Blenner-Hassett, Roland, 'Lawman's London', Mediaeval Studies 10 (1948): 197–200.

Blenner-Hassett, Roland, 'A nature-name puzzle in Lawman's Brut', Studia Neophilologica 14 (1941–2): 53–57.

Blenner-Hassett, Roland, 'Two Old Norse Motifs in Lawman's Brut', Studia Neophilologica 21 (1949): 211–215.

Blenner-Hassett, Roland, A Study of Place Names in Lawman's 'Brut', Stanford: Stanford U.P., 1950.

Blenner-Hassett, Roland, 'Middle English Muggles, Muglinges', PMLA 68 (1953): 917–920.

Blenner-Hassett, Roland, and F.P. Magoun, 'The Italian Campaign of Belin and Brenne in the Bruts of Wace and Lawman', Philological Quarterly 21 (1942): 385–90.

Bogholm, N., The Layamon Texts. A Linguistical Investigation, Travaux du Cercle Linguistique de Copenhague 3, Copenhagen: Einar Munksgaard, 1943.

Borges, J.L., 'The Innocence of Layamon', in Other Inquisitions, transl. Ruth L.C. Simms, New York: Washington Square Press, 1966.

Brook, G.L., 'A Piece of Evidence for the Study of Middle English Spelling', Neuphilologische Mitteilungen 73 (1972): 25–28.

Brown, A.C.L., 'Welsh Traditions in Layamon's Brut', Modern Philology 1 (1903–4): 95–103.

Bruce, J.D., 'Some Proper Names in Layamon's Brut Not Represented in Wace's Roman de Brut', Modern Language Notes 26 (1911): 65–69.

Bruce, J.D., 'The Mort Arthur Theme in Mediaeval Romance', Romanic Review 4 (1913): 403–472.

Burrow, J.A., 'Laȝamon's Brut 10.642: Wleoted', Notes and Queries 27 (1980): 2–3.

Cook, A.S., 'Layamon's Knowledge of Runic Inscriptions', Scottish Historical Review 11 (1914): 370–5.

Cross, T.P., 'The Passing of Arthur', in J.M. Manly Anniversary Studies, Chicago: Univ. Chicago Press, 1923, pp. 284–294.

Davies, H.S., 'Laȝamon's similes', Review of English Studies 11 (1960): 129–142.

Dobson, E.J., 'Two Notes on Early Middle English Texts', Notes and Queries 21 (1974): 124–126.

Donahue, Dennis Patrick, Thematic and Formulaic Composition in Lawman's Brut, Ph.D. New York: 1976. Abstract in DAI 37 (1976–1977): 5808A–5809A.

Donahue, Dennis Patrick, 'The Animals Tethered to King Arthur's Rise and Fall: Imagery and Structure in Lawman's Brut', Mid Hudson Studies 6 (1983): 19–27.

Everett, Dorothy, 'Laȝamon and the Earliest Middle English Alliterative Verse', in *Essays on Middle English Literature*, Patricia Kean ed., Oxford: Oxford U.P., 1955, pp. 23–45.

Fletcher, R. H., 'Some Arthurian Fragments from Fourteenth Century Chronicles', *PMLA* 18 (1903): part 3, pp. 84–94: 'Did Layamon make any use of Geoffrey's *Historia*?'.

Fletcher, R. H., *The Arthurian Material in the Chronicles. Especially Those of Britain and France*, Boston: Franklin, 1906; esp. ch. 5, 'The Arthurian Story after Geoffrey', pp. 147–166.

Frankis, P. J., 'Laȝamon's English Sources', in *J. R. R. Tolkien, Scholar and Storyteller. Essays in Memoriam*, ed. Mary Salu and Robert T. Farrell, Ithaca and London: Cornell U.P., 1979; pp. 64–75.

Friedlander, Carolyn VanDyke, *The Structure and Themes of Layamon's Brut*, Ph.D. Yale, 1973. Abstract in *DAI* 34 (1973): 272A.

Friedlander, Carolyn VanDyke, 'The First English Story of King Lear: Layamon's *Brut* Lines 1448–1887', *Allegorica* 3 (1978): 42–76.

Friedlander, Carolyn VanDyke, 'Early Middle English Accentual Verse', *Modern Philology* 76 (1979): 219–230.

Fries, Maureen, 'Rhetoric and meaning in Geoffrey of Monmouth and Layamon', *BBIAS* 24 (1972): 194–195.

Geist, Raymond Herman, *The Vocabulary of Layamon's Brut. With Particular Reference to Semantics*, doct. diss. Harvard, 1918. Abstract in *DAI* SOO84.

Gibbs, A. C., 'The Literary Relationships of Laȝamon's *Brut*', Unpubl. doct. diss. Cambridge, 1962.

Gillespy, Frances Lytle, 'Layamon's *Brut*: a Comparative Study in Narrative Art', *University of California Publications in Modern Philology* 3 (1916): 361–510.

Glowka, Arthur Wayne, *Rhyme and Rhythm in Layamon's Brut: a Study in Prosodic Decorum*, doct. diss. Univ. of Delaware, 1980. Abstract in *DAI* 41 (1980): 1064A.

Gray, J. M., 'Tennyson and Layamon', *Notes and Queries* 15 (1968): 176–178.

Hamelius, Paul, 'The rhetorical structure of Layamon's verse', in *Mélanges Godefroid Kurth II, Mémoires Littéraires, Philologiques et Archéologiques*, Liège: Vaillant-Carmanne, 1908; pp. 341–349.

Heather, P. J., 'Layamon's *Brut*', *Folklore* 48 (1937): 339–365.

Heather, P. J., 'Gleanings from Layamon's *Brut*', *Folklore* 53–54 (1942–3): 57–71.

Hilker, Wilfried, *Der Vers in Layamons 'Brut'; Untersuchungen zu seiner Struktur und Herkunft*, Ph.D. Westfälischen-Wilhelms-Universität, Munster: Gadderbaum, 1965.

Hinckley, H. B., 'The date of Layamon's *Brut*', *Anglia* 56 (1932): 43–57.

Hoffmann, Paul, *Das grammatische Genus in Layamons 'Brut'*, (Studien zur englischen Philologie 36) Halle-a-S.: M. Niemeyer, 1909.

Imelmann, Rudolf, *Layamon. Versuch über seine Quellen*, Berlin: Weidmannsche Buchhandlung, 1906.

Keith, W. J., 'Layamon's *Brut*: the Literary Differences Between the Two Texts', *Medium Aevum* 29 (1960): 161–172.

Kellner, L., 'Zu Layamon (Calig.) 13857', *Archiv fur das Studium der Neueren Sprache und Literaturen* 114 (1905): 164–165.

Kennedy, Christopher Brian, 'Per ovra delle rote magne: Mutability and Providence in *Beowulf*, Layamon's *Brut* and *Morte Arthure*', doct. diss. Duke Univ., 1979. Abstract in *DAI* 40 (1979): 6266A.

Kirby, I. J., 'Angles and Saxons in Laȝamon's *Brut*', *Studia Neophilologica* 36 (1964): 51–62.

Kolbe, M., *Schild, Helm und Panzer zur Zeit Layamons und ihr Schilderung in dessen Brut*, Ph.D. Univ. Breslau, Trebnitz: Maretzke & Martin, 1891.

Kossick, Shirley, 'The *Brut* and English Literary Tradition', *Unisa English Studies* 15 (1977): 25–32.

Krautwald, H., *Layamon's 'Brut' Verglichen mit Wace's 'Roman de Brut' in Bezug auf die Darstellung der Culturverhältnisse Englands*, Breslau: A. Schreiber, 1887.

Lange, Heinrich, *Das Zeitwort in den beiden Handschriften in Layamon's 'Brut'*, Ph.D. Strassburg, s.l.: Elsass-Lothringische Druckerei, 1906.

Leslie, R. F., 'Laȝamon's *Brut*: Its Formulaic Systems and Imagery', *BBIAS* 34 (1982): 300.

Loomis, R. S., 'Notes on Laȝamon', *Review of English Studies* 10 (1934): 78–84.

Loomis, R. S., 'Laȝamon's *Brut*', in *ALMA*, pp. 104–111.

McNary, Sarah Jane, 'Studies in Layamon's verse', doct. diss. Univ. New York 1903, Baltimore: J. H. Furst, 1904. Abstract in *DAI*, SO 146.

Marquardt, H., 'Kannte Layamon Runen?', in *Indogermanica: Festschrift für W. Krause*, Heidelberg: Carl Winter, 1960, pp. 114–120.

Martin, Lynn S., 'Arthur as Pendragon in Geoffrey of Monmouth, Wace and Lawman', *BBIAS* 24 (1972): 184–185.

Maynadier, G. H., *Arthur of the English Poets*, Boston: Mifflin, 1907, esp. ch. XII: 'From Layamon to Malory', pp. 197–215.

Monroe, Benton Sullivan, 'Studies in the Phonology and Vocabulary of Layamon's *Brut*', doct. diss. Cornell Univ., 1901. Abstract in *DAI*, SOO58.

Monroe, Benton Sullivan, 'French Words in Laȝamon', *Modern Philology* 4 (1907): 559–67.

Morse, William Russell, 'The Modal Syntax of the Finite Verb in Layamon's *Brut*', doct. diss. Harvard Univ., 1914. Abstract in *DAI*, SOO84.

Nearing, Homer Jr., 'The Legend of Julius Caesar's British Conquest', *PMLA* 64 (1949): 889–929.

Noble, James Erwin, 'Layamon's *Brut* and the Continuity of the Alliterative Tradition', doct. diss. Univ. of Western Ontario, 1981. Abstract in *DAI* 43 (1983): 2683A.

Noble, James Erwin, 'Variation in Laȝamon's *Brut*', *Neuphilologische Mitteilungen* 85 (1984): 92–4.

Noble, James Erwin, 'The Larger Rhetorical Patterns in Laȝamon's *Brut*', *English Studies in Canada* 11 (1985): 263–72.

O'Sharkey, Eithne M., 'King Arthur's Prophetic Dreams and the Role of Mordred in Layamon's *Brut* and the Alliterative *Morte Arthure*', *BBIAS* 27 (1975): 216–217.

Pilch, Herbert, *Layamon's 'Brut'. Eine literarische Studie*, Heidelberg: Carl Winter, 1960. Reviews by Schirmer, W. F., *Anglia* 79 (1961): 76–81; Leslie, Roy F., *Medium Aevum* 31 (1962): 212–213; Bolton, W. F., *English Studies* 46 (1965): 341–344.

Pilch, Herbert, 'Layamon und die kymrische Literatur. Eine Erwiderung an W. Schirmer', *Zeitschrift für Celtische Philologie* 39 (1962): 193–197.

Ringbom, Håkan, *Studies in the Narrative Technique of 'Beowulf' and Lawman's 'Brut'*. Åbo: Åbo Akademi, 1968.

Roach, Bruce V., 'A Concordance to Layamon's *Brut* lines 1–8020, with Introductory Essay Descriptive and Illustrative of the Structure and Uses of the Concordance for Literary Scholars', doct. diss. Washington Univ., 1973. Abstract in *DAI* 33 (1973): 4361A.

Le Saux, Françoise, 'Laȝamon's Welsh Sources: A Critical Review of Herbert Pilch's thesis', unpubl. M.A. diss., Swansea, Univ. of Wales, 1984.

Le Saux, Françoise, 'Laȝamon's Welsh Sources', *English Studies* 67 (1986): 385–93.

Schirmer, Walter F., 'Layamon's *Brut*', *Bulletin of the Modern Humanities Research Association* 29 (1957): 15–27.

Schirmer, Walter F., *Die frühen Darstellungen des Arthurstoffes*, Arbeitsgemeinschaft für Forschung des Landes Nordrhein-Westfalen, Geisteswissenschaften 73, Köln und Opladen: Westdeutscher Verlag, 1957. Esp. pp. 54–82.

Schreiner, Katherina, *Die Saga von Hengest und Horsa. Entwicklung und Nachleben bei den Dichtern und Geschichtsschreibern Englands*, Berlin: E. Ebering, 1921.

Seal, Jonathan Roger, 'Kings and Fated Folk: A Study of Lawman's *Brut*', doct. diss. Univ. Washington, 1977. Abstract in *DAI* 38 (1977/8): 3522A.

Serjeantson, M. S., 'Dialects of the West Midlands in Middle English', *Review of English Studies* 3 (1927): 54–67, 186–203, 319–333.

Seyger, R., *Beiträge zu Layamon's 'Brut'*, doct. diss. Halle-Wittenberg: Ehrhardt Karras, 1912.

Smith, R.M., 'Gernemuðe and the Benighted Geography of the Minstrels', *Modern Language Notes* 64 (1949): 70–72.

Smith, R.M., 'Lawman's Gernemuðe', *Modern Language Notes* 60 (1945): 41–42.

Standop, Ewald, 'Der Rhythmus des Layamon-verses', *Anglia* 79 (1961): 267–286.

Stanley, E.G., 'Laȝamon's Antiquarian Sentiments', *Medium Aevum* 38 (1969): 23–37.

Stanley, E.G., 'The Date of Laȝamon's *Brut*', *Notes and Queries* 213 (1968): 85–88.

Stanley, E.G., 'Review of *Facsimile of the Owl and the Nightingale*, ed. N.R. Ker', *Notes and Queries* 11 (1964): 191–3.

Stern, Gustav, *Old English æ in the Earlier Text of Layamon*, Göteborgs Högskolas Årsskrift 47, s.l.: Elander, 1941.

Stroud, Theodore A., 'Scribal Editing in Lawman's *Brut*', *Journal of English and Germanic Philology* 51 (1952): 42–48.

Sundén, K.F., 'Notes on the Vocabulary of Laȝamon's *Brut*', *Studia Neophilologica* 14 (1942): 281–300.

Swart, J., 'Laȝamon's *Brut*', in *Studies in Language and Literature in Honour of Margaret Schlauch*, ed. M.Brahmer, S.Helsztynski, J.Krzyzanowski, Warsaw: Polish Scientific Publishers, 1966, pp.431–435.

Tatlock, J.S.P., 'Laȝamon's Poetic Style and its Relations', in *The J.M. Manly Anniversary Studies in Language and Literature*, Chicago: Univ. Chicago Press, 1923, pp.3–11.

Tatlock, J.S.P., 'Epic Formulas, Especially in Laȝamon', *PMLA* 38 (1923): 494–529.

Tatlock, J.S.P., 'Irish Costume in Lawman', *Studies in Philology* 28 (1931): 587–593.

Tatlock, J.S.P., 'Greater Irish Saints in Lawman and in England', *Modern Philology* 43 (1945): 72–76.

Tatlock, J.S.P., *The Legendary History of Britain*. Berkeley: Univ. California Press, 1950; esp. ch.23, 'Lawman', pp.483–531.

Van der Ven-ten Bensel, E., *The Character of King Arthur in English Literature*, Amsterdam: H.J.Paris, 1925; esp. ch.III, 'King Arthur in the Chronicles', pp.52–75.

Trautmann, Moritz, 'Über den Vers Layamons', *Anglia* 2 (1879): 153–73.

Visser, G.J., *Laȝamon. An Attempt at Vindication*. Assen: Van Gorcum, 1935.

Willard, R., 'Laȝamon in the Seventeenth and Eighteenth Centuries', *Texas Studies in English* 27 (1948): 239–278.

Wülcker, Richard, 'Über die Quellen Layamons', *Beiträge zur Geschichte des Deutschen Sprache und Literatur* 3 (1876): 524–555.

Wyld, Henry Cecil, 'Laȝamon as an English Poet', *Review of English Studies* 6 (1930): 1–30.

Wyld, Henry Cecil, 'Studies in the Diction of Laȝamon's *Brut'*, *Language* 6 (1930): 1–24; 9 (1933): 47–71 and 171–191; 10 (1934): 149–201; 13 (1937): 29–59 and 194–237.

E. General

Arnold, Matthew, *On the Study of Celtic Literature and Other Essays*, London: Dent; New York: Dutton, 1976.

Arnold-Forster, F., *Studies in Church Dedications: or England's Patron Saints*, London: Skeffington & Son, 1899; 3 vol.

Atkins, J.W.H., *The Owl and the Nightingale*, New York: Russel and Russel, 1971 (first publ. 1922).

Bassnett-McGuire, S., *Translation Studies*, London/New York: Methuen, 1980.

Bathgate, Ronald H., 'A Survey of Translation Theory', *The Incorporated Linguist* 20 (1981): 113–4.

Benton, John F., 'Clio and Venus: An Historical View of Medieval Love', in *The Meaning of Courtly Love*, ed. F.X.Newman, Albany: State University of New York Press, 1968, pp. 19–42.

Bethune-Baker, J.F., *An Introduction to the Early History of Christian Doctrine to the Time of the Council of Chalcedon*, London: Methuen, 1949.

Blair, P.H., *An Introduction to Anglo-Saxon England*, Cambridge: Univ. Press, 1970.

Bromwich, Rachel, 'The Character of the Early Welsh Tradition', in *Studies in Early British History*, ed. H.M.Chadwick, Cambridge: Cambridge U.P., 1959, pp. 84–136.

Brown, A.C.L., 'The Round Table before Wace', *Harvard Studies and Notes in Philology and Literature* 7 (1900): 183–205.

Bullock-Davies, Constance, 'Marie de France and South Wales', unpubl. doct. diss., Univ. of Wales, 1963.

Bullock-Davies, Constance, *Professional Interpreters and The Matter of Britain*, Cardiff: Univ. Wales Press, 1966.

Caldwell, Robert A., 'Wace's *Roman de Brut* and the *Variant Version* of Geoffrey of Monmouth's *Historia Regum Britanniae'*, *Speculum* 31 (1956): 675–82.

de Certeau, Michel, Dominique Julia, Jacques Revel, *Une Politique de la Langue. La Révolution française et les patois: l'enquête de l'abbé Grégoire*, Paris: Gallimard, 1975.

Chambers, E.K., *Arthur of Britain*, London: Sidgwick & Jackson, 1927.

Curtius, E.R., *Europäische Literatur und lateinisches Mittelalter*, Bern: Francke, 1966.

Denomy, A. J., 'The Round Table and the Council of Rheims, 1049', *Mediaeval Studies* 14 (1952): 143–149.

Ditmas, E. M. R., 'Geoffrey of Monmouth and the Breton Families in Cornwall', *Welsh History Review* 6 (1972–3): 451–61.

Dobson, E. J., *The Origins of Ancrene Wisse*, Oxford: Clarendon Press, 1976.

Le Duc, Gwenaël, 'L'*Historia Britannica* avant Geoffrey de Monmouth', *Annales de Bretagne* 79 (1972): 819–35.

Dumville, David N., 'Brittany and Armes Prydein', *Etudes Celtiques* 20 (1983): 145–159.

Ellis, George, *Specimens of the Early English Poets. To which is Prefixed an Historical Sketch of the Rise and Progress of the English Poetry and Language*, London: G. and W. Nicol, 1801, 3 vol.

Fleuriot, Léon, 'Breton et Cornique à la fin du Moyen Age', *Annales de Bretagne* 76 (1969): 705–721.

Fleuriot, Léon, 'Les fragments du texte brittonique de la *Prophetia Merlini*', *Etudes Celtiques* 14 (1974–5): 43–56.

Fleuriot, Léon, *Les origines de la Bretagne. L'émigration*, Paris: Payot, 1980.

Fleuriot, Léon, 'Sur quatre textes bretons en latin, le "liber vetustissimus" de Geoffroy de Monmouth et le séjour de Taliesin en Bretagne', *Etudes Celtiques* 18 (1981): 197–213

Fontenrose, Joseph, *Python. A Study of Delphic Myth and its Origins*, Berkeley/ Los Angeles/ London: Univ. of California Press, 1980.

Gallais, Pierre, 'La *Variant Version* de l'*HRB* et le *Brut* de Wace', *Romania* 87 (1966): 1–37.

Guest, Edwin, *A History of English Rhythms*, ed. W. W. Skeat, New York: Haskell House: 1968 (repr. of 1882 ed.).

Holmes, Urban Tigner Jr., 'Norman Literature and Wace', in *Medieval Secular Literature: Four Essays*, ed. William Matthews, Berkeley/Los Angeles: Univ. California Press, 1967.

Jarman, A. O. H., 'The Welsh Myrddin Poems', in *ALMA*, pp. 20–30.

Kaluza, Max, *A Short History of English Versification*, transl. A. C. Dunstan, London: George Allen, 1911.

Keller, H.-E., 'Wace et Geoffrey de Monmouth: problème de la chronologie des sources', *Romania* 98 (1977): 1–14.

Korrel, Peter, *An Arthurian Triangle*, Leiden: Brill, 1984; esp. ch. 2, pp. 166–72.

Leckie, R. William Jr., *The Passage of Dominion. Geoffrey of Monmouth and the Periodization of Insular History in the Twelfth Century*, Toronto/ Buffalo/ London, Univ. of Toronto Press, 1981.

Lord, Albert B., 'Homer and Huso II: Narrative Inconsistencies in Homeric and Oral Poetry', *Transactions and Proceedings of the American Philological Association* 69 (1938): 439–45.

Luick, Karl, 'Geschichte der Heimischen Metra', in *Grundriss der Germanischen Philologie*, ed. Hermann Paul, Strassburg: Trübner, 1893; 2 vol.

MacCana, Proinsias, *The Learned Tales of Medieval Ireland*, Dublin: Dublin Institute for Advanced Studies, 1980.

McCulloch, Florence, *Mediaeval Latin and French Bestiaries*, Chapel Hill: Univ. North Carolina Press, 1960.

Magoun, F.P. Jr., 'Recurring First Elements in Different Nominal Compounds in *Beowulf* and the Elder *Edda*', in *Studies in English Philology in honor of F.Klaeber*, ed. Kemp Malone, Minneapolis: Univ. Minnesota Press, 1929: 73–8.

Magoun, F.P., 'The Oral Formulaic Character of Anglo-Saxon Narrative Poetry', *Speculum* 28 (1953): 446–67.

Micha, Alexandre, *Etude sur le 'Merlin' de Robert de Boron. Roman du XIIIe siècle*, Genève: Droz, 1980.

Minnis, A.J., *Medieval Theory of Authorship. Scholastic Literary Attitudes in the Later Middle Ages*, London: Scolar Press, 1984.

Morris, Rosemary, 'Uther and Ygerne: A Study in Uncourtly Love', *Arthurian Literature* 4 (1985): 70–92.

Mossé, Fernand, *A Handbook of Middle English*, transl. James A.Walter, Baltimore: John Hopkins Press, 1952.

Nida, Eugene A., *Towards a Science of Translating. With Special Reference to Principles and Procedures involved in Bible Translating*, Leiden: E.J. Brill, 1964.

Oakden, J.P., *Alliterative Poetry*, Manchester: Manchester U.P., 1930; 2 vol.

Piggott, Stuart, 'The Sources of Geoffrey of Monmouth', *Antiquity* 15 (1941): 269–86.

Pilch, Herbert, 'Zu der Quellen der *Roman de Brut*', *Zeitschrift für Celtische Philologie* 27 (1957): 1–9.

Pilch, Herbert, 'Galfrids *Historia*. Studie zu ihrer Stellung in der Literaturgeschichte', *Germanisch-romanisches Monatsschrift* 8 (1957): 254–273.

Reiss, Edmund, 'The Welsh Versions of Geoffrey of Monmouth's *Historia*', *Welsh History Review* 4 (1968–9): 97–127.

Richards, Melville, 'The Population of the Welsh Border', *Transactions of the Honourable Society of Cymmrodorion* (1970): 77–200.

Roberts, B.F., 'Geoffrey of Monmouth and Welsh Historical Tradition', *Nottingham Medieval Studies* 20 (1976): 29–40.

Roberts, B.F., *Brut Tysylio: Darlith Agoriadol*, Swansea: Coleg Prifysgol Abertawe, 1980.

Robertson, D.W., Jr., 'The Concept of Courtly Love as an Impediment to the Understanding of Medieval Texts', in *The Meaning of Courtly Love*, ed. F.X.Newman, Albany: State University of New York Press, 1968, pp. 1–18.

de Rougemont, Denis, *L'amour et l'occident*, Paris: Plon, 1972.

Schipper, Jakob, *Grundriss der Englischen Metrik*, Wien: Braumüller, 1895 (Wiener Beiträge zur Englischen Philologie 2).

Saintsbury, George, *A Historical Manual of English Prosody*, New York: Schocken Books (repr. of 1910 ed.).

Stanley, E. G., *The Search for Anglo-Saxon Paganism*, Cambridge: D.S. Brewer; Totowa, N.J.: Rowan and Littlefield, 1975. First publ. as articles in *Notes and Queries* 209–10 (1964–5).

Stenton, F. M., *Anglo-Saxon England*, Oxford: Clarendon Press, 1947 (2nd ed.).

Taylor, Rupert, *The Political Prophecy in England*, New York: Columbia U.P., 1911.

Thomas, Gwyn, 'Sylwadau ar Armes Prydein', *Bulletin of the Board of Celtic Studies* 26 (1976): 263–7.

Thorpe, Lewis, 'The Last Years of Geoffrey of Monmouth', in *Mélanges de langue et littérature françaises du moyen-âge offerts à Pierre Jonin*, Aix-en-Provence: CUERMA, 1979 (Sénefiance 7), pp. 663–72.

Wilson, R. M., *The Lost Literature of Medieval England*, London: Methuen, 1970.

Wright, C. E., *The Cultivation of Saga in Anglo-Saxon England*, Edinburgh/London: Oliver and Boyd, 1939.

Wright, C. E., *English Vernacular Hands From the Twelfth to the Fifteenth Centuries*, Oxford: Clarendon Press, 1960.

Zumthor, Paul, *Merlin le Prophète*, Lausanne: Payot, 1943.